MW01090039

PICATRIX

THE MAGIC IN HISTORY SERIES

FORBIDDEN RITES
A Necromancer's Manual of the Fifteenth Century
Richard Kieckhefer

CONJURING SPIRITS
Texts and Traditions of Medieval Ritual Magic
Edited by Claire Fanger

RITUAL MAGIC
Elizabeth M. Butler

THE FORTUNES OF FAUST
Elizabeth M. Butler

THE BATHHOUSE AT MIDNIGHT
An Historical Survey of Magic and Divination in Russia
W. F. Ryan

SPIRITUAL AND DEMONIC MAGIC
From Ficino to Campanella
D. P. Walker

ICONS OF POWER
Ritual Practices in Late Antiquity
Naomi Janowitz

BATTLING DEMONS
Witchcraft, Heresy, and Reform in the Late Middle Ages
Michael D. Bailey

PRAYER, MAGIC, AND THE STARS IN THE ANCIENT AND LATE ANTIQUE WORLD
Edited by Scott Noegel, Joel Walker, and Brannon Wheeler

BINDING WORDS
Textual Amulets in the Middle Ages
Don C. Skemer

STRANGE REVELATIONS
Magic, Poison, and Sacrilege in Louis XIV's France
Lynn Wood Mollenauer

UNLOCKED BOOKS
Manuscripts of Learned Magic in the Medieval Libraries of Central Europe
Benedek Láng

ALCHEMICAL BELIEF
Occultism in the Religious Culture of Early Modern England
Bruce Janacek

INVOKING ANGELS
Theurgic Ideas and Practices, Thirteenth to Sixteenth Centuries
Edited by Claire Fanger

THE TRANSFORMATIONS OF MAGIC
Illicit Learned Magic in the Later Middle Ages and Renaissance
Frank Klaassen

MAGIC IN THE CLOISTER
Pious Motives, Illicit Interests, and Occult Approaches to the Medieval Universe
Sophie Page

REWRITING MAGIC
An Exegesis of the Visionary Autobiography of a Fourteenth-Century French Monk
Claire Fanger

MAGIC IN THE MODERN WORLD
Strategies of Repression and Legitimization
Edited by Edward Bever and Randall Styers

MEDICINE, RELIGION, AND MAGIC IN EARLY STUART ENGLAND
Richard Napier's Medical Practice
Ofer Hadass

The Magic in History series explores the role magic and the occult have played in European culture, religion, science, and politics. Titles in the series bring the resources of cultural, literary, and social history to bear on the history of the magic arts, and they contribute to an understanding of why the theory and practice of magic have elicited fascination at every level of European society. Volumes include both editions of important texts and significant new research in the field.

MAGIC *in* HISTORY

PICATRIX

A MEDIEVAL TREATISE ON ASTRAL MAGIC

TRANSLATED WITH AN INTRODUCTION
BY DAN ATTRELL
AND DAVID PORRECA

Based on the Latin edition by David Pingree

THE PENNSYLVANIA STATE UNIVERSITY PRESS
UNIVERSITY PARK, PENNSYLVANIA

Library of Congress Cataloging-in-Publication Data

Names: Majriti, Maslamah ibn Ahmad, -1004?, author. | Attrell, Dan, 1988- editor, translator. | Porreca, David, 1974- editor, translator.
Title: Picatrix : a medieval treatise on astral magic / edited and translated by Dan Attrell and David Porreca ; based on the Latin edition by David Pingree.
Other titles: Ghayat al-hakim wa-ahaqq al-natijatayn bi-altaqdim. English | Magic in history.
Description: University Park, Pennsylvania : The Pennsylvania State University Press, [2019] | Series: Magic in history | In English; translated from the Latin, which was translated from the original Arabic. | Includes bibliographical references and index.
Summary: "An English translation, with accompanying introduction, commentary, and notes, of the medieval treatise on astrological magic known as Picatrix, a guide for constructing magical talismans, mixing magical compounds, summoning planetary spirits, and determining astrological conditions"—Provided by publisher.
Identifiers: LCCN 2018044815 | ISBN 9780271082127 (cloth : alk. paper)
Subjects: LCSH: Magic—Early works to 1800. | Alchemy—Early works to 1800. | Astrology—Early works to 1800.
Classification: LCC BF1618.A7 M3513 2019 | DDC 133.4/3—dc23
LC record available at https://lccn.loc.gov/2018044815

Printed in the United States of America
Published by The Pennsylvania State University Press,
University Park, PA 16802-1003

10 9 8 7 6 5 4

The Pennsylvania State University Press is a member of the Association of University Presses.

It is the policy of The Pennsylvania State University Press to use acid-free paper. Publications on uncoated stock satisfy the minimum requirements of American National Standard for Information Sciences—Permanence of Paper for Printed Library Material, ANSI Z39.48-1992.

Though I speak with the tongues of men or of angels, but have not love, I am but a resounding gong or a clanging cymbal.

1 Corinthians 13:1

Therefore I say to you, if you wish to apply your intellect to those lofty, noble, and important realms of knowledge, then spare no zeal, and do not neglect studying the books and words of the wise for it is by that path that you shall reach your desire.

Picatrix 2.8.4

CONTENTS

TABLES

ACKNOWLEDGMENTS

A project such as this one does not come to fruition in a vacuum. We are grateful for the support of a number of colleagues and peers who have contributed their time, effort, and expertise to make this volume both a reality and better than it would otherwise have been. Any remaining omissions or errors are, of course, the result of our own shortcomings.

We acknowledge and appreciate the assistance of Brett Bartlett, Leonard Curchin, Sophie Page, Liana Saif, and Ziad Wadi for their detail-level contributions to the introduction, annotations and/or editorial adjustments. We thank Ashley Street for her work on the images that appear throughout the text. We thank Matthew Hyde for his work in rendering part of the original handwritten translation into an electronic format.

We would like to thank all our friends and colleagues in the Societas Magica who contributed so much along the way in terms of encouragement and opportunities to share ideas.

We are grateful to our friends and colleagues in the department of classical studies at the University of Waterloo who have endured the repeated progress reports and casual references to black magic in conversation over the years. Porreca thanks his friends and colleagues in the faculty association of the University of Waterloo for the same reasons; he is particularly grateful to Erin Windibank, who bore the brunt of the updates.

All of our Latin teachers over the years deserve particular thanks—*inter alios/-as*, Leonard Curchin, Greti Dinkova-Bruun, Riemer Faber, Lucinda Neuru, Padraig O'Cleirigh, George Rigg, and Andrew Sherwood. This translation represents the culmination of their labors as much as that of the authors.

We acknowledge the individuals—giants of scholarship, one and all—whose pioneering efforts form the bedrock of this work: David Pingree, Martin Plessner, and Helmut Ritter. We are likewise grateful to the more recent translation efforts of Davide Arecco, Ida Li Vigni, Paolo A. Rossi, Stefano Zuffi, Béatrice Bakhouche, Frédéric Fauquier, Brigitte Pérez-Jean, John Michael Greer, and Christopher Warnock, whose work we inevitably had to take into account.

We would like to thank S.O.S. BBQ in Kitchener, Ontario for the hecatombs of chickens that kept us fed over the several years of collective effort we invested.

Last, yet first by priority, we thank our families and partners for their patience and support over the entire length and breadth of this project. Our gratitude goes well beyond words.

INTRODUCTION

The book you are holding in your hands is an English translation of a manual of astral magic known as the *Picatrix*, itself a medieval Latin rendition of the Arabic *Ghāyat al-Ḥakīm* (غاية الحكيم, *The Goal of the Sage*), which was written circa 954–59. The confluence of ideas that formed this eclectic tome draws its sources from numerous geographical tributaries: Spain, North Africa, Greece, Egypt, Nabataea, Arabia, Babylon, Persia, India, and beyond. Its scope is encyclopedic. As a general overview of long-lost beliefs, occult worldviews, and ritual practices, the work is fascinating to intellectual and religious historians. As a compendium of material that reflects the personal needs, ambitions, fears, and desires of magicians and their clients, the *Picatrix* is no less interesting to critical social historians, who might tease from it a great number of subtle observations. Its importance as a primary source lies in its incorporation of the vast magical, philosophical, and astrological heritage of antiquity and the Islamic Middle Ages, setting them within an internally consistent theoretical framework.

The chief factor in the *Picatrix*'s complexity and comprehensiveness as a treatise of medieval magic is its twofold nature. The author of the *Ghāyat al-Ḥakīm*, Abū 'l-Qāsim Maslama ibn al-Qāsim Ibrāhīm al-Qurṭubī al-Zayyāt (905/6–964), an Andalusian ḥadīth scholar described by his contemporaries as "a man of charms and talismans" (henceforth referred to as al-Qurṭubī), tells us clearly that "magic is divided into two parts, namely, the theoretical and the practical" (1.2.2).[1] That is to say, the *Picatrix* is no mere compendium of disassociated bits and pieces of decontextualized operations, though large portions of the work do indeed strictly apply to the practical application of magic. Such practical portions generally involve recipes for the material ingredients necessary for rituals, prayers for invoking the planets and their spirits, instructions for the crafting of talismans, formulas for suffumigations, remedies for specific conditions, and so forth. These sections, however, are quite distinct in character from their theoretical counterparts, which explain the system underlying the efficacy of practical magic. These theoretical discourses include admonishments to initiates, aphorisms of famous sages, astrological instructions pertaining to the figures of the heavens (decans, constellations, planets, etc.), and exposés on the theoretical underpinnings of magic and ritual image-crafting.

Although some might dispute the *Picatrix* as belonging to any kind of reified tradition (such as "Hermeticism" or "Gnosticism"), this work can be neatly encompassed by an historiographical concept recently come to be known as Platonic Orientalism.[2] This concept circumscribes the belief that there exists one single perennial wisdom tradition (such as Ficino's *prisca theologia*) that unites all the sages of every nation, and whose origins can be traced back to the likes of Plato, Pythagoras, Orpheus, Moses, Hermes Trismegistus, Enoch, Zoroaster, and ultimately, to a pre-lapsarian Adam. In reality, this "wisdom tradition" is a manifestation of late antique mystical Platonic idealism more or less veiled in and syncretized with the pre-existing religions of assorted peoples conquered and bound together by Hellenism.[3] We must not, however, overstress the purely Platonic character of the *Picatrix* at the expense of pseudo-Aristotelian causality that was an Arabic innovation to the science of magic not present in Late Antiquity (e.g., al-Kindī's theories of rays and Abu MaʿShar's extension of the theory to include souls).[4] This development is rooted in a quasi-mechanistic, natural magical worldview that contrasts with a more mystical late antique "theurgy" that is centered on the statues of temple gods. The *Theology of Aristotle* was the most prominent source of Neoplatonic ideology in the medieval Arabic world, and it is an adaptation of Porphyry's *Enneads* IV–VI as translated by al-Kindī's scholarly circle in Baghdad during the ninth century.[5]

Our translation is based on David Pingree's Latin edition of the *Picatrix*, and is specifically intended for students and scholars of the history of science and magic.[6] This introduction offers a detailed history of the text and its various versions and editions, a discussion of the author and his worldview, a caveat on the problematic term *nigromancia*, a numerical breakdown of the *Picatrix*'s rituals, and a number of observations on the poisonous and psychoactive ingredients contained therein. Finally, our translators' notes lay bare the inevitable trade-offs involved with idiomatically rendering a medieval text into a modern language, in addition to other editorial issues.

A Prehistory of the Latin *Picatrix*

The word "Picatrix" itself, according to the Latin text's prologue, is the name of the original author: "one wise philosopher, the noble and honored Picatrix," who "compiled this tome from over two hundred books of philosophy and then named it after himself" (Prologue .1). By and large, this was the title most familiar to the magicians, astrologers, and occultists of western Europe. From at least the time of the renowned Arab historian Ibn Khaldūn (ca. 1332–1406) until quite recently, the *Ghāyat al-Ḥakīm* had traditionally been attributed to Abū 'l-Qāsim Maslama ibn Aḥmad al-Faraḍī al-Ḥāsib al-Majrīṭī al-Qurṭubī al-Andalusī (d. 1007), the Madrilenian polymath, or alternatively to one of his disciples under the name of Pseudo-Majrīṭī. More recently, however, Maribel Fierro has argued forcefully for attributing the work to al-Qurṭubī, an attribution we accept as being most plausible.[7]

Al-Qurṭubī lived in Islamic Iberia, where he not only had access to over 224 books of both ancient and contemporary philosophy but also benefited from the great intellectual ferment and relative tolerance toward unusual scholarly and spiritual pursuits of the time. This author with *bāṭinī* aspirations traveled widely and accessed many of his sources from within the broader Islamic world beyond Spain, in particular while undertaking his *riḥla* during the early 930s when he passed through major cities and met the sages of distant lands.[8]

One may ask how al-Qurṭubī and the Latin version of his text came to be called "Picatrix." If we take the Latin prologue at face value, which says "hunc librum . . . quem suo proprio nomine nominavit" (this tome . . . [which he] named after himself), we run into a problem in the body of the text. While the author writes in an initiatory style, in the first person, the work cites a few operations of a so-called Picatrix that refer to the author in the third person (2.10.10–11, 16, 24, 27, 33, 37). Though this could be a strategy to embed himself among the ranks of such ancient sages as Empedocles, Hermes Trismegistus, Aristotle, and Plato, we cannot be certain that this is not a mere rhetorical device used by the author. Furthermore, in a section concerning magical stones (2.10.2–8), there are at least two correspondences between the Latin edition's "Picatrix" and the *Ghāyat al-Ḥakīm*'s "Buqrātīs/Biqrātīs." Béatrice Bakhouche and her collaborators report the theory that this name "Picatrix" could merely have been a corruption or transliteration of "Buqrātīs," while Ritter had suggested that this "Buqrātīs/Biqrātīs" was a simple corruption of Hippocrates (Ἱπποκράτης), the father of Western medicine.[9] Nevertheless, Ritter's hypothesis was abandoned for two reasons: first, the Periclean-era physician can already be found cited twice in the *Picatrix* under the name

"Ypocras" (3.3.32; 4.4.58); and second, this would be the first instance of a book on astral magic ascribed to the Hippocratic tradition.[10] Others proposed Harpocration (Ἁρποκρατίων), the second-century Greek grammarian who lived in Alexandria, on account of his interest in magical stones; they believed it was the Spanish translator of the original Arabic (and thus the author of the prologue) who attributed the name "Picatrix" to the text.[11] Johannes Thomann, however, suggests an alternative hypothesis that would reconcile the titles of the Latin *Picatrix* and the Arabic *Ghāyat al-Ḥakīm*. He believes the feminine noun "Picatrix" was first translated in Spanish as "Picatriz," the feminine form of *picador* (from the Latin *picator*, meaning goader or stinger). This was done as a sort of pun in imitation of the Arabic first name "Maslama" on the basis of the Spanish verb *picar* (to sting, prick, or bite), a crude rendering of the Arabic stem *s-l-m*, which can mean "to prick, sting, or bite like a snake."[12] Thus, "Picatrix" would not be a corruption of "Buqrātīs," but rather a corrupted translation of "Maslama" into Spanish. The appearance of "Picatrix" for "Buqrātīs" in Book 2, then, was merely a confusion in the scribal tradition between the translation of the Arabic "Maslama" and the transcription of the name "Buqrātīs." Ultimately, this association between the word "Picatrix" and the concept of pricking or stinging remains conjectural, although it seems to stand as the least implausible of the ideas put forth so far.

A Brief History of the Latin Text

In its prologue, the *Picatrix* declares that the Christian King Alfonso "the Wise" was the first to have the original Arabic text translated into Castilian Spanish "in the year of the Lord 1256 (in the year of Alexander 1568, in the year of Caesar 1295, and in the Arab year 655)" (Prologue .1). These dates, however, as pointed out by Pingree, do not align with one another perfectly. Nevertheless, it seems safe to assume that this work was translated into Spanish sometime between 1256 and 1258.[13] The translation (and transliteration) from Arabic to Spanish to Latin was not without its problems. Although the passages regarding lunar mansions and planetary images were written in fairly simple Arabic, Pingree believed that the Spanish translator "often blundered" and that "he did far worse in philosophical passages, and in passages such as the prayers to the planetary deities, where the Arabic is more complex."[14] He maintained that the Spanish *Picatrix* was not a very accurate rendering of the *Ghāyat al-Ḥakīm*, abounding in elaborations, errors, and omissions, which is not unusual for translations of the time. Some of these omissions include longer segments that were either just too difficult for the translator (including some theoretical sections) or were otherwise too offensive to Christian sensibilities (e.g., rituals involving homosexual relations or passages from the Qur'an).[15] Pingree cautiously speculated that the identity of the Spanish translator was a Jewish scholar named Yehudā ben Moshē (one of the translators at King Alfonso's court) while proposing even more cautiously that the individual responsible for the Latin text was Aegidius de Tebaldis of Parma (an imperial notary).[16] The Spanish version only survives in a short fragment, so a full detailed comparison of the three versions of the text remains impossible.[17] Charles Burnett has recently undertaken a detailed reevaluation of the Latin translation itself, revealing it in a more positive light as a *translatio ad sensum* (i.e., a translation faithful in meaning rather than a literal word-for-word rendering).[18]

It is unknown how long it took for the Spanish version to be translated into Latin. Nicolas Weill-Parot argues that an interpolation in 2.12.39–51 (and in particular 2.12.44) originated from Montpellier in southern France around the year 1300, thereby establishing a terminus ante quem for the translation since the Latin text must have already existed when the interpolation was added.[19] Fortunately, the Latin version is very nearly a literal rendition of the Castilian.[20] Ultimately, the Latin edition that is the basis of our translation is shorter than its Arabic original despite several additional interpolations.[21] Nevertheless, it was undoubtedly this Latin version (in its various and divergent manuscript traditions) that circulated widely throughout Europe from the mid-fifteenth century onward. Accordingly, we have consciously worked toward a translation that captures the spirit of the text's reception in Europe rather than in the Arabic world.

The history of the text in the period between its first appearance in Latin and the earliest surviving manuscripts is largely obscure since no precise references to the text have so far been found.[22] The widespread circulation of the *Picatrix* only begins around 1450, as evidenced by the large number of manuscripts extant in the libraries of Paris, Florence, Oxford, London, Kraków, Hamburg, Prague, and Darmstadt, all copied between the fifteenth and the seventeenth centuries.[23] Aside from the scribe of the illustrated Kraków manuscript,[24] Italian scholars appear to have been the first to engage with the text on an extensive basis. Galeotto Marzio (1427–1497) is among the original users of the *Picatrix* in the context of his medical, philosophical, and astrological work.[25] Marsilio Ficino (1433–1499) relied on it heavily for the elaboration of his theories of natural, astral magic in his *De vita coelitus comparanda*.[26] The great Christian kabbalist Giovanni Pico della Mirandola (1463–1494) kept a handwritten copy in his library, and the text was also known to a contemporary, the poet and Hermeticist Lodovico Lazzarelli (1447–1500).[27] Pico's nephew,

Giovanni Francesco Pico (1470–1533), appears to have possessed some degree of knowledge concerning the *Picatrix* according to a work he wrote after his uncle's death.[28] For each of these Renaissance men, however, this work was not entirely seen in a favorable light. As a testament to the *Picatrix*'s illicit reputation in Europe, the text never received a printed edition during the Early Modern period.

North of the Alps, the earliest citation of the *Picatrix* occurs in the commonplace book written in 1477 by John Argentine (ca. 1442–1507), doctor of medicine at Cambridge and personal physician to King Edward V and his brother Richard, Duke of York.[29] Heinrich Cornelius Agrippa (1486–1535) made extensive use of the *Picatrix* in his magnum opus, *De occulta philosophia*. The widespread infamy of this textbook throughout western Europe is attested by the fact that François Rabelais (d. 1553) condemned a certain Picatris as a "reverend father in the devil" and "rector of the diabolical faculty" in one of his novels.[30] His contemporary, the French thinker Symphorien Champier (1471–1539), railed against the *Picatrix* in the following terms: "It is a very pointless book, full of superstitions, and structured like a ladder toward idolatry."[31] Agostino Nifo (ca. 1473–1538 or 1545) called Picatrix "the foremost among the magi," while Gabriel Naudé (1600–1653) accused him of being a "Spanish charlatan who writes about magic."[32] The Benedictine abbot and occultist Johannes Trithemius (1462–1516) was also vehement in his criticism of the *Picatrix*.[33] Despite all this, even the Holy Roman Emperor Maximilian I owned two copies.[34] Moreover, according to Pingree, there were a number of vernacular translations: "The Latin version was translated, in whole or in part, into English, French, German, Hebrew, and Italian."[35] The clandestine circulation of such manuscripts is evidenced by a letter composed circa 1575 by the French poet Agrippa d'Aubigné (1552–1630), wherein he claims to have been secretly given access to a number of magical books imported to France from Spain by King Henry III. Among these were "les commentaires de Dom Joüan Picatrix de Tollede."[36]

More recently, Aby Warburg brought fresh attention to the Latin *Picatrix* in the period before the First World War. Starting in 1910, Warburg was on the lookout for manuscripts of the text, and in 1912, he borrowed two Latin versions from the Bibliothèque nationale de France in Paris. That very year, Fritz Saxl confirmed and revealed the close relationship between the *Picatrix*'s planetary invocations and the prayers of both al-Ṭabarī and Sabaean authors from Harrān.[37] In 1914, Wilhelm Printz established that this so-called *Picatrix* was in fact a copy of a much older Arabic text, the *Ghāyat al-Ḥakīm*. On account of this discovery, Ritter, then a young orientalist living in Hamburg, turned his interest toward the subject. In 1926, the only extant fragment of the

Castilian version of the text was published by Antonio Solalinde.[38] When this fragment was first discovered, Warburg refused to believe it.[39]

Despite the puritanical sentiment expressed in 1897 by Rev. J. Wood Brown that "it is to be hoped [the *Picatrix*] may never be translated into any modern language,"[40] projects were established for creating two distinct critical editions (one Latin and one Arabic) and a translation of the Arabic into German. These, however, were beset with all manner of delays, due both to the intervening wars and to assorted personal crises in the lives of the individuals involved. Among other complications, Ritter was twice arrested for homosexual activity under the repressive legal system prevailing in Germany at the time. After being released from prison by virtue of general amnesty on August 13, 1926, both he and Martin Plessner were forced into exile. In the summer of 1929, Plessner reconnected with Ritter in Istanbul but fell into a deep bout of depression. In a letter to Saxl, Ritter declared that Plessner was suffering from a nervous breakdown and would not make an able collaborator.[41] Not long after, Plessner himself bemoaned to Saxl how Ritter had stopped working on the *Ghāya* and would probably contribute nothing more to the project.[42] In 1933, after all these disastrous setbacks, Ritter's edition of the Arabic version appeared without any introduction. An early draft of an introduction had been published separately back in 1926. It was reprinted, along with updates, in Plessner's German translation of Ritter's Arabic text, which had been ready by early 1927 but never published. Only a single copy of the page proofs of Plessner's German translation would survive World War II. During this time, the Kulturwissenschaftliche Bibliothek Warburg moved to London and eventually became the Warburg Institute.[43] The translation project was put on standby for many years, but in 1949, Plessner could finally resume where he had been forced to abandon the project sixteen years prior. It took Plessner another thirteen years to publish an authoritative, thoroughly annotated German translation of the text in 1962.[44]

In the summer of 1971, he asked Pingree, an ardent orientalist and professor of the history of mathematics at Brown University, a "knight without fear, without reproach, [an] erudite connoisseur and enthusiast of ancient magic,"[45] about the possibility of publishing an edition of the Latin *Picatrix* while Plessner himself was busy working on an edition of its Hebrew versions.[46] As a man who had long been captivated by the Arabic version, Pingree agreed. The Warburg Institute, under the direction of Ernst Gombrich, gave its assent and support to the publication project. Pingree was given the copy of the Latin text made by Wilhelm Printz from a Hamburg manuscript (designated as *H* in Pingree's edition) and extensive notes concerning the *Picatrix* collected over decades by Elspeth Jaffé.[47] In 1986, the work was finally published.

On Knowledge, Wisdom, and Self-Legitimacy in the *Picatrix*

The magical operations and desired effects listed in the *Picatrix* are by no means set within the bounds of today's conventional morality or "political correctness."[48] Scattered throughout are rituals or operations calling for cannibalism, coprophagia, animal sacrifice, and genital mutilation. Inasmuch as there are numerous rituals for acquiring friendship, benevolence, and healing, there are also a large number designed toward coercion, abduction, violence, and ruin. The text abounds with the realities of magic being weaponized in power politics, war, patriarchal dominance, mind control, manipulation, and cruelty to both humans and animals. More hair-raising still for many today is the very theoretical basis upon which the *Picatrix*'s astral magic operates.

The *Picatrix* presents us with an unseen world of cosmic energy currents that radiate down from the firmament of stars and pass through the planetary spheres. They are augmented and diminished before pouring into the people, places, and things disposed to them. Hiding behind these rays, however, are spiritual entities with whom "wise" individuals can communicate given the fulfillment of complex ritual conditions. Ultimately, in the world of the *Picatrix*, we see a seamless integration of practical magic, earnest piety, and traditional philosophy. There is no incompatibility between traditional monotheistic beliefs and the invocation of planetary spirits that might, at first glance, be reminiscent of pagan gods—particularly in name. The unity of God is preserved since the planetary powers are understood as astral volitional forces that constitute the hidden inner workings of a cosmos ruled entirely by God's will.[49]

For al-Qurṭubī, magic is the inevitable consequence of a zealous philosophical life.[50] Regarding the question of efficacy, the practical elements of the *Picatrix* concerning ritual magic are founded upon a consistent syncretic philosophical worldview. The praises of wisdom and true science in the opening portion of the work are no mere rhetorical embellishments. A complete understanding of the work necessitates a thorough knowledge of Pythagorean, Platonic, and Aristotelian philosophy, to say nothing of the teachings of certain Arabic, Indian, Babylonian, and Egyptian sages. The *Picatrix* often imparts its wisdom in an esoteric style, as if a cult hierophant, chief initiator, or Sufi master were addressing his sole acolyte. Wisdom, ritual purity, and discretion are constantly advised to the practitioner.

But what makes someone wise according to the *Picatrix*? Who is eligible, according to our author, to learn how to bring the heavens' forces down to Earth and consort with astral entities? The answer is, of course, the righteous man—and the man who is astrologically predisposed. When asked "what do science and philosophy have in common?" the wise Hermes answered: "perfect nature" (3.6.5) (Arabic: *al-ṭibā al-tār*). The Hermetic concept of a Perfect Nature is a recurring theme throughout the *Picatrix*, and it refers to a kind of *telos* built into the seven liberal arts. It constitutes a state of mystical fulfillment that the magician achieves by aligning himself with the planets governing his own nativity and closely adhering to ceremonial scruples such that a personal informing *daimon* or guardian spirit is generated (not unlike the one with whom Socrates is said to have dialogued in his mind).[51] Through this ritually purified, guiding intellect, which is empowered both by an understanding of the ebbs and flows of cosmic forces and by drawing upon the rays cast down by the spirits of the celestial spheres, the magus performed effective magic.

The path of the sage contained within the *Picatrix* appears to be based upon the notion of a self-legitimizing cycle: the individual who is righteous becomes wise by adhering to religious law; through this wisdom, the sage becomes naturally inclined toward acquiring *sciencia* and thus turns toward the handiwork of God (botany, geometry, arithmetic, astronomy, metaphysics, etc.); the natural outcome, then, of living a righteous life with an eye fixed upon the orderly nature of creation is a sort of *gnosis*—an awareness of a holistic Neoplatonic cosmology that places humankind as mediator between God and the material world. To the *Picatrix*'s ideal sage, however, the study of creation is the study of the creator, and the love of nature (imperfect though it may be) is the love of God. Once the knowledge is revealed on how the world is actually organized (with its threefold division of matter, spirit, and intellect/mind), one attains the metaphysical framework within which to perform magical operations.

In the *Picatrix*, magic is the inevitable outcome of a life lived in holy contemplation. Magic is the thread that ties together the wisdom of the likes of Moses, Plato, Aristotle, Geber, and Hermes—it is an emergent property of the righteous life. It is the mark of the true mystic, not of the madman lost in diabolical pacts and Faustian bargains. The opening prayer, which prefaces the entire work, states that God "must be praised since it is by His light that secrets are revealed and things concealed are made manifest. It is through God's power that all miracles occur, and by Him that all prayer and science is understood" (Prologue .2). By putting God at the forefront of the work, by making Him the fount of all miracles and all science, the author ultimately stands justified in the pursuit of magic as a pious act of knowing God and His creation.

Due to this heavy emphasis on divinely imparted knowledge, the author puts great stress on prohibiting the foolish (i.e., the impious and therefore ignorant) from having any access to his enigmatic compilation (1.1.2; 1.4.33; 2.1.3; 2.2.7; 3.8.4). The cryptic and labyrinthine nature of the *Picatrix* is one of the more evident aspects of its composer's heightened sense of esoteric elitism.

"If this knowledge were revealed to humankind," he writes, "it would destroy the universe" (Prologue .3). We are told that its obscure style and figurative speech is in the interest of "honesty and goodwill" and that this is done to protect humankind against its own ambition—against men who would operate for themselves rather than "for the good, and in the service of God" (Prologue .3–4). A more cynical interpretation would see these methods as thinly veiled attempts to preserve trade secrets. Admonishments against the unwise abound throughout the work, as is traditional in the discourse of magic. Cynicism aside, exhortations to secrecy are a well-known trope in all esoteric literature, Hermetic or otherwise.[52] Such warnings recall Pico della Mirandola's caution to would-be practitioners of Kabbalah: "Si errabit in opere aut non purificatus accesserit, devorabitur ab Azazele" (If he errs in the work or comes to it unpurified, he will be devoured by Azazel).[53] Likewise, the fool who errs in the operations of the *Picatrix* or delves into them unpurified risks destruction by evil spirits. Such admonishments were not idle threats either. A great number of operations contained within the work include ingredients for suffumigations, potions, pills, capsules, and confections that would render a human sick, blind, insane, or dead if improperly handled or consumed. Great caution is expected of the user throughout the work, yet few specific precautions are noted.[54] To the sage, the noxious qualities of mercury, hemlock, and human excrement are *a priori* information; to the fool, they can be a fatal oversight. For the individual who is righteous, with a consequently keen interest in natural philosophy and insight into the inner workings of creation, the work should pose no problems.

On *Nigromancia*

A recurring term that has caused much confusion in the study of the *Picatrix* specifically and medieval magic in general is *nigromancia*, the word used to render the Arabic *siḥr* (سحر).[55] By the High Middle Ages, this word emerged due to a gradual corruption of the Greek adjective νεκρός, νεκρά, νεκρόν (dead) into the Latin *niger, nigra, nigrum* (black, dark). Thus, the word *nigromancia* stood as a composite of the Latin adjective *niger* and the Greek noun μαντεία (*manteia*; prophecy, divination). As to its meaning, the term had essentially lost its original connection with the narrow sense of the ancient term "necromancy," a form of divination based on communion with the dead. Although we certainly recognize these etymological transformations, the magic in the *Picatrix* is strictly concerned with invoking the powers of spirits belonging to specific heavenly bodies, and there are no forms of divination pertaining to the dead in its pages (though the dismembered body parts of humans and sacrificial animals do occasionally appear as ritual components).[56] While this word *nigromancia* pertains to the invocation of occult forces, the spirits invoked are not necessarily malefic beings conjured up to worship or to make pacts with, as a Faust does with a Mephistopheles. Contemporary conceptions in popular culture of the word "necromancy" elicit images of dark wizards summoning skeletons and living in dank crypts, yet these connotations are absent from the *Picatrix*, where the term is practically synonymous with "natural magic."[57]

As such, we would give a wrong impression if we were to interpret nigromancia as "necromancy" or even "black magic." The astral magic of the *Picatrix* is laid out (as discussed) as a consequence of a righteous life and an act of devotion to the one true God. It is God who moves the creative spiritual forces to act on behalf of the righteous magician, not the magician who compels either nature or the spirits of the dead to work in his favor. Magic in the *Picatrix* is noble and hieratic, not base and hubristic.[58] Nevertheless, such kinds of magical operations were only considered true and valuable through an appeal to antiquity, insofar as they gained legitimacy from being passed down directly by the sages of old. After all, the star-worshipping Sabeans were granted protection by the Qur'an, although somewhat tenuously, as "a people of the book" (أهل الكتاب, 'Ahl al-Kitāb).[59] We should always keep in mind that our author was very aware that the material he was passing on to unforeseeable readers could be objectionable in the face of contemporary religious law, though he assures us that his intentions are pure (3.8.4). This explains the numerous exhortations to secrecy throughout the work, because for the true sage, the ends justify the means.

Nigromancia then, in a European context, might best be understood simply as ceremonial magic. In their own translation of the *Picatrix*, Greer and Warnock use the expression "black ops" to emphasize the element of secrecy.[60] It is comprised of scrupulous work with talismans (Latin: *telsam*) or "images" meant to channel stellar rays down from the macrocosm into the microcosm. It is the art of binding spirit into matter and is not therefore "demonic" in the Christian understanding of the term. The *Picatrix* should also not be retrojected with the same air as an "evil grimoire," like H. P. Lovecraft's fictional *Necronomicon*. Those who secretly practiced nigromancia considered it the natural outcome, the consummation, of all medieval science, wisdom, and philosophy. Thus, in our opinion, it is not entirely correct to connect the *Picatrix* with necromancy, black magic, or any form of objectionable sorcery. For this reason, we have ultimately opted to render nigromancia with the nebulous word "magic" in our translation, and we hope this interpretation will serve to clean up the sullied reputation that easily misunderstood words like *nigromancia* gave to this great treatise of medieval astral magic.

The Cosmology of the *Picatrix*

The practice of magic described in the *Picatrix* assumes from its practitioner a high degree of knowledge in the sciences of the time. By the late thirteenth century, medieval theories of physics were based predominantly on Aristotelian thought, and they were as fundamental to the *Picatrix* as they were to any contemporary treatise on natural philosophy. The four elements (fire, water, air, and earth) compose the whole material portion of the cosmos. Further pairs of opposite qualities (hotness and coldness, wetness and dryness) cause these elements to interact with one another in a vast array of combinations according to Empedoclean notions of Love (attraction) and Hate (repulsion).[61] As it was until Johannes Kepler's time, the circle/sphere was believed to be the shape synonymous with perfection and thus figured extensively in systems of medieval astronomy. Its simplicity appealed both to the scientific perspective of the time and to theologians. In the *Book of 24 Philosophers*, Hermes Trismegistus defines God as "an infinite sphere whose center is everywhere and whose circumference is nowhere."[62] Implicit to the *Picatrix* is a vision of the world that Aristotle had organized and that later figues such as Ptolomy, al-Kindī, and Abu Ma'Shar would expound upon in much detail. It is a vision of the universe as a series of concentric spheres made of some ethereal substance. Nestled in the center of the cosmos, the gross material world is fixed in place yet ever changing in its elemental constitution. The four elements organize themselves naturally according to their density. The grosser elements (water and earth) fall naturally to the very center, and the lighter ones (fire and air) rise heavenward. Ascending beyond the realm of the four elements, one leaves behind the microcosmic (lesser) world and enters the macrocosmic (greater) world.

The first of the planetary spheres, that of the Moon, is like a silvery gate leading out from the sublunary world (the world of matter and corruption) into the supralunary world (the world of spirit and source of generation). From here onward, the cosmos is no longer comprised of elemental matter—the planets are formed out of an immaterial spiritual substance that radiates power downward. They are ordered as follows above the Moon: Mercury, Venus, the Sun, Mars, Jupiter, and finally Saturn. All passages in the *Picatrix* that concern the planets specifically follow this pattern in reverse order. Beyond the planetary spheres is the eighth sphere, the ring of the Zodiac, through which the planets appear to make all their wanderings.[63] Beyond this eighth sphere lies the ninth, the *Primum Mobile* or the veil covering the Empyrean, which gives us the daily revolution of the firmament and shields us like a perforated black canvas from the light and total glory of the One. God dwells in the infinite space beyond these cosmological spheres. This very specific cosmology, rooted in centuries of Greek, Egyptian, Babylonian, Arabic, and Indian natural philosophy, is absolutely essential to the internally consistent theoretical foundations of the magic in the *Picatrix*.[64]

From Neoplatonism the *Picatrix* borrowed the concept of a "hierarchy" or "great chain of being" that emanates downward from a single divine principle.[65] The path to achieving any degree of union with, or understanding of, this divine principle, is an ascetic, rather than a hedonistic, one. We find three distinct hierarchies of being scattered throughout the *Picatrix*, each no doubt stemming from different textual sources. The first hierarchy of being is described as follows: God, the intellect/mind, spirit, matter, the sphere of nature, the sphere of fixed stars, the planetary spheres, prime or universal matter, the elements; within the latter, there is another progression from stones up through plants, animals, and finally, beings endowed with reason (1.7.1). The second hierarchy takes a slightly different form: the Principle, high matter, elements, matter, form, nature, body, growth, animals, humankind, men, individuals (1.7.2). The third hierarchy has another variation: God, *Prima Materia* and the First Form, sense perception or mind, spirit, the nature of the heavens, the elements, and that which is composed of them (4.1.1). All of these cosmologies share a process of emanation downward from a divine principle through successive phases of emergent properties that ultimately result in the formation of the rational human. It is by employing this rationality that the human manifests his predisposition for achieving righteousness, thus aligning himself to the divine principle and creating a feedback loop of awareness between the microcosm and the macrocosm.

Everything that exists on the great hierarchy of being between the just, righteous, and rational human and the divine principle at the root of all things is subject to the workings of magic. This heavily stratified vision of the cosmos lies at the root of the *Picatrix*'s ambiguous oscillations in content "between astrolatry, angelology, and monotheism."[66] It is unclear exactly at which level of existence magic operates, if any such single level does exist, since each level in the hierarchy of being seems to effect it.

It is the burden of the magician to understand the intricate interrelationships that exist between the various things on the chain of being before embarking on any of the operations laid out in the *Picatrix*. From this foundation of knowledge, the magician will learn the hidden or occult correspondences (also known as "sympathies" or "dispositions") between the plants, animals, and minerals of the lower world and the spiritual forces of the heavenly bodies in the upper world. With this awareness, he can gather up all the requisite sympathetic materials and use them to invoke the planetary spirits pertaining to the nature of his objective. For example, copper plates, saffron suffumigations, and "things of moderate heat and excess humidity" may be necessary to invoke Venus in rituals for love or seduction (1.3.2). By the sympathetic resonances between the gathered objects and their respective heavenly bodies, the magician can draw upon their power to effect change in worldly affairs. This function operates in the same manner that a note on one stringed instrument will cause, at a distance, another string tuned to the same note to resound in sympathy. The magician tirelessly gathers materials (whether through trade or foraging); crafts elaborate images or talismans; spends countless nights staring up into the night sky; pores over astrological charts, tables, and star maps; pays close attention to the slightest details of astronomical position (down to the seconds of arc); and then, by the grace of God, can move nature to act. The practitioner comes to Mercury with issues concerning knowledge or study; he looks to Venus to liven up his existence with games, pleasures, and love affairs; he seeks Mars in times of war or in legal battles; he calls upon Jupiter or the Sun in order to charm kings and noblemen; he turns to Saturn when he wishes to create enmity between friends. Every planet governs its own set of plants, animals, and minerals, but also its own psychologies, professions, places, languages, and people. Astrological considerations are foundational to the operation of magic; the practitioner must potentially wait years for the occurrence of the right celestial circumstances to enact his desired outcome. In the meantime, he would prepare himself by selecting the right locations, clothing, suffumigations, sacrifices, tinctures, and, most importantly, magical images. The *Picatrix* relies on the idea that all particulars contain universals (2.3.17). All things in the lesser, material world reflect those of the greater, celestial world (1.6.1; 3.5.1). Thus, bringing together various ritual components is an act of devotion, a work that the sage performs as a sort of Plotinian "flight of the alone to the alone."[67]

One word used for the magical images is "talisman," from the backward reading of the Arabic word *musallaṭ*, yielding *ṭillasm*, which means "that to which power over something is conferred."[68] The talisman is a composite object that, by nature of its constituent parts, draws down the influx of *spiritus* from the upper world by means of a hidden cascade of physical rays, as theorized by al-Kindī in his *De radiis* (also known as *Theorica artium magicarum*).[69] The Latin *Picatrix* tells us the word *telsam* may be translated as "force-bearer"—a thing that operates by force—since the magician who makes a talisman does so through force, conquering the substances from which it is composed (1.2.1). The talisman is built out of appropriate substances and at appropriate times, and it is consecrated with the appropriate ritual actions. Then, it is strengthened by the appropriate suffumigations and sacrifices that will attract the spirits to the image. Throughout the text, all the magic described in the *Picatrix* is self-consistent within its own theoretical parameters. There is a definite cosmological system that all practitioners are expected to understand, and the effectiveness of all the magic in the *Picatrix* depends upon a thorough understanding of that *physis*.

The most powerful action in magical ritual is animal sacrifice. The sacrificial act forces a resonance upon external things through its very solemnity in combination with the power of the human will. The choice of sacrificial victim is determined by the astrological influences that constitute it—influences that the magical operator is in essence seeking to harness. Liana Saif has aptly described how al-Kindī's model of the mechanics behind this process sits at the foundation of the *Ghāyat al-Ḥakīm*'s magical system:

> As part of the elemental world, a living animal emits rays and so when it dies from natural causes, the rays do not cause any discernible modification on the natural world. Al-Kindi here does not elaborate on what happens to the rays upon natural death, perhaps they dissipate or even get reabsorbed into the universal network of rays. However, if the death is unnatural and achieved by human intervention, then the rays will have a strong impact on the material world. The implication here is that the violence of the action will result in a sudden release of the animal's rays, causing a kind of ripple in the universal harmony thus affecting the immediate natural world. Even the efficacy of animal sacrifices is given natural reasons (*rationem naturalem habere*) by al-Kindi.[70]

This surprisingly mechanistic-seeming theory is the result of a Neoplatonic cosmology that is imbued with a system of Aristotelian natural causation. The rays are transmitted by "vital and volitional agents . . . which are called *rūḥāniyyāt*, [or] spiritual powers."[71] Such a combination of Aristotelian and Neoplatonic elements did not coexist in antiquity, and their synthesis in the theory of rays must be understood as an innovation of the Arabic world. Nevertheless, we know only of these theories from the Latin translation of *De radiis* as no Arabic version has yet been found. The Latin readers of the *Picatrix*, therefore, were likely familiar with the idea that all earthly processes were caused by the influx of variously conditioned stellar rays that emanate downward from heavenly bodies as "proximate efficient causes," though ultimately from the divine principle as the "far efficient cause."[72]

The *Picatrix*, Social History, and Material Culture

Magic in Western culture (at least according to some scholars)[73] comprises activities that breach social norms.[74] While many of the authors of medieval magical texts, including al-Qurṭubī, claim higher and more salubrious goals for their magic, this section aims to unpack and compare the specific, operative objectives of the magical rituals described in the *Picatrix*. In other words, what were its intended users so desperate to achieve, yet so powerless to bring about (keeping in mind the often reprehensible and illegal nature of the magical practices in question)?

Before examining the details of the materials in the *Picatrix*, it is important to observe the common thread that unites virtually all of the rituals in this book: the attempt to control what lies beyond the grasp of whoever is requesting or performing the magic. By repeatedly questioning the intent, purpose, or objective of each ritual in the text and then compiling and aggregating the results, one can also get a generic sense of what kind of person would need the rituals described in the book and, therefore, of the intended audience of the book itself—at least as far as its Latin version is concerned.

In the *Picatrix*, a total of 2,325 different objectives for the magical rituals can be identified and categorized. This high number was reached on account of a methodological choice, namely, to separate out different elements or components within larger rituals. For example, *Picatrix* 3.7.26 is a lengthy description, complete with an extensive prayer to be spoken aloud, of how to invoke the planetary spirit of Mars. One could have taken that at face value and treated it as a single objective, but a number of additional, more precise purposes emerge by examining the details within the ritual, which are consonant with the inherent properties attributed to Mars elsewhere in the text. The more detailed list of objectives in this instance includes killing, spreading sadness and anger, attracting the fury of kings, suffering the victory of enemies and that of wild, savage beasts, among many other analogously negative goals. In the tabulations presented below, each of these specific objectives is treated as a separate entry. In essence, since the author would not have bothered to include all these details merely by accident, the specifics become important, especially once they are aggregated over the entire text. The large sample size allows for conclusions based on the proportion of rituals dedicated to one or another of the broad categories of objectives.

When attempting to make sense of such a large data set, one is confronted with the task of creating categories that both make sense and are helpful. Details of interest might be neglected if the categories are too few, yet multiplying them to excess retains too much of the incoherent complexity of the original text. We are in the presence of the classic "lumper" versus "splitter" debate that perpetually dogs the fields of biology and the data-based social sciences. The tabulation presented here does not attempt to resolve that debate, but rather to offer a balanced presentation of the materials. This analysis is akin to the one done by Jean-Patrice Boudet specifically regarding sex magic in his article "L'amour et les rituels à images d'envoûtement dans le *Picatrix* latin." We are extending the scope to all types of magical operations in the entire text rather than focusing only on one particular type.[75]

Now, the results: in table 1 below, all 2,323 rituals are divided into fourteen categories. While the categories are meant to be self-explanatory, they also bear further detailed investigation, which follows.

Before examining the principal categories listed in table 1, a few general observations arise. The most challenging facet of life for those inclined to practice magic is clearly what one might call "dealing with others" (roughly one-third of the rituals involve such concerns), whether these "others" be family, spouses, lovers, friends, associates, or social superiors, as can be seen in table 8. It is also a category of rituals where the combination of the practitioners' intently focused wills with their targets' beliefs in the effectiveness of magical

TABLE 1 *Picatrix* ritual objectives by category

Category	Number of ritual objectives noted
Interpersonal relations	751
Healing/health	372
Knowledge/skills	229
Apotropaic magic	132
Commerce and wealth	124
Occult sciences	120
Elements/properties of matter	117
Agriculture	97
Military	84
Travel	56
Infrastructure	52
Foraging	40
Illusion/sense perception	29
Outliers/others	120

operations more reliably creates conditions for real-world effects than is the case for most of the other categories in the table.[76]

Personal health is a matter of abiding concern—approximately one-sixth of the rituals are devoted to this topic. The assortment of ailments listed makes explicit which sorts of health problems were most widespread, as is detailed in table 6. It is nevertheless surprising that such a critical matter as personal health would solicit less concern than interpersonal relations.

Shortcuts to becoming knowledgeable and/or skilled at performing certain tasks were also a major priority (just under one-tenth of the total number of rituals). While this category could be entitled "achievement without effort," this also may be a misnomer considering that the complexity of some of the rituals involved rivals that of acquiring the skill in the first place—analogous to the *Ars Notoria*'s supposed "shortcuts" to knowing the seven liberal arts.[77] The additional paradox here is that the *Picatrix* repeatedly recommends a thorough knowledge of nature as a prerequisite for the practice of magic, while knowledge of nature—via the seven liberal arts, *inter alia*—is one of the more frequently seen objectives of the rituals that fall under this category (see diagram 1 below).

The "elements/properties of matter" category encompasses rituals that attempt to control the raw materials that were thought to make up the material universe, i.e., the four elements and their primary effects on human activities: air in terms of storms and weather; earth and fire in terms of how they interact with each other; and water in terms of precipitation, flooding, and related effects. Rituals for levitation, cleansing, and creating light or darkness have also been included under this category since they also represent attempts to control the behavior of inert matter.

Under "foraging" appear such things as hunting, fishing, and finding treasure, which collectively represent the vast majority of rituals in this category. The relatively small number of these rituals compared to some of the other categories indicates that these interests were fairly minor in the author's mind, reflecting urban concerns rather than rural ones.

The *Picatrix* was not written by a famished individual: only a small fraction of the rituals (roughly one twenty-fifth of the total) are related to agriculture. Basic subsistence, relatively speaking, was not a primary concern for those social elites interested in reading about or performing these magical rituals. The fact that concerns surrounding commerce and the accumulation of wealth do not make any mention of agricultural productivity further confirms that the author was chiefly concerned with urban life. Military affairs appear even less prominently than either urban or rural issues.[78]

As was pointed out above, there is a certain arbitrariness in the choice of groupings. "Sex magic" could have been a category of its own that currently overlaps with "interpersonal relations," "healing/health," and even "military," which contains rituals to induce sex for weakening an enemy and to avert sex for one's own greater strength in war.

One must be mindful that the target audience of this text is literate but a practitioner's clients need not be. Nevertheless, any conclusions that arise from an analysis such as this one by definition reflect the interests of those elements of society that could afford the leisure time and effort necessary for cultivating literacy.

One methodological weakness in this approach must be acknowledged: equal weight is attributed to each of the rituals' objectives, and conclusions are drawn based on their aggregate numbers. This approach can tell us nothing about the popularity or frequency of use for any given ritual. Thus, the conclusions drawn in this section are applicable to the concerns of the author and consequently his intended readers in the aggregate, not to what any particular reader may have done with any specific ritual or even with the entire book.

Now, we can turn to examining some of the categories in table 1 in more detail in order to draw conclusions from them. Note that not all of the rows necessarily yield anything noteworthy.

Agriculture

Table 2 reveals that magic dedicated to agriculture splits roughly into two-thirds that focus on plant crops and one-third on animal husbandry, with about one-fifth of the total rituals in this category devoted to harming others' crops or animals. In terms of specific crops, vines are mentioned five times while figs, wheat, and broomrape are each mentioned once, with the latter specifically referred to as a weed. Animals are mentioned as follows: sheep four times; cattle three times; bees, chickens, dogs, goats, and horses each two times; and cats and pigs each once.

TABLE 2 Agriculture rituals in the *Picatrix**

	Harvests/crops (66)	Animal husbandry (31)
Improve/increase/protect (77)	52	25
Harm/decrease/destroy (20)	14	6

*In this and all subsequent tables, the numbers in parentheses indicate the specific number of rituals falling under that category.

Apotropaic Magic

Table 3 shows that nature and its fauna were still an immediate threat to personal safety in our author's world—more so even than hunger when one compares the number of apotropaic rituals to those devoted to agricultural concerns. Controlling the deadly aspects of nature was—not unreasonably—more of a concern than its merely noisome effects. Small, poisonous creatures (like snakes and spiders) were definitely seen as a greater threat than large, predatory ones (like bears, lions, or wolves), which serves to reinforce the impression that the author and his intended audience lived principally urban lives: rural people have reason to fear predators, whereas cities tend to be safe from them (a fact which increases the intensity of insect and vermin infestations). Rituals for depopulating places of human habitation also fall under this category since they effectively function like warding rituals against people rather than beasts.

Commerce and Wealth

This category includes rituals concerning profit, commercial goods, theft, inheritances, and other similar concerns (see table 4). Of note here are some of the specific sources of profit that are mentioned along the way: law, battle, medicine, scribal work, and the trade of perfumes. The sharp difference between the high proportion of rituals directed at destroying or diminishing wealth as opposed to those directed against the means of its acquisition sug-

TABLE 3 Apotropaic rituals in the *Picatrix*

	Kill/bind/ ward off	Protect from bite/harm	Assemble/ empower/make
Nuisances (ants [1], bedbugs [5], bees [3], birds [10], dogs [3], fleas [6], flies/ bugs [7], frogs [2], leeches [1], lice [1], mice [7], wasps [5])	33	7	2
Deadly animals (reptiles/snakes/serpents/adders/ vipers [39], scorpions [8], tarantulas [6], wolves [4], bears [4], lions [1], wild/ harmful/ poisonous animals [19])	51	12	18
People (9)	8 (for depopulating, + others under "anti-healing")	1 (from wicked folk)	n/a

TABLE 4 Commerce and wealth rituals in the *Picatrix*

	Trade/commerce/ profit/goods	Wealth/abundance/ finance/ fortune/ riches/inheritance	Other
Improve/increase	45	35	-
Diminish/destroy	2	24	-
Other	–	–	18 (includes theft & fraud [8]; arranging debts [3], spendthrifts [2], honesty, estimates, balance of things, expanding a city for prosperity, crumb collectors [1 ea.])

gests that, for our author and his intended audience, jealousy was more intently directed at the former than the latter.

Occult Sciences

Table 5 demonstrates that divination was the primary concern of those willing to practice magic in order to harness supernatural powers in a sort of self-reinforcing, bootstrapping process. The relative absence of alchemy should be no surprise since the elder sibling volume to the *Ghāyat al-Ḥakīm* was the *Rutbat al-Ḥakīm*, which focuses on alchemy as opposed to astral magic.[79]

Healing and Health

As the second-largest category of rituals, the need for healing looms large for the *Picatrix*'s author and his intended audience. Table 6 reveals that those ailments that are hidden from view (i.e., those that are psychological or that affect internal organs) are most predominant. Here as well we see that inflicting ill

TABLE 5 Occult science rituals in the *Picatrix*

Type of ritual	Number of occurrences
Divination (including astrology and geomancy)	39
Spirit/demon summoning	29
Magic (unspecified)	20
Curses	Bestow: 6; remove/prevent: 12
Alchemy	2
Other	12

TABLE 6 Healing and health rituals in the *Picatrix*

Disease/ailment type	Improve/cure/ prevent illness (280)	Cause/induce illness (92)
General health	28	30
Mental/psychological (insomnia, epilepsy, anxiety, melancholy, depression, irritability)	55	18
Organ health (head and fevers, eyes, ears, throat, spleen, heart, blood, gallbladder, kidneys, liver, gastric system, skin)	63	12
Limb health (teeth, tongue, back, hips, groin, arms, hands, legs, feet [incl. gout], paralysis, agility, strength/weakness, wounds, rheumatism)	25	11
Poisons	30	7
Sex and childbirth	29	7
Aging	9	1
Other (laughing to death, drinking/appetite, planetary illnesses, pain, children's illnesses, dryness, old ailments)	41	6

health upon others represents roughly one-third of these rituals, one of the higher proportions of such harmfully oriented rituals among the categories examined here. This ratio is fully consonant with the proportion of bestowing versus removing curses that was revealed in table 5 and surpassed only by the ratio of creating versus destroying infrastructure in table 7 below.

Infrastructure

Table 7 reveals the breakdown of the rituals relating to physical infrastructure (i.e., the built environment). Here, we see that wrecking other people's property is almost as desirable as maintaining or protecting one's own. In terms of attempts to do harm with rituals in the *Picatrix*, targeting others' wealth and homes is preferred proportionally over doing direct harm to their health—although the latter is certainly also featured, just less prominently in terms of relative numbers. Some peculiar methods include a ritual to curse a bath so that no one frequents it (4.9.55), a ritual for populating a deserted place (4.7.8), and several other rituals that do not fit neatly into table 7, such as protecting roads, ancient sites (3.7.9), and places of faith (3.7.10); opening doors (3.7.11); or making a house appear red or shine like a ruby (4.9.18).

TABLE 7 Infrastructure rituals in the *Picatrix*

	Buildings/homes	City/village	Prison	Wells/channels
Building/strengthening/ protecting	15	2	10	4
Destroying/preventing	12	8	0	1

Interpersonal Relations

Representing a significant plurality of the rituals contained in the *Picatrix*, the category of interpersonal relations deserves close attention (see table 8). The large number of rituals directed at promoting—or more particularly, gaining the help or favor—of social superiors exemplify how important social hierarchy was to the author and intended readership of the *Picatrix*. Furthermore, this high number—roughly one-fourteenth of the rituals in the entire book—reflects the fact that those who were interested in these magical rituals were not at the apex of the social pyramid and were very cognizant of the need to appeal to social superiors in order to benefit materially or socially. This disproportion attests to the power social superiors exerted over their subjects, as well as the seeming inscrutability of the superiors' decisions, favors, and dislikes—why else would one resort to the risky, often frowned-upon, and largely illegal practices of magic to influence them? That rituals directed at social superiors should exceed the number dedicated to love, sex, or relationships is a surprising find that underscores the importance and power of the social hierarchy at the time our author and his intended readers lived. These rituals conferred a perception of agency in the minds of those who otherwise lacked it so desperately.

TABLE 8 Interpersonal relations rituals in the *Picatrix*

	Promote/ enhance/help	Vengeance/enmity/ discord
Social inferiors (slaves, children, "the masses")	46	36
Peers/allies/friends	36	18
Social superiors (kings, noblemen, lords, prelates, ministers, elders, judges)	158	16
Love/sex/relationships (husband/wife, man/woman)	115	30
Fear (cause/remove)	14	5
Unspecified	94	83
Unspecified (e.g., "for kings," "for sons," without indication of intent)	100	

Knowledge/Skills

Diagram 1 divides the realm of knowledge and skill into three broad categories: theoretical knowledge, applied skill (*techne* in the Greek sense, as it pertains to the working of material objects), and public performance. The numbers to the right of the slashes represent rituals devoted to diminishing or destroying that skill. Note that the seven liberal arts span the intersection areas of the diagram marked 1 and 2. The strong numeric predominance of theoretical knowledge combined with the observations made above regarding the literacy of the *Picatrix*'s audience explains its appeal to a readership among the junior ranks of the Western medieval academic system. The relatively small numbers devoted exclusively to applied skills that do not belong to the seven liberal arts (only sixty-one rituals fall in the bottom right-hand lobe of the diagram) emphasize how the *Picatrix* reflects primarily intellectual and academic concerns rather than those of individuals engaged with practical apprenticeships; indeed, guild-based crafts are nigh absent.

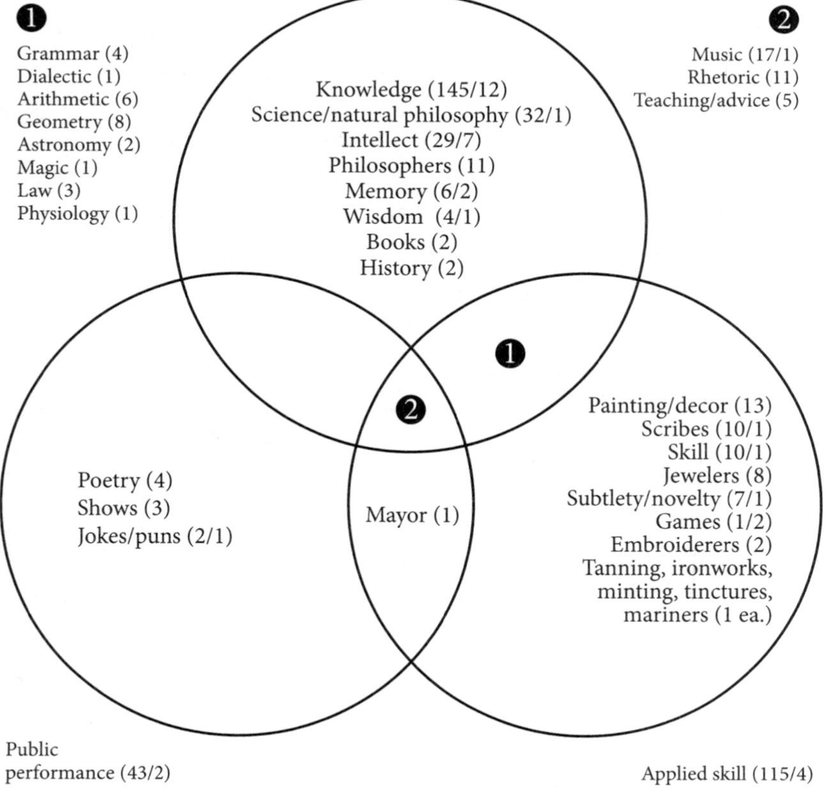

Diagram 1 Knowledge and skill rituals in the *Picatrix*

TABLE 9 Travel rituals in the *Picatrix*

	On land	By water	Undetermined
Make safe/help/assist	13	13	20
Harm/hinder	0	4	6

Travel

Table 9 reveals that our author and his audience are just about equally concerned with travel by water as by land. That travel should appear at all on this list reveals that the intended readership of the *Picatrix*, despite generally not being from the apex of the social pyramid, did have substantial opportunities for personal mobility. At the same time, these rituals show that travel of any sort—maritime or land-based—was a risky and hazardous enterprise on account of brigands and pirates. We have included two borderline cases: a ritual for teleportation (2.12.59) and one specifically for military travel (2.12.37).

Other/Outliers

The only large-scale concern with respect to the "other" category is methodological: none of its subdivisions is larger than the smallest category in table 1, as table 10 shows.

So, after examining all the data, what sort of impression emerges of the *Picatrix*'s values and priorities? The typical reader for whom the *Picatrix* would have been most relevant occupied the middle rungs of the medieval academic or clerical ladder, desirous of both material and social elevation: someone rather envious of others, especially of their accumulated wealth and physical surroundings. The author assumed his readership was familiar with the practice of medicine on some level, considering how prominently healing and health concerns of a variety of sorts arise in the text, especially concerning the hidden ailments of the psyche or of the internal organs. The book reflects the needs of those who predominantly inhabited an urban, built environment resulting in few encounters with large wild animals, and many more with poisonous and/or harmful pests. The text offers methods for magical control over both physical matter and the spirit world in roughly equal measures, but a greater priority than either was the acquisition of knowledge by any means, fair or foul. It represents a world with only occasional need for travel, in the case of a magus perhaps to gather and trade material components for rituals or for religious pilgrimage, both of which remained risky enterprises. It reveals

TABLE 10 Other/outlier rituals in the *Picatrix*

Good/evil	26
Motion/laziness	16
Law/governance (abstract)/justice	16
Animal friendship/control	15
Achievement (otherwise unspecified)	13
Beauty	8
International relations	4
Food	4
Shape changing	3
Purity	3
Grief/burial	2
Manual labor	2
Returning borrowed item, good belief, benefit, necessity, hope, truth, virtue, crowds	8 (1 each)

that our author was only peripherally involved in military conflict and marginally concerned about the source of his next meal. Indeed, commercial success was a greater worry than bountiful harvests: the latter must have been regular enough occurrences. This situation corresponds to what is known about the environment in the Medieval Warm Period, during which the text was first composed and translated into Castilian and shortly thereafter into Latin.

Although it is impossible to go beyond these sorts of general observations based on a study such as this one, the portrait that emerges from all these particular interests coexisting in a single book serves to explain the *Picatrix*'s eventual success in and among what Richard Kieckhefer has called the "clerical underworld" of Europe's magical practitioners—with literacy being the *sine qua non* of the learned magic tradition, a skill largely guarded and maintained by the Church.[80] It should be mentioned that this conclusion applies to the use of the Latin *Picatrix*, and it is not necessarily transferable to the use of the Arabic *Ghāyat al-Ḥakīm*.

Psychoactive and/or Poisonous Substances in the *Picatrix*

Homemade concoctions, suffumigations, pills, ointments, potions, and incenses abound throughout the text, particularly in books 3 and 4. Most suffumigation magic in the *Picatrix* seeks the assistance of planetary spirits. The ingredients composing these compounds, however, have hitherto received little specific attention, perhaps being deemed less important than the astrological or theoretical elements in the *Picatrix*. Throughout the work's magical recipes there are instructions for fashioning concoctions from variegated combinations of both inert materials (such as animal parts, human excrement, pine resin, and tarragon) and explicitly psychoactive ones (like opium, mandrake, datura, and cannabis). At times, suffumigations appear to contain no known psychoactive ingredients at all, while others are veritable cocktails of drugs mixed with binding agents to enhance the product's combustibility (e.g., mastic gum, frankincense, storax, and balsam). When the magician wished to speak with a planet, he dressed himself in robes dyed with the colors of that planet and made with an appropriate cloth, he found and abided by its hours, he prayed its prayers, and he "suffumigated" with its ingredients (3.7.1). Every ingredient found in a magical recipe (whether psychoactive or not) was selected according to its sympathetic nature with the particular planet governing the operation at hand. Since most scholars and students of history are typically not trained in the pharmacology of exotic compounds, we do not recommend that anyone try to recreate any of the following mixtures at home.

The operations in the *Picatrix* assume the body of the sage itself to be a magical vessel, taking in and synthesizing various spiritual powers and physical materials, at times in order to elicit a sensory experience and thereby accomplish the sage's aims. If the degree of complexity inherent to each ritual is indicative of the intensity of its practitioner's intent, the user of the *Picatrix*'s magic was compelled to possess what William Blake famously called a "firm perswasion [that] removed mountains."[81] The astral spirits can only appear to the individual who truly believes in them, not to those who are merely testing or toying with the book. Like the initiate of some preliterate cultures' shamanic rites, the sage, who spent months planning his work, collecting an array of ingredients, and charting out the right astrological hours to perform his work, was doubtless assisted—in certain cases—with achieving what he desired through the help of psychoactive substances. The substances for certain rituals involving suffumigation in the *Picatrix* are often required in such large quantities that a powerful mind-altering experience would have been inevitable for the practitioner. In these dreamy (or delirious) states, the planetary spirits cascaded down into the mind of the adept, who straddled the realm of common experience and the abstract realm of forms hidden within the subconscious. Nevertheless, through the perturbation of regular consciousness, the well-prepared sage perceived himself not as falling into a state of madness or delirium but into a perfected rationality (2.5.4), which granted access to otherworldly spirits. This world was opened to the sage alone who—refined by fasting, ritual, and intention—had studied the ways of the wise and could harness the effects of these mind-altering experiences without becoming overwhelmed. We do not, by any means, wish to suggest that all magic in the *Picatrix* can be explained away as drug-addled delusion; we merely wish to stress the ingredient lists' frequent reliance on psychoactive substances, which has received far less scholarly discussion than the text's underpinning astrological postulations.

Suffumigation is the chief method of ingestion for most psychoactive substances in the *Picatrix* (at least for those not meant as offensive poisons). Ointments, confections, and pills made of strange mixtures are not so rare either, but their use is more generally relegated to medicinal mixtures (e.g., for healing the stings of scorpions or the bites of vipers) or as composite poisons (e.g., for causing sleep or "ruining someone spiritually"). From a list of aphorisms attributed to Hermes Trismegistus, the twenty-seventh states simply: "Rituals performed with suffumigations and prayers are more effective than those in which suffumigations are lacking or the will is divided" (4.4.28). Among those practicing the science of suffumigation, the *Picatrix* recognizes the Indians and the Nabataeans (*Naptini/Neptini*) as the most proficient (2.5.1). The alleged masters of this art, the Indians, say that "suffumigations must correspond to the nature of the planet to which the request is made" (4.2.18). Ritual suffumigation, therefore, when used as a means of altering states of consciousness demands explicit and focused intent. It requires the magician to willfully remain standing over a smoldering mixture, sometimes in an enclosed area, as the world around him becomes progressively hazier and more bizarre, and the drama of his ritual reaches its apex. It is unclear, however, if any given magician would know which of the many substances they had compounded was responsible for the psychotropic effects. Although the effects of indirectly inhaling vapors would admittedly not be as potent or economical as direct consumption (e.g., through a pipe), it appears that the quantities required in some of the recipes would provide more than ample fumes to produce visionary experiences, at least given a confined space or close proximity.

One suffumigation, for example, is created for the purpose of conjuring Saturn (3.7.16), and is one of many recipes containing opium. We have isolated at least two substances that are known to be strongly psychoactive (opium and wormwood).[82] The ritual suffumigation of opium in braziers stretches back to at least the Neolithic Age.[83] Its addictive properties were not recognized until an epidemic of laudanum addiction swept over Europe during the nineteenth century due to its overprescription, especially to children. During this time, romantic poets like Thomas De Quincey wrote about their profound experiences with the drug, sensing within it a strong association with the far-off and mysterious "Orient." In his visions, he experienced communion with Egyptian and Indian gods and "was buried for a thousand years in stone coffins, with mummies and Sphynxes, in narrow chambers at the heart of eternal pyramids."[84] Smoked opium produces a relaxation to the point of disassociation wherein one falls in and out of waking dreams and becomes prone to visions.[85] In both waking and sleeping dreams, the planetary spirit could come to the magus all the more easily. With the addition of other known psychotropic substances, such as wormwood, this suffumigation would undoubtedly have induced profound mind-altering effects.

In many other suffumigations, such as the "suffumigation of the hermits" (3.7.27), nutmeg plays a prominent role. Intoxication from the essential oil of nutmeg (i.e., from the phenylpropene called myristicin, aptly named for its production from the *Myristica fragrans* tree), has a long history in India and Indonesia. It is traditionally used medicinally as a sedative, an aphrodisiac, a remedy for asthma symptoms, and a treatment for digestive problems. Nevertheless, its rather potent psychoactive effects are manifest after consuming as little as five to ten grams; in its early stages, its effects have been likened to a deliriant mix of alcohol and cannabis, while in its later stages, to a nauseating and sedative combination of LSD and tropane alkaloids.[86] Malcolm X, in his autobiography, famously reported that nutmeg use was a popular method of intoxication among prisoners.[87] In one account recorded by the *British Medical Journal*, a nineteen-year-old girl reported her experience with nutmeg in some detail: after a few hours she felt cold and nauseous; she saw faces and the room appeared distorted with flashing lights and loud music; she felt like a different person and everything seemed unreal; time appeared to stand still; and when she shut her eyes, she saw lights, black creatures, and red eyes.[88]

Throughout the *Picatrix*, a number of toxic ingredients appear that seem to be meant to test the subtlety of the magus's intellect in properly preparing the recipes. The *Picatrix* is clear that not every mind can bend without breaking and that its secrets should never be privy to any weak-minded individuals. Many plants listed among the ritual ingredients have parts with psychoactive effects and parts with deadly ones. Nevertheless, these details are rarely laid out in the ingredient lists. Other ingredients ought not to be consumed by humans at all. In one ritual for Saturn drawn from the works of a pseudo-Aristotle, the magician is advised to use a suffumigation made from "the brain of a black cat, euphorbia, hemlock, myrrh, and St. John's Wort" (3.9.11). Although quantities here are unspecified, it is certain that inhaling the fumes of hemlock (*cicuta*) would be injurious at best and lethal at worst.[89] This toxic herb, infamous for ending the life of Socrates, appears numerous times in the planetary suffumigations. It is indeed possible that a number of recipes such as this one were inserted by the author as a ploy to weed out the unwise readers of his cherished compendium of secrets.[90] Such ploys would have certainly reinforced the notoriety surrounding the use of magical books like the *Pictarix*.

Undoubtedly the most accessible and regularly consumed psychoactive substance at the time of the *Picatrix*'s rendering into Latin was alcohol, in the form of beer in northern Europe and wine in the south. The relative absence of this substance in the *Picatrix*'s recipes reflects the religious strictures against it due to the Islamic context of its origins. Indeed, the vast majority of the instances where wine is mentioned in the text feature its use as a moistening and binding agent for the manufacture of pills intended for combustion as suffumigations. That being said, there are a few rituals where the actual consumption of wine is integral, and a state of drunkenness appears necessary for its proper performance. Most prominently, we see among the instructions to invoke the power of Mars that the operator is instructed to "drink as much wine as possible," clearly leading to an altered state of consciousness (3.9.13).[91] The rarity of such instances serves to highlight the intentionality behind them.

The most psychoactive and dangerous of the substances used in the *Picatrix* come from the family of solanaceous plants, such as various *Daturas*, *Mandragora officinarum*, and *Hyoscyamus niger*, which are infamous for their uses in European witchcraft.[92] These, and a handful of other plants appearing throughout the work, contain the tropane alkaloids scopolamine, hyoscyamine, and atropine, which are each powerful deliriants even in small doses. Mandrake, henbane, and datura (also known as jimsonweed or thorn-apple) are known to provoke bizarre deliria, nightmarish hallucinations, out-of-body experiences, and so-called "flights." In some recipes containing solanaceous plants to be eaten or drunk, warnings are given of the mixtures' lethal potency in order that the magician might use them as poisons against enemies.[93] They can also cause death by respiratory paralysis. These substances can be lethal in low doses and must be prepared with extreme care. For this reason, they have not gained much popularity as recreational drugs despite their widespread availability. Modern connoisseurs of these plants tend to come from the ranks of Wiccan and Neo-Pagan revivalists willing to risk their sanity in recreating the rituals of medieval magical practitioners, whereas the average "psychonaut" or ritual magician shies away from them, preferring to stick to the safer, more predictable illegal drugs. Therefore, we neither advise nor encourage any reader to perform the operations described in this book. We cannot vouch for the safety of any one recipe, although we can acknowledge the inherent danger and/or illegality of many.

Translators' Notes

This section is provided as a caveat for those who may have been expecting a word-for-word "literal" rendering of the Latin text. The fact is, all translations are interpretations. Any attempt at such a literal translation of a medieval Latin text would yield, at best, what we like to call "latinese"—or at worst, outright gibberish. In other words, there is no such thing as a literal translation, and what is ultimately desired is equivalent meaning. For this reason, we as translators have taken some liberties (which will be elucidated below) in order to breathe some degree of life, clarity, and elegance into an old, recondite, and esoteric work. Our intention behind this translation is to combine the two seemingly contradictory concepts of scholarly rigor and ease of accessibility. Our desire is to make the text appear to a twenty-first-century English reader as we believe it might have been understood by a typical European medieval or Renaissance magus, aspiring to be well-schooled in the seven liberal arts. Our version does not in any way aspire to give an account for the original work in Arabic (the *Ghāyat al-Ḥakīm*); it is admittedly (and unabashedly) Eurocentric in this sense. Others are at work on the Arabic text itself, leaving us to focus on the version of the text that was so influential to its readers in medieval and Renaissance Europe.[94] Our interest in the *Picatrix*, at least as far as this book is concerned, lies with reception rather than inception (though admittedly, the latter phase is not entirely isolated from the former).

In translating the obtuse prose of the *Picatrix*—which at times is extremely prolix and at others, extremely terse—we chose to adhere to a number of stylistic conventions that, in our opinions, do not detract readers from the sense of the Latin text but rather elucidate the intentions of its original translator. In this sense, we are acting as "de-occultists" of sorts, surely much to the chagrin of the original author, al-Qurṭubī. As a monumental compilation of carefully curated sections drawn from 224 separate sources, according to the author himself (3.5.4), the *Picatrix* was intentionally designed to be elusive and difficult to read. The intention was to dissuade those common men merely interested in a casual perusal and attract only those who thrive in dealing with abstruse, esoteric texts. We can infer this from a claim the author himself makes: "The ancient sages who wrote in their books about mystical knowledge and magic did so as obscurely as possible such that few or none might benefit from them except for the wise and those who study and work with them assiduously" (3.4.1). Evidently, the author's intent was to carry on with this ancient tradition.

As a result, in our efforts to illuminate the obscurities in the text, we have eliminated a great number of redundancies that often clutter the text while providing virtually no additional clarity or meaning; if we sensed that they contributed anything to the meaning of a sentence, we retained them. Another regular practice was to eliminate the excessive use of self-referential expressions (e.g., "the aforementioned," "the aforesaid," "the things said above," "the things discussed")—these are often simply rendered (if at all) as "these things." Likewise, we liberally cut out extraneous adverbs and conjunctions that fulfilled the function of punctuation in medieval Latin, while trying to maintain the text's imperious feel.

Since the punctuation of the Latin text depended on Pingree's interpretation of numerous variant manuscripts, we often took the liberty of subdividing excessively long sentences into more manageable parts and resupplying subjects in place of pronouns. For intelligibility's sake, we have been very cautious to employ the Oxford comma. At times, we provide brackets to disambiguate particular examples from general principles, which often run seamlessly in succession. Other times, we simply supply brackets to break up a lengthy sentence for clarity. In order to produce a clearer and more idiomatic text, we rendered into an English active voice a countless number of sentences hinging upon Latin passive verbs. In most cases, we distilled the three different types of Latin imperative formulations (imperative, second person subjunctive, second person future) into simple present imperative English commands. For example, "take such-and-such a thing, and grind it into a powder" instead of "you should take such-and-such a thing and you should grind it into a powder" or "you will take such-and-such a thing and you will grind it into a powder" or, most turgid of all, "let such-and-such a thing be taken and ground into a powder." This seemed far more concise and appropriate, especially in magical recipes.

In regards to the planets, we have supplied gendered pronouns where necessary in accordance with astrological tradition: Moon (female), Mercury (male or hermaphrodite), Venus (female), Sun (male), Mars (male), Jupiter (male), and Saturn (male). The signs of the Zodiac, however, are left gender-neutral.

In those instances where the Latin was impenetrable or nonsensical, or for particularly complex and technical astrological passages, we consulted a number of other translations into modern European languages (German, French, Italian, and English) and then exercised our judgment accordingly. These translations are listed in the "*Picatrix* Editions and Translations" section of the bibliography. In cases where the identification of specific ingredients was unclear, we checked the manuscript variants from Pingree's critical apparatus to see if any meaning could be gleaned from them or left the terms in their transliterated form, as it is likely these would have appeared alien to the text's medieval and Renaissance readers as well.[95] All translations into English from both ancient and modern languages are our own.

Pingree's edition includes a full table of contents at the beginning of the text as well as at the beginning of each of the *Picatrix*'s four books. We judged the tables at the beginning of the text and those before each of the individual books to be redundant and have thus left them out of this volume. In including selected materials from Pingree's appendices, we inserted the passages where they belong in the sequence of the text, but used square brackets to distinguish them from the main text since they only appear in a minority of manuscripts. Typically, we excluded excerpts that added little relevant content. Furthermore, we also excluded marginalia from various manuscripts, as they represent the idiosyncratic interests of individual readers and/or copyists. Lastly, the numbers in square brackets that appear throughout the translation correspond to the page numbers in Pingree's Latin edition, while elision marks between pointed brackets (< . . . >) indicate lacunae or corrupt sections of the Latin text.

In recipes that include specific measures for ingredients, Pingree's edition ubiquitously uses the medieval apothecary's symbol for "dram" (ʒ). All available translations have interpreted this as "ounce," yet the recognized symbol for ounce is ℥. The extant manuscripts of the Latin *Picatrix* are inconsistent with respect to their use of these symbols, so wherever our translation reads "ounce," the reader should be aware that the intent may equally well have been "dram."

PICATRIX

[1] PROLOGUE

§1 To give praise and glory to the highest and omnipotent God, who commands us to reveal the secrets of the sciences to His chosen ones (and for the enlightenment of Latin scholars who lack works published by ancient philosophers), Alfonso, most illustrious king of Spain and all of Andalusia, by the grace of God, ordered that this book entitled "Picatrix" be translated from Arabic into Spanish with the utmost zeal and diligence.[1] This undertaking was accomplished in the year of the Lord 1256 (in the year of Alexander 1568; in the year of Caesar 1295; and in the Arab year 655).[2] One wise philosopher, the noble and honored Picatrix, compiled this tome from over two hundred books of philosophy and then named it after himself.

§2 In the name of our Lord, amen. Here begins the book that this most wise philosopher Picatrix composed about the magical arts with the help of a great many volumes. As the wise have said, the first thing we must do in all worldly affairs is give thanks to God.[3] I proclaim that God must be praised since it is by His light that secrets are revealed and things concealed are made manifest. It is through God's power that all miracles occur and by Him that all prayer and science is understood. At his command, the day was separated from the night. Through God's power, all things were created from nothing and proceed toward their perfection—and by His potency all creatures are renewed.[4] God himself is not confined by other things, nor is He separate from them. He has no definite location, nor is there anything outside of Him, since He is space itself. All the languages in the world could not bear witness to God's works or proclaim His powers. Indeed, God's wonders are infinite and nothing is novel to Him. For that reason, let us praise Him. Let us obey Him, His prophets, and His saints, who were illuminated by His command and who revealed to humankind the ways of the world through which they might attain that knowledge and wisdom of God. So, let us implore Him to receive us into His grace and lead us to eternal reward for His glory. Amen.

§3 O you who wish to direct your attention toward the knowledge of the philosophers, to know and ponder their secrets, first you must seek out the great wonders of the art that they set forth in their books, and you must strive to focus on the wonders of the science of magic. Before that, however, you must know that these philosophers kept this knowledge secret and were sworn not to divulge any of it to humankind. More precisely, they occulted this knowledge on account of its powers and discussed it through shrouded words, [2] images, and symbols, as if discussing some other sciences. This decision to hide their knowledge is indicative of their honesty and goodwill, since if this knowledge were revealed to humankind, it would destroy the universe. On this account, the philosophers shared their knowledge figuratively, in such a way that none could understand it unless they were as enlightened in this knowledge as these philosophers were. Despite all their efforts at concealment, they nevertheless shared the paths and rules by which a sage might attain this knowledge and make progress in all the subjects they discussed esoterically. It is for this reason that I compiled this book, and in it I intend to explain the means and ways to this knowledge, to outline what sages have said about it, and to reveal what they concealed in their works through exotic and deceptive words.

§4 I therefore pray to the highest creator that this work of ours fall into the hands of no sage lest they be capable of following everything I am about to say herein—and consider it beneficial—such that everything done through it be done for the good and in the service of God.

§5 Furthermore, this tome is divided into four books and each of these is divided into their own chapters. In the first book, we discuss the nature of the heavens, as well as their effects that ensue from the signs therein. The second book discusses the figures of the heavens in general, the motion of the eight spheres, and their effects upon this world. The third book discusses the properties of the planets and signs, laying out their figures and forms in their appropriate color, revealing how one might speak with the spirits of these planets, and many other magical affairs. The fourth book discusses the faculties of spirits, the necessities of this art, and how one might be assisted by images, suffumigations, and other things. [3]

BOOK 1

Chapter 1

On the Science of Knowing Where You Are

§1 Know, dearest brother, that the ability to possess knowledge is a very great and noble gift that God bestowed on humankind since through knowledge one can become acquainted with ancient things, the causes of everything in this world, which causes are more immediate than others, and how one thing influences another. In this way, everything in existence can be understood (i.e., why it exists, why one thing is set in order above another, and where that singular root and foundation of everything exists). Through God all things are reconciled, and through God all things both new and old are discerned. He Himself is first in truth. Nothing is lacking in Him, nor does He lack anything. He is the cause of Himself and everything else, and He receives qualities from no other. God is neither a body, nor composed of any matter, nor mixed with anything outside of Himself. Rather, God is whole in and of Himself. He cannot be described except as *The One*. One sole truth and one unique unity pertain to Him, and through His unity each thing has unity. He Himself is the first Truth, nor is He lacking the truth of another; everything receives its truth from Him. Indeed, everything other than God is imperfect. God alone is perfect. Truth is incomplete without God's unity and vice versa, for only His truth or unity can be considered perfect. All things exist below God and from Him receive their truth, unity, generation, and corruption.[1] On this account, one can discover how every part of each thing [4] receives its properties from Him, how this happens, and why. God alone understands the order and rank of generation for all creatures (which of them are first, which are middling, and which are lowest). Those creatures in the lowest rank are a source for corruption to other creatures but never a source of generation to them. Those creatures in the middle have a source of corruption within themselves but only cause corruption in all the creatures that exist beneath them. Those creatures ranked highest are the source of generation and corruption for all the creatures that exist beneath them, but nothing is higher and more perfect than that which is the source of its own generation and corruption. There is nothing aside from *The One* that seeks to know perfectly the proper order of created things, how those lowest creatures are exalted by their similarity to another until they are conformed with the first, and how they proceed from the first in due order until they conform with the last. God alone is the first—perfect philosophy and knowledge of Truth. Understand that knowledge is the utmost noble thing and strive in God every day—in His commandments and in His goodness—since knowledge, sense perception, and goodness all proceed from Him. God's spirit is a boundless and excellent light. Anyone who intends to be deeply devoted to Him must despise the concerns of this world, since they are transient and lack permanence. As if from a celestial world, the human spirit descends from God. As such, one must desire to return to that place whence one came, where the root of one's existence lies. There, he will understand the nature of the world, what its powers are, and how it was made by its creator. The source of this knowledge is true wisdom. Know that God Himself is maker and creator of the entire universe and that everything existing within it was created by Him, the most exalted. The mind of God is too deep and powerful to be understood, and that which can be understood from it must be grasped through study and knowledge. Dedication to knowledge and understanding—this is the greatest gift that God gave to humanity. Therefore, to study is to serve God. Understand that knowledge has three properties: the first is that it always grows and never diminishes; the second is that it is always praised and never devalued; and the third is that it is always clear and never ambiguous. Likewise, knowledge has three more properties: the first is that it causes humans to spurn the concerns of this world; the second is that it promotes good character; and the third is that it does not exceed what it desires to learn while seeking out its wishes through reason and will.

§2 Know, therefore, that the secret we mean to divulge in our book cannot be understood without the prerequisite knowledge. Whoever intends to understand it must focus on knowledge and pursue it exhaustively.[2] The secret will not be revealed except by a sage—one determined to study these disciplines in the right order. This secret is most pure and will be of great advantage to you. [5]

Chapter 2

What Magic Is and What Its Properties Are

§1 Know that this science is called "magic."[3] We call "magic" any act someone performs in which the spirit and all the senses are engaged throughout the whole process and through which miracles are produced to the extent that the senses are driven to their contemplation and wonder. Magic is difficult to perceive through the senses and lies hidden from sight on account of its similarity to sense perception. This is because divine powers have been set aside for perceiving these things and using them. This knowledge, however, is too deep and powerful for the intellect. One part of this magical science is practical, on account of how it works by operating from spirit into spirit, making those things similar that are not so by their essence. Working with images, however, involves spirit in matter, and alchemical work involves matter in matter. Generally, we use the term "magic" for everything hidden from the senses whose causes most of humanity cannot perceive. The wise call the images "talismans" which literally means "force-bearers" because those who fashion images do so through force, by conquering the substances from which they are composed. To succeed, one builds images with mathematical proportions, influences, and celestial effects. Such talismans are composed from substances appropriate for receiving the celestial influences.[4] This is done at appropriate times, and the influences are further fortified by suffumigations that attract specific spirits to those particular images. This works similarly to the Elixir that overcomes matter and, by transmutation, reduces it to another purer matter.[5] In the same way, magicians craft images that operate through force. Poison works similarly when coursing through a body, changing it, and reducing it to its base state (since poison changes one body into a different body through the power of its composition). Know that the power of purification, which is called the Elixir, arises from earth, air, fire, and water. These four elements are united into one and reduced to the union's original state because once the purification process begins and penetrates matter, the Elixir scatters throughout its makeup such that the altered matter becomes more perfect, more potent, and changed in state. This Elixir likewise functions in alchemy insofar as it effortlessly transmutes matter from one nature into another nobler one: first by overcoming the spirit, then the hardness, and then the resonance by removing the dross and the noise. This is the secret of the Elixir according to the wise ancients. The word Elixir means "power" because it shatters other powers by overcoming them and transmutes them from one state to another until reducing them to a state similar to its own.[6] The Elixir can only be produced if one combines animals, trees, plants, and minerals throughout every step of the process since they say the Elixir is a reflection of the world, and the world is composed of all these things. Moreover, the Elixir must be composed of like things because each part influences [6] every other part, and each part depends on every other (just as trees cannot stand on their own, plants and animals cannot subsist without other plants, and minerals need heat and the power of fire with humidity and air); this is how the Elixir is made. This we discovered in a book called *On Ordinations*.[7] Now let us return to our proposed topic.

§2 I say that magic is divided into two parts, namely the theoretical and the practical.[8] The theoretical part is the knowledge pertaining to the positions of fixed stars since the celestial signs and the forms of heaven are derived from these. The theoretical also pertains to how the fixed stars project their rays onto the planets that move themselves about. It is the science of knowing the signs in the heavens when they (the astrologers) do what they intend to do. Under this topic we include all the debates of the ancient sages regarding the selection of hours and times for the crafting of images. Know that one who truly understands the construction of images is aware that their power relies entirely on the correct selection of astrological hours and times appropriate to the things for which the images are made. Another aspect of magic is concerned with words since words hold in themselves the strength of magic. And Plato agreed, saying: "friends are made foes through callous and cruel words, and so too are foes made friends through kind and pleasant ones."[9] From this it is clear that words have inherent magical power. Moreover, this power is augmented when many powers are coordinated; this is how the power of magic is manifest. All this encompasses the theoretical part.

§3 Now, the practical part pertains to three natures in combination with the power that pours down from the fixed stars. The wise call this "power," but they do not understand what type it is nor how it links with the powers mentioned above. Once these things have been brought together (i.e., those that have the abovementioned properties), they ought to have elemental heat. This is the heat that in suffumigations helps perfect that imperfect power. Therefore, suffumigations must be lit with a natural heat to be used for consumption. Ultimately, these two things are useless and impossible to perform without the spirit of man and animal.

§4 Know that magic is performed through works and deeds and also through other subtle means. Indeed, the magic accomplished through works and deeds emerges from the disciplines that the sages of the world carry out below the sphere of the Moon (as one sage said in the *Liber Alfilaha*, where it is written to trap four birds).[10] The part of magic acquired from subtle means, however, comes from the works written by that sage who labored on the movements of the sphere of Saturn and so too from the writings of that wise man who labored on the movements of the sphere of Venus. Both these wise men wrote in this *Liber Alfilaha*.

§5 Ancient Greek sages used to perform tricks for altering vision and making things appear that do not exist. They called this science of images *yetelegehuz*, which translates as "the attraction of celestial spirits."[11] [7] The sages applied this name to all facets of ceremonial magic. They came to such knowledge by no means other than astrology, and they could not proceed beyond astrology until they knew (i) all the figures on the eighth sphere,[12] (ii) their motion, (iii) the motion of the other spheres, (iv) the division of the twelve signs with their own degrees and natures, (v) the qualities of each sign and the implications of each upon worldly affairs, (vi) the parts of each of the planets in those twelve signs, (vii) the movements of the Zodiac and at what times other bodies are conjoined with them, (viii) the natures of the seven planets and the Head and Tail of the Dragon, (ix) their location in the heavens and the meaning of each relative to the things of this world, (x) how to predict each of their ascendants and descendants, (xi) which ones rise and fall before the others, and (xii) their radical significations; these are the fundamentals of astrology. Furthermore, one must know which of the seven planets dominates in which sign, one must understand their proper order in that dominion, and one must determine the parts of the planets from the Zodiac. These are the things without which one cannot attain a working knowledge of this science; and all these things are found in the books of astronomy.[13] This is what the first sage said in the *Liber Alfilaha*, where we read: "They exalted me above the seven heavens." What he meant was that he understood all the motions of the heavens and their qualities through the power of contemplation and sense perception. This is what God meant when He spoke: "Let Us exalt man on high." Indeed, He means to say: "Let Us give him sense perception and understanding such that he might grasp profound knowledge."

Chapter 3

On What the Heavens Are and of What Substance They Are Made

§1 The shape of heaven is spherical, round, and smooth in its surface area and so is everything in it with respect to their qualities and rotations.[14] Certain people believe that at one time the heavens did not appear round. This is false: the shape of heaven is its own shape and cannot be otherwise because that is the shape of spirit, and one must admit that spirit is first, and nothing in the universe is older. Doubtless, what is first and oldest in the world ought to have a perfect shape. The perfect shape and figure is a circle because it is the first of all the shapes and is itself made up of a single line.[15] None of the generation and corruption in the matter that constitutes this world can occur in the heavens. On the contrary, no part of the heavens can have its essence undergo the generation and corruption of here on Earth; and all this is because of the heavens' power and superiority. The firmament is, as we have said, a round sphere in all its parts, truly symmetrical in its roundness and contained by the line of a circle, in whose middle is a point from which all the lines that lead to the line of the circumference are of equal length; that point is called the center. [8] They say that those lines symbolize the rays that the stars project onto the Earth, as if into its core. From these rays arise the effects and powers of the images, and this is how they work. As we said, the heavens are a round sphere containing the whole world within itself (i.e., within its capacity). Such a sphere has neither bumps nor holes—it is form, permanent in itself, and from it, all the spirits' powers arise. The heaven of fixed stars is beneath it, and its center is separate from it, for in fact, its center is the same as the center of the Earth. The nature of the heavens is of one single nature, and all motion, both of bodies and of nature, follows the motion of the heavens. All heat pours down from them, and by this we mean that all of Earth's heat comes from the heavens. The degrees of heaven are 360 in the first division, and the figures are the same in number. Through these, all of the judgments of astrology are determined, since the judgments follow the images of the heavens, and the heavens are the cause of all processes below.

§2 The effects and powers manifest when the planets are in these figures. Both the aspect and the conjunction that they have with one another and the effects of the planets that govern over earthly affairs in the world are of the same type. So, if it were Saturn, cold and dry things would be affected; if Jupiter, hot and humid; if Mars, hot and dry; if Venus, things of moderate heat and excess humidity; if Mercury, things of low heat and high dryness; but if it were the Moon, cold and humid things would be affected, and if it were the fixed stars, then they would be affected through their own powers (like the Moon). When any planet enters some degree of heaven within which it has power and if the planet were itself clearly hot yet lacking in humidity and dryness, and if the Sun were drawing upon its power, we ought to conclude that its effect must increase and grow. Similarly, if we find that a planet is acting by empowering something through its own nature and power, that thing will be stronger and more potent in its effects on Earth. If the planet were affecting a contrary thing, its effect would be weakened according to the planet's power in that function.

According to this, understand the effects of planets, and you will not go astray. This you can find in the books of astronomy.

Chapter 4

On General Theories and the Arrangement of the Heavens for Fashioning Images

§1 When the sages of old wished to craft magical images, they could not ignore the constellations, which are fundamental to the science of images. The constellations are the very things by which the images' effects are made manifest. What we mean is that there are fundamentals to those constellations that will support you in all rituals with these images. These fundamentals are the heavens' workings toward the effects of the images. Those who seek to make images should have knowledge of the relationships of planets, the other constellations, and also of the motion of the heavens. They must firmly believe in the rituals they perform with the magical images such that the work they implement will be genuine and without doubt. They must not [9] doubt a single thing concerning the rituals' effects and not perform them for the sake of testing or probing whether or not they are efficacious. Through this, the rational spirit is strengthened and united to that power of the upper world whence the spirit acting upon the image came. Thus, what is sought shall be. [Firmly believe that a combined action of the intellect and of the first and principal among all intelligences and intermediaries is required for the image to have power. Among all intelligences, the human soul or intellect seems to be the lowest, whose combined action is also required. It, however, acts alone and collectively with firm and total concentration, diligence, and the utmost concern. In our parlance, this is called "faith." In matters of craft, if the craftsman does not make his product with diligence, concern, and total concentration, he will seldom bring about and complete his task skillfully.][16]

Now, I want to teach you a most necessary component to these operations, and that is performing your ritual when the conditions on this world are favorable for magic. Indeed, I say that you should have nothing to do with these operations unless the Moon is sitting in a favorable and appropriate degree relative to those tasks you intend to accomplish since the Moon, to whom nothing lies hidden, has power and obvious effects upon the things beneath her. Afterward, I will explain to you the most splendid results in these processes that will profit you greatly in those works; but at present I intend to talk about the effects and works of the Moon within the boundaries of her own mansions according to what every sage in India agreed upon regarding the Moon's twenty-eight mansions.[17]

§2 The first mansion of the Moon is called *Alnath*. It begins from the first minute of Aries and ends in the position of the twelfth degree, fifty-first minute and twenty-sixth second of the same sign. The sages of India would begin journeys and take medicine when the Moon was in this mansion. Place this mansion as a foundation to all the images that you intend to make for those going on a journey so that they may come and go safely. Also, this mansion ought to be placed as a foundation to creating discord and enmity between a man and a woman and between two friends so that they become enemies and also to sow discord between two associates; and do this similarly when you wish to cause a slave to flee. I shall demonstrate to you the fundamental source that must be observed in all beneficial works and rituals: namely, that the Moon be well-positioned, safe from Saturn and Mars, and safe from the combustion of the Sun. On the other hand, in every ritual bent on causing harm, know that the Moon must be in combustion from the Sun and in conjunction with Saturn and Mars or at least be facing one of them.

§3 The second mansion is called *Albotain*. It begins in the twelfth degree, fifty-first minute, and twenty-sixth second of Aries and ends in the same sign at the twenty-fifth degree, forty-second minute, fifty-second second. In this mansion, make images when you wish to dig channels or wells, to discover lost treasures, to plant a mass of wheat, or to destroy the completed buildings of households; and similarly, make an image in this mansion to make one man rage against another and also to make a prison stronger and securer for its captives.

§4 The third mansion is called *Azoraya*. It begins in the aforementioned degree and ends in the eighth degree, thirty-fourth minute, and second second of Taurus. In this mansion, make images to protect those sailing by sea such that they might return safely, to reinforce the prison cells of captives, to accomplish works of alchemy, to carry out any work done with fire, to pursue hunting expeditions on land, and to create affection between husband and wife. [10]

§5 The fourth mansion is called *Aldebaran*. It begins in the eighth degree, thirty-fourth minute, and second second of Taurus and ends in the same sign, namely in the twenty-first degree, twenty-fifth minute, and forty-fourth second. In this mansion, make an image to condemn a city or village or some other building you wish to destroy, to make a master abhor his slave, to instill discord between husband and wife, to contaminate springs and wells, to find buried treasures, and to kill or bind every kind of reptile and poisonous animal.

§6 The fifth mansion is called *Almices*. It begins at the twenty-first degree, twenty-fifth minute, and forty-fourth second of Taurus and ends in the fourth degree, seventeenth minute, and tenth second of Gemini. In this mansion, make images for children learning a craft or profession, to protect those on journeys that they may return quickly, to protect those travelling by sea, to improve buildings, to destroy the alliance of two men, and to instill affection between husband and wife. This happens when the Moon is rising in a human sign, safe from Saturn and Mars and safe from the combustion of the Sun, as we have mentioned above regarding the first mansion. These are the human signs: Gemini, Virgo, Libra, Sagittarius, and Aquarius.

§7 The sixth mansion is called *Athaya*. It is from the fourth degree, seventeenth minute, and tenth second of Gemini all the way to the seventeenth degree, eighth minute, and thirty-sixth second of the same constellation. In this mansion, make images to destroy cities and villages, to position armies around them, to enable the enemies of kings to exact vengeance, to condemn harvests and trees, to spark friendship between two associates, to improve hunting in the countryside, and to curse medicines such that they fail to work on those taking them.

§8 The seventh mansion is called *Aldirah*. It begins in the seventeenth degree, eighth minute, and thirty-sixth second of Gemini and ends at the end of the same constellation. In this mansion, make images to increase trade and profit and to travel safely, to increase harvests, to sail safely, to generate friendships between one's friends and one's associates, to prevent flies from entering a location you wish, and to ruin someone's career. The mansion is effective for going before a king or some other notable person, for gaining royal favor, or for getting whatever you wish from some lord.

§9 The eighth mansion is called *Annathra*. It begins in the first degree of Cancer and lasts until the twelfth degree, fifty-first minute, and twenty-sixth second. In this mansion, make images for love and friendship, to ensure that whoever goes through villages in a wagon may proceed safely, to spark friendship between two associates, to reinforce a captive's jail cell, to curse and afflict captives, and to expel mice and bedbugs from wherever. [11]

§10 The ninth mansion is called *Atarf*. It begins in the twelfth degree, fifty-first minute, and twenty-sixth second of Cancer and ends in the twenty-fifth degree, forty-second minute, and fifty-first second of the same constellation. In this mansion, make images to condemn harvests, to curse travellers and all those seeking to do harm, to erect divisions and enmities between allies, and to force a man to defend himself from another man who wants something from him.

§11 The tenth mansion is called *Algebha.* It begins in the twenty-fifth degree, forty-second minute, and fifty-first second of Cancer and ends in the eighth degree, thirty-fourth minute, and eighteenth second of Leo. In this mansion, make images to incite love between man and wife, to curse enemies and travellers, to reinforce the jails of captives, to reinforce and complete buildings, to create benevolence between associates, and to help one another.

§12 The eleventh mansion is called *Azobra.* It begins in the eighth degree, thirty-fourth minute, and eighteenth second of Leo and ends in the twenty-first degree, twenty-fifth minute, and forty-fourth second of the same constellation. In this mansion, make images to liberate captives, to position armies outside cities and villages, to organize trade and the wealth it yields, to protect travelers on the road, to reinforce buildings for stability, and to increase the wealth of friends.

§13 The twelfth mansion is called *Acarfa.* It begins in the twenty-first degree, twenty-fifth minute, and forty-fourth second of Leo and ends in the fourth degree, seventeenth minute, sixth second of Virgo. In this mansion, make images to improve harvests and plants; to ruin someone financially; to curse ships; or to bolster allies, authorities, captives, and slaves that they may be stable and prosperous.

§14 The thirteenth mansion is called *Alahue.* It begins in the fourth degree, seventeenth minute, and sixth second of Virgo and lasts until the seventeenth degree, eighth minute, and thirty-sixth second of the same constellation. In this mansion, make images to increase trade and its profits, to enlarge harvests, to protect travelers by road, to complete buildings, to free the incarcerated, and to charm noblemen for one's benefit.

§15 The fourteenth mansion is called *Azimech.* It begins in the seventeenth degree, eighth minute, thirty-sixth second of Virgo and ends at the end of the same constellation. In that mansion, make images to instill love between man and wife, to heal the infirm with knowledge of the body and medicine, to curse harvests and plants, to empower kings such that they may be strong and take the throne, to protect those sailing, and to win the friendship of associates.

§16 The fifteenth mansion is called *Algafra.* It begins in the first degree of Libra and ends in the twelfth degree, fifty-first minute, twenty-sixth second of the same constellation. In that mansion, make images to dig wells, to seek buried treasures, to impede travelers on their journeys, to put a division between a husband and his wife so that they may never have sex, to induce [12] discord between friends and associates, to scatter enemies from their positions, and to destroy their homes.

§17 The sixteenth mansion is called *Azubene.* It begins in the twelfth degree, fifty-first minute, and twenty-sixth second of Libra and ends in twenty-fifth degree, forty-second minute, and fifty-second second of the same constellation. In this mansion, make images to curse merchandise, harvests, and plants; to induce discord among friends or between man and wife; to curse a woman you desire; to impede those on a journey such that it might fail; to induce discord between friends; and to free captives from jail cells.

§18 The seventeenth mansion is called *Alichil*. It begins in the twenty-fifth degree, forty-second minute, and fifty-second second of Libra and ends in the eighth degree, thirty-sixth minute, second second of Scorpio. In that mansion, make images to heighten deceptions so that one might excel through them, to position armies around cities and villages, to reinforce and stabilize buildings, and to protect those navigating on water. Everyone agrees that the Moon should be in this mansion while forging friendships; the friendship will endure and never be destroyed. In this mansion, make everything for the arrangement of lasting love.

§19 The eighteenth mansion is called *Alcalb*. It begins in the eighth degree, thirty-eighth minute, and second second of Scorpio and lasts all the way to the twenty-first degree, twenty-fifth minute, and forty-fourth second of the same constellation. In this mansion, make images to rouse conspiracy against kings, to inflict vengeance upon desired enemies, to build and reinforce buildings, to free captives from prison cells, and to divide friends.

§20 The nineteenth mansion is called *Exaula*. It begins in the twenty-first degree, twenty-fifth minute, and forty-fourth second of Scorpio and ends in the fourth degree, seventeenth minute, and tenth second of Sagittarius. In this mansion, make images to position an army around cities and villages, to enter and take them, and seize what you will, to ruin the wealth of whomever you please, to drive men from a place, to benefit men going through villages in wagons, to increase harvests, to make captives escape, to destroy and shatter ships, to divide and ruin the riches of associates, and to kill captives.

§21 The twentieth mansion is called *Nahaym*. It begins in the fourth degree, seventeenth minute, and tenth second of Sagittarius and ends in the seventeenth degree, eighth minute, and forty-sixth second of the same constellation. In this mansion, make images to domesticate wild and untamed beasts, to cause those travelling by carriage to return swiftly, to make any man come to wherever you wish, to associate good men with one another, to reinforce prison cells for captives, and to bring evil and ruin upon the riches of friends.

§22 The twenty-first mansion is called *Elbelda*. It begins in the seventeenth degree, eighth minute, and forty-sixth second of Sagittarius and lasts all the way to the end of the same constellation. In this [13] mansion, make images to reinforce buildings, to increase harvests, to retain profits firmly, to protect those travelling through villages, and to separate a wife from her own husband.

§23 The twenty-second mansion is called *Caadaldeba*. It begins in the first degree of Capricorn and lasts all the way to the twelfth degree, fifty-first minute, and twenty-sixth second of the same constellation. In this mansion, make images to heal infirmities, to set discord between two men, to make slaves and captives flee, to cause goodwill between associates, and to cause captives to escape.

§24 The twenty-third mansion is called *Caaddebolach*. It begins in the twelfth degree, fifty-first minute, and twenty-sixth second of Capricorn and ends in the twenty-fifth degree, forty-second minute, fifty-second second of the same constellation. In that mansion, make images to heal infirmities, to unite friends, to divide a man from his wife, and to make captives escape from their jail cells.

§25 The twenty-fourth mansion is called *Caadacohot*. It begins in the twenty-fifth degree, forty-second minute, and fifty-second second of Capricorn and lasts all the way to the eighth degree, thirty-fourth minute, and twenty-eighth second of Aquarius. In this mansion, make images to improve commerce and its profits, to induce goodwill between husband and wife, to give soldiers victory over enemies, to ruin the riches of friends, and to disrupt enterprises such that they might not come to fruition.

§26 The twenty-fifth mansion is called *Caadalhacbia*. It begins in the eighth degree, thirty-fourth minute, and twenty-eighth second of Aquarius and ends in the twenty-first degree, twenty-fifth minute, and forty-fourth second of the same constellation. In this mansion, make images to position armies around cities and villages, to take vengeance upon enemies and to inflict evil upon them as you please, to hasten envoys to deliver their messages and return quickly, to separate a wife from her husband, to wither harvests, to bind a man and his wife or a woman and her man such that they cannot have sex, to bind any limb of the human body you wish so as to render it useless, and to further reinforce the prisons of captives; it is good for making buildings.

§27 The twenty-sixth mansion is called *Almiquedam*. It begins in the twenty-first degree, twenty-fifth minute, and forty-fourth second and ends in the fourth degree, seventeenth minute, and tenth second of Pisces. In this mansion, make images to unite men in mutual esteem, to protect those travelling by carriage, to reinforce the prisons and cells of captives, and to inflict evil upon them.

§28 The twenty-seventh mansion is called *Algarf almuehar*. It begins in the fourth degree, seventeenth minute, and tenth second of Pisces and ends in the seventeenth degree, eighth minute, and thirty-sixth second of the same constellation. In this mansion, make images to improve commerce and its profits, to unite associates, to increase harvests, to heal infirmities, to ruin someone's riches, to impede the construction of buildings, [14] to imperil those sailing, to prolong the incarceration of captives, and to inflict harm on whomever you desire.

§29 The twenty-eighth mansion is called *Arrexhe*. It begins in the seventeenth degree, eighth minute, and thirty-sixth second of Pisces and lasts unto the end of the same constellation. In that mansion, make images to improve commerce, to besiege cities, to increase harvests, to balance things, to ruin jokes, to cause someone to lose treasure, to protect those travelling by carriage and ensure their return in good health, to instill peace and harmony between husband and wife, to reinforce the prison cells of captives, and to inflict harm upon those who sail by ship.

§30 The wise Indians held these twenty-eight mansions as foundational in all of their rituals and elections.

§31 The fundamental part of this text is that you ensure that in all benevolent rituals, the Moon is safe from both Saturn and Mars, from their aspects, and from the combustion of the Sun; and that she is tied to the fortunes by favorable aspects (i.e., the trine and sextile aspects). In all these affairs, ensure that the Moon is separate from one fortunate planet and joined to a different fortunate planet. Make sure you do the opposite in malevolent rituals.

§32 A practitioner of magical arts should be one who puts faith in his own actions without any doubt regarding the rituals. That is how the practitioner becomes well-disposed to receiving the effects and powers through which he intends to do magic. This disposition exists within humans alone. The disposition exists in other sensible creatures, however, it is such that they receive sensations according to their own individual natures (just as wax effortlessly takes the forms pressed into it, or a demonically possessed man is invaded by other demons since his body is disposed to receiving such demons given that his broken body is powerless to resist them). Similarly, a disposition toward weakness is found in a place of power, just as the disposition suited to the materials from which images are fashioned is found in those materials; for all materials are predisposed to receiving some effect harmonious to them. This is a fundamental to these rituals, and everyone agrees on it. When a disposition exists for receiving influence, it will be received; and when the reception has occurred, the effect will be clear and manifest, and the figure will receive power. The effect will be as you desire insofar as matter and form will be united as one, just as the image of a man is united with a mirror or a pool of water or just as the unity of spirit and body.

§33 If you wish to undertake a ritual during daytime, ensure that the Moon is ascendant and—while she is ascending—that she is in one of the diurnal signs. If the ritual is at night, she should be ascending in a nocturnal sign. If she will be ascending out of the signs of direct ascent, the effect will be swifter and surer. If the Moon is ascending in a sign of tortuous ascent, the task will be more difficult.[18] This can be improved or impeded by [15] aspects toward the fortunate planets, such that if the Moon were ascending out of a sign of direct ascent and an unfortunate planet were also in it, it would curse, cancel, and suppress the effect. If the Moon were ascending out of a sign of tortuous ascent and a fortunate planet were to look toward her or gaze upon her with a good and favorable aspect, that effect would be effortlessly brought about. Likewise, when diurnal signs ascend at night or nocturnal signs by day with a fortunate planet in aspect with them, the fortunate planet directs and fortifies them; and if unfortunate planets are in aspect with them, they bring about ruin. One who intends to craft an image must thoroughly understand: the signs of direct and tortuous ascent; the fixed, mobile, and impartial signs; the diurnal and nocturnal signs; the fortunate and unfortunate planets; the times when the Moon is safe from the influences opposed to her; and which images are appropriate to each planet and sign. As much as possible, beware of performing magic pertaining to beneficial effects when the Moon is eclipsed or beneath the rays of the Sun by twelve degrees ahead and behind. Likewise, guard her from Saturn and Mars and beware lest the Moon herself be setting in a northern latitude when she goes out of the twelve degrees mentioned above; and that same thing is true concerning southern latitudes in opposition. Be sure that the Moon is not in a slow, waning course, that is, when she proceeds less than twelve degrees in a day because she is assimilated to the motion of Saturn; and beware that she not be in a combusted path, which is also to be avoided (i.e., from the eighth degree of Libra all the way to the third degree of Scorpio). Moreover, make sure the Moon is not on the edges of the signs, which are the boundaries of the unfortunate planets, nor falling from the angle of the mid-heaven (i.e., in the ninth house). If an emergency arose and there were some important desired effect that could not wait until the Moon was free from all unfortunate planets, have Jupiter and Venus in the ascendant or in mid-heaven because they rectify the unfortunate influences of the Moon. Know that whatever we say, we do not say to profane the secrets that are written in the books of the wise. We beseech God omnipotent that, by His piety and grace, this book may reach the hands of none but those who are wise and good. You must, therefore, be the custodian of everything written herein; never reveal it to any unworthy person.

Chapter 5

On Examples of Cases for Discussion and the Requirements for Making Images

§1 When you wish to craft an image for inducing love between two individuals (and to give their love and joy the strength of an oak), make images in both of their likenesses. Make them in the hour of Jupiter or Venus with the Head of the Dragon ascending.[19] Let the Moon be with Venus or looking toward her with a favorable aspect. Let the lord of the seventh house look upon the lord of the first house in a trine or sextile aspect. Afterward, join the images together in an embrace, and bury them at the home of one of the two people (i.e., at that person's home whom you wish to feel most in love). Whatever you desire shall come about. [16]

§2 *Images for generating peace and love between two individuals.* Make two images under the ascendant of the querent's question. Let the ascendant and the tenth house be fortunate. Remove the influence of unfortunate planets from the ascendant. Let the lord of the tenth house be fortunate, facing the lord of the ascendant from a trine or sextile aspect.[20]

§3 Here I intend to clarify other key concepts about the aspects. The trine aspect pertains entirely to love because all signs of a fiery nature gaze at each other in a trine aspect; the same applies to aerial and aquatic signs. This aspect creates perfect friendship. The sextile aspect, however, concerns lukewarm friendships because the signs gazing upon each other in that aspect are congruent with one another in their active but not their passive natures; thus, it is called an aspect of "moderate friendship." The square aspect pertains to moderate enmity because the signs gaze upon each other from two contrary natures. The opposite aspect is one of extreme enmity because the signs gazing upon each other are opposed in all four natural qualities. Now, let us return to our proposed topic.

§4 Make a second image: were it for two friends, make the eleventh house of the first image the ascendant of the second; were it between a man and a woman you wish to make friends, make the ascendant of the second image be the seventh house of the first image. Let the lord of the ascendant of the one who seeks to return to friendship be facing the lord of the other image's ascendant with a favorable aspect, and let it be well received. Afterward, join the images, and bury them at the home of the one who seeks the friendship; henceforth they will be friends as before.

§5 *An image to cause two individuals to fall in love.* Make two images with Venus ascending in the first face of Cancer and the Moon in both the first face of Taurus and the eleventh house. Once you have, join the images in an embrace, and bury them in the home of either one. They will like each other, and a durable love will prevail between them. They call these the figures of alteration, and Ptolomy speaks about this in proverb thirty-three of his book *Centiloquium*.[21] We shall speak of this in the fourth book of this tome. There, if God wills it, we shall further explain.

§6 *An image to cause a durable love.* Make two images, and place a fortunate planet in the ascendant and the Moon in Taurus joined with Venus. Using the figures of al-Khwarizmi (the ones that employ 0s), write "220" on one image and "284" on the other.[22] Join both images in an embrace. Then there will arise a perfect, durable love between the two. [17]

§7 *An image to cause kings and nobles to favor whomever.* Make an image in the shape of that man, in his name, in this way: make the ascendant fortunate with a fortunate planet that is strong and not waning, retrograde, or combusted. Let the lord of the ascendant be strong and in good condition, direct, and in its exaltation. Let the lord of the tenth house gaze upon the lord of the ascendant in a trine or sextile aspect with a strong reception. Place the lord of the ascendant in commanding signs and the lord of the tenth house in obedient signs.[23] As long as that man for whom this image was made will hold it close, he will be esteemed and honored. Whatever he seeks from the lords with whom he interacts, he will obtain.

§8 *An image to cause a lord to be esteemed and obeyed by his men.* Make two images. Make one in the hour of Jupiter with the Moon facing the Sun in a favorable aspect and separated from the unfortunate planets with the Head of the Dragon in the ascendant. Next, make the other image whose ascendant should be the fifth house from the ascendant of the first image in the hour of Venus; let the Head of the Dragon be in the ascendant or facing it while ascending with a favorable aspect. Do this in the hour of the Moon, when the Moon is free from unfortunate influences. Bury the images beneath the ascendant of one of the fixed signs in the hour of Saturn. Join them in an embrace, and bury them in the place of that man who seeks the love of another.

§9 *An image to cause a slave to favor his master.* Make two images. Make one in the hour of any of the superior planets; let the ascendant be outside the houses of any of the superior planets with the Moon waxing and the Head of the Dragon in the ascendant, fourth, seventh, or tenth house.[24] Make the second image in the hour of any of the inferior planets, whose ascendant should be the tenth house of the first image's ascendant, and place the Tail of the Dragon in the ascendant, fourth, seventh, or tenth house. Once you have made those two images in this way, join them in an embrace, and bury them in the home of the man who seeks the love of the other.

§10 *An image for being promoted by a lord.* Make an image, and let the ascendant, the tenth house, and likewise the lord of the ascent be fortunate. Remove the unfortunate influences from the ascendant and its lord, and let the fortunate planet be in the eleventh house gazing toward the ascendant and its lord with a favorable and praiseworthy aspect. Let the lord of the tenth house be facing the lord of the ascendant with a favorable aspect and reception. Once the image is completed, keep it near and secret, out of sight; when you go before a lord and seek an office or promotion from him, you will have it.

§11 *An image for increasing wealth and trade.* Make an image, and let the ascendant, the tenth house, their lords, the lord of the house of the ascendant's lord, and the lord of the house of the tenth house's lord, the Moon, the lord of her house, also the second house and its lord be fortunate; let the lord of the second house receive [18] the lord of the ascendant in a trine or sextile aspect. Let a fortunate planet be in the second house. Let the Part of Fortune be in the ascendant or the tenth house, with the lord of that Part of Fortune facing it with a favorable aspect.[25] Let the eleventh house and its lord likewise be fortunate. Once this image is complete, guard it, keep it secret and out of sight. You will profit in whatever you do, and you will succeed in all your efforts.

§12 *An image for expanding cities so that they may prosper.* Make an image; let the ascendant, the tenth house, and its lord be fortunate; let them face a fortunate planet. Let the lord of the second house, the lord of the eighth house, and the lord of the ascendant be fortunate, and face a fortunate planet. Let the lord of the house of the ascendant's lord, the Moon, and the lord of the house of the Moon be fortunate. Once this image is completed as described, bury it in the middle of the city, and what you seek will unfold.

§13 *An image for acquiring the love of another.* Make two images. Make one in the hour of Jupiter with Virgo ascending and the Moon waxing. Let the Moon be in the ascendant, fourth, seventh, or tenth house. Make the second image in the hour of Venus, herself facing Jupiter; let the unfortunate planets be receding from the ascendant; let the ascendant of the second image be in the seventh house and the lord of the ascendant facing the lord of the ascendant in a trine or sextile aspect. Once this is done, join them together in an embrace, and bury them in the home of that man who wants to acquire love and goodwill.

§14 *An image for destroying an enemy.* Make an image in the shape and appearance of the man upon whom you wish to inflict evil in the hour of Mars with the Moon in Scorpio. As much as possible, let the ascending planet be unfortunate by placing an unfortunate planet on the ascendant or facing it with a bad aspect. Let the unfortunate planet and the lord of the ascendant face each other. As much as possible, let the lord of the fourth house and the ascendant's lord be unfortunate, and let them face each other. Let the lord of the ascendant in the fourth house be unfortunate, or have it be received by an unfortunate planet in the fourth house or in the ascendant. Once you have done this, bury the image upside down outside the city wherein your enemy resides. Your wish will unfold.

§15 *An image for destroying a city.* Make an image in the hour of Saturn (since it is an unfortunate planet) under the ascendant of that city. Let unfortunate planets be in the ascendant, present with the lord of the ascendant, and the lord of the house of the ascendant's lord. Let the fortunate planets be removed from the ascendant, its lord, the lord of the triplicity of the ascendant, and also from the fourth, seventh, and tenth houses. Once this is done, bury it in the middle of the city, and you will see wondrous things.

§16 *An image for hindering the construction of buildings.* Make two images, one in the hour of the Sun with Leo ascending and the other in the hour of the Moon with Cancer ascending. Do this when the Moon is waxing and safe from the unfortunate planets [19] and swift in its course. Once this is done, bury them in the hour of Venus, and the building will be impeded.

§17 *An image to cause a prisoner to escape.* Make an image in the shape of the incarcerated individual whom you wish to free in the hour of the Moon, while she is waxing, swift in her course, and free from unfortunate planets. Bury the image under the ascendant of the tenth house of that city by placing the face of the image toward the building where the imprisoned is detained.

§18 *An image for destroying an enemy.* Make two images, the first in the hour of the Sun with Leo rising and the Moon receding from the ascendant; make the other in the hour of Mars with both Cancer ascending and Mars receding from the Moon. Make the images look like one is striking the other. Bury them in the hour of Mars with the face of Aries ascending. Once this is done, you will be able to act against your enemies by whatever means.

§19 *An image for making a man flee from his home.* Make an image under the ascendant of any of the signs ascending tortuously. Let its lord be receding from the ascendant, fourth, seventh, or tenth house. Let the Moon be receding likewise. Bury the image at a crossroad under a combust path. Place the face of the image towards the place from which you wish to make the man flee, and you shall see wondrous things.

§20 *An image for separating two friends.* Make an image beneath any ascendant, and let the ascendant and the tenth house be unfortunate; let the lords of the ascendant and the tenth house be unfortunate; let an unfortunate planet face them with a square or opposite aspect. Then let the fortunate planets recede from the ascendant, the tenth house, and their lords. All in all, make the other image just as was described above. Bury it in the place of the other image under the ascendant of the fixed sign made unfortunate by the Tail of the Dragon or when another unfortunate sign rises. Once this is done, those friends will hate each other and never love one another again.

§21 *An image for directing the wrath of a king upon someone.* Make two images according to the instructions for the images above. Let the lord of the ascendant be receding from the lord of the tenth house or be made unfortunate by him and facing the lord of the fourth house from a square or opposite aspect. Bury them under the unfortunate ascendant of any of the fixed signs. Once this is done, the king will hate that man.

§22 *An image for catching many fish.* Make an image in the shape of a fish living in that specific river. Do this with Pisces ascending and Jupiter within it, and make Venus the lord of this hour. Make it this way: first make its head and body, then a tail, and join them together at the hour discussed. Make one thin silver stylus, and place the image on the head of the stylus; then make a jug or another vase made of lead with a narrow spout. Place the stylus upright in the middle of the spout and the image of the fish on the very top of the stylus. Next, fill the vase [20] with water, and plug its spout with wax lest the water escape the vase. Afterwards, throw the vase to the bottom of a river. All the fish from that area will be gathered to it.

§23 *An image for catching fish.* Al-Hanemi spoke in a certain book of his concerning an art that he himself possessed, tested, and found to be true.[26] He spoke thus: make an image in the shape of a fish, cast it with the second face of Pisces ascendant, and let the Moon and Mercury be in the ascendant. Do this in the hour of the Moon. When this image has been made thus, throw it in the river when fishing; you will see wondrous things because of the multitude of fish that will gather there.

§24 *An image for repelling scorpions.* Make an image of a scorpion out of the purest gold in the hour of the Sun; place the Moon in the ascendant, fourth, seventh, or tenth house, in Taurus, Aquarius, or Leo (the best of which is Leo because its nature is more contrary to the scorpion). Let the Sun be in Leo and Saturn retrograde. First craft a tail, then the feet, next the claws, and finally the head. Pay close attention to the order, and understand it well for it will help you in many tasks. Once you have crafted those limbs, place the left claw in the place of the right claw and the right foot in place of the left foot; then place its head in its proper place and likewise the tail. After this, craft the stinger, and attach it to the tail upside down; then place the tip of the stinger in such a way that the scorpion can only strike itself with its tail. Once the image is made, bury it in a perforated stone from a mine. Subsequently, bury the stone in an important part of the city; scorpions will flee and no longer come within forty-five miles of the site of the image from any direction.

§25 *An image for healing scorpion stings.* Make an image of a scorpion in a bezoar stone. Do this in the hour of the Moon in the second face of Scorpio, with Leo, Taurus, or Aquarius ascending. Bind that stone to a gold ring, and impress the seal into softened incense under the abovementioned constellation. Give one of those impressed pieces of incense to the stung man in a drink; he will be healed at once, and the pain will subside.

§26 There spoke a certain man from the land of the Blacks who made it his life's work to prove the above and its understanding.[27] He recommended writing a single name on a tin tablet that one holds on his person. When someone was stung by a scorpion, this man soaked the tablet in water, which he gave to the stung man to drink. He was healed at once, and the pain subsided. This man also said that when he did not have a tin tablet, he wrote the names of things that can be drunk (such as saffron) on a clear glass plate with writing chalk. He gave the drink to the sick man, and his pain ceased immediately.

§27 Were it not from fear of being verbose, I would recount the wonders that he performed with those names; because he gave those drinks [21] to numerous men, I could not name them all in brief. Nevertheless, since I saw those names put to the test, I have decided to relate them in this book here. They are:

ZAARE ZAARE RAAM ZAARE ZAARE
FEGEM BOHORIM BORAYN NESFIS ALBUNE
FEDRAZA AFFETIHE TAUTUTA TANYN ZABAHAT
AYLATRICYN HAURANE RAHANNIE AYN LATUMINE
QUEUE ACATYERY NIMIERI QUIBARI YEHUYHA
NUYYM LATRITYN HAMTAUERY VUERYN
CATUHE CAHUENE CENHE BEYNE ✡[28]

These names must be written in precisely seven lines—no more no less—and with Solomon's seal at the head of the seventh line.[29] Some say that they must be written on the first Thursday of the month of May, and others say that could be written on the first Thursday of any month. I have seen them written whenever. Beware lest you make a mistake in those names, in their forms, or in their figures; they must be transcribed accurately. Among the names written, I have seen a wise man write "BOHORIM" or "NOHORIM" with an "n," but I recall it with a "b" as I said above. I say this to you so as to reveal the secrets of this science.

§28 *An image so that men may be loved by women.* Make an image of a girl out of a cold and dry metal, and make it with Mercury ascending in Virgo, increasing in the circle or being the *almutaz* of the chart.[30] Do this in the hour of Mercury until the image is complete. Afterwards, make another image in the form of a young man while Mercury is in Virgo and returning to the place of the first image or in Gemini. Watch for the diversity of the ascendant (that is, when Mercury is in Gemini, do not put Virgo in the ascendant, but whichever one you do put in the ascendant, put Mercury in it). Once you have made both images thus, join them in an embrace, and wrap the hands of each around the sides of the other. Do all this in the hour of Mercury with Virgo or Gemini ascending. Encircle the images with a band of that metal from which you created them, and bury the images in the most densely populated quarter of the city. Once you have done this, men will be joined with women and have high quality sex. Similarly, do this when a man desires the favor of a woman so that she might fancy him; bury the images in the place where you want them to be joined.

§29 *An image for destroying cities, homes, and similar things.* Make an image under the ascendant of that city, if you know it, or under the ascendant of the question. Let the ascendant, the fourth house, the lord of the ascendant, the Moon, the lord of the Moon's house, the lord of the house of the ascendant's lord, the tenth house, and its lord be unfortunate. Once you have made the image, bury it in the middle of the city, and what you seek will happen.

§30 *An image for making a physician profit.* On a tin lamella make an image of a man sitting on a throne, performing the task of a physician. Make [22] another image of a man standing on his feet with a urine sample in his hands in front of the physician performing a diagnosis. Make both of those images under the ascendant of Taurus or Libra with Mars in the ascendant and with the Head of the Dragon in mid-heaven. Once you have done these things, set that lamella and the images together in that place where you wish men to come, and you will see men drawn to that place miraculously.

§31 *An image for multiplying harvests and plants.* Make an image on a silver lamella of a man sitting surrounded by harvests, trees, and plants. Make this with Taurus ascending, when the Moon is in Taurus journeying away from the Sun toward Saturn. Bury it anywhere, and all the seeds and plants there will grow quickly and well, without loss from beast, bird, storm, or any manner of pest to the harvest.

§32 *An image for healing kidney stones.*[31] On a lamella of the purest gold, make an image of a lion with a stone in its paws as if in a war dance with it. Make it in the hour of the Sun in the first degree of the second face of Leo ascending. Let the sick man carry this lamella with him. Immediately, he will be cured. This has often been verified. [Regarding the construction of the image of a lion, Hermes adds that the Moon must not be facing the sixth and the Sun not be facing Saturn or receding from it.][32]

§33 *An image for casting out depression and irritability.* If you want to cure someone's depression, to strengthen health thoroughly, or to withdraw curses from whomever you want, make an image out of the purest silver in the hour of Venus, the Moon being in the ascendant, fourth, seventh or tenth house, and facing Venus with a favorable aspect. Let the lord of the sixth house face a fortunate planet in a trine or opposite aspect, and let the lord of the eighth house face Mercury with a square aspect. Beware lest Mercury be retrograde, combusted, or faced by an unfortunate planet. Make that image in the last hour of the day of the lord. Let the lord of the hour be in the tenth house from the ascendant. Once it is made, these ills will abate.

§34 Know that the qualities of the images, the powers and effects that they have within them, come solely from the celestial bodies. When the images are made according to the celestial motions, nothing can hinder or stop them. One must observe when casting images for love and friendship that the Moon be fortunate and full. Avoid making anything while the Moon is unfortunate and waning. A similar example: make an image for love and affection and for the visitation of kings or of lords of a superior rank, on Monday, with the full Moon in Sagittarius, Taurus, Cancer, or Pisces (and were she in the Head of the Dragon, the image will be more effective) and always in a fortunate house, appropriate for the task. Let the Moon be joined to Venus in the hour of Jupiter with Jupiter himself in Pisces, [23] Sagittarius, or Cancer, the Moon being with him. On the other hand, if you want to make an image for evil, do it with the Moon in an unfortunate house and conjoined with unfortunate planets or facing them with a square or opposite aspect; thus your work will be completed. In everything mentioned, note that the crafting of images is better done at night than during the day.

§35 What is necessary to these magical operations—without which one cannot complete anything—is to link one's whole will and belief to the operation such that the power of the spirit be joined to the power of the heavens; only then will everything actually be fulfilled. Plato said in his book of aphorisms that when one speaks a word with intention—and it agrees with one's belief—those who hear it will be moved (and vice-versa if one did the opposite). This is the basis for joining the will with belief during prayer, and this is of utmost importance in seeking our desires from the Lord when we pray.

§36 The specifics of these magical rituals must be hidden from humankind and the light of day. They should not be performed anywhere the Sun might enter. Let no other individual know about these rituals unless he be faithful in his friendship and persuaded in the work. Let him be neither a scoffer nor a disbeliever in the works and powers of celestial spirits, in their potencies which have effect upon this world, or in the belief that these works ensue from these spirits. Thebit ben Corat stated in the book he composed, *On Images*: "Knowledge of the images is the most excellent part of astronomy," to which he added:

"A body without life has no spirit."[33] He said this concerning images not made at the right and opportune times, which as such were not suited to receiving the spirits of the planets and were therefore akin to dead bodies wherein dwells no spirit. When crafted at the right and opportune times, the magical images receive spirits and the pouring down of planetary powers and thus are akin to living bodies from which ensue wondrous effects.

§37 Aristotle said in his books on magical images: "The best and most excellent effects that images can have come from the seven planets. The effects are more durable when a fortunate planet is looking on." He meant this in regards to drawing the spirits and powers down from heaven to Earth. Furthermore, he said that there are names of spirits that if one were to invoke and draw them down, their powers in their respective hour would kill the invoker unless he was wise and well-instructed in the nature of that spirit (and of the planet appropriate to this ritual for drawing it down) that he might receive it into his body.

§38 This is how those who perform rituals with very powerful names bring about miracles in the world, and they say that their power to change themselves exists according to their own natures. Most of those who practice with the name above disagree. I myself have completed one book on this name and how [24] we ought to understand it. I have laid this out in explanations on each of these.

§39 I wish to return to the statement of Aristotle on magical incantations. He said that none of them exceed the circle of heaven, nor should they have such an ability to draw down spirits since words do not have such power except at the behest of the glorious and high God, who moves the spirits by His command by diverting them toward Earth and sending them to its core. Thus spoke Aristotle.

§40 Every sage who discussed this body of knowledge agrees that words coupled with prayers in image-based rituals may serve toward the completion of works and tasks. The wise Thoos said:[34] "Words on images are like spirits in a body, mobilizing spirits and powers to working effect. How powerful is the word of one who, while performing a ritual, applies his own will and confidence!" Therefore, it is this noble factor that allows for the completion of the images and words we discussed. The following things we intend to say are relevant in all the rituals that we will cover in these books.

§41 *An example.* If you wish to make an image for love and unity, speak this:

> Let such a man, N, be joined with such woman, N, just as fire and air and water and earth are joined. Let the spirit of such a man be moved toward such a woman, just as solar rays move the light of the world and its inner capacities. Let this woman and her actions become as important to such

> a man as the stars are to the heavens or the blossoms are to the trees. Place the excellent and sublime spirit of such a man atop the spirit of such a woman just as water sits atop the earth!

That said, such a man should refuse to eat, drink, dance, or feel any joy without such a woman.

§42 If your image were made to separate people or put enmity between them, speak this: "Through the powers of those spirits and planets, divide and rend asunder such and such, just as light is divided from darkness; let enmity and hatred arise between them, just as fire and water are opposed!"

§43 If your image were made to bind some man to some woman (or to many others), say this: "Let the spirit of desire for such and such a woman bind you (if you are doing this for a single woman) or for all the others (if you are doing this for a group); through the strength and power of the spirits and planets, may this work seize you in the same way mountains accumulate and bind stone!"

§44 If your image were for dissolving this magical binding, say this: "Through the power of the spirits and planets, may the fetters of such a bound and constricted man or woman's spirit be broken, dissolved, and destroyed, just as fire melts wax, the Sun dis-spells the darkness and its spirits, and snow is consumed by the heat of the Sun!" [25]

§45 If you wish to prevent individuals from putting curses on you or anyone else, say this: "May you blanket such an individual with a cover of shining light, cut the tongues of men from their mouth, and blind their eyes with a cover of spirits that drive out evil incantations. Let their evil tongues and desires be cut out!"

§46 If your image were made to curse someone such that everyone might hate them, say this: "Through the strength and power of those spirits and planets, let such an individual be corrupted and destroyed, just as a solar ray dissolves or breaks down the thickness and density of clouds. Let their spirits be affixed to the malign tongues of men until they be ruined, just as bodies are ruined by the arrows loosed from bows! "

§47 Beware while you perform any aforementioned works lest you err in using things unsuited to the chosen operation. Instead, speak the words that reinforce and perfect your rituals.

§48 Guard these words well and diligently since they offer great profit and utility in the use of images. With these words, and by adhering to those instructions, you will be able to create all the images in the world. A magical image should be crafted in a similar manner and in proportion to the thing for which the image was made, whether for good or evil. Hereafter, I intend to relate which things are governed by each of the planets, from metals to animals, trees, colors, suffumigations, sacrifices, and so forth. From these you will benefit in all your operations, just as the physician works with many medicines and diagnoses in addition to the cooperation of the patient toward observing diets and taking medicines. This is how a physician reaches his intent. The entire basis of these procedures is the observation of the planets' and constellations' movements. Ancient Greek sages would observe a planet, waiting until it entered its own appropriate node.[35] Once the planet reached the point of midheaven, they would suffumigate it with the suffumigations suited to that planet and make sacrifices with suitable prayers. They requested their desires and fulfilled them. Similarly, when they worked with an ascending planet, they got what they desired. It should be noted that the rituals discussed are more effective if the planet has power in the nativity of the one for whom the ritual is performed. Know this because through it, you will fulfill your desire.

Chapter 6

In What Degree Everything in the World Exists and How We Know That Humans Are a Microcosm Similar to the Macrocosm [26]

§1 Recognize that knowledge is most excellent and exalted. Whoever pursues and applies it receives its excellence and splendor. Knowledge is like a ladder in the sense that once one thing is known, a new thing becomes immediately apparent to the knowledgeable individual. Perfect is the one who reaches the ultimate degree of knowledge—who rejoices and delights in those degrees of knowledge. Such men are called "lovers of wisdom" in Greek, but in Latin they are called "lovers of knowledge." One who does not pursue knowledge is defective and lacking in authority. That individual should be considered human in name only, merely possessing a human form and shape. Nevertheless, should one happen to pursue knowledge, one should recognize what a human actually is and how humankind itself is a microcosm analogous to the macrocosm—a body perfected by a complete, animate, and rational spirit. By those three spirits, humans are set apart, insomuch as they have reason, from the animals and all the other things of this world. Reason is like an attorney: it can recognize contingencies and determine which ones are false. Reason directs itself to any place in the world and takes it in through its own knowledge and sense perception. Reason retains the things it perceives through its own strength and power. Through this, humans perceive with their senses things that may happen throughout the day and to other humans (who are microcosms similar to the macrocosm, corresponding in form and contents). Humans are similar to animals in all their inherent characteristics but set apart by their knowledge and expertise. They have six motions; they have hard bones (all naturally set in straight lines and moved by the parts beside them); they have fingers and palms set out in straight lines; they have round heads and a capacity for reason. Humans engage both the sciences and the scriptures, attain mastery, and reject all things animal, while they themselves are not rejected by anything. They laugh, cry, and make sorrowful sounds in lamentation. God's virtue and the knowledge of justice for governing cities dwells within them. Humanity is an image, bearing an internal light, since the human body is an image. Humans are both powerful in spirit and well-proportioned in shape. They understand which things are beneficial and which are harmful.[36] They work with diligence and skill and are distinguished thereby. They learn subtle disciplines in fine detail, perform miracles, make wondrous images, and preserve all forms of knowledge. From all the other sensible creatures, humanity is distinct. God made humanity the author and explorer of His wisdom and knowledge, the expounder of His qualities, the receiver of all worldly things through His prophetic spirit, the treasure of His wisdom, and the knower of all things (including the conjunctions that exist in the macrocosm). Through their senses, humans comprehend all intelligences and how the things of this world work, yet the intelligences themselves cannot comprehend humanity. All things serve humankind, and humankind serves none of them. With their voice, at any time, humans can imitate every single animal. With their hands, they fashion shapes similar to them, and with their words, they recount, relate, [27] and explain the animals' natures and actions. There is no other animal with the ability to understand humans nor any that can change their voices and imitate others. The cock, the dog, and the lion, for example, cannot change their voices. Humans, with their own intrinsic voice, have the power of replicating the sounds of all the animals and of shaping their forms and likenesses as desired. Humans conduct themselves with good habits, impart them to the animals, and direct them accordingly. Humans possess a gross body and a subtle spirit since they are one part physical and another part spiritual. The subtle part pertains to life, the gross one to death; the essence of the one is changing, and the essence of the other is immutable; the one's essence is formed, the other is formless; the essence of one is night, the other's is day. One is light, the other darkness; one is openly visible, the other secret; one perceives, and the other is perceived; one weighs down, and the other is weighed down. Humans feel ashamed of their evil deeds, which they do by freewill, and repent for some. They are composed of both gross and subtle matter, having within themselves the density of earth, the subtlety of air, the heat of fire, and the coldness of water, all of which make humankind well-proportioned in the motions of its vital power. The heat of fire is discerned relative to the heat in humans, and the coldness of water is discerned relative to the coldness in humans. From this process, humans discern the other elements of this kind.[37]

§2 The shape of the human head is analogous to the shape, appearance, and roundness of the heavens. Generally speaking, all manner of subtleties are bound together in the human form.

§3 The universal human form is a vessel in the form of universal spirit; universal spirit is a vessel of generalized consciousness; and generalized consciousness is a vessel of the light whence proceed the senses. Light is the material of universal consciousness, which belongs to a higher degree than all inferior things. Matter is always inferior to it and relatively simple. In this way, humans were created from the composite form of humankind, given that they rule over all other bodies, all the while being themselves united with another nature.[38]

§4 Whoever desires to understand this must live simply, be inclined to goodness, be ritually cleansed, and be free from all fleshly impurity and concerns, since anyone disposed as such possesses the capacity to search and behold with their own consciousness to confirm the matter.

§5 We mentioned that we have deviated from the intent of this book. This intent—the knowledge of magic and the awareness of it—are the very foundations of this book. If you strive diligently in the pursuit of knowledge, in the understanding of things and how they are perceived (whatever they may be), then regardless of what happens, you will be able to employ and understand ceremonial magic and the occult arts. Plato said this in the book he assembled called the *Timaeus*, wherein he explained the forms at great length. He put forth his reasoning very adeptly given that [28] he spoke in riddles, as it was customary for sages to obfuscate and conceal their knowledge such that fools could never understand it. A certain other sage, Zadealis by name, wrote of similar things in his book, which he conveyed secretly and profoundly.

§6 The subtlety of the wise in their explanations resides in the occult and profound nature of words. Consequently, wise men's words cannot be understood without great concentration. Concepts lie dormant in those words until the hidden meaning is extracted from them. Then the meaning is extracted from other scenarios that are understood from the outset through the intellect and vision. This knowledge is divided into two parts, of which one is manifest, the other hidden. The hidden part is boundless. Boundless perceptions are those that cannot be well understood without first understanding the others that precede them. Only then is this explanation clear and revealed. If anyone were to study these things thoroughly, they would get what they desired: secrets would be revealed to them, and they would satisfy their will. The paths and methods for obtaining these things are many. Some of them are for sending manifest phenomena back into occultation, for tracing back branches to a root such that they may be integrated, or even for aligning your mind and thoughts with the reliable proverbs of holy men or saints. In this way, you will achieve completion and perfection and attain your desires. The hidden senses will be manifest and revealed to you in those words. Accept what is suitable from these paths such that you might achieve, reach, and reveal the things hidden to human understanding—through one of these paths, you will be able to obtain your desires, understand the sciences and their reasoning, and recognize everything and every sense in its proper order.

Chapter 7

In What Degree Everything in the World Exists and on Many Other Profundities Hidden by Sages That We Intend to Reveal in This Book

§1 Everything in this world is connected and organized in accordance with its proper order. The first of all things in this world—the most excellent, splendid, and complete—is God, the maker and creator of all. After God, in descending order, is mind or intellect; after mind, spirit; after spirit, matter. Matter is inert, unalterable, and unchanging from place to place. Next is the sphere of nature, which is called the prime mover of motions, and it is the source of the generation and corruption that besets the world. Next is the sphere of fixed stars wherein are found the other spheres, according their proper positions, all the way down to the sphere of the Moon. Below that is found common matter—namely, the *Prima Materia*—which is inherent to every material thing in this world, though it is not apparent.[39] After matter are the elements that are part of that common matter, since the elements have no [29] processes nor operations in matter. After the elements follow (in order): minerals, plants, animals, and finally, the rational animals. The discernment of this order is different from others because other orders are discerned by the intellect, which is more excellent and splendid than everything else.[40] And so, by descending, the other orders proceed toward baser things until they reach the sphere of the Moon; then by proceeding from the lower to the higher, they reach humans, who are more excellent than all sub-lunar things. For in humans, knowledge, wisdom, and inquiry are openly brought to fruition. Know that whoever intends to pursue knowledge must work scientifically. Whoever does so will secure an improved fortune and avoid becoming what one sage warned against in saying that there is nothing worse than people who want to appear sophisticated without having the knowledge.[41] Since these types cannot acquire understanding, unlike those who strive for it faithfully, a human deprived of true knowledge is only human by equivocation.

§2 Know that the things encountered in this world have other orders and divisions that I intend to relate here for sharpening the intellect so that it might have more practice in the pursuit of knowledge. Focus upon it, and you will understand the secrets of the wise. They are organized in this way: first there is the Principle, then high matter, then the elements, then matter, then form, then nature, then the body, then growth, then the animal, then humankind, then man, then the individual person named. The First Principle is more universal than high matter because it is said to be above matter and above the capacity to be acted upon. It is not called matter except as matter in a body. Matter is more universal than the elements because matter is without combination, and the elements cannot exist without combinations. The elements are more universal than other materials because an element is a simple body, and it receives qualities, whereas matter is an orderly unification of the elements for receiving form. Matter is more universal than form because it is simple before receiving form. Once it receives form, it becomes matter-and-form—just as brass is the matter constituting the form of a vessel, and wood is the matter constituting the form of a chair.[42] When matter-and-form receive motion and applied intent, their quality is changed, and nature unfolds thus. When their natures are joined together, they receive color, growth, and diminution. Growth is divided into animal and non-animal; the animal is divided into human and nonhuman; human is divided into man and woman; and man is recognized individually as such-and-such a man.

§3 Matter is a union of elements organized for receiving form. Matter is divided into two parts of which one is simple matter that does not receive anything but the form of the elements—earth, air, water, and fire—and is transmuted from one material to another. The other part is universal matter disposed to receiving every form composed of simple qualities [30] (heat, cold, dryness, and wetness).[43] It cannot be transmuted from one material into another. One sage called it this: that which is disposed for receiving all diverse forms. It is also known by a different name, after that part of nature called the body where it is governed and perfected in all things.

§4 In so far as we have discussed this design, we have only done so to sharpen the intellect and illuminate consciousness because the words and explanations discussed are spiritual images—the very words that Adam received from the

Lord God. They are intelligible to none but the sages who have faithfully labored in the pursuit of knowledge and those who have understood how they are beings predisposed to the truth. Understand all these things, and tuck them away in your mind, since what we have said in this book thus far is fundamental to the magical art, if you understand it well.

The first book ends [31]

BOOK 2

The Second Book Begins Wherein Stands a General Discussion on the Heavens' Signs, the Motion of the Eighth Sphere, and Their Effects in This World

Chapter 1

How One Can Grasp This Knowledge

§1 Sages naturally endowed with sense perception always seek to know and understand the secrets of the wise. These they hid in their books written with occult words. They discovered such things by means of diligent [32] inquiry to the extent that they achieved their desire. Fools, however, and those lacking in intelligence are unable to achieve or reach these things. The motion of my will advanced to the exploration of magic and the occult at the time of my youth. I studied the *Centiloquium* of Ptolomy, wherein he states that everything in this world obeys the celestial forms. It is obvious that all sages agree on this: the planets have influences and powers in this world, through which everything in it exists and is altered by the motions of the planets through the zodiacal signs. Thus, they believed that the root of magic is the motion of the planets. I wish to put forward this example I learned from one sage who worked in these realms of knowledge. While he was sojourning in Egypt in the household of the king, he met a certain young man who had come from India, who also had been very interested in these realms.

§2 He said to me that while he and that youth were talking they heard the voice of a man crying as if he were about to die from the sting of a poisonous scorpion.[1] When the youth heard this, out of his bag he took a cloth wherein a great many sigils were wrapped, which were similar to incense in smell. He ordered one of these sigils to be given to that man to drink, and at once that man would be healed, as he said. I, desiring to learn and for curiosity's sake, stood up and took the sigil from his hands and gave it to him as a drink as he had ordered. Immediately, the shouts and pains were calmed, and the man became healthy. Now, I myself had inspected the sigil; on it was the figure of a scorpion. I asked the visitor what he had inscribed it with, and he showed me a golden ring with a bezoar stone on it, bearing the figure of a scorpion. I asked him what that figure was and by what secret influences that healing occurred. The young man answered that the figure had been made with the Moon in the second face of Scorpio, and this was that ring's secret power. Thus the sage spoke to me. I myself have made an image of that figure in this hour. I impressed some incense and some other imprintable things and with those I have accomplished miracles at which everyone has marveled.

§3 For this reason, know and understand that nobody can know or comprehend the powers and works of the heavens upon this world below unless they have been instructed in the natural *quadrivium* and mathematics.[2] Whoever has disregarded these things will have an imperfect knowledge regarding the movements of the heavens; they will be incapable of understanding them or attaining their desires since their structure and foundations are drawn from these things. Whoever disregards arithmetic and geometry will be unable to calculate the motions of the celestial bodies, to retrace their trajectories, or to observe their movements since their understanding emerges from arithmetic and geometry. Similarly, it is fitting to have music for understanding the proportion and number of things, how celestial affairs are harmonized in love and hatred with earthbound actions, and how the works of the celestial bodies are more apparent on Earth in one thing [33] than in others. Indeed, whoever neglects those proportions cannot understand the operations and their types, nor is he able to discern their similarities to each other. Likewise, whoever overlooks the natural sciences cannot comprehend the processes of generation and corruption nor their causes. If one did not know these things, one would be unable to apprehend or discern the works of the celestial bodies or their powers upon terrestrial bodies. Similarly, one who ignores metaphysics cannot know or understand into which terrestrial locations the power of the celestial bodies flows and into which ones it does not. For this reason, one necessarily concludes that one cannot understand or know that science perfectly unless one knows its proper order and foundation, which none but a philosopher can comprehend, for all this was extracted from the branches of philosophy, as discussed. Therefore, none can grasp that science perfectly except the perfect philosopher.

Chapter 2

On the Figures of the Heavens and Their Secrets

§1 It is very difficult and burdensome to speak about the figures of the heavens because all the sages occulted and concealed their work as much as possible. I shall relate the cause of this concealment. Anyone who seeks and desires greatly to study this body of knowledge and who desires to reach an understanding of all the forms and figures should study the great book of figures that the wise Rozuz wrote.[3] He wrote well and thoroughly about all the figures and forms in that book. The ascensions of the celestial signs are of two kinds, one of which concerns the forty-eight forms taken from the constellations.[4] This is what we see changing according to the rising and falling of the fixed stars, just as the signs and other heavenly figures, such as the Dog, the Bear, the Cock, and the like, are changing. All those figures change from sign to sign and place to place, and they do not move merely according to the nature of the heavens. The shapes of signs in the Zodiac change much more than other figures since they move from one decan to another over a thousand years. In the constellations that are around the poles, however, no noticeable motion can be discerned in them during those thousand years since they move together in a small circle. Thus, even through many thousands of years, no observable motion can be discerned in them. Such are the ways of the signs.

§2 The second motion of the celestial signs is according to the opinion of the Indians, who spoke about them in the following way. What ascends in the first face of Aries is a man with red eyes and a great beard, wrapped up in a white linen garment, making great gestures in his gait, covered with a great white cloak belted with rope, and standing on one foot as if he were looking at something he held in front of him. What ascends in the second face of Aries is a woman covered in a linen cloak, dressed in red garments, having only one foot; her face is similar to that of an angry horse, [34] and she is seeking clothes, jewelry, and a son. In the third face of Aries ascends a red and white man with red hair, angry and worried, with a sword in his right hand and a staff in the left, dressed in red clothes; he is learned, a perfect master of iron work, desiring to do good, yet unable to do so. In this way, one may proceed all the way to the last decan of the signs.

§3 Know that the Indians did not determine those figures except from the nature of the stars and signs. Thus, you may understand what was said above concerning the second face of Aries. All their writings are of that kind. What I have said up to now, one might apprehend by the senses and the faculty of imagination; everything you desire, you shall achieve.

§4 Abenoaxie[5] in his book translated from Nabataean, which he called *Timachanin*, spoke on the triplicity of signs. One of these he named the triplicity of water, when he discussed the northern signs. He says this: "When someone wishes to invoke a body of water, a river, a well, or some other similar thing, know that their work belongs to water. Through this method, know that other figures of triplicities are assigned to fire, earth, or air, when you seek to invoke them." Along that path went Tymtym and all the sages who discussed the celestial figures and degrees.[6]

§5 This is what they said concerning the names of the degrees and also what they said in the examples of their forms in their places, since all those things are signs by which you may understand the powers and the effects of the degrees. Thus, understand the following in the same way. As an example, when one says "mutilated head" or "severed hands," one means to symbolize death, weakness, and the paths of one planet among the others since all those things are means for understanding the effects of the planets and how they empower other bodies such that miracles and their effects manifest. This is how you should understand the entire art of magic.

§6 Know that the effects of the planets are numerous and diverse. Their effects change in each degree of the heavens when a particular planet stands alone in a particular degree or when it is conjoined with another planet. If you wish to know the sum of their effects, namely those of every planet in every degree of the heavens, multiply 360 seven times, and the sum will be 2,520. Each of these aspects has diverse effects by itself. If you were then to multiply 360 six times, the result will be, from the conjunctions of any two planets in a single degree: 2,160. These aspects have potency and wondrous effects in this world. If you were to multiply 360 five times, the result would be the number of conjunctions of any three planets in a single degree: 1,800. If you multiply 360 four times, the result is the number [35] of conjunctions of any four planets in a single degree, or 1,440. Likewise, these aspects have power and wondrous effects in this world. If you were to multiply 360 three times, the result is the number of conjunction of any five planets in a single degree, or 1,080, and these aspects similarly have wondrous effects in this world. If you were to multiply 360 twice, the result would be the number of conjunction of any six planets in one single degree: 720; these aspects, as above, have wondrous effects in this world. If you were to multiply 360 once, then the result is the number of conjunctions of all seven of the planets in one degree: 360; similarly, these aspects have powers and wondrous effects in this world. This is the method that the First Teacher[7] accepted when he spoke on the figures of the heavens, their judgments, their significance, and also the motions of the seven planets and the degrees of the signs. Indeed, the total sum of those aspects is 10,080, which has powers and wondrous effects.

§7 After this, moreover, the First Teacher himself said that when you want to make those figures, do this: when you place one of the seven planets in one degree and another in a second degree, divide it over the seven planets, then place them two degrees apart; do it in this way for every degree of the heavens, of which there are 360. While this task is longer than the first we have described, nevertheless, it is more precise; through this method you will be able to understand the powers and effects of the figures on this world. Once you have done this, return to the conjunctions of the seven planets moving through the degrees of the fixed stars; and return to the application of the fixed stars, the separation of those moving by themselves, and the separation of the fixed stars by themselves. Then memorize all this, and understand it well for the sake of learning the decans.[8] Beware lest you disclose the special character of those figures to anyone except one who recognizes their importance.

Chapter 3

All the Works of the Planets, the Sun, and the Moon

§1 Some sages, discussing these matters, said that the heavens' effects and powers upon this world do not exist except through the waxing and waning of heat. They said this because they did not understand the heavens' wondrous occult properties. Accordingly, the sages said that the effects of the Sun, the Moon, and the other five planets operating in this world support and empower the heavens' effects. They also said that we ascertain all other motion from the heavens' motions (namely, those of the seven planets together). Likewise, all the qualities of things being born are collectively demonstrated by the qualities of the Sun. They said that the Moon has qualities that demonstrate and reveal all her qualities and effects. The first of her qualities is her distance from the Sun (i.e., she is separated from conjunction with the Sun until after her first square aspect). Then her power [36] is in augmenting humidity and heat, but she affects humidity more than heat. During that time, her effect appears upon the growth of trees and plants. The effect of her augmentation, however, appears more in the herbs creeping on the ground than in the trees that rise above the Earth. The second of her qualities runs from the end of the first quarter until her opposition with the Sun. At that moment, her influence has been well established to augment heat and humidity equally. During this time, her effect has been demonstrated well to increase the humidity and heat in vegetables and minerals. Once she recedes from opposition to the second quarter, her strength is in augmenting humidity and heat (though she augments heat more than humidity). Her effect is more manifest in augmenting the bodies of animals, vegetables, and minerals that grow in all their parts; thus she works more with heat than humidity. From that second quarter until her combustion by the Sun, her effects, motions, and works seem considerably reduced in heat, so much less than all three abovementioned periods, so that her effects are opposite to those other operations, drying moderately and becoming very cold. They say this on account of her state that is then moderate in humidity; as such we can say that that the fourth quarter is moderately dry and very cold.

§2 When she is conjoined to the Sun, within one minute, the Moon then has a fifth quality, which the Chaldean sages say is better than all the Moon's other qualities and more powerful than all her other figures. The sages from Persia, however, say that the power and weakness, growth and diminution, of the effects of the fifth quality depend on the nature of the sign wherein they are conjoined. The Greek and Egyptian sages, however, are in agreement about this for they say, as we have said before, that the conjunction of the Sun is stronger while denying what we have said, namely that the quality of the conjunction is better. That is, they place that before the opposition of the Sun and the Moon (i.e., when the Moon is full). Nevertheless, all our sages agree that the best quality of the Moon is her aspect when conjoined to the Sun within one minute. They believe that this fifth quality belongs to the Sun and should have other interpretations from the other four qualities since it is better and stronger in all its effects. The reason is such: when the Moon is conjoined to the Sun, she rejoices and is gladdened, just as a traveler returning home from a journey. Thus, the operator will be more experienced toward the making of all things, most of all when premeditating their effects. When the Moon is conjoined to the Sun, she completes her works, which are to diminish what is in excess and to augment what is lacking. The sages said that she then has the power of generating effects similar to those of the Sun. This is a great thing and an excellent quality. Then they said all composite bodies [37] receive the powers that they ought to receive. And it should not be concluded from the foregoing that the Moon generates power and effects other than what comes from the Sun. Rather, the Moon generates those results and draws upon the effects produced by the Sun. They do not appear until the Moon reveals what was previously concealed and illuminates what had been in darkness.

§3 These five qualities of the Moon, which she owes to the Sun, exist according to the qualities of all living things in their lifespans. In the same way, there are five ages: infancy, childhood, youth, old age, and decrepitude. Similarly, there are four times of the year—spring, summer, autumn, and winter—just as there are four parts of the world—east, west, south, and north, and each of those parts has a predominantly appropriate wind. Correspondingly, there are four humors in the body: blood, yellow bile, phlegm, and black bile.

§4 Understand these perspectives and opinions, especially since all the foundations of magical operations arise out of the powers of the planets, the Sun, and the Moon, and out of their motions according to the qualities of the degrees of the signs that receive the strength and power of the planets in their own course because the power crosses over to those planets from the planets sitting in their respective signs. Therefore, the planets will have other qualities with the meanings of the other figures distinct from their own figures (which they had from their own dispositions). When those aspects are thus, it is obvious that all composite bodies are changed and altered in all their changeable qualities for a period in whatever time and in whatever hour, relative to the interaction of planetary motions and mutual aspects. Those changes are distinctly called mutations. The other fundamentals discussed, the foundations and properties of all things, are called common and permanent mutations. These are not changed or altered for if they were to receive some alteration or mutation, all the universal forms of things in the cosmos would be corrupted and destroyed; for this reason, there are permanent and common ones.

§5 The conclusion we ought to accept from everything discussed is that all things in the world, in all their qualities, orders, and boundaries, arise from the aspects of the Moon with the Sun since whatever constitutes vegetation and composite bodies exists thanks to the stars and the Moon. This is the greater power they receive and the harm they suffer because of an eclipse of the Moon or other eclipsed planets <. . .> from the Sun, the Moon, and the fixed stars come the permanent mutations, being altered and receiving benefit from good qualities and harm from bad ones. An eclipse affects the Sun and the Moon and the other planets, and it is likened to the harm done to other composite bodies. Disregard the idea that the Sun or the Moon can suffer any loss by nature or accident. Know that we call those "the impediments of the heavens" because they are the causes [38] of harm to animals, trees, and other bodies composed of the four elements. These are altered, changed, and harmed by the eclipse of the Sun and Moon and of the other planets.

§6 Next, find an appropriate place suitable to your rituals and relevant to your work. Do this by taking account of the signs' truthful and deceitful influences (as much with respect to generation as to corruption). Doing so is the greatest power in this world and in all its qualities. Similarly, seek freedom from the impediments and unfortunate influences, and do not be in a combust path since every operation set up while the Moon is in a favorable condition and on a direct path will be fulfilled and brought to a favorable end. Whatever you desire will effectively appear, and its duration will be relative to the motion of the Moon (slow or swift). This duration will be relative to what the signs reveal when joined to unfortunate planets descending from mid-heaven or being in the end of signs (the last or second last degree) since all these things harm and weaken the Moon. This is likewise when the Moon is descending to her descendant, falling[9] from the lord of her house and not facing him, falling from the ascendant or any other angle, or is with the Head (of the Dragon) since anything begun under these circumstances will not be completed nor last long. The house of the Moon must not be a planet from which she is separating nor one to which the Moon travels in angles or successions of angles since she is unsuitable for any operation in that state. If the location of the Moon's descent is in opposition to the house from the ascendant on account of the circle of houses with the Moon herself in the ninth house and with the lord of the same house falling from the ascendant, the result will be similar to the aforesaid. If you found the lord of the Moon's house in the ascendant, in mid-heaven, the eleventh or fifth houses, easterly and direct, everything will be suited and compatible to the things you have set out to do. An example: just as the benevolence of Venus is present for all rituals pertaining to the action of youths, to pleasures, and to women with painted faces, so too the benevolence of Jupiter is appropriate to the works of clergymen, kings, and lords. Similarly, as the benevolence of Mercury is appropriate to messengers and scribes and the benevolence of the Sun is appropriate to great royal achievements and kings, so too is the benevolence of the Moon attributed to students and messengers. As such, pay heed to all the works and dispositions that you wish to enact effectively. Consider the Sun, the Moon, the lords of their exaltations, and also the lords of their own boundaries. Then watch the ascendant and mid-heaven because you will find them calm and free from unfortunate planets with their lords situated in favorable positions. This will be a good ritual; it will go well, come to fruition, and the result will ensue; this will occur all the more if the fortunate planets are shining, appearing out of the right, and with the lord of the ascendant from the east because when the planets are [39] easterly, they signify victory and the fulfillment of things with no difficulty nor hindrance. When they are westerly, especially in one of the four angles, they signify sluggishness, tardiness, and the delay of things. If you find the Moon in a favorable position with her lord descending, it indicates that the disposition of this affair will start well but end poorly. If you find the Moon and the lord of her house in a favorable position, that operation will be good all around and completed in its entirety; you shall obtain your desire within it, and it will come to fruition. This effect will be greater if the lord of the ascendant is fortunate and in the ascendant or in another of the angles of the ascendant, or if it is unfortunate and situated in a favorable position. Therefore, what can be better and more useful than Jupiter or Venus being in the ascendant or facing the ascendant with a favorable aspect? That affair will be easily fulfilled and reach a good end—your intent will be effortlessly and quickly completed (all the more so if the Moon is conjoined with fortunate planets, and those fortunes are neither waning in light nor retrograde since such conditions are appropriate for all operations except for those done on the behalf of prisoners struggling to escape their masters or for those wishing to steal things that are not theirs).

§7 Heed the Moon in all your works since she is more important than all the other planets. The Moon has more noticeable effects and authority over everything in this world. Hers is the power of generation and corruption, and she is mediatrix in those processes. She receives influences and impressions from the stars and planets, and she pours them into the lower things of this world. Therefore, heed what we have said regarding her fortunate and unfortunate influences and regarding the augmentation and diminution of light because after she is separated from the Sun, her powers are balanced; thereafter, they change when she is in sextile, square, trine, and opposite aspects. Her strength will exist according to the nature of the planets and stars with which she is conjoined (while she herself sits in the aspects discussed). If you find the Moon waxing in light, then her strength and power will be enhanced and more useful toward everything that you wish to perform regarding augmentation. If you find her waning in light, then she will be apt and congruent in all the tasks you want to perform regarding diminution. After the Moon is separated from a conjunction with the Sun all the way to the left square until it reaches opposition, she will always be favorable and beneficial for purchases and sales, for seeking opinions and duties, for disputes, and for seeking advice. After she is separated from opposition, crossing from the right-hand square all the way to her conjunction with the Sun, she will be favorable and beneficial for seeking those debts we ought to pursue, for those who borrow things from others and return them, for philosophers, and for those searching and probing for truth.

§8 Know that a better and stronger fortune of the ascendant is one that has a fortunate planet in an ascendant sign and also in the second house. Moreover, do not [40] conceal from yourself the fact that the mobile signs, especially Aries and Capricorn, are favorable and appropriate for everything you wish to overcome and acquire.[10] The common signs are apt for magic and miracles.[11] The fixed signs are effective toward and apt for binding, attracting, and performing magical effects.[12] Everything you wish to be long-lasting, and in even greater works, should be suited to attracting spirits inwards and binding them. In these affairs, ensure that the ascendant be in a common sign and the Moon be in a mobile sign, facing the ascendant. Similarly, in all long-lasting operations, place the ascendant toward a fixed or common sign, the Moon being in a fixed sign, facing the lord of her own house in a trine or sextile aspect, being free from unfortunate influences, combustion, and retrogradation. If all those conditions cannot be met, see to it rather that the Moon be facing a fortunate planet and the lord of the ascendant be in a trine or sextile aspect. In everything, be aware of the square and opposite aspects since the trine and sextile are better aspects (the worst, however, are square and opposite). Similarly, when the lord of the Moon's house is facing her with an amicable aspect and with an unfortunate planet in it, it will be useful in your request and in everything you have done for the operation. In all rituals, beware lest the Moon be conjoined with the Tail of the Dragon or facing away from the unfortunate planets by a square or opposite aspect. Likewise, pay very close attention in all your works to the waning of the Moon since when she wanes, she reveals and shows harm, detriment, delay, and impediment, upon all the affairs of this world. These are the wanings of the Moon, that is, when she is diminished in light and reckoning and delayed in her motion. A superior state and condition for the Moon is when she is waxing in light and reckoning and swift in her course. She should not be facing Mars by any aspect since when she faces Mars while waxing in her light, she is considered a misfortune. When the Moon is faced by Saturn and waning in light, she becomes a serious misfortune. Nevertheless, at night, she stands alone among all others in her strength and powers over the Earth. Know then that it is evidently better and more useful in everything we do whenever the Moon and the ascendant are in directly ascending signs. When they are thus, those tasks will be easily and quickly completed with effect, especially when they are in common or fixed signs.

§9 Among the mobile signs, the most mobile is Aries, then Cancer, and then Libra, which is the most powerful of the inimical signs. In the same way, know that the angles are quicker in all operations followed by those that follow; the descending ones, however, are the slowest. The quickest of all is when a fortunate planet is ascending and the Moon is waxing in light and reckoning. Note that the boundaries of things cannot be known except through the triplicity of the Moon and the lord of the ascendant (through the calculation of their locations and qualities and through their mutual aspects [41] with their planets in their respective times). Thus, the boundaries of things can be determined.

§10 In his writings, Dorothius teaches us this.[13] In considering judgments and the arrangement of things, heed the ascendant and its lord, the Moon, and the lord of the Moon's house. Beware in these dispositions, and heed the ten judgments of the Moon. As much as possible, ensure the Moon is not falling from the ascendant. Even more so, ensure that the lord of the ascendant and the lord of the Moon's house are not two unfortunate planets facing the Moon from the ascendant or from their own houses. In all works and dispositions, make sure that the Part of Fortune not be falling away from aspect or conjunction with the Moon. Let neither the lord of the Part of Fortune's house nor the Part itself be falling from the ascendant after facing the ascendant and the Moon. Nevertheless, if a lord of the ascendant is conjoined with the Part, it will be better for all your works and dispositions. In everything you do, see to it diligently that the Moon not be in the third, sixth, eighth or twelfth houses from the Part of Fortune for then she will be ineffective and ill-suited in all affairs. In all your works, always make sure the Moon and the ascendant are in the signs ascending directly. Know and understand that the ascendant and the fourth house collectively signify and demonstrate all the dispositions. If you find the Moon poorly positioned, and it happens that your work is urgent, and you can in no way delay it, make sure the Moon is falling from the ascendant with no part in it. Then place a fortunate planet in the ascendant, and make fortunate this same ascendant and its lord. Thus spoke Dorothius.

§11 Know that the strength and effectiveness of the ascendant consists of two things, namely the configuration and the fortunate planet. The same applies to the lord of the ascendant. The configuration is what you put ascending, akin to nature's designs and the qualities of the intended request. The similarity of quality is of this kind: if you needed to perform your work quickly, easily, through the power of motion, and in the halls of kings and nobles—in all these affairs—place the ascendant outside the fiery signs. Likewise, if your operation were related to war and martial affairs, place one sign from the houses of Mars in the ascendant. Make fortunate the house of the request and the lord of that house because the place or house of the request reveals and demonstrates what will happen at the beginning and in the successive steps. The lord of the request signifies and demonstrates what will happen in effect in the middle of the request. The lord of the lord of the request's house signifies the end and outcome of the affair. In the same way, the ascendant demonstrates what will happen in the beginning of the affair, and the lord of the house of the lord of the ascendant signifies the end of the affair.[14] Heed the part of the request for it reveals the nature of the request itself, its lord, and the lord of the house wherein the lord of the part stands. Consider diligently how you should direct the locations as we have described them [42] above, and place fortunate planets in them from among the fortunes that grant strength when standing together in that house and facing these things with a favorable aspect. Make sure the unfortunate planets are falling from those places. Never place a retrograde planet as the lord of the ascendant or as the lord of the request; if either of them is retrograde, that request will be delayed, prolonged, and incomplete. This is what it reveals and demonstrates. Similarly, all other positions are safe in all their qualities. If any of them were retrograde, their effect would be ruined from the start and would not be completed except by means of effort and risk. Again, pay attention lest any of these be in conjunction with the Sun or the Moon or in their opposition. Rather, they should be in the ascendant, in the position of the request, or with the part of the request itself. A fortunate planet should be in the ascendant, in any of the ascendant's angles, or in the place of the request itself. Know that the Greater Fortune has greater strength and power in all requests concerning the high sciences and laws.[15] The Lesser Fortune operates and is concerned with all requests pertaining to women's disputes, adornments, womanly pleasures, their vices, and similar things.[16] Never place the Moon in the ascendant for anything you intend to do because she is an enemy of the ascendant. The Sun himself, however, is not an enemy of the ascendant because he reveals entities and melts apart frozen things.

§12 Similarly, do not place any unfortunate planet in the ascendant nor in any of its angles, especially not if the unfortunate planet itself has power in any of the malign places[17] as if it were the lord in the eighth house (which signifies loss in trade-related matters, in change, and in great kingdoms). If that unfortunate planet holds dominion in the sixth house, it signifies a detriment to requests concerning enemies, slaves, illnesses, prisoners, or beasts. If, however, the unfortunate planet governs in the twelfth house, it signifies hindrance and loss in affairs concerning misery, conflict, enemies, or prisoners. If the unfortunate planet has dominion in the second house, it signifies improvement in affairs concerning riches, subservience, eating, or drinking. In all this, see to it that you not forget these instructions—hold them as foundational to the entire magical art. In all daytime operations, place a diurnal sign in direct ascent in the ascendant; in nighttime operations, place a nocturnal sign in direct ascent in the ascendant. Heed the Sun and the Moon if you can, and see that their hours and lords are in strong and fortified places. Do this so that these powers and qualities may be unified and joined together. Wherefore, inspect and direct the status of what the planets reveal and their significance to your works, then aggregate them before you begin to work. In all works [43] for love and benevolence toward a man or woman, see to it that the Moon be received by Venus in a trine or sextile aspect. This is more effective if she is in her own house or exaltation.

§13 Note that the trine aspect is the one that is joined as an equilateral triangle such that each side has 120° of the circumference of the heavens. The sextile aspect is the one that is joined in the shape of an equilateral hexagon, and each side has 60° of the circumference of the heavens. The square aspect is the one that is joined in an equilateral square, and each side has 90° of the circle of heaven. Opposition is when the planets are at opposite ends of the heavens' diameter.

§14 Now, however, I return to the explanation I was putting off. If some task came your way that you were unable to delay until the time when the Moon is received by Venus, make sure she is received by Jupiter in a trine or sextile aspect or the lord of his house in a trine or sextile aspect. If you cannot do this, let the Moon be on the boundary of Venus, fortunate from Jupiter, and free from unfortunate influences. If your work were for love and goodwill, place as the ascending degree one from the boundary of Venus. If your work were for acquiring the shares of an inheritance, let the boundary of Venus be on the cusp of the fourth house. If your work were for acquiring profit from the law, let her be in the ninth house. If your work were regarding finances—for which you think and toil—let her be in the eleventh house, and in that strong place, make sure the Part of Fortune is fortunate, and its lord is received by a fortunate planet. If your work were more oriented toward profiting from a lawsuit, battles, and similar things, ensure that Mars is also received by the Moon with an amiable aspect. If your work were for sorting out debts, make Saturn the receiver instead of Mars. If your work were on account of numbers, writing, or study, let Mercury be the receiver. If your work were for pleasing or battling with kings and nobles, let Jupiter be received as above. If your request were for other reasons, namely the remaining reasons, let the lord of the ascendant be the receiver. This reception belongs to the Moon, the ascendant, the Part of Fortune, and the part of substance. Direct the lord of the Moon's house, the lord of the ascendant, and also the lord of the fourth house (as said above); make sure all their positions are free from the unfortunate planets, at rest, and made fortunate by the fortunate planets inasmuch as possible since these locations demarcate the boundary of things.

§15 If you are trying to have goods allotted and granted to you, let the lord of the ascendant and the Moon be received by the *almuten* and the lord of the request.[18] Let the Moon be with the lord of the ascendant in the location of the request. If your request concerned the elderly or those working the earth, let Saturn be the lord [44] of the request. If your request concerned officials, judges, prelates, or rich and honest individuals, the lord of your request should be Jupiter. If your petition were about soldiers, men-at-arms, and chiefs, tested by iron or fire, let the lord of your request be Mars. If your request concerned kings or noblemen, let the Sun be the lord of your request. If your request were about women or people having fun together, decorators, painters, decorations, pantomimes, and those who work on embroideries of silk cloth, gold, or similar things, let Venus be the lord of your request. If you request were concerning merchants, scribes, officials, and clever geometricians, let Mercury be the lord of your request. If your petition were about cold things, things of an aquatic nature, messengers, cases to be brought before a king, fishermen, and so forth, let the Moon be the lord of the request. Similarly, in all your requests, let the lord of the ascendant and the Moon be equally fortunate. If your request were on account of a question of wealth and sustenance, direct the Part of Fortune so that it is received by the fortunate planets. Beware lest the unfortunate planets cut off the Moon's light from the lord of the ascendant or the contrary. Do not allow any of the unfortunate planets to be conjoined with the lord of the request nor the Moon nor the lord of the ascendant—nor should any unfortunate planet be in conjunction with or have anything to do with the lord of the request. Let that reception we mentioned be from a trine or sextile aspect with the planets, whether fortunate or unfortunate. Let there be a conjunction with the fortunate planets. Beware that the lord of the request, the Sun, the Moon, and the lord of the ascendant not be falling from any of the angles. If unable to heed all of this, pay attention to the movement of one of the five lords of the request. It should have an aspect and reception according to the request, as mentioned. Let those two locations be well received by the fortunate planets. Beware lest any of the unfortunate planets be with the lord of the Moon's house, with the lord of the fourth house, or with the lord of the ascendant. If any of the unfortunate planets were to be in these houses, this would damn, destroy, and impede the purpose of your request.

§16 If you wish to operate toward something concerning professions and bureaucracy, let the Moon and the ascendant be in common signs, free from unfortunate influences. If your task were for gold, fortify the Sun, and let him be with the fortunate planets at the beginning of your work. Observe the same in all qualities.

§17 Until now, we have spoken generally on the judgments of the stars. If you heed and understand them as you should, you will have their assistance in whatever works you will perform through this science. Through generalities, you will be capable of comprehending and discerning particulars. Be very cautious not to reveal or show the things discussed here to anyone, except to those who understand and study these matters. Know [45] that these are the roots and foundations of the images, and those are the things by which one's own secrets are plainly manifest. It is for this reason that the profound study of the art of astronomy was prohibited by the Law, since a profound knowledge of it overlaps with the study of the magical art. On this account, Aristotle said to King Alexander: "O Alexander, be wary in every moment and action you perform! Do them according to the motions, aspects, and qualities of the celestial bodies. If you have done your research, your request will be fulfilled effectively, and you will have whatever you had reckoned in your will." This example is very good and useful because it demonstrates the difference between the motives of the wise and those of fools who can understand nothing beyond their mundane thoughts (and thus are cut off from the contemplations of another world).[19] These contemplations of another world are nothing less than the hidden secrets of the wise encompassed by knowledge and wisdom.

Chapter 4

On the Motion of the Eighth Sphere and the Fixed Stars

§1 The ancient sages who were learned in the magical sciences perceived how the four quarters of heaven moved from west to east by eight degrees, then returned from east to west by another eight degrees.[20] They called this motion the movement of the eighth sphere. Many of those who write astronomical charts have forgotten that sphere's movement, making no mention of it. This motion has great advantages in the magical arts. Some of those who make charts write that motion into them, in addition to the numbers and calculations by which its movement can always be found at will. Do not forget this because it is an utmost fundamental to magical science (since the figures of heaven are changed by this motion, which is one of the secrets of that science). That eight degrees motion is completed in 640 years, whereupon it returns to its original position. It has already been said, and you have seen how fitting it is to heed this motion in the science of magic as well as in the science of the heavens' effects. This movement is the motion of the constellational sphere's poles, moving from east to west and back again, and it cannot move otherwise except in those two ways. When that motion proceeds from east to west, it reveals and signifies some things coming about in this world, and when it proceeds from west to east, it reveals and signifies other effects that occur in this world. This motion is the movement of the eighth sphere, the sphere of the signs and the fixed stars, a motion that, however, is not the movement of the whole heavens. It is fitting that you understand this motion and diligently review it in all your undertakings.[21] [46]

Chapter 5

The Division of This Science Among the Nations and Which Part Is Allotted to Each Nation

§1 I say to you that I have heard from a certain sage of old a very great miracle pertaining to that science that I have decided to discuss here. He said that this science is divided into three parts. The first of these is the science of magic; those who study it in detail and operate in it are those whom we have named "the Sabeans"—the captured slaves of the Chaldeans. The second is the science of the stars (praying to them with suffumigations, sacrifices, prayers, and scripture). Those who studied this science are the Greeks, who are very skilled, knowledgeable, and understanding of it (i.e., astrology). They possess true knowledge since the science of astrology is presumed to be the foundation of all magical knowledge. The third part, however, is the science that operates through suffumigations, incantations, and words particularly appropriate to those things. It is likewise a science of binding spirits together and loosening them with these words. The Indians are well-versed in this science. Some people from Yemen and the Nabataeans from Egypt have also worked most successfully in this manner. Each of these parts has a foundation and an essence that are both theoretical and practical.

§2 It is noted and clear that the Indians have strength and power through words with which they can treat and cure themselves from deadly venoms without medicine. Similarly, they have incantations and words by which, whenever they desire, they can cause a man to be horribly vexed by demons. Solely by hearing those words, it is also possible to alter the senses. By virtue of these words, they provoke desired motions. Similarly, they have an instrument for the composition of music they call *alquelquella*, with a single chord of harmonies.[22] With this they produce sounds and perform all sorts of subtleties according to their wills. Similar miracles are wrought upon women whom they cause to conceive without having had sex, through gestures, rituals, and medicines. Some Indians make a kind of drinkable wine that they consume; by its virtue, it both prevents them from growing old and keeps them from being racked by the feebleness of old age (such that they never die lest by natural causes).[23] In all these things, the Indians are the most powerful because they were granted these abilities by nature, whereas others achieved them through toil and diligence alone. The Indians possess greater power in the arts of magic and the other mysteries of this world.[24] Some Indians claim and assert in common parlance that there exists a group south of the equinoctial line whom they call devils. They are most subtle beings as they neither reproduce nor die, a fact in accordance with scripture.[25] The dominant planet and celestial body in strength and power over these devils are Saturn and the Tail of the Dragon. One sage I mentioned says that all the forms and figures of generation and corruption in this [47] world exist by the powers and influences of the fixed stars. They are laid out and organized according to the aspects and dispositions of the fixed stars within those signs. He says that the other figures and forms are in the heavens and not upon Earth. These are neither known nor understood except by the wise (who have been educated in the science of the art of magic and the spirits), and they are demarcated by defined proportions. Sages gave them the names by which they are now known but not because those names reveal any quality nor anything about those figures. Those names are figures and seals like this:[26]

Then they are joined together with lines. Those lines that connect one point to another are to be thought of as rays that extend from one to the next, through which the figures and images are then calculated. These dwell in the eighth sphere and the fixed stars.

§3 This same sage said that there are other imagined figures in the heavens that are not seen except in the mind, in the same way that the degrees of heaven have bodies.[27] The wonders that this sage spoke about cannot be comprehended nor grasped except through the books of the Indians, who themselves brought much to this science. They say that those figures must be made in the appropriate and opportune hours, times, and constellations with the due and appropriate ascendants. The Indians similarly sought oracles through severed heads and birds or interpreted dreams by gazing into mirrors and swords. They did these things to aid themselves in their requests or to discover subtleties and secrets. With such things the Indians benefit themselves just as astrologers benefit themselves with the circles made around the planets and the Moon, the rainbow or celestial arc appearing in the heavens, the apparent twinkling in the stars, and the storms in the Sun.[28] The astrologer assists himself using all of these in judging and discerning the heavens' effects. They said that there exist in the heavens lovely and beautiful forms; likewise there exist others that lack beauty, emerging from the fixed stars' dispositions and aspects. Those individuals born under the ascensions of lovely and beautiful signs (while the Sun and Moon also stand in such magnificent signs)—are shown to be fortunate in their deeds and activities. If, however, during the hour of someone's nativity, there were a negative and deformed figure on the ascendant (while the Sun and the Moon also stand in such negative ones), it would reveal that a person born in this condition will be unlucky in all their endeavors, business ventures, and activities. So, heed the revolutions of nativities and every conjunction; do the same for works of magic. Moreover, the sages say that among the constellations and their motions, there exist things that reveal nothing in any judgment, just like pointless dreams that have neither meaning nor significance. Regarding these constellations, pay them no heed; [48] rather, seek your request from any other constellation. It is appropriate to look for these in nativities, conjunctions, and revolutions. Similarly, the wise have said that the knowledge of dreams is a kind of power residing in the soul by which it becomes bound up with the spirits of heaven. The forms and figures of things corresponding to potential scenarios on Earth are seen through the soul, and through them the power of the spirit is informed. These are the truthful dreams from which we obtain information. This knowledge of dreams is compatible with the science of astronomy and similar to it because it draws upon the science of astrology. This power and influence arises out of the powers of Mercury because when Mercury is strong in the root of a nativity, he allows for the divination of dreams. Some dreams are produced during rest, others by the humors, and yet others by vapors rising into the brain, as the physicians assert and confirm; such dreams signify nothing.

§4 Know that dreams are actually demonstrations of things that are simple, discrete, and dissimilar from material bodies. Dreams arise when the soul cuts itself off from sensory impressions and receives no input from the senses. Indeed, dreams are formed according to the cognition of the mind and the shaping powers of entities (those that hold power over the perceivable). Furthermore, dreams have a third property: they are like a memory of things after they have occurred—while the rational spirit exists in a perfected state, it envisions entities that the individual has seen before. The entities enter the dream, appearing no different than how they were seen beforehand. If the power by which the entities are formed is stronger than the rational spirit, however, that individual will envision an image of what he had previously seen with his eyes but not the exact same thing. Here is an example for one of these two types: one individual who has a perfected rational soul will envision some sort of bear or dog hounding and approaching him in a dream, and this will actually happen. For the other type: in that same dream, another individual will envision a bandit or a diseased person running alongside him; and similarly, this will also happen. If one's nature were strong and powerful—that is, strong in regards to such natural things as eating, drinking, dressing, and having sex—then the spirit would be impeded by that nature. In dreams, this individual will only envision things pertaining to the body and disproportionately so. If one's body were predisposed to sex (that is, full of semen), that man would envision himself having sex with a woman. This is because nature wishes to expel the fullness of that matter from itself.[29] If the body were full of wet humors, one would envision rivers and waters in dreams. If it were full of yellow bile, then fire, burning, and similar things would appear in the dreams. If it were full of black bile, one would envision frightful and terrifying things in dreams and so forth. Diviners are similarly confirmed; they are right when the accuracy of their predictions is supplemented by those things that the diviner has understood by seeing, hearing, dwelling upon, [49] and contemplating what is perceived in the augury. If the power of those things in which entities are formed were strong and pure for individually shaping those entities that have being—in the same way that a sage beholds entities in a mirror, guiding himself according to what he saw and heard—then by all those things, one may attain the power of knowledge and an understanding of things that have being. All of this exists by the power and fortitude of spirit. Thus, one produces the power or strength that forms entities when they are separated from the perceptible and relinquish the sensible realm. The spirit is made into a medium between the sensible realm and the visible act at hand. They are united by the powers of the spirit. From this proceed dreams and divination; that is: if the body were purged of bad humors and balanced in its complexion, whatever one envisions will be certain and true. If one were in the opposite state, whatever one envisioned would be pointless and deceiving.

§5 Clearly, divination is a power of the quintessence and is what we call "prophecy." It is one of the faculties of the spirit, wherein things formed out of discrete objects are seen. One perceives and understands this while sleeping or waking. When that faculty in which entities are formed is perfect and pure from all dross and impurity, one will envision discrete objects just as images in a mirror. Thus, images are revealed in the spirit when it is unpolluted and perfected. On this account, none who predict the future from purely abstract things or things purely perceptible to the senses can be a diviner. One is hardly "wise" if one has merely mastered perceptible things while lacking the other requirements discussed. If one mastered both of these, one would be a prophet. This does not happen, however, except to unique individuals into whom flow perfectly prophetic spirits from the first creator of entities, God Himself. He transmits those prophetic spirits and pours them down using consciousness as a medium.[30] Thus, God Himself naturally places such a virtue into a prophet, and from that consciousness, the strength and power of humanity's perception or intellect emerge. The senses themselves are bound to the powers from which entities are formed; then, on account of the binding of that power, human sense perception is adorned with wisdom. On account of being engaged with the powers that form entities, such men are called prophets. Whoever is so disposed is more excellent, perfect, and fortunate than any other. This is the good we seek that through it we may reach such a state for we do not desire blessedness unless we have a better fate through it. Thus, we should be versed in good morals and habits lest our character turn evil. The prophets teach humanity laws and beliefs about the future so that they may unite them to one mind in blessedness. This is how to attain that greater fortune and to understand the things of the world, their qualities, and how they are united and divided. We call this part prophecy, [50] whose path proceeds from the perceptible up to higher things by wandering until reaching a metaphysical knowledge wherein humanity's power is fulfilled; through theoretical knowledge, a human is perfected. This is the good that humans seek, and one can find no greater thing since there is nothing better than a perfect lot. Albunasar Alfarabi says in his book on the work of the craft that the proper order and layout of universals will be the way of understanding splendor and the sublime.[31] He says that those things by which we attain a better lot are good character and virtuous deeds that beget blessings. One who has reached those things has a solid start devoid of misfortune. They will have joy, delight, and durable wisdom forever and without end. Alfarabi upholds the Founder of the Law,[32] saying that his is not a life worth remembering lest there be some future life in another world (since, in his view, the present life is worthless).

§6 Now, however, let us return to the proposed topic. I say that according to the Indians, spirits reveal themselves as bodies that speak and make demonstrations such that they cause kings to love and hate whomever they wish or to produce and withdraw whatever they desire through their effects. This was done according to the procedures of the ancient sages who made images of various figures, including prayers at the correct hours relative to whatever they sought. They say that images are the spirits of the chosen time because the works done through them are like miracles (or things that seem miraculous). This is because their works are established by natural powers for the natural powers produce wondrous effects just as the red stone jacinth (that is, the ruby), by its innate virtue, supports and reinforces bearers against evil, sickness, epidemics, and many other ills. Thus, an image with two united powers (i.e., the strength and power of celestial bodies that the image received from occult bodies) makes other impressions from natural powers, as happens with the expulsion of fleas, bugs, and flies. This comes about from the mastery and the magical works of the constellations and celestial bodies. The images must be fashioned out of the materials at the hours and minutes naturally appropriate to the desired effect. Know and understand the property of the natural virtues of the materials used to craft images, and build them according to the power and effect you desire. Know also that everything we do in this world is for the sake of understanding something or knowing some fact or piece of information—all have their respective types of images. If you have looked diligently into everything discussed so far, you will go far in reaching perfection in this science. [51]

Chapter 6

On the Powers of Images; How They May Be Harnessed; How Images Can Receive Planetary Power; How Images Produce Effects; and How This Is Fundamental to the Knowledge of Magic and Images

§1 Know that the thing that is called "a virtue" is that which is evidenced by nature and experiment. If an agent acts according to its own power, its nature will be manifest in its work—especially when such an action exists with power over those things, not over the manifest nature it has within them. Then that work will be stronger and more visible, and what actually appears from it will be truer and more clearly perceived. For example, the virtue of scammony, which attracts cholera by its special power, exists on account of the harmony that cholera has in and of itself with hotness and dryness, through which it is assimilated to the nature of cholera. It is also clear in simple medicines that when they do something by the power and similitude of the nature existing within them, then that process will be more visible, effective, and apparent. Thus, the images operate by the power of similitude because an image is nothing more than the power of the celestial bodies flowing into matter. So when the matter of that body is disposed to receiving the influence of those celestial bodies or planets, and likewise the body is disposed to influencing the material bodies of the images, then that image will be stronger and more disposed to effect everything sought and desired; similarly, the gift of the planet will be more perfect and complete. For example: when you wish to begin crafting an image, consider the shape and the reason for which you wish to fashion the image as well as the material. Let all these things be harmonious with one another in similitude. Similarly, let them be in the powers and influences of the planets governing that work. When things are ordered thus, the image will be strong and complete, and its effects will follow and be visible. The spirit that has been placed in the image will manifest with effect. Then the effects of that planet will be clear to you as is, and its mode of reception (namely, to what house it belongs) will be manifest and apparent. Indeed, practitioners of any era who make images and ignore these things do wrong. Moreover, when you wish to craft an animal from animals or something from plants or something from stone, take the first parts of that composition and join them with other parts of a similar nature. Mix and combine them into an appropriate blend. Carry on like this until your objective is reached. While doing this, nature does not stop operating in this effect. The stars augment and increase the effect until an appropriate end is reached (just as beings come about in many ways and can be created as much through paints as through animal parts that humans [52] can bring to life through effort; these include reptiles, serpents, scorpions, and many similar things fabricated according to the dispositions of nature and the planetary powers). Works that are done through decoctions and mixtures of species, from which come medicines with the necessary and appropriate ingredients, are like a decoction of live sperm cooked in a womb until it reverts to a state suitable to the essence of that creature. Thus, nature accomplishes its work through the respective planetary powers until the work is perfected in its own proper order. Thus, stones are also composed of minerals and water. At first, water is fresh; then winds race down upon it, striking and beating it until it is curdled like milk; then it is cooked by the nature of the mineral and by the natures existing within it; finally, it is solidified by cooking and rendered similar to the appropriate stone; then it receives the form and shape of that mineral. This is how plant material is made (all things born beneath the earth are ordered in such a fashion). It happens like this: at first, the material rots until returning to the state that is needed for a plant to be generated. It receives the form and shape suited for the fulfilling of its own form. It receives this form and fulfillment from the nutrients of humidity received from that material acquired at the time of rotting. All artificial things are made in this way: at first, we must remove the form and shape that first existed in that matter. With its initial form stripped, it will be disposed to receiving another form and shape. No material can receive another form and shape except by being stripped of the form and shape that it had before. Through this method, all artificers who intend to do anything proceed by acting in this way. First, they collect the components for their operation, and then they work on these things until the latter return to that composite material that is disposed to receiving another form. In this way, we see how the brewmaster works by means of fermentation; the same is done by makers of cheese, butter, and other things made from milk or honey. The same applies to craftsmen who make silk by spinning and all the other specialized craftsmen who convert one thing into another and transform them. This happens because any material with form and shape cannot receive another form unless it loses or gives up the first one. Thus, matter disposed to receiving a second form receives it. When matter receives a form and is shaped, it is free and unrestricted by all other forms besides that one. We say this only concerning the matter existing here below since in the superior world, matter is formed by eternal forms that can never be separated from matter nor can that matter take [53] other forms.[33] Understand that rituals with images are of that sort because the creators of images look first to collecting the things from which the image itself is made. These materials should be disposed and suited to receiving the form in question. Some examples: laurel berries, which heal and assuage adder venom; saffron, which causes scorpions to flee; and wasps, which flee from sour and bitter things. Wasps love and seek rosewater and are attracted to the odor of the herb called thyme. Many other things like this exist, such as eating chickpeas, and other appropriate things causing growth in the volume of sperm and increase in virility for a man having sex with a woman. Thus, the body of an image is a composite of many things joined together. By putting these things together, its form comes about disposed to receiving the powers and qualities of the things for which that image itself is fashioned and created.

§2 Physicians work in this same way when they combine medicines with the intention of healing pain and disease. The medicinal work of physicians consists of two types. The first of these is work with simple medicines. According to what Johannitius says in his *Physics*, a good and perfect physician should always be able to heal with simple medicines and not with the use of composite ones.[34] The second type, however, involves combining many medicines prescribed as a single medicine. This is how the electuaries and theriacs of the elder Galen come about, which are composed of many medicines.[35]

§3 I say to you that a single planet produces various effects distinct from one another, just as fire makes honey take on a good flavor when properly cooked—indeed, better than the original. If cooked too much, it might burn and taste unpleasant. This happens with the planets when they stand in light and dark degrees. The heavens have two effects: the first is motion and natural effect, and the other is the accidental heat (which is generated by motion). Heat ensues consequently from motion, and motion ensues from the heavens. This teaching is true and obvious. What appears to the senses, however, is caused by the movement that comes from the motion and spirit of the eighth sphere (the sphere of the constellations). This occurs on account of the power of the fixed stars since it certainly appears that heat ensues from motion and that motion ensues from the power and strength of the fixed stars. The power of the fixed stars was the first thing ever created with nothing preceding it in primacy.

§4 Understand that the same applies to all the parts and motions of the heavens and the heat generated by them. Accordingly, the stars' effects follow the effects of the heavens because the heavens produce their own effects along with the stars themselves. The stars do not produce their own effects except through or from the heavens since the stars have no [54] motion in and of themselves but have works and wondrous effects according to the heavens' motions. *Prima Materia* is the first nature and is itself the author of truth—thus, the garments and tinctures we make are in accordance with the works of the stars. Consequently, *Prima Materia* is more excellent and splendid than any other thing. The degrees of heaven are nothing more than imagined place markers for there is no distinction between active and inert parts in the heavens. It is one whole in form, power, effect, and sense, with no variability or distinction in its own parts. Since the whole is of a single type, it therefore cannot at any time have diversity in any of its qualities.

§5 No degree of the heavens or the firmament can lack the quality and essence of the fixed stars because the entire sphere of fixed stars is filled with them. Those who say that some degree of the heavens is devoid of stars at any given time only do so because those stars cannot be perceived by sight or sense. Only the greater among them can be seen while the rest are invisible. Furthermore, it can happen that a star stands in another place where it produces no manifest effects, namely, when it is not in its boundary or exaltation, not ascending nor in opposition to ascent, not retrograde nor direct (unless going to any of the abovementioned locations); neither should it have any aid nor aspect from any of the planets suited to the same nature nor its contraries. This is because those places, especially those that are active and have effects contrary to the fixed stars' active places, are similar to inert places because the planets never lack motion and therefore cannot lack effects. What we said here is very obscure and profound. So pay attention, and study it diligently until you understand how it is linked with the effect because once strengthened in their effects, the planets operate in two ways: the general and the particular. The general effect does not pertain to one distinct part, whereas the particular effect does. Thus, they say such a planet is a giver, or it has an aspect, connection, or reception, and so on.

§6 Another example: when food is in the stomach and is drawn by the liver through the mesentery, it is converted into blood. When the blood is sent by the liver to the other organs, it is formed in the likeness of other organs according to their differences. Thus, in every organ blood loses and gives up its form as if it never had it; then it becomes the bone in bones, the nerve in nerves, and so on in the other organs. In their motions, the planetary effects are similar: when they travel toward some aspect, conjunction, or any place from those mentioned, they proceed by converting themselves in accordance to the nature and effect of that place toward which they are traveling. Similarly, the planets have other excellent effects as they are conjoined. When a planet is ascending, it works according to the action of the fixed stars standing directly above it and is associated with them in their effects—and then it makes wonders. Similarly, [55] when it is in opposition to the ascendant, it works according to the planet standing beneath it. Pay good and very close attention to what we have said here. We say this for this reason: the sphere of fixed stars operates according to the operations and effects of the First Mobile.[36] The sphere of the Moon influences and works through the nature of fire and air (on account of their subtlety) more than through the other elements. Thus, we say that when ascending, Saturn produces the effects of the fixed stars above him. When Saturn is in opposition to an ascendant, he produces the effects of Jupiter. Likewise for the other planets, namely when a planet is ascending, its effects and its works will be according to the actions of the planet existing ahead of it in order. Were the planet opposite to ascending, it would operate according to the actions of the planet existing behind it in order. This principle is of great value in the magical art. Sages of old hid these things with all their might. Were we not to convey them, it would be totally unacceptable. Know well that a planet that moves more slowly in its motion is more powerful in its effects, and on the other hand, a planet swifter in its motion will be weaker in its effect. One that is moderate in motion is moderate in its effect. On this the sages of old are not in agreement. Some have said diverse and contrary things, stating that a planet slow in its motion is weaker in its effect, and one swifter in its motion is stronger in its effect. Here is the explanation of these things: those who accept the latter theory do so according to the order and disposition of the First Moved toward the sphere of fixed stars. The former theory is according to the dispositions of the motions of generation on the Earth, according to which the slower planet is stronger in its effect while the swifter is weaker. According to another opinion now touched upon regarding the disposition of the First Moved toward the sphere of fixed stars: a swifter planet will be stronger in effect and a slower one weaker, because it is a similar analogy. On this the wise disagree to the extent that one party of ancient sages held a contrary position, suggesting this analogy and attributing it to the First Moved and the sphere of fixed stars. According to this the slower planet is closer and more analogous in its similitude to the First Moved and to the sphere of fixed stars in its slowness because the latter is slow in motion. Thus, the slow motion will be similar to the slow motion, and the swift to the swift. Many ancient sages have spoken in their books secretly and covertly concerning these things. Now we intend to state the secrets of the ancient sages on the magical art here. Know that when the Moon is conjoined with Saturn, her effects will be in accordance with the effects of Saturn. This happens because the effects of Saturn are more powerful than the effects of the Moon. Similarly, when any of the planets are conjoined with Saturn, their effects will be in accordance with the dispositions and effects of Saturn. This is because the power of Saturn is the strongest of all the planetary powers. [56] This arises from the reasons and causes given above, which are on account of Saturn's uppermost altitude and proximity to the highest heavens (namely, the First Moved and the sphere of fixed stars). Saturn is very slow because his motion is likened to that of the First Moved and to the other qualities discussed above. Everything that is said on these conjunctions of Jupiter, the Sun, and Venus is changed or altered by great transformations or modifications when they are mixed with the effects of Saturn. It happens in the same way for Jupiter with the fixed stars and generally to all the planets all the way down to the Moon. Next, the effect of those fixed stars appears in fire and air, and the effect of fire and air upon water and earth is clear. The effects of these four elements are clearly visible upon the processes of generation that they generate.

§7 The conjunction of any two planets can have three qualities in their union: augmentation, diminution, and balance between one another. For example, when the Moon is conjoined to Saturn, the effect of the Moon will be weak and shrouded. This is because the power of Saturn exceeds the power of the Moon—that is, when she has been conjoined to Saturn in the same degree of longitude and latitude, in their *hayz*, in their exaltations, or in similar qualities such that the Moon and Saturn proceed in one path and are in one of those places, not otherwise.[37] This quality of Saturn among the other planets appears in other places. It could well occur that the effect of the Moon and her power be greater and stronger than the power of Saturn. This occurs when the Moon is in one of the dignities discussed, and Saturn is in opposition thereto. However, if the Moon were conjoined to Saturn in opposition to the dignities mentioned above, then the effects of the Moon will be according to the effects of Saturn as in the other abovementioned conditions. If Saturn were in those dignities and the Moon were in its contrary, the effect of the Moon would be very weak and suppressed. If the Moon were equal in motion or slowness to Saturn and in other places similar to Saturn's, then the power of the Moon and of Saturn would be equal and similar in quality—more so when the Moon is soon to be ascending, which is the greatest possible dignity for the Moon (although such a dignity is unequal to the greater descent of Saturn) and even more so if Saturn were about to proceed directly. The quality of Saturn with Jupiter, however, is unlike the quality of Saturn with the Moon, being always equals in a great many things. This occurs when Saturn and Jupiter are both dignified. At that point, the effects of Jupiter will be stronger than the effects of Saturn. If Jupiter were dignified and Saturn were equal in motion, direct, and in exaltation, then the effects of Jupiter will not be greater than Saturn's. When the opposite is the case, then the power of Saturn will be above Jupiter's, and the power of Jupiter himself will be weak and diminished. This does not appear in the conditions of

Saturn with Mars when they are conjoined for the effects of Mars would appear more clearly unless, perchance, he were in the conditions and dispositions discussed above. Venus and Mercury, however, have dispositions and similarities with every planet, and the Moon has no similitude or correspondence since she [57] shares neither similitude nor correspondence with any planet. That is some sort of great fundamental to be guarded carefully since it is highly essential in magical procedures.

§8 Know that the effects of the planets are effects in and of themselves; this is because planets are simple bodies.[38] Those things that are simple suffer neither accident nor any corruption for if they did, they would be unrecognizable. Harm and corruption can only befall bodies made out of diverse things. Know that the effect of the First Moved is a perfect effect and the foundation of all the processes of the heavens, planets, and fixed stars. This is on account of the power and fortitude that moves the other heavens. It is said that the First Moved is the mover of everything, and there is nothing that moves within it. Those who claim it moves oppose the truth. The sphere of fixed stars, however, is distinguished from the motion of the First Moved, particularly because its motion is general. Thus, it moves all the other spheres. Know that the motion of each of the heavens, the motion of the spheres, and that of the fixed stars is an equal motion in each case, and the motion of the planets exists in accordance with the essential motion of their own spheres by which they are moved. The stars have no motion in and of themselves except by accident. The effect of heaven is twofold, as we have discussed. There is the motion that a planet has in and of itself, and the heat that it possesses by accident. After heat proceeds motion, and motion is natural to the heavens themselves as we have said. Then proceed the gift and the pouring in of the planets, which are harnessed by magical images, to move things and powers and redirect them so that they may be manifest. This is because the similitude of things resides in form, and matter has the capacity of receiving powers. Each substance has a form for every complexion, and each form has a substance for every complexion. For example: a fire, although small, grows until it becomes great; thus it grows and is increased since a small flame draws out the fire from the matter upon which it is burning since fire lays hidden in matter until one manifests it; thus, it is increased and grows.

§9 Know that corruption does not enter visible things for the sake of destroying them; rather, it enters into invisible things and corrupts them without appearing to do so. Everything that exists according to nature is balanced, and everything unbalanced exists contrary to nature. On this account visible heat naturally provokes hidden heat, and likewise, hidden heat provokes visible heat. This is because hidden heat is disposed to the effects of heat, thus it is the generation of itself. Study these explanations diligently since you shall draw support from them. [58]

Chapter 7

On How to Work Dialectically in the Science of Images, and Which Part of It Is Fitting to That Science

§1 From what we have said so far, it should be obvious that the reception of form is by matter, that the gift of planetary influence is in magical images and the reception of their powers, and also that the forms of similarity and dissimilarity appear evidently enough (since similarity emerges from a kind of union within the images' effects). This is because rituals with a magical image require similarity to the stars' effects, similarity in the property of the metal from which the image is composed, similarity in the time when it is crafted, and similarity in the place where such an image is cast and prepared. From all these things conjoined in their appropriate similarities, the effect of the image itself will ensue. If these things were dissimilar in some way, the image itself would be deficient in effect. From this, it appears that unification is some great foundation toward the effects to be acquired by magical art.

§2 Similarly, "quantity" is a foundation of that science because it operates in the *quadrivium*. According to its own first division, "quantity" is divided into two parts, which are "continuous quantity" and "discrete quantity." "Continuous quantity" is divided into five parts, which are lines, surfaces, volume, time, and space. "Discrete quantity" is divided into two parts, namely number and word.[39] All parts of "quantity" are very important to magical works, just as a line is necessary to a magical image on account of the aspects and the symbolism that we demand from an image insofar as we seek to receive the image's effects by similitude or dissimilitude. These two parts wherein we divide the line according to aspect and suitability is discussed in the *quadrivium* (in the chapter on the straight line). Therein it is said: "A straight line directly connects two points placed at a distance from one another." This definition is better than any other definition for the images because the straight line upon which something is set travels on a single path from the beginning of the first point of the line passing through the remaining others until it reaches the other point placed directly opposite to it. For this reason, we say that such a thing is "facing" a thing in a straight line; this happens when it encounters something that, on its own path, pours down and proceeds through the straight line. For example, the projection of planetary rays from a single point flows directly upon a point on the surface of a body disposed to receiving the projections of such rays. The reason why that is better for magical images is on account of the influence of the stars that is sought in the effect of the image. This projection of rays is also suited for entering the metal or whatever the image is made of in order to fulfill that effect for which the image was fashioned and assembled by contrariety or similarity. Thus, it appears that a line coming directly out of a planet into an image's form must be straight so that what is contributed may be whole and complete, for it would not be called a straight line were it oblique—that indeed would be weak and diminished. [59]

§3 A surface is forcibly the "figure" of the influence because a surface is an extension of an image's effect on that location. Then, when it is extended, it necessarily becomes a surface; for everything that extends, even the most subtle thing, is a surface. Thus, water, in and of itself, is effectively transmuted and altered just as it is changed by heat, cold, light, odor, colors, and other similar things. The lines poured in by the planets proceed from above into images. These lines poured into the images by the planets and those lines arising from the magical image itself make a surface. For this reason, learn and understand those secrets. Nevertheless, the ancient sages have not yet revealed their reasons for operating in this way.

§4 Time is certainly relevant and necessary to the work of magical images because it follows the motions of bodies. As such, I shall categorize and explain the effect of the image itself. Time is divided into parts by the effects of images; then the time of the aspects is divided according to the location and influence of that effect, whether or not you wish it to be completed out of the parts of the planetary declinations. What we mean is to observe the time of the planets in the proper and suitable hour and to know the conjunctions that this planet has with the other planets when sharing in a single degree, or possibly in some other aspect, whether opposite, square, trine, and otherwise. Other important things to consider regarding the locations of the planets are the production of effects, both complete and incomplete, which must be discerned according to the mode and form of the ritual: that is, whether a planet be direct, descending, or in its exaltation; where the planet's influence will be found; where this influence is cut off by the fortunate or unfortunate planets; and also when the planet is in light, pitted, and dark degrees, or others described in astrology.[40] This is, by far, the greatest secret in magical teaching (that is, this kind of diversity, as they say, in similarity and contrariness). The latter is the time for examining what the specific given effect will be, and the former is the time in which we must consider the preparation of magical images, the place where they should be prepared, and what things are akin to each other at that time.

§5 Location, however, is the final component of our division of "continuous quantity." Location is an aspect toward the goal that the ease of the ritual endure all the way until one reaches the desired end at the opportune time. The location of the image, its materials, whether it is in the air or on land, whether hidden or in the open, and other such factors (such as the places where the images are constructed and where practitioners lay out and work the material from which their image must be made)—all these things are worthy of consideration among the works of magic since it is on account of such factors that the planetary influences and effects arise. Greater and more wondrous effects will arise that are hard to believe in the opinions of those who behold them. Amen. I am telling to you the truth about the nature of miracles and wondrous effects (since those are the effects of magical images). This is especially the case since their effects are not similar to those of animals. Rather, they are like [60] removing sands; polishing jewels; holding back plague, floods, and clouds; changing winds; and other such things that we will not cite here on account of the inconvenience of a prolix discourse.

§6 Words and numbers, which are from the category of "discrete quantity," are necessary in predictions, divinations, dream interpretations, speeches for the masses, and the like; these things also pertain to one branch of the art of magic. "Quantity" per se is necessary and essential to those procedures because it delineates time, which indeed does not exist except through the calculation of the heavens' movements. This is what we mean when we say "from such a time until such a time," that is, some number for calculation; when the heavens' movements reach this given position, then the calculation is complete. The same applies when we say "such an operation will be from this hour for the next forty-two days." This statement clarifies that we wish to express some calculation of number.

§7 Proportion pertains to the method of that science since it constitutes the image's form. The location of the effect itself receives the strength and power that the sages claim is a determining factor in an image. For the most part, these factors pertain to the measure of proportion and the configuration for preparing images in a place where that quality must be present. This whole thing pertains to the category of proportion, and others of other qualities similar to these pertain to this category of proportion.

§8 "Quality" per se is the cause of a magical image's effects because what is done through an image's effects should have virtue and complete power similar to its own effect and to that "quality" that should be included in the image itself for the manifestation of that power and effect sought in the image. This is the capacity and composition it should have: impressions upon the nature of lower things from the nature of higher things, such that the resulting image is adjusted for the planets' endowment and complements their effects on your requests, which we have often discussed in this book. This is because planets participate more in some things than in others, just as some planets govern a particular city, certain types of plants, animals, stones, and other similar things. When, for example, a stone is arranged into another image—composite and disposed for receiving that planet's effects—or likewise something similar to it for the reception of a planet's effects and nature contained within, it should be similar to the effect and reception of that planet operating therein. Thus, that stone or substance from which an image is made should be composite since if the nature of the stone (or the other substance from which the image is made) is strong and enduring such that it is entirely fortified in itself until achieving victory over nature, then the effect manifests and is extended. Those laboring faithfully in this science never managed to discover how they could do this except the one who would grasp the nature of a stone (or something of the same or a similar quality) until his nature was strengthened such that it overcame and vanquished all other natures (for example, in electuaries and theriacs, which by their own virtue find and conquer illness). Such [61] a victory arises from the power of many medicines combined together since many wondrous things occur by combining medicines, as in physiology, the Great Work, and the other works employing nature, such as fashioning images, repelling plague, and using the effects of stones upon one another. Always remember the sayings of the sage who claimed that—in all your works and effects—look to sympathy and mutual love; avoid differences and mutual dissonances by which natures resist one another.

Chapter 8

On the Orderly Arrangement of Nature and How It Affects This Science

§1 The ancient sages believed that ranks exist among the degrees of nature; they pursued these beliefs until they knew the rank and nature of species and how everything else was governed. Thereafter, they related species to each other until the use of medicines and the effects that they produced by their combinations were understood. Here we cannot omit one necessary thing, which is the disagreement among the ancient sages concerning simple natures (of what sort, and how many there are). One party, which I believe to be the correct one, says that the simple natures are the mothers of and beginnings to all other things. There are four of these natures: coldness, wetness, dryness, and hotness, which are appropriately named the first and simple qualities.

Second, other composite natures follow the simple ones, which are these: the hot, the cold, the wet, and the dry. That which we call "hot" expresses when matter is joined with hotness, and the same is to be understood regarding the others. It is very clear from this opinion, namely, when we say "hot" or "cold," it is not similar to what we mean when we say "hotness" and "coldness." Then that composite material follows according to another composite, which we call "hot" and "dry," "hot" and "wet," "cold" and "dry," or "cold" and "moist," which are pairs of composite natures. Clearly, the latter are not equal to the former (that is, the "hot" without the "dry" and the "wet," and the "cold" without the "dry" and the "wet"). Third, other composite natures follow, namely fire, air, water, and earth, which are the third composite natures produced from the union of the first and second qualities. Other composite natures situated in the fourth rank follow those natures, which exist in bodies that are divided into many parts—that is to say, the four seasons of the year (namely, winter, spring, autumn, and summer) or the four humors found in humans as in other animals (namely, blood, phlegm, yellow bile, and [62] black bile).[41] The material of humankind is more delicate and more subtle than all the other materials of animals because the nature of those animals is grosser and much more chaotic than the nature of humankind. Third in order behind humans and animals are the natures of trees and plants born from soil, such as oil, tinctures, seeds, roots, and similar things; the qualities of stones are in natures of this kind. One must understand what we have spoken about thus far: what we have said regarding plants and stones is equally true concerning humans and animals. In the subtlety of nature, plants follow after the other animals. These composite matters ensue from craft. They are the ones that we say are composed out of composites and are the final composites (for example, medicines and other amalgamated things). Nevertheless, all things wherein the natures of simple and composite things stand together are divided into seven parts, which then by extension make twenty-eight parts.[42] I wish here to give a second example of the same so that we may clarify what is divided in the first explanation.

§2 The simple natures are hotness, coldness, wetness, and dryness; the first composite natures are the hot, the cold, the wet, and the dry; the second composite natures are hot and dry, hot and wet, cold and dry, cold and wet; the third composite natures are the elements themselves, namely, fire, air, water, earth; and the fourth composite natures are the seasons of the year, namely spring, winter, summer, and autumn; and the fifth composite natures are the four humors, namely blood, yellow bile, phlegm, and black bile; and the sixth composite natures are tinctures, oils, roots, seeds, and such things.

§3 Thus, I say that hotness, coldness, wetness, and dryness are similar to fire, air, water, and earth when they are divided into many parts by sense perception and their perceptibility. For they say that fire is hot because it is hot and dry; they do not say that hotness itself is fire nor that it is composed with fire and another thing because every composite thing is joined together out of the things preceding them and named in them (it is composed in such a way that heat precedes fire, humidity precedes air, coldness precedes water, and dryness precedes earth). The example we gave in the foregoing applies also to the liver, the lung, the gallbladder, the heart, the head, the legs, the hands, and all the other organs. Hotness, as we said above, ensues from the motion of the heavens, coldness is generated from its center (i.e., the Earth, which is called the center of the First Mobile) from which terrestrial materials produce all the generation in all types of matter; thus, coldness is opposed to hotness in all of its fundamental qualities, in rest and in motion, because hotness is a quality that joins similar things and divides opposites. Thus, we say that contrary things are joined by coldness, and similar things are divided by the same. It must be so in those things that are opposed in all their qualities; were this not the case, their definition would be harmed and lost. [63]

§4 Therefore I say to you, if you wish to apply your intellect to those splendid, excellent, and important realms of knowledge, then spare no zeal, and do not neglect studying the books and words of the wise for it is by that path that you shall reach your desire. The other things that I discussed thus far on mixing and joining things were taken from the sayings of the wise and from all the sciences. I used them only as an explanation and in order to dispose your spirit and intellect such that you be benevolent, easily taught, and attentive.

Chapter 9

On Examples of Figures and Forms of Images Made for Planetary Assistance

§1 Now I propose to return to the previous topic we were discussing on the figures of the heavens and on the effects they produce with the stars' help and influence. There are six images that we shall discuss directly below; they have virtues, powers, and effects upon the world. Here, I intend to discuss and describe these figures, namely that which is tested from its results and its effects, about which the ancient sages working upon this were in agreement with one another.[43]

§2 *The first of these figures is for driving off mice from wherever you desire.* Write the figures below on a thin sheet of red bronze, with the first face of Leo ascending. These figures were bound to the fixed stars within the sign of Leo.

When this is done, place the thin sheet where the mice are, and they shall all flee from that area. These are the figures:

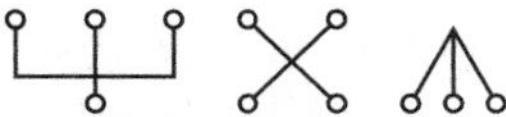

§3 *For repelling insects.* Make the following figures on a sulfurous stone with the second face of Taurus ascending. Place this stone wherever you desire. No insects shall ever be able to come there for as long as the stone shall remain. These are the figures:

§4 *For repelling flies from wherever you want.* Inscribe the figures below on a thin sheet of tin with the third face of Scorpio ascending. Place that thin sheet wherever you desire, and the flies shall recede from there. These are the figures of the stars that drive them off:

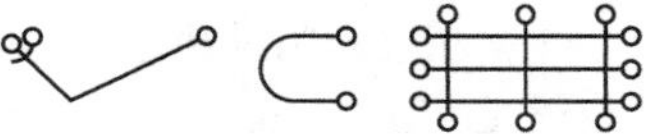

§5 *So that a person you desire comes running to you or to a specific place.* Make these figures on a linen rag in the day and hour of Venus when the second face of Taurus is rising with Venus standing in it. On that very hour, [64] write the name of the one whom you wish to come to you. Then set the head of the linen rag on fire. At once, the person who you suggested will come to you. These are the figures:

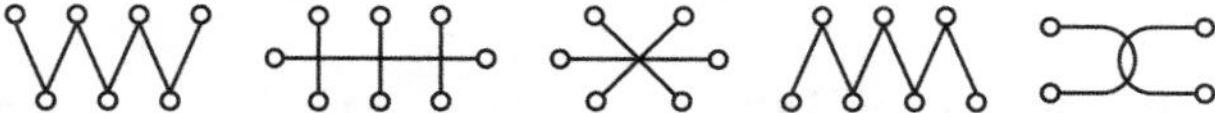

§6 *For creating enmity.* When you wish to separate two individuals such that they never love one another again, draw the figures inscribed below with the tooth of a black dog on a thin sheet of black lead in the day and hour of Saturn with the third face of Capricorn ascending and Saturn standing in it. Put the thin sheet in the place of either of them or in a place where they are accustomed to get together. Their friendship will dissolve, and they will never again love one another. These are the figures:

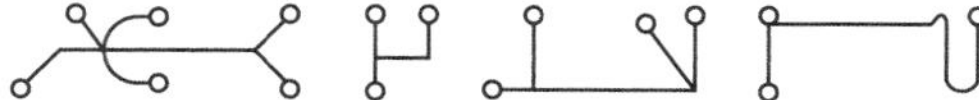

§7 *For cursing a place you never wish to be inhabited.* Make these figures on a thin lead sheet with the brain of a pig on the day and hour of Saturn with the second face of Capricorn ascending with Saturn standing in it. Place the thin sheet in the place that you desire to be depopulated. The harmful power of Saturn will flow into it, and it will never be populated for as long as the thin sheet shall stand there. These are the figures:

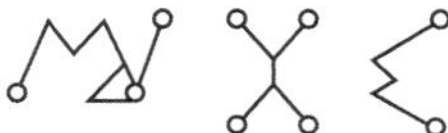

§8 All six of these work through the power of the planet or planets when they have been physically joined to the aforesaid constellations. Know that there are no figures that invoke the help of the fixed stars other than those six nor have any of the sages said more.[44] This is why I have decided to completely lay this science out in this book.

Chapter 10

On the Stones Suited to Each Planet and on the Formation of Figures

§1 Here, I intend to clarify what each planet governs, as much in metals and stones as in the figures of the planets and their wondrous operations.

§2 First regarding Saturn: out of the metals, Saturn governs iron and part of gold; out of the stones, he governs diamond, onyx, cameo, jet (which is black and clear), iron, and magnesium. He governs partly over red stones, golden marcasite and also hematite.

§3 Out of the metals, Jupiter governs lead and out of the precious stones, those that are white and yellow. He governs partly over carnelian, emerald, beryl, crystal, and all white and clear shining stones, as well as gold. [65]

§4 Out of the metals, Mars governs red bronze and all types of sulfur and has a part in glass. Out of the stones, he governs *premonada*[45] and the bloodstone, and partly over carnelian and onyx, as well as all red and speckled stones.

§5 Out of the metals, the Sun governs Egyptian glass and arsenic.[46] Out of the stones, he governs garnet, diamond, red pearls, and all shining and clear stones. He governs partly over hematite, *azumbedich*,[47] Balas ruby, and yellow marcasite.

§6 Out of the metals, Venus governs red bronze and has a part in silver and glass. Out of the stones, she governs azure, coral, and malachite, and partly over beryl and magnesium.

§7 Out of the metals, Mercury governs quicksilver and has a part in tin and glass. Out of the stones, he governs emerald with all its types, and partly over *azumbedich*.

§8 Out of the metals, the Moon governs silver, and out of the stones, she governs silver marcasite and minute pearl, and partly over crystal, azure, onyx, and beryl.

§9 These are the figures of the seven planets:

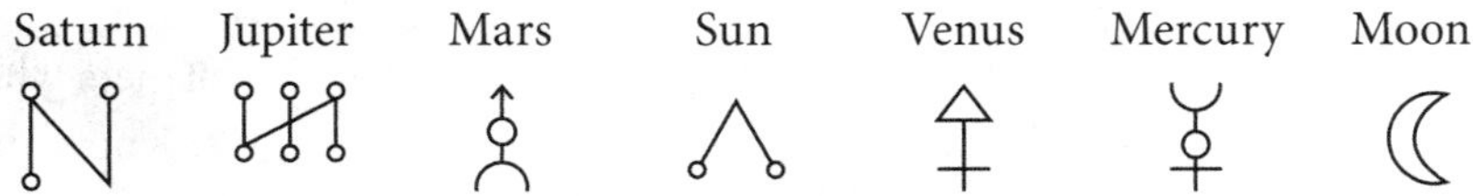

§10 These are the figures of the planets as we found them translated in the *Lapidary of Mercurius*, the *Book of Apollonius*,[48] and in the *Book of Spirits and Images*, which the wise Picatrix translated.

§11 The image of Saturn, according to the opinion of the wise Picatrix, is the shape of a man with a crow-like face and the feet of a camel, sitting upon a throne, with a spear in his right hand and a lance or dart in his left. This is his shape.

§12 The image of Saturn, according to the wise Apollonius, is the shape of an old man sitting erect on a tall throne. This is his shape.

§13 The image of Saturn, according to the opinion of the wise Mercurius, is the shape of a man standing, raising his hands above his head and holding a fish in them. Below his feet is a lizard. This is his shape.

§14 The image of Saturn, according to the opinion of other sages, is the shape of a man standing upon a dragon, holding a scythe in his right hand and a spear in his left, dressed in black and tawny clothes. This is his shape.

[*The ring of Saturn*. Saturn governs turquoise among the minerals and lead among the metals. Therefore, on Sunday during his hour, with the Moon in Capricorn, inscribe on turquoise set in a lead ring a man riding upright upon a dragon, holding a sickle in his right hand, with an egg-like stone in the middle of his hand. The one wearing this ring must avoid eating dilled meats and entering dark places. The spirits that dwell in dark and obscure places will be well-disposed to the wearer; bulls will assist the wearer. Even profound secrets, humans, scorpions, serpents, mice, all the reptiles upon the earth, and all the operations of Saturn will be revealed to the wearer.][49]

§15 The image of Jupiter, according to the opinion of Apollonius, is the shape of a man sitting on an eagle, wrapped in a cloth, with his feet on the eagle's back, and a head, covered by a cloth, held in his right hand. This is his shape. [66]

§16 The image of Jupiter, according to the opinion of Picatrix, is the shape of a man with a leonine face and the feet of a bird; beneath his feet he is holding a dragon that has seven heads, and in his right hand he holds a dart as if he wished to throw it at the head of the dragon. This is his shape.

§17 The image of Jupiter, according to the opinion of Mercurius, is the shape of a man covered in a single linen cloth, riding upon a dragon, holding a lance or a dart in his hand. This is his shape.

§18 The image of Jupiter, according to the opinion of other sages, is the shape of a man riding an eagle, holding a cloth in his right hand and nuts in his left; all his clothing is yellow. This is his shape.

[*The ring of Jupiter.* Jupiter governs tin among the metals and chalcedony among the minerals. Therefore, on a Thursday, during his hour, with the Moon being in Sagittarius, inscribe on chalcedony set in a tin ring a man sitting atop an eagle with noble or high-class clothes, holding his mouth with his right hand. Whoever wears it will see the sons of men, eagles, vultures, lions, and all the operations of Jupiter be favorable to them.][50]

§19 The image of Mars, according to the opinion of the wise Apollonius, is the shape of a crowned man holding an inscribed sword in his right hand. This is his shape.

§20 The image of Mars, according to the opinion of Mercurius, is the shape of a naked man standing erect on his feet, holding on his right a beautiful virgin standing on her feet, which is an image of Venus with her hair fastened back. Mars is placing his right hand on his own neck and his left hand extending above her chest; he is facing her and admiring her. The sage says that this figure has great powers and, indeed, great effects. God willing, we shall speak about it later.[51] This is his shape.

§21 The image of Mars, according to the opinion of other sages, is the shape of a man riding a lion, holding a sword in his right hand and brandishing the head of a man in his left; his clothes are of iron and mail. This is his shape.

[*The ring of Mars.* Mars governs iron among the minerals. On Tuesday in his hour, inscribe on iron a man dressed in a breastplate, equipped with arms, grasping an unsheathed sword in his right hand, and holding in his left the head of a man. Anyone wearing this ring will subdue in battle and triumph over enemies. Elephants, lions, and vultures will be well-disposed to the wearer, and all the works of Mars will favor them.][52]

§22 The image of the Sun, according to the opinion of the wise Apollonius, is the shape of a standing woman, placed on a chariot drawn by four horses, holding a mirror in her right hand and a staff bound above her breast in her left hand; above her head she has the likeness of a flame. This is her shape.

§23 The image of the Sun, according to the opinion of Mercurius, is the shape of a man standing on his feet as though wanting to salute those around him, and he is holding in his left hand a round shield; beneath his feet he has the image of a dragon. This is his shape.

§24 The image of the Sun, according to the opinion of Picatrix, is the shape of a king sitting on a throne with a crown on his head, with the image of a crow in front of him, and beneath his feet is the figure of the Sun that we depicted above.[53] This is his shape.

§25 The image of the Sun, according to the opinion of other sages, is the shape of a baron standing in a chariot that is drawn by four horses; in his right hand he is holding a mirror, and in his left a shield; all his clothes are yellow. This is his shape.

[*The ring of the Sun*. The Sun governs gold and adamant among the minerals. On Sunday, at the first hour of the day with the Moon in Aries, inscribe in adamant set in a gold ring the Sun riding a chariot led by four horses, holding in his right hand a *marcha* (which is an Arabic name), that is, a mirror or a gallbladder, and in his left hand a stick knotted with pelts, with a wax seal above his head. Anyone wearing the ring should not eat a white dove, nor should they have sex with a white woman. While wearing this ring, the sons of men and magnates will be well-disposed to you, and whatever you say will be obeyed reverently, and all the operations of the Sun will be favorable to you.][54]

§26 The image of Venus, according to the opinion of the wise Apollonius, is the shape of a woman standing on her feet and holding an apple in her right hand. This is her shape. [67]

§27 The image of Venus, according to the opinion of the wise Picatrix, is the shape of a woman holding up an apple in her right hand and, in her left, a comb similar to a tablet with these characters written on it: ΟΛΟΙΟΛ. This is her shape.

§28 The image of Venus, according to the opinion of the wise Mercurius, is a shape with the body of a man, the face and head of a bird, and the feet of an eagle. This is its shape.

§29 The image of Venus, according to Ptolomy, is the shape of a naked woman, and in front of her neck she has the shape of Mars with a single chain. This is her shape.

§30 The image of Venus, according to the opinion of other sages, is the shape of a woman riding a stag with her hair down, and in her right hand she has an apple, and in her left she has flowers; her clothes are of white colors. This is her shape.
[*The ring of Venus.* Venus governs bronze and copper among the minerals. Therefore, on a Friday, in her hour, with the Moon in Libra, inscribe on *acuty* set in a red bronze ring a woman standing upright with a comb in her right hand. Anyone wearing the ring should avoid having sex with an old woman. Women, kings, flying animals, forest creatures, cocks, locusts, all birds with pretty feathers, and all the works of Venus will be well-disposed to the wearer.][55]
§31 The image of Mercury, according to the opinion of the wise Apollonius, is the shape of a bearded youth holding a dart in his right hand. This is his shape.
§32 The image of Mercury, according to the wise Mercurius, is the shape of a man with a cock on his head, standing on a throne; his feet are similar to the feet of an eagle; he is holding fire in the palm of his left hand and under his feet are the figures that are reproduced below.[56] This is his shape.
§33 The image of Mercury, according to the opinion of Picatrix, is the shape of a man standing with wings extended to his right side, and a small cock on his left. He holds a dart in his right hand and a round seashell in his left; in the middle of his head is a cock's crest. This is his shape.
§34 The image of Mercury, according to the opinion of other sages, is the shape of a crowned baron riding on a peacock; in his right hand he holds a pen and in his left a sheet of paper; his clothes are a mixture of every color. This is his shape.
[*The ring of Mercury.* Mercury governs quicksilver among metals and magnetite among the minerals. Therefore, on Wednesday, in his hour, with the Moon in Virgo, inscribe in magnetite a man seated upon a throne, with a round tray covered in books placed before him, at his feet men are seated and students are listening attentively. Anyone wearing the ring must avoid eating fish. The wearer will understand more profoundly and speculate more loftily. Rivers, seas, all things living within them, all nations, and all the works of Mercury will be well-disposed to the wearer.][57]
§35 The image of the Moon, according to the opinion of Mercurius, is the shape of a woman with a beautiful face, encircled by a dragon, with horns on her head, encircled by two snakes (on her head there are two snakes and on each arm a snake is entwined); above her head there is one dragon and another beneath her feet; each of these dragons has seven heads. This is her shape.
§36 The image of the Moon, according to the opinion of Apollonius, is the shape of a woman standing upon two bulls; the head of one is next to the tail of the other. This is her shape.

§37 The image of the Moon, according to the opinion of the wise Picatrix, is the shape of a man with a bird upon his head, balancing himself on a cane, with a tree in front of him. This is his shape. [68]

§38 The image of the Moon, according to the opinion of other sages, is the shape of a crowned youth, standing on a chariot drawn by four horses; in his right hand is a crook and in his left a mirror, and all his clothes are green and white. This is his shape.

§39 Any of these figures, whether of the Sun or of other planets, have wondrous powers and effects in magical operations that, God willing, we shall explain in this book.

§40 These are the images just as the ancient sages, that is, those who delved into this knowledge, set them out in their books. Each of those figures has wondrous effects and the greatest possible powers. Now I intend to speak about their effects and powers.

§41 *Image of Saturn for excessive drinking.* From the works of Saturn, engrave into a turquoise[58] stone the shape of a man elevated on a tall throne, with a muddy linen cloth on his head, and a scythe in his hand (in the hour of Saturn while he is in the ascendant). The power of this image is such that whoever carries it will be able to drink excessively but not die except in old age.

§42 If, from the works of Saturn, you wish to place discord between anyone, make these figures on a diamond (with Saturn in the ascendant, in his hour):

If you were to impress pitch with that image and place this seal in the dwelling of the two friends or in that of one of them, they will hate each other. Beware not to carry this image with you at all.

§43 *The image of Jupiter.* From the works of Jupiter, make the shape of a man crowned and sitting on a throne with four feet, each of the feet should be on a man's neck, and all those four men should have wings; the man who sits on the throne should raise his hand just as those giving a speech do. Do this in the hour of Jupiter while he is in the ascendant and in his own exaltation. Engrave this on a clear and white stone. Whoever carries this image will be raised into riches and honor. He will live out the best life and have many sons; he will accomplish what he desires; all endeavors wherein his effort is spent will end well; and no enemy will be able to harm him.

§44 If you want to be esteemed by officials and judges, engrave on a stone of crystal from the works of Jupiter the shape of a handsome man with ample clothes riding an eagle; do this in the hour of Jupiter when he is in the ascendant and in his exaltation. Whoever carries this image will be esteemed by officials and judges.

§45 If you desire to prevent a woman from conceiving or if you wish to catch birds, engrave on a stone that is called <. . .> from the works of Jupiter the image of a vulture; do this in the hour of Jupiter with the first face of Sagittarius [69] rising and Jupiter ascending in it. If a bird hunter were to carry this stone, birds would gather around, and he could catch as many of them as he wished. The practitioner will also be loved by people and well received. This stone that we have mentioned leans toward red in color; when it is shaken in the hands, inside it another stone rattles; when it is polished, a white water comes out of it. If you were to place this stone on a woman, she would never conceive so long as it remains upon her.

§46 Hermes said: "Whoever makes the image of a fox on this stone (in the day and hour of Venus, with Jupiter ascending in Pisces facing the Moon) and holds it will be feared by humans and devils."

§47 If one makes on this stone the shape of a crane (in the hour of Jupiter in exaltation) and soaks it in any liquid and gives it as a drink to anyone, the drinker will behold spirits and from these they will accomplish their desires. Hermes mentioned these two powers.

§48 *An image of Mars to do what you will, whether for good or ill.* Engrave upon a diamond the shape of a man from the figures of Mars riding a lion and holding an unsheathed sword in his right hand, brandishing the head of a man in his left. Do this in the hour of Mars with the second face of Aries ascending, with Mars ascending therein. Whoever carries this stone will be potent in both good and evil but particularly more potent in evil.

§49 If you wish to make your appearance terrifying, engrave upon stones of Mars the shape of a man covered in mail and holding two swords, one on his neck and the other unsheathed in his right hand while holding the head of a man in his left. Do this while Mars is in his own house. Whoever carries the stone will be feared by all those who see them, nor will anyone approach them.

§50 *The image for diverting blood from whichever body part you desire.* From the works of Mars, engrave upon onyx the image of a lion, and in front of it these figures or signs:

3 I M

Do this in the hour of Mars with the second face of Scorpio ascending. Whoever carries this image, the blood flowing out of any part of their body will at once be staunched.

§51 *The image of the Sun.* If you wish that a king overcome and conquer all other kings, engrave in a ruby or a balas ruby the shape of a king sitting on a throne made out of the shape of the Sun, having a crown upon his head and a crow before him; beneath his feet are these figures:

b o ⫯ o

Do this when the Sun is in his exaltation. The king who carries this stone will conquer all other kings opposed to him. [70]

§52 If you wish that someone not be vanquished but that they achieve what they set out to do and not see pointless dreams, engrave upon a ruby a lion from the figures of the Sun and above it the four abovementioned figures when the Sun is rising in Leo with the unfortunate planets descending and not facing the Sun. Whoever carries this image will never be overcome by anyone, and what they begin they will bring to a close.

§53 From the figures of the Sun, engrave upon a stone of adamant a woman sitting upon a chariot drawn by four horses with a mirror in her right hand, a rod in her left hand, and seven candelabra above her head. Do this with the Sun in exaltation. Whoever carries this image will be feared by everyone who sees or encounters them.

§54 Engrave the figures of the Sun written below upon a stone of hematite when the Sun is standing in the first face of Leo ascending. Whoever carries this image will be safe from all lunar illnesses that come from the combustion of the Moon.

I Ϛ 4 3 O ⊂∘∘⊃

§55 *The image of Venus.* Make from the figures of Venus the shape of a woman with a human body but with the head of a bird and the feet of an eagle, holding an apple in her right hand and a wooden comb similar to a tablet in her left, which has these figures written upon it: ΟΛΟΙΟΛ. Whoever carries this image will be well received and esteemed by all.

§56 From the forms of Venus, inscribe upon a white stone the figure of a woman holding an apple in her right hand and a comb in her left, with the first face of Libra ascending. Whoever holds or carries this image will always be laughing and cheerful.

§57 From the forms of Venus, inscribe upon a stone of lapis lazuli the figure of a naked girl holding a chain around her neck with a man next to her and the form of a small boy raising a sword behind her, in the hour of Venus. Whoever carries this image will be loved by women and will achieve their desire.

§58 From the forms of Venus, inscribe on a stone of crystal or beryl the figure of a snake, above which is a tarantula, and before which is rising water (with Jupiter in his exaltation). Whoever carries this stone will not be bitten by snakes, and whoever bathes this image in a liquid and gives it to drink to a bitten individual, at once that person will be cured. [71]

§59 From the forms of Venus, inscribe the figures written below in the hour of Venus; all the children will love and follow you. In some other book I found this second set of figures; you may write whichever you desire.

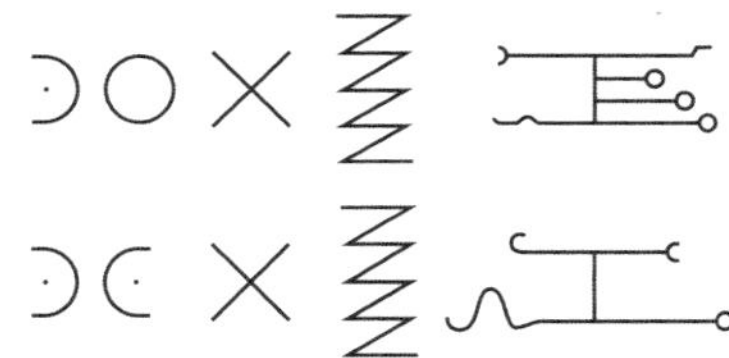

§60 From the forms of Venus, inscribe on beryl the shape of a woman with wings sitting, her hair drawn back in two tresses, and two children in her left hand (in the hour of Venus in her exaltation). Whoever carries this stone will travel easily and without harm.

§61 From the forms of Venus, inscribe on a stone of crystal the figure of three people joined to one another. Whoever carries this figure will be fortunate in commerce and make great profit from it.

§62 From the figures of Venus, inscribe on a stone of coral the figures of two male cats and one mouse (in the hour of Venus with her ascending). No mouse will remain where you place the figure.

§63 From the figures of Venus, inscribe on a carnelian the figure of a fly flying (in the hour of Venus with herself ascending). No fly will remain where you place the figure.

§64 From the figures of Venus, inscribe the figure of a leech on part of a stone of malachite, and on the other part inscribe two leeches, the head of one holding the tail of the other (in the hour of Venus with herself in the ascendant). Make a wax seal or something else with this image and throw that seal in the place of those leeches, and none of them will remain there.

§65 From the figures of Venus, inscribe on a stone of crystal the figure of a woman standing with the figure of an idol standing in front of her. Do this in the hour of Venus, herself in the ascendant. Whoever carries this image will be loved by women.

§66 From the figures of Venus, inscribe on a carnelian stone the figure of a woman standing on her feet with the likeness of hair on her thigh, with a folded sheet of paper in one hand and an apple in the other (in the hour of Venus, herself in the ascendant). Make a seal from this image with wax and give it to children in food, they will be freed from colic.

§67 From the figures of Venus, inscribe upon a carnelian stone the head of a wild ass with a fly above its head and atop that a little something (that is, what could be a small head covering), in the hour of Venus with Venus herself in the ascendant. Make a wax seal with this image and you will overcome all gastric ailments. [72]

§68 *The image of Mercury.* From the figures of Mercury, inscribe upon an emerald the shape of a baron sitting on a stool with a cock above his head, with his feet like those of an eagle, with the likeness of fire in his left hand, and with these signs under his feet:

Do this in the hour of Mercury when he is ascending and in exaltation. If a prisoner were to carry this stone, he would be freed from prison.

§69 From the works of Mercury, inscribe the signs below on an emerald (in his hour, Mercury himself in the ascendant). Whoever carries this stone will be served by scribes, notaries, and all those of mercurial nature.

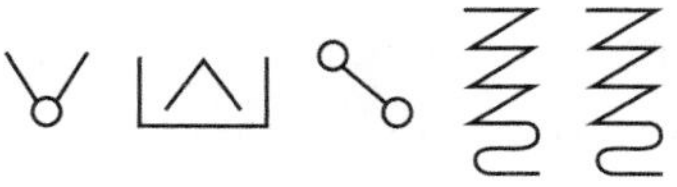

§70 From the works of Mercury, inscribe the figure of a frog on an emerald (in the hour of Mercury, himself in the ascendant). Whoever carries this stone will be offended by none; nay, people will speak well of them, and they will say good things about all their works.

§71 From the works of Mercury, make the figure of a lion on an emerald and another figure in the shape of a lion's head (in the hour of Mercury, with the sign of Gemini ascending, with Mercury standing there). Above its head, write an 'A' and below its head a 'D.' Whoever holds this image will avoid sickness, be feared, and good things will be spoken about them.

§72 From the works of Mercury, inscribe on an emerald the figure of a scorpion (in the hour of Mercury, with himself ascending). A pregnant woman carrying this stone will give birth easily and without danger, neither for her nor the child.

§73 From the works of Mercury, inscribe on a marble stone the figure of the hand of a man holding scales (in the hour of Mercury, with himself in the ascendant). By imprinting a wax seal with this image (or by inscribing another suitable object) and giving it to a sick man, he will be cured quickly from any kind of fever; this is proven against fevers.

§74 *The image of the Moon.* From the forms of the Moon, inscribe the figure of a man with the head of a bird holding himself up on a cane and holding in his hand the image of a flowering plant (in the hour of the Moon with her ascending in her exaltation). Whoever carries this image will never tire on a journey, wherever they may go.

§75 From the forms of the Moon, inscribe these signs on a lapis lazuli (in the hour of the Moon, with herself in the ascendant). If you soak this image in any liquid and give it to drink to two or [73] more people, then they will love each other greatly, and will not be able to be separated from one another:

§76 From the works of the Moon, inscribe on a stone of crystal the figure of a woman with scattered hair drawn back, standing upon two bulls, holding one of her feet on the head of one and the other foot on the other. On another part of the stone, inscribe the figure of a woman standing with the likeness of a crown on her head and a cane in her right hand. Write these signs around her:

Do this in the hour of the Moon with her in the ascendant. Imprint a wax seal with this image, and then place it in a dovecote. Many doves will gather there.

§77 From the works of the Moon, inscribe on lapis lazuli the figure of a lion with the head of a man, and this sign above his back:

Do this in the hour of the Moon with her in the ascendant. You will cure children from all their illnesses with this image.

§78 From the works of the Moon, inscribe the figure of an adder on bezoar stone or green malachite, with these signs on its head:

Do this in the hour of the Moon with herself in the ascendant. Neither adder nor snake will ever come wherever these figures are.

§79 From the works of the Moon, inscribe these signs on an emerald stone in the hour of the Moon with herself in the ascendant. Imprint incense with this stone and give that seal to a man, and he will have a good retentive memory:

§80 These are the images suited to each planet:

§81 *First regarding Saturn.* In the hour of Saturn with Saturn ascending in the third face of Aquarius, make an image for a healing stone that heals the pangs of a virgin and holds back a woman's blood or menstrual fluids. [74]

§82 *Regarding Jupiter.* In the hour of Jupiter with Jupiter rising in the second face of Sagittarius with an aspect from the Sun, make an image for preventing excessive rain and diverting the losses thereof.

§83 *Regarding Mars.* In the hour of Mars with Mars ascending in the first face of Scorpio, make an image for strengthening the timid, humbling the wrath of a king, and diverting damages caused by thieves, wolves, wild beasts, and all wicked folk.

§84 *Regarding the Sun.* In the hour of the Sun with the Sun rising in the first face of Leo, make an image for banishing wicked thoughts and healing stomach and liver problems. This image will be effective for these things and even for healing old ailments.

§85 *Regarding Venus.* In the hour of Venus with Venus ascending in the first face of Pisces, make an image for healing women's gynecological illnesses, cheering up an unhappy individual, curing melancholy, eliminating wicked thoughts, and having more and better sex. In the first face of Taurus are made images of great and wondrous effects regarding love and human goodwill.

§86 *Regarding Mercury.* In the hour of Mercury with Mercury ascending in the first face of Gemini, make images for sharpening the memory and the intellect regarding knowledge and wisdom or for acquiring mercy from individuals.

§87 *Regarding the Moon*. In the hour of the Moon with the Moon ascending in the first face of Cancer, make an image for improving harvests, vegetation, and all things that are born in the earth.

Chapter 11

On the Images of the Constellations' Faces and Their Effects

§1 The ancient sages who discussed this knowledge related so many things (and proved them through so many arguments) that if we wished to relate everything, it would be excessively prolix and verbose, thus causing us to deviate from our proposed topic. Nevertheless, we must discuss those explanations that are necessary—those without which we would be unable to pursue our topic. I myself will teach you what you must study for your advantage, you who intends to study this knowledge and draw from its benefits. Reveal this to no one. The sages had no intrinsic knowledge about the spirits, nor did they come to any except through great difficulty, study, and toil. They achieved what they could from this effort, first in quietude, removed from all anxiety or concern for this world, and they studied with continued zeal and the good minds and memories they possessed. Indeed, the spirit and the senses are strengthened through intelligence and memory. A profound knowledge is attained by the individual who has a better capacity for discerning and verifying matters that not everyone understands. [75] Discerning the veracity of a speaker hinges upon good memory and intellect; for this reason, the wise have said that there is a type of conviction that is made totally clear by the rational spirit, given for improving our capacity to prove things with certainty. What illuminates the rational spirit is its ability for and disposition toward receiving the things it seeks to receive, thus easily fulfilling pursuits. On that account, intellect is vigorous, efficient, and strong, as opposed to opinion, which is feeble. Here is an example of a strong intellect versus a feeble one: the strong one acts without difficulty, without great effort; the weak one is subject to change, easily and suddenly. In the same way, an individual with a good intellect and memory effortlessly understands the sciences and learns in a short time by natural perception, study, and insight what must be understood. Good learning and comprehension of this kind arises from an acuity of the spirit until, in a small amount of time, the individual obtains what he seeks. Indeed, this intellect and agility, or disposition, is drawn from the acuity of fire, which acts swiftly in its effects. Likewise, it is drawn from the Sun's acuity, which scatters parts of the atmosphere and illuminates and grows brighter in his own hour. This kind of acuity belongs to the intellect, which, on account of its sharpness and clarity, subdivides the thing sought, searching within all its parts until it leans toward certitude and, in a brief time, understands the thing sought *as is*. Therefore, the sharper the intellect, the more easily does it comprehend a thing sought or whatever is brought before it. All this is necessary for understanding the following.

§2 Note that each of the twelve signs is divided into three equal parts, and each division is called a "face." As proclaimed by the sages of India, each of these faces has images, forms, and figures; is allocated to one of the seven planets; and these faces are divided and distributed according to the position and order of the planets, beginning from the highest, proceeding in order down to the lowest, then returning to the highest.

First regarding Aries, whose first face is attributed to Mars, the second to the Sun (who follows him in the order), and the third to Venus (who comes after the Sun). The first face of Taurus is to Mercury, and thus it proceeds through the order of the planets unto the end of the signs.[59] These faces have natures and forms suited to the natures and forms of their lords. Here we propose to relate the ascending forms in each of these faces as follows.

§3 The first face of Aries is Mars, and in it (according to the opinion of a great sage in that science) there ascends the image of a black man, anxious, with a large body, red eyes, holding a chopping axe in his hand, and girded in a white cloth. There is great worth in him. This is the face of strength, nobility, and worth without modesty. This is its form. [76]

§4 In the second face of Aries ascends a woman dressed in green clothes and missing a leg. This is the face of splendor, excellence, value, and rule. This is its form.

§5 In the third face of Aries ascends an unsettled man, holding a golden bracelet in his hands and dressed in red clothes, desiring to do good yet incapable. This is the face of subtlety, subtle crafts, novelties, instruments, and the like. This is its form.

§6 In the first face of Taurus ascends a woman with curly hair, with a single son wearing clothes similar to fire, and she also is dressed in similar clothes. This is the face for plowing and working the land, science and geometry, sowing and crafting. This is its form.

§7 In the second face of Taurus ascends a man looking like a camel, with hooves in place of his fingers like cattle. He himself is wholly covered with a torn linen cloth. He wishes to work the earth, sow, and craft. This is the face of nobility, political power, and rewarding the people. This is its form.

§8 In the third face of Taurus ascends a red-colored man with very large, white teeth visible outside his mouth and with a body similar to an elephant with long legs. With him ascends one horse, one dog, and one calf. This is the face of wickedness, poverty, misery, and fear. This is its form.

§9 In the first face of Gemini ascends a beautiful woman, the mistress of stitching, and with her ascend two calves and two horses. This is the face for scribal work, computation and number, giving and receiving, and science. This is its form.

§10 In the second face of Gemini ascends a man whose face is similar to an eagle, and his head is covered by a linen cloth. He is covered and equipped with lead chainmail and on his head is an iron helmet, above which is a silken crown, with a bow and arrows in his hand. This is the face of oppression, evils, and subtleties. This is its form.

§11 In the third face of Gemini ascends a man covered in chainmail with a bow, arrows, and a quiver. This is the face of daring, honesty, the division of labor, and encouragement. This is its form.

§12 In the first face of Cancer ascends a man with crooked fingers and a bent over head. His body is like a horse. He has white feet, and fig leaves cover his body. This is the face of instruction, knowledge, love, subtlety, and craft. This is its form.

§13 In the second face of Cancer ascends a woman with a beautiful face with a crown of green myrtle on her head and the stem of a plant that is called the water lily in her hand, singing songs of love and joy. This is the face of games, riches, rejoicing, and abundance. This is its form. [77]

§14 In the third face of Cancer ascends a turtle[60] with a serpent in his hand and golden chains before him. This is the face of running, riding, and acquiring profit in war, disputes, and conflict. This is its form.

§15 In the first face of Leo ascends a man dressed in dirty clothes. With him ascends the figure of a master of the horse looking northward. His figure is that of a bear and of a dog. This is the face of strength, largesse, and victory. This is its form.

§16 In the second face of Leo ascends a man with a crown of white myrtle on his head and a bow in his hand. This is a face of beauty, of riding, and of the rise of ignorant and rude men. It is the face of war and unsheathed swords. This is its form.

§17 In the third face of Leo ascends an old man, black and filthy, holding fruit and meats in his mouth and a bronze pitcher in his hand. This is the face of love, delight, feast platters, and health. This is its form.

§18 In the first face of Virgo ascends a virgin girl covered in an old, soft linen cloth, holding a pomegranate in her hand. This is the face for sowing, plowing, germinating trees, collecting grapes, and a good life. This is its form.

§19 In the second face of Virgo ascends a man of handsome complexion dressed in hide; above the clothes of hide is another covering of steel. This is the face of petitions, desires, loot, tribute, and denying fair things. This is its form.

§20 In the third face of Virgo ascends a white man with a large body dressed in a white linen garment. With him there is a woman holding black oil in her hand. This is the face of weakness, old age, sickness, laziness, the cursing of body parts, and the destruction of people. This is its form.

§21 In the first face of Libra ascends a man holding a lance in his right hand and a bird hanging by its feet in his left. This is the face of justice, truth, good judgments, perfect justice for the people and weak persons, and doing well to those in need. This is its form.

§22 In the second face of Libra ascends a black man with a fiancée and a joyful path ahead. This is the face of quietude, rejoicing, abundance, and good life. This is its form.

§23 In the third face of Libra ascends a man riding upon an ass, and a wolf is before him. This is the face of evil works, sodomites, adultery, songs, rejoicing, and flavors. This is its form.

§24 In the first face of Scorpio ascends a man holding a lance in his right hand, the head of a man in his left. This is the face of power, sadness, ill will, and enmity. This is its form. [78]

§25 In the second face of Scorpio ascends a man riding a camel, holding a scorpion in his hand. This is the face of knowledge, modesty, power, and of one speaking ill of another. This is its form.

§26 In the third face of Scorpio ascends a horse and a hare. This is the face of evil works, flavors, and joining oneself by force with unwilling women. This is its form.

§27 In the first face of Sagittarius ascends three bodies of men of whom one is yellow, another white, and the third red. This is the face of heat, manumission, bearing fruit in fields or gardens, sustaining, and separating. This is its form.

§28 In the second face of Sagittarius ascends a man leading two cows with a monkey and a bear before him. This is the face of fear, lamentation, sorrow, pain, misery, and restlessness. This is its form.

§29 In the third face of Sagittarius ascends a man with a hat on his head killing another man. This is the face of swiftness in ill wills, inimical and evil effects, wicked wishes of enmity, dispersion, and poor conduct. This is its form.

§30 In the first face of Capricorn ascends a man holding a reed in his right hand and a hoopoe in his left. This is the face of joyfulness, rejoicing, and dissolving businesses, as well as laziness, weakness, and poor process. This is its form.

§31 In the second face of Capricorn ascends a man with a typical monkey before him. This is the face for seeking impossibilities or things that nobody has prevailed in achieving. This is its form.

§32 In the third face of Capricorn ascends a man holding a book for himself to open and close; before him, he has the tail of a fish. This is the face for riches, the accumulation of money, and for gathering and growing businesses inclined toward a positive end. This is its form.

§33 In the first face of Aquarius ascends a man with a mutilated head, holding a peacock in his hand. This is the face of misery, poverty, and crumb cleaners. This is its form.

§34 In the second face of Aquarius ascends a man similar to a king who permits himself much and abhors those he sees. This is the face of beauty and position, the achievement of desires, fulfillment, detriment, and weakness. This is its form.

§35 In the third face of Aquarius ascends a man with a mutilated head and an old woman with him. This is the face of abundance, the fulfillment of the will, and affronts. This is its form.

§36 In the first face of Pisces ascends a man with two bodies, appearing as if he were greeting with his hands. This is the face of peace, humility, weakness, long journeys, misery, the search for riches, and the taking of pity on other ways of life. This is its form.

§37 In the second face of Pisces ascends a man with a second upside-down head, [79] his feet raised on high, and a platter in his hand for eating. This is the face of great value, strong will, seriousness, worthiness, and contemplation regarding splendid matters. This is its form.

§38 In the third face of Pisces ascends a gloomy man with evil thoughts, considering deceits and betrayals. In front of him there is a woman with an ass climbing atop her, and a bird in her hand. This is the face for mounting and having sex with yearning women, or for seeking quietude and rest. This is its form.

§39 Know that in the signs' faces is the greatest secret and a great profit that cannot be grasped except by those most studious in the art of astrology and who have a good comprehension of it—sharp and subtle in extracting fundamentals and profound subtleties. This is because one planet can impede the effects of another. The power of a boundary is stronger than the power of a face, and the power of a face is stronger than the power of a house. Through their natures, one encroaches upon the other just as water extinguishes the heat of fire, and fire carries away the coldness of water, or as water softens and moistens the dryness of earth, and earth dries up the wetness of water. When pure natural things are joined together, the stronger overcomes and prevails. Even if many weak natural things were conjoined, the stronger ones would overcome them all. If they were equal in their powers and effects, that process and its effects would have a mixed nature. If there were one very strong nature removed from its appropriate place, it would lessen and damage its purity. In the same way, when health is at its height, then illness is generated; or when the fruit is ripe and ready for harvesting, it falls from the tree by itself; or when a small snake overcomes and kills large snakes; or how tiny worms kill a snake when working together; and this is especially so when the stronger things are weakened and more hampered in their natures. Pay diligent attention to the things discussed. The properties of those faces are such that you might observe what is important regarding the effects and bodies of each planet. When you craft any of the images with the faces mentioned above, do it with the material suited to the planet that rules in that face. Then, if the image was made with that face's planet, that process will be complete and manifest in the world. If perchance the Sun were in the ascendant in the hour of that planet or it had another desirable combination with him, then its effect would be more stable and stronger. In all the above, beware that a planet's nature not be overcome by the Sun. Nevertheless, if you have understood everything discussed, you should be able to craft and perfect the faces' images with the stated effects. [80]

Chapter 12

On the Figures and Degrees of the Signs and Their Effects According to the Indians; How One Contemplates This Knowledge; and How, According to Their Opinion, the Powers of Superior Bodies Are Drawn Down (with Notable Secrets)

§1 Some sages from India claim that the foundation of the magical art regarding effects is a dignity called *adorugen*, which they assign and distribute among the seven planets; they also call the planet that governs each part an *adorugen*.[61] The *adorugen* are found in this way: an ascending sign is divided into three equal parts, and its first part is attributed to the lord of the ascendant, the second to the lord of the fifth house, and the third to the lord of the ninth house. This is because the ascendant, the fifth, and the ninth belong to the same triplicity. Works of magical art must be brought about through the faces of the signs according to the sages of India, as it will be told below in sequence.

§2 At first let us begin from Aries. We say that its first face belongs to Mars, wherein images are made so that those individuals for whom the images are cast may always overcome and succeed in battles, litigations, and controversies and that they might never ever be overcome. Furthermore, images are made in it for preventing the milk of beasts and cursing their butter.

§3 The second face of Aries belongs to the Sun, and in it make images for kings and lords, for acquiring their love, and for diverting their nuisances.

§4 The third face of Aries belongs to Jupiter; in it make images for officials, vicars, city judges, prelates, and for fostering peace and benevolence between them and also for reconciling them when they are in disagreement.

§5 The first face of Taurus belongs to Venus; in it make images for fostering love between a man and his wife.

§6 The second face of Taurus belongs to Mercury; in it make an image for causing enmity, binding wills, and introducing discord among women.

§7 The third face of Taurus belongs to Saturn; in it make an image for binding men so that they cannot copulate with women and, on the other hand, for making women ill and separating men from women.

§8 The first face of Gemini belongs to Mercury; in it make images for cursing the senses and the intellect.

§9 The second face of Gemini belongs to Venus; in it make images so that the absent may come, and the fugitive may be returned to his place.

§10 The third face of Gemini belongs to Saturn; in it make images so that evil things may be said about whomever you desire and that they may be laid low in infamy.

§11 The first face of Cancer belongs to the Moon; in it make images for invoking clouds and [81] rains at a time of necessity or so that the absent may return by land or sea.

§12 The second face of Cancer belongs to Mars; in it make an image for preventing destructive rains and snows and diverting harmful snakes and wild beasts on land or sea.

§13 The third face of Cancer belongs to Jupiter; in it make an image for evading nautical dangers.

§14 The first face of Leo belongs to the Sun; in it make an image for acquiring the love and benevolence of lords and for gathering wolves, bears, and wild beasts in a place you desire.

§15 The second face of Leo belongs to Jupiter; in it make an image for diverting wolves and bears so that they may not do harm to the beasts of the herds.

§16 The third face of Leo belongs to Mars; in it make an image for bringing together bears, wolves, and wild beasts into whatever city, village, or place you desire.

§17 The first face of Virgo belongs to Mercury; in it make an image so that scribes may do well and profit in their business dealings.

§18 The second face of Virgo belongs to Saturn; in it make an image for cursing instruments and scribes' tools.

§19 The third face of Virgo belongs to Venus; in it make an image for fostering the peace and love of women and their husbands.

§20 The first face of Libra belongs to Venus; in it make an image so that whomever you desire be afflicted with love for a woman, or vice versa.

§21 The second face of Libra belongs to Saturn; in it make an image for love in all things according to the above.

§22 The third face of Libra belongs to Mercury; in it make an image so that a fugitive may return from wherever he was.

§23 The first face of Scorpio belongs to Mars; in it make an image for gathering tarantulas, snakes, and vipers to whichever place you desire.

§24 The second face of Scorpio belongs to Jupiter; in it make an image for expelling tarantulas and snakes from whichever place you desire.

§25 The third face of Scorpio belongs to the Moon; in it make an image for diverting and preventing rains and damages from the rain itself or from the sea.

§26 The first face of Sagittarius belongs to Jupiter; in it make an image for love, benevolence, and community.

§27 The second face of Sagittarius belongs to Mars; in it make an image for afflicting and infecting whomever you desire. [82]

§28 The third face of Sagittarius belongs to the Sun; in it make an image for acquiring the love and grace of kings and social superiors.

§29 The first face of Capricorn belongs to Saturn; in it make an image for hunting birds and beasts and so that the milk of the herds may be improved and increased.

§30 The second face of Capricorn belongs to Venus; in it make an image for increasing the milk of goats, improving bees and multiplying them in their dwellings, and calling birds to the place you desire.

§31 The third face of Capricorn belongs to Mercury; in it make an image for cursing everything contained in the previous face.

§32 The first face of Aquarius belongs to Saturn; in it make an image for love and friendship; for gathering the elderly, the upper class, and servants; or for discovering and seizing treasures.

§33 The second face of Aquarius belongs to Mercury; in it make an image for the love and company of boys.

§34 The third face of Aquarius belongs to Venus; in it make an image for the friendship and benevolence of women.

§35 The first face of Pisces belongs to Jupiter; in it make an image for fishing in the sea and for having safe journeys in doing so.

§36 The second face of Pisces belongs to the Moon; in it make an image for promoting vegetation and fruits, for provoking rain at a time of need, and for gathering fish wherever you desire, whether in rivers or seas.

§37 The third face of Pisces belongs to Mars; in it make an image for having safe journeys in military affairs and in hunting birds and beasts.

§38 The Indians call these faces *adorugen*.[62]

§39 Hermes Trismegistus wrote the book *On Images for Renal Stones*, wherein he posits that one by one each image is connected to an organ of the human body and formed under the faces of the signs. Take pure gold, and make a seal on which you should inscribe the figure of a lion with the Sun being in Leo in the first or second face and in the ascendant or mid-heaven, with the Moon not in her house, and the lord of the ascendant neither facing Saturn nor Mars nor receding from them. This seal should be bound on the back or around the kidneys. I have tested that whoever carries it never suffers. I even saw some doctor imprint frankincense with that seal as if it were wax. He gave that seal to a patient in a drink, and at once he was cured. I myself have made imprinted pills from the blood of a goat according to those instructions, and they worked miraculously. This same thing occurs regarding pain in other limbs relative to their function and shape and their connection with the planets.

§40 *Aries*. Its image is a standing ram without a tongue. Its properties are for all the illnesses of the head. To whomever was born with the Sun in the first, third, or fifth degree of Aries, this figure is not profitable unless it is made in the waxing or the fullness of the Moon. [83] These are the conditions of the figure: Saturn and Mars must be direct, Jupiter must not be in Aquarius, and Venus must not be in Virgo because it is the house of her descent, and Mercury should not be in Taurus; this figure should be made between the first degree of Aries all the way to the fifth degree of the first face, and it should not be made in the second face (for some say that the second face pertains to the eyes and the third to the ears, whence it must be examined in succession) and when the Sun or Jupiter are entirely above the Earth. Make it in the hour of the Sun. Others say that it is good on the day and hour of Jupiter. The seal should be made of gold or silver to the weight of seven grains of ordinary wheat. This has been verified.

§41 *Taurus*. Its image is placed on the liver and on all its infirmities. Make it in the first face from the first degree to the ninth. Saturn should not be in Pisces nor the Moon in Scorpio, and Mars should be direct; it is indeed subject to change a lot. The seal should be made the day and hour of the Sun; the Sun should not be beneath the Earth. It should not be made in the second face of

Taurus (for some say that the second face is for illness of the gallbladder, and the third face is for illness of the windpipe). Its image should be made in the shape of an ox with a large tail, a small mouth, and large eyes. Make the seal out of red bronze.

§42 *Gemini.* Its image is placed upon the spleen and all its illnesses. Make it between the first degree and the tenth. The Sun should be above the Earth; if Jupiter is in Gemini, it will be more effective because he diminishes the spleen. The Gemini are two twisted bodies in the shape of two men down to the navel and one body from the navel downward; and in one hand it holds a staff. The seal should be made out of silver on the day and hour of the Sun in the first face of Gemini; in the second or third faces you will find damage to other organs.

§43 *Cancer.* Its shape is placed over all illnesses of the abdomen. Make it in the first face between the first degree and the fifth; the second face does not apply to that illness for it governs every illness of the large intestine. Make sure Saturn and Jupiter are not retrograde, that Mars is in Taurus, and the Moon is waxing in her light. The Sun should be in descent (that is, after midday), and Leo should be above the Earth. It should not be made except on Sunday nor should it be made except between or in the first and eighth hour. Make it out of gold or silver. Its image is the form of a crab. Make sure Capricorn is not in the middle house (according to the opinion of the teachers of doctrine, the middle house is the sixth or eighth house). Taurus should not be in the fourth house; pay attention to these conditions because they are all necessary. It is placed over one suffering from colic. If the seal is made in the night of the Sun and its hour, it will be very good.

§44 *Leo.* Its image is placed over the right kidney and above every illness of the kidneys. Make its image in the shape of a lion without a tongue, straight and upright. It should be made in the day and hour of the Sun, and it should be made between the first degree and the tenth of the first face. Mars should be direct; and if Saturn and Jupiter are in the same sign, there can be nothing better. If the Moon were in Leo, she should be waxing; if she were in the other signs, we should not fear her, though she should not be in the fourth, fifth, or sixth houses. Saturn should not be in the eighth house. The seal should be made out of gold or silver, and it should be made [84] by engraving or impressing it in a single strike. The weather should not be cloudy nor should the seal be made between the middle of the fifth degree or higher; the Sun should be above the Earth. The second face is used for carrying away every illness of Mercury and the Moon, and the third face is placed over the ribs, which are in front of the kidneys; and it is tested. Some say that if the seal is impressed into mastic gum with the Sun in Leo and re-softened in wine for ten days and drank whole at the time of need, it cures every disease of the right kidney for that entire year.

§45 *Virgo.* Its image is of a woman covered and riding on a lion, holding in her hand a staff or a sword. It is placed over all the illnesses of the left kidney for an individual over five years old. There are many other conditions that are posited in the *Book of Images*,[63] but here I shall relate those that are most essential. Saturn, Jupiter, and Mars should be retrograde; the Moon should not be in the fifth house nor the Sun in the eighth house nor Jupiter in Aquarius nor Saturn in Leo nor Aldebaran under the Earth; nor should Algamidirus be with the Moon nor in her aspect; nor should Saturn and Mars be contrary (that is, opposite); nor should Jupiter be in mid-heaven. The seal should be made with the Sun between the first and fifth degree of the first face of Virgo. Make the shape of a man riding a lion. In this it will have great power: the Indian sages who are experienced in this agree on it. The seal should be made from gold or silver on the day and hour of the Sun. Do not change anything written here, and be cautious in the number.

§46 *Libra.* Its image is placed over all illnesses of the stomach. Make it in the first face between the first degree and the tenth. Venus should not be retrograde nor should Jupiter be in Libra, and let the Sun be above the Earth. Craft it on the day of Jupiter between the first and fifth hour. The seal should be made out of gold or silver to the weight of seven ordinary grains of wheat. Indian sages never varied the custom; on the contrary, they made it on the day and the hour of the Sun, and they have demonstrated that it should not be made on a cloudy day. If you can have the Sun shine upon the image, there can be nothing better, just as Enoch wrote; and it was verified. It is said that the form of Libra must be a man climbing or walking upright, holding accurate scales in his hand, and with a bird upon his head, half-white and half-black. The men from the south wrote that the Moon should not be waning in her light. If she were in Libra, be very cautious in number and form; this is verified. Whoever tested it discovered that it is better in the first degree. According to them, it was because Jupiter was above the Earth and the work was during daytime. The seal was improved because it was wrought by engraving rather than stamping.

§47 *Scorpio.* Some posit that its image is the shape of a crow, and some that it is the image of a man holding a crow in his hand; both have been verified to be the case. It is placed over illnesses of the upper intestine. The Moon should be waxing in her light on the day and hour of the Sun; the Sun should be above the Earth; it should be made in the first face; and it should not be cloudy. The Indians posit that Saturn should be above the Earth. Make it in the first face of Scorpio between the first degree and the eleventh. [85]

§48 *Sagittarius.* Its image is that of a man firing arrows with a bow. Enoch says that it ascends tortuously such that its head is bent, and in his left hand is a bird. It is placed over all infirmities of the right hand. He greatly recommends it against amnesia because it is useful for expelling all the illnesses of Saturn, Mars, and Venus. Saturn should not be retrograde nor should Mars be in the twelfth house nor Jupiter in the fourth house; the Sun should be above the Earth; and the weather should not be cloudy. The seal should be made from gold or silver in the first face between the first degree and the fifth in the day and hour of the Sun.

§49 *Capricorn.* Its image is of a single white goat, and the middle of its belly is black. It is placed over all illnesses of the left hand and used for expelling illnesses of Mercury and the Moon. Mercury should be above the Earth and not retrograde; Saturn should be beneath the Earth and Venus ascending above in the East, as Enoch says. The Indians say that it should be made in the day and hour of the Sun or on Wednesday in the hour of the Sun; but the latter is not as good as the former. The seal should be made in the first face between the first degree and the tenth. Some propose that its property is for laughter and tears (that is, for use against laughter and tears); some posit that it calms an angry individual, reducing them to graciousness.

§50 *Aquarius.* Its image is that of a man holding two pitchers. It is placed upon all infirmities of the right foot. Saturn, Jupiter, and Mars should not be retrograde; the Moon should be above the Earth and Venus beneath the Earth. Some have posited this figure for all illnesses of the feet. It should be made in the first face between the first degree and the fourth. It is for carrying away all wicked feelings of the heart. Others have posited that it is for making one joyful. Make it in the day and hour of the Sun; Jupiter should not be combusted by the Sun, and the Sun should not be higher than Jupiter; and let Saturn be in the degree of the ascendant.

§51 *Pisces.* Its image is placed upon all infirmities of the left foot. Make it while the Moon is in mid-heaven; Mars should not be in mid-heaven, Jupiter should not be retrograde, and the Sun should be above the Earth. The weather should not be cloudy. Make it entirely in the first face; the second face is posited for the shins, and the third for the hips. Some have posited that this third is against human cruelty, as the Indians have verified. The seal should be made out of gold and not out of any other metal. Others say that tin is good for this or mastic gum. Do this during daytime. Hermes laid out these figures in his book on renal stones.

§52 One great Indian sage says that the pouring down of the fixed stars' power is not brought to effect except by the ordering, purification, inquiry, and evaluation of the will. The powers of the bodies above are the forms and forces of those below; the forms below are like matter disposed to the powers of the forms above; they are bound to one another as one draws upon the other. This happens because physical matter is one substance alone and spiritual matter is also one substance. [86]

§53 Other Indian sages claim that these powers are subtle things that God created and placed in the world above His creatures in mercy and piety. Those sages who wrote much on these topics also discussed a subtlety and sharpness of the mind. When they sought to achieve the level of the higher ones who established the laws, they first had to punish their bodies and purify themselves of all uncleanliness. This they began in the first hour of Sunday, which day and hour are properly attributed to the Sun. They fasted for forty days without meat and were nourished by the things grown in the earth, seeds, and herbs. They would diminish their food intake each day unto the fortieth day; then, on the last of the forty days, they ate one fortieth part of what they had eaten on the first day. Throughout the whole fast and afterward, drugs were employed by which the desire for eating and drinking was removed (the opportunity for which they never lacked). After they did this, they discovered a subtlety and sharpness of mind in their spirit. They understood everything they wished while strengthening and enhancing their spirit and senses. Within them the earthly and gross parts were diminished; then subtlety and insight manifested clearly within them. The taste or longing for ascending to the higher world and the place from which the spirit comes became evident. They abhorred the tastes, comforts, and delights of the world. Once they did this, it was fitting that they draw upon the powers of the heavens for they would say and do wondrous things. They realized their desires in past and future things by knowing the periods of their lives. Thus, they had the power of establishing laws as they pleased, and the spirits of the stars were obedient unto them. In this book are contained the great secrets that they call the truth of things through which to understand God on high and recognize Him as maker and creator of all. They assert that everyone using this work did so only to come to an understanding of God Himself and His unity, that they be illuminated by His light. As much as we have said above, we have said nothing other than to reveal the sages' origins and the aggregate of their effects and organizations, which they enacted in their laws.

§54 So great were their wonders that if we wanted to relate them, it would be as difficult for the listeners as for the narrators, and this work of ours would become too prolix and verbose, deviating from our proposed topic. Therefore, let us return to our proposed topic by profitably leaving behind the things discussed.

§55 I say that the wise al-Razi[64] wrote a book on magic, and in it he posited one set of astrological conditions that he had tested: in all works of magic made for love, friendship, and fellowship or anything similar to these, see to it that the Moon be conjoined to Venus or facing her [87] in the sign of Pisces or that the Moon in Pisces be facing Venus in the sign of Taurus. When we will have observed that set of astrological conditions in such things, we shall obtain our intent wondrously and achieve what we desired. When wishing to perform some kind of harm, see to it that the Moon be in Cancer or Libra, facing Mars or conjoined to him in the ascendant or seventh house, and what we sought will be wrought in evil. In all the rituals for bloodshed from any source, place the Moon in an aquatic sign. In all rituals for discord and enmity, place the Moon in Aries or Cancer facing Saturn from a square aspect or conjoined with him. In the rituals to bind tongues, place the Moon under the rays of the Sun, and operate at night. In every ritual for kings, elders, and noblemen, place the Moon in aspect with the Sun in his house or exaltation, also in mid-heaven; and when it is like this, our request will be fulfilled. In all rituals for prelates, judges, and rectors and of those dealing with laws, place the Moon facing Jupiter in Pisces or Sagittarius and in mid-heaven, by which their business is strengthened and fulfilled. In all rituals for laws, scribes, and kings' servants and of the debts of kings' tenants, place the Moon facing Mercury in Gemini or Virgo; let the Moon be in her full light; then you will be able to complete the transaction.

§56 Understand that the square aspect of the Moon with any of the planets is more apparent according to nature. This is when she is in any of the four angles, the stronger of which is the angle of mid-heaven. Thus, in all beneficial works, see that there is an aspect to the fortunate planets, but for evil works she should have an aspect with the unfortunate planets alone. If you wish to perform some sort of evil ritual, see to it that the unfortunate planets are in aspect with her because the aforesaid effects are fulfilled by the powers of Saturn and Mars for they are stronger in these kinds of operations.

§57 Likewise, know that the aspect of the Moon with the planets is stronger when the Moon is east of the Sun or before him, not when she is behind him. When the aspect of the Moon with the Sun is trine or sextile, it is favorable in all noble works such as seeking treasure, great riches, rule, honor, and victory. However, if in all these works the Moon were in the tenth house, the execution would be better and far stronger in implementing the effect itself, which cannot occur with the Moon in the fourth or seventh houses. The Moon herself is good for nothing mentioned here if deprived of light or combusted by the Sun. The trine or sextile, square, or opposite aspects of the Moon toward Venus are compatible with all [88] effects. However, it is not as useful as the aspect of Jupiter, which is indeed better and stronger in all rituals, except in those of crafting, love, long-lasting friendship with women, and in all similar things where the aspect of Venus is better and stronger than Jupiter since all these things are properly attributed to Venus (particularly when her aspect is trine and the Moon is in a terrestrial or aquatic sign). If per chance the Moon was in a fiery or an airy sign, she should be ascending in them.

§58 The sage who voiced the things above, al-Razi, was a man worthy of credence regarding all those sciences since he was a sage, an inquirer into the sciences, and a tester of things, taking a great interest in the books of the ancients. Geber Abnehayen was also a great sage who wrote many books on this body of knowledge.[65] He wrote a book called the *Book of the Secrets of Magic*; another, *Great Book,* divided into eighty chapters; and another that he named the *Book of Keys*, with the figures of the degrees and their effects and astrological judgments; then another, *On the Astrolabe*, which he divided into a thousand chapters wherein he explains the many rituals and wondrous effects that none other has discussed. He also wrote this great book he entitled the *Complete Book of Magic*, wherein he compiled the sayings of sages concerning all the knowledge and other wonders that the wise keep hidden. Geber observed all the sciences of images, the effects of the figures of the heavens, the planetary powers, and the works of nature. In fact, this sage wrote all the above material, having drawn out the Sun's motion and effect, which he discovered by means of the arithmeticians' calculations. For these things I have deservingly titled him "wise," accepted him into my teaching, and made myself his disciple (though there exists a great gap of time between us). I pray God that He grant him eternal life and place him loftily among the souls of the blessed.

§59 Plato, the great sage, made two books of magic, namely the Greater and the Lesser. In the Greater, Plato discussed the effects of the heavens' figures, from which arose great wonders, he said, such as walking on water; transforming into the form of any animal (or some composite shape unheard of throughout the ages); provoking rain at a time when it ought not to rain; holding back rain at a time when rain is expected; making stars run and cast their rays outside of their appropriate hours; burning down enemy cities, seaborne ships, and far off regions you wish to be consumed with fire; ascending into the air; causing the stars to appear at an awkward time such that they seem to be falling from heaven; speaking with the dead; making the Sun and Moon appear divided into many parts; causing ropes and spears to seem like snakes or serpents, eating everything set before them; and crossing distances, great or small, in the blink of an eye. All these things ensue from the figures' powers and from the attraction of the spirits' fortitudes such that they may be obedient to us. These ensue from [89] the composition of their fortitudes with the bodies' figures composed from the matter of this inferior world. From these things follow the spiritual motions that move all bodies, through which motions arise wondrous effects (and works from the category of miracles usually not appearing among humankind).[66] In fact, for this reason, all the books composed by Plato are full of figures' descriptions and exhortations for us to identify them and learn their properties and effects and how we might be able to achieve their effects and describe them intimately in every way. This is what Pythagoras said speaking about the figures of the heavens: they are examples signifying other figures of the world. He also said that there exists in the upper world a durable and spiritual matter that sense perception cannot perceive. Geber Abnehayen composed one book on this science that he called the *Complete Book*. In it he spoke of what comprises a rational and an irrational animal. Concerning natural reason, he said that it conforms to the effects of nature. What Plato said about the reason of heaven, however, he said about the powers and effects of the spirits' figures, which are composed of natural matter. In our book, God willing, we will discuss all these things with explanations of the effects of the heavenly figures. These we will discuss in an appropriate place according to our own judgment, according to what we have discovered in the books of sages, and according to what I have tested recently regarding the effects of the figures, signs, and planets.

The second book of Picatrix ends. [90]

BOOK 3

Here Begins the Third Book of Picatrix Concerning the Properties of the Planets and Signs; Their Forms and Figures Shown in Their Respective Colors; How One Can Speak with the Spirits of the Planets; and Many More Magical Matters [91]

Chapter 1

On the Roles of the Planets in Plants, Animals, and Metals

§1 After having spoken in the preceding book on the images and figures of the heavens and the other matters therein, now let us discuss how the figures or faces of this world are likened to those celestial figures similar to them. Know that according to the fact that the Sun crosses from place to place in the circle of signs, his effects are diversified. They are also diversified on account of the variety of planets and fixed stars. When you wish to make preparations, see to it that the timing be compatible with the necessary rituals by paying attention to the celestial figures, then the works should transpire with the intended effect by the nature and similarity of terrestrial to celestial things and the congruence of the two natures to each other (namely, the celestial and the terrestrial). The celestial power is poured into the terrestrial, and in it the spiritual motion and alteration is greatest according to what is desired. Thus, the works of images are of two kinds, namely, by the power of the heavens and by the natural power of the Earth. In this third book, we will relate the entire picture concerning magical images. Here follows the knowledge of images and its high nobility.

§2 Here I shall tell in fuller detail the effects and powers that each of the planets has individually within itself vis-à-vis the effects and properties of magic.

§3 First I shall speak about Saturn. Saturn is the source of retentive power. He governs an aspect toward profound knowledge; the science of law; the search for causes, effects, and the origins of things; the utterance of magical words; and the knowledge of deep and occult properties. From the languages, he governs Hebrew and Chaldean. From the external appendages, he governs the right ear. From the internal organs, he governs the spleen, which is the source of melancholy conjoining all organs. From the religions, he governs Judaism. From cloth types, he governs all black cloth. From the crafts, he rules working the soil, plowing, digging, extracting and working minerals, and the building trades. From the tastes, he governs the bitter. Among locations, he governs black mountains, murky rivers, deep wells, ditches, and desert places. From the stones, he governs onyx and all black stones. From the metals, he governs lead, iron, and all black musty metals. From the trees, he governs elderberries, oaks, carobs, palms, and vines. From the herbs, he governs cumin, rue, onions, and all the plants that have deep leaves. From the kinds of aloe, myrrh, and similar things, he governs white lead and colocynth. From the incenses, he strongly governs cinnamon and storax gum. From the animals, he governs black camels, pigs, monkeys, bears, dogs, and cats. From the birds, he governs all those with a long neck [92] and a powerful cry, like cranes, ostriches, *duga*,[1] and crows. He governs all the animals that live beneath the earth, all the tiny, juicy, and foul-smelling creatures. From the colors, he governs every black and tawny color.

§4 Jupiter is the source of growing power. He governs an aspect toward law, legality, jurisprudence, and the ease of acquiring requests, reparations, and restraints. He guards against mortal illnesses. He governs wisdom, philosophy, and the interpretation of dreams. From the languages, he governs Greek. From the external appendages, he governs the left ear. From the internal organs, he governs the liver, by which combinations and humors are regulated. From the religions, he governs the faith of the One. From cloth types, he governs expensive white garments. Among the crafts, he governs ruling, jurisprudence, and selling pristine merchandise. From the tastes, he rules the sweet. Among locations, he governs places of prayer and all famed and distinguished holy sites. From the stones, he governs the emerald, all white and yellow stones such as crystal, and every shining and all precious white stones. From the metals, he governs tin and calamine. From the trees, he governs nut and hazelnut trees, pines, and all pistachio and fruit-bearing trees, as well as those whose fruits have shells. From the herbs, he governs white mint, all fruitful herbs, and those with a smell. From the spices, he governs saffron, yellow sandalwood, musk, camphor, amber, and mace. From the animals, he governs all beautiful animals used for their beauty, from which people tended to make sacrifices, and all the harmless animals that are clean and not speckled, such as camels, beavers, stags, and gazelles. From the birds, he governs all the beautiful and colorful ones, such as peacocks, cocks, mountain doves, and quails. From the insects, he governs those that are profitable, such as silkworms and similar things. From the colors, he governs red fading to white.

§5 Mars is the source of attractive power. He governs an aspect toward knowledge of nature. He rules surgery and the taming of wild beasts, extracting teeth, bloodletting, and circumcision. From the languages, he governs Persian. From the external appendages, he governs the right nostril. From the internal organs, he governs the gallbladder whence comes yellow bile and heat. From the instincts, he governs those that cause anger and war. From the religions, he governs heretical sects and those people who switch from one religion to another. From cloth types, he governs linen, the pelts of rabbits and dogs, and other various pelts. From the crafts, he governs ironworking with fire, warfare, and banditry. From the tastes, he governs the hot, the dry, and the bitter. Among locations, he governs army camps; forts; defensible places; battlefields; places where fires are lit; where animals are beheaded; where wolves, bears, and wild beasts gather; and places of judgment. From the stones, he governs carnelian and all dark and red stones. From the metals, he governs arsenic (i.e., a red pigment of gold), sulfur, naphtha, glass, and red bronze. From the plants, he governs every hot plant, such as pepper, pine, scammony, cumin, caraway, laurel, euphorbia, hemlock, and [93] trees that are good for burning. From the spices, he governs all those with a poor balance of humors which kill all those who eat them due to an excessive heat within. From the incenses, he governs red sandalwood. From the animals, he governs red camels, all animals with large red teeth, and dangerous wild animals. From the small animals, he governs those doing harm such as vipers, scorpions, mice, and similar things. From the colors, he governs bright red.

§6 The Sun is the light of the world by which the universe is governed and the source of generative power. He governs an aspect toward philosophy, divination, and the exposition of jurisprudence. From languages, he governs the Gallic tongue and is a participant with Mercury in the language of the Greeks.[2] From the external appendages, he governs the eyes. From the internal organs, he governs the heart, which is the lord of the bodily limbs and the source of heat, granting life to the entire body. From the religions, he rules the faith of the gentiles and those who pray to the spirits of the planets.[3] From cloth types, he governs the precious and noble into which gold is woven. From the tastes, he governs the thick and the sweet. Among locations, he governs great, regal, and beautiful cities wherein kings reside (elevated and valuable places). From the stones, he governs the ruby and the jacinth. From the metals, he governs gold. From the plants, he governs the distinguished and beautiful ones, such as palms placed on high. From the herbs, he governs saffron and the rose. He is a participant with Saturn in wheat, grain, and olives. From the spices, he governs aloewood, sandalwood, lac tree resin, and all those that are hot and sharp in their composition. From the incenses, he governs the best aloewood. Among the beasts, he governs the valuable and powerful, such as humans, bulls, horses, camels, rams, cows, and all large animals with strength and power. From the birds, he governs those that kings tend to hold, such as hawks, falcons, and eagles. He participates with Mars in peacocks and bears and also governs large snakes. From the colors, he governs ruby red and yellow gold.

§7 Venus is the source of the power of taste. She governs an aspect toward grammar, the art of poetic meter, sounds, and songs. From the languages, she governs Arabic. From the external appendages, she governs the right nostril. From the internal organs, she governs the vagina, the projection of sperm, and the stomach whence emerges the ability and taste for eating and drinking. From the religions, she governs the faith of the Saracens. From cloth types, she governs all those with decoration. From the crafts, she governs all the skills of painting, illustrating, selling perfumes, playing instruments pleasantly, singing, dancing, and producing harmonies with instruments. From the tastes, she rules all the sweet ones that taste delicious. Among locations, she rules places of vice where men tend to relax, where men do ritual dances, in places of merriment where singing and music arise, in places of beautiful ladies and women, as well as in places of eating and drinking. [94] From the stones, she governs pearls. From the minerals, she governs lapis lazuli and litharge.[4] From the plants, she rules all those with a pleasant smell, like the crocus, the *arhenda*, roses, and all the flowers with a good odor, taste, and beautiful appearance.[5] From the spices, she governs balsam and good grains of very fragrant julep mint, nutmeg, and amber. From the animals, she governs women, camels, beautiful things, all the handsome animals, and those balanced in their bodies, like gazelles, sheep, deer, and rabbits. From the birds, she governs all the beautiful and famous ones and those with beautiful singing voices, like partridges, calandra, larks, and similar ones. From the insects, she governs the decorated and beautiful ones. From the colors, she rules sky blue and gold lightly fading to green.

§8 Mercury is the source of intellectual power. He governs an aspect toward learning knowledge and wisdom, dialectic, grammar, philosophy, geometry, astronomy with its processes, geomancy, notarial science, the augury of birds according to tradition, and the interpretation of Turkish and other languages. From the outward appendages of humankind, he governs the tongue. From the inner organs, he governs the brain and the heart from which emanate the intellect, the powers by which beings are organized, and the sensory memory. From the religions, he rules all forbidden faiths, speculations on religion, those who love the philosophers' faiths, and those faiths that exist according to sense perception.[6] From cloth types, he governs linen. From the crafts, he governs preaching, writing in verse, carpentry, geometry, dream interpretation, flute playing, illustrating, and all the realms of knowledge that are discovered by means of subtle, innate talent. From the tastes, he governs the bitter. Among the locations, he governs the house of preaching, the places where subtle craftsmen work, and springs, rivers, lakes, and wells. From the stones, he governs all those shaped and engraved. From the minerals, he governs quicksilver and all the minerals that are sublimated and worked into nobler substances. From the plants, he rules the reed, the cotton tree, flax, pepper, all bitter plants like the clove, and all those with fruits having shells on the outside. From the spices, he governs all the gums. From the incenses, he governs those that are useful as medicines and setting the mind straight, such as ginger, spikenard, and the like. From the animals, he governs men, small camels, wild asses,[7] ruminants, monkeys, wolves, all animals swift in leap and gait, and all those that eat by means of deception. From the birds, he governs those that are nimble in flight, looking like everything they do is done consciously and intelligently, and those with beautiful voices. From the insects, he governs those that move easily, such as ants and the like. From the colors, he rules the blue and the multicolored.

§9 The Moon is the one that receives the powers of the planets and pours them into the world, and she is the source of natural power. She governs an aspect toward geometry and arithmetic; the concourses of waters, weights and measures; the noble sciences; magic; physiology and the research thereof; and ancient things. From the languages, she governs Alemannic.[8] From the external appendages of humankind, she governs the left eye. [95] From the internal organs, she governs the lungs out of which emanates the breath. From the religions, she governs those who worship idols and images. From cloth types, she governs pelts and canvases. From the crafts, she governs polishing, tanning, coin minting, and sailing. From the flavors, she governs those things lacking taste, such as water. From the stones, she governs tiny pearls. From the metals, she rules silver and those with white bodies. From the plants, she governs iris, reeds, all white plants, those with a pleasant smell, all those born in the ground that do not rise up above their roots, all tiny plants, all cabbages, and all pastures. Among the locations, she governs springs, lakes, swamps, snowy places, and wherever water might flow. From the spices that are medicinal and for managing the body, she governs those like cinnamon, ginger, pepper, and such. From the animals, she governs red rounceys,[9] mules, asses, cows, and rabbits. From the birds, she governs all the birds that are agile, all animals born in the air and living therein, all the water birds, and white birds. She governs white snakes. From the colors, she governs the mixture of yellow and red.

§10 Know that the nature of the Head of the Dragon is to augment. When it is with fortunate planets, they are augmented in their honors and powers. If it were with the unfortunate planets, their damage and misfortune are augmented. Likewise, the Tail of the Dragon concerns the nature of diminution. If it were with fortunate planets, it would diminish their benefits, but if it were with the unfortunate planets, it would diminish their damages and misfortunes. I urge you to understand these things diligently.

Chapter 2

On the Roles of the Signs in These Three Categories: Plants, Animals, and Metals

§1 Just as each of the planets governs their own properties in things, thus each of the signs also governs their own properties in things. Let us begin first from Aries.

§2 From among the limbs of the body, Aries governs the head, the face, the pupil of the eye, and the ears. From the colors, it governs yellow mixed with red; from the flavors, bitter things. Among the locations, it governs sandy places, fiery places, and thieves' dens. From the metals and minerals, it governs those worked by fire. From the animals, it governs those whose feet are hooved.

§3 From the parts of the body, Taurus governs the neck and the passages of the voice. Among the locations, it governs all populated lands, gardens, and plowed areas. From the plants, it governs all the tall trees, those bearing edible fruit, those not requiring water, and all those with pleasant smells and tastes. From the animals, it governs all the quadrupeds and those with hooves.

§4 From the parts of the body, Gemini governs the shoulder blades, the arms, and the hands. From the colors, it governs green fading to yellow. From the tastes, it governs the sweet. Among the locations, [96] it governs the home and plowed areas in high mountains. From the plants, it governs the tall ones. From the animals, it governs humans and monkeys. From the birds, it governs water birds and all those with good voices making pleasant songs.

§5 From the parts of the body, Cancer governs the chest, breasts, stomach, lungs, ribs, and the hidden places of the torso. From the colors, it governs the tawny and smoky colors. From the tastes, it governs the salty. Among the locations, it governs lakes, swamps, and places where waters meet, the seashore, and rivers. From the stones, it governs those in water. From the plants, it governs the tall, aquatic ones. From the animals, it governs those emerging in water, tiny fish, snakes, scorpions, vipers, and the reptiles of the earth.

§6 From the parts of the body, Leo governs the upper part, the heart, the chest, and the thin and back ribs. From the colors, it governs red, yellow, and brown. Among the locations, it governs defensible places and forts, royal cities, strongholds, and holy sites. From the tastes, it governs the bitter. From the stones, it governs ruby, diamond, and jacinth. From the metals, it governs gold. From the animals, it governs those with long teeth. From the birds, it governs raptors.

§7 From the parts of the body, Virgo governs the belly and the hidden places, which are the intestines, the pelvic bones, and the viscera. From the colors, it governs white and tawny. From the tastes, it governs the astringent. Among the locations, it governs those where women gather and places of joking and singing. From the plants, it governs those bearing seeds. From the animals, it governs humans. From the birds, it governs those born in water.

§8 From the parts of the body, Libra governs the hips, the buttocks, the sexual organs, and the upper stomach. From the colors, it governs green, violet, and tawny. From the tastes, it governs the sweet. Among the locations, it governs desert wastes, sandy places, hunting grounds, and all elevated places (from which much can be seen all around). From the plants, it governs tall and straight ones. From the animals, it governs humans. From the birds, it governs those with large heads.

§9 From the parts of the body, Scorpio governs all the genital organs of men and women. From the colors, it governs green, red, and tawny. From the tastes, it governs the salty. Among the locations, it governs wetlands, prisons, places of mourning, and the rocks where scorpions gather. From the stones, it governs coral and water pearl. From the plants, it governs the tall and straight ones. From the animals, it governs scorpions, vipers, snakes, tiny moist creatures in the earth, and aquatic beasts.

§10 From the parts of the body, Sagittarius governs the buttocks, the shins, and the superfluous, extra marks on the body. From the colors, it governs pink fading to reddish and every tawny and mixed color. From the tastes, it governs the bitter. Among the locations, it governs gardens, places of kings, and fire places. From the stones, it governs the emerald. From the minerals, it governs lead. From the animals, it governs humans, birds, snakes, and small worms.

§11 From the parts of the body, Capricorn governs the knees, tendons, and below the knees (under the kneecap and under the calves). From the colors, it governs peacock blue, cardinal red, and every tawny color tending toward black. From the tastes, it governs the astringent. Among the locations, it governs the palaces of kings, gardens, irrigation ditches, riverbanks, kennels, hospices, inns, places where captives are assembled, [97] places of great beauty, and forts. From the plants, it governs all strong trees, such as the olive, nut-bearing trees, oaks and all aquatic plants, such as the reed, sweet flag, and all thorny plants. It governs some aquatic beasts, reptiles of the earth, and snakes.

§12 From the parts of the body, Aquarius governs the part under the calves and the heels and their tendons and joints. From the colors, it governs green, grey, and yellow. From the tastes, it governs the sweet. Among the locations, it governs the places of running water, seas, and places where wine is sold. From the stones, it governs glass and similar things. From the plants, it governs the tall ones. From the animals, it governs humans and every animal whose appearance and form is as repulsive as the Devil's.

§13 From the parts of the body, Pisces governs the feet, the nails, and the tendons. From the colors, it governs green, white, and every good color. From the tastes, it governs the bitter. Among the locations, it governs hermitages, riverbanks, seashores, lakes, and irrigation ditches. From the stones, it governs pearls, white and transparent stones (such as crystal), and pearls grown in whatever kind of water. From the plants, it governs those of middling height and all the aquatic ones. From the animals, it governs the aquatic and the slow-moving.

§14 These are the properties of things that the planets and signs govern and that are suited to them. Take heed because this is the groundwork for magic.

Chapter 3

On the Figures, Colors, Clothes, and Suffumigations of the Planets; Also the Tinctures of the Signs' Faces

§1 Let us now speak about the colors of the planets.

§2 The color of Saturn is like burnt wool; that of Jupiter is green; that of Mars is red; that of the Sun is like yellow orpiment; that of Venus is saffron-colored; that of Mercury like lac tree resin and the color of orpiment mixed with green; and that of the Moon is white.

§3 Here are the images of the planets according to Mercurius in the book that he sent to King Alexander and named *The Book of the Seven Planets*. They are described below and are very essential in this science.

§4 The image of Saturn is the shape of a black man wrapped in a green cloak with a dog-like head and a sickle in his hand.

§5 The image of Jupiter is the shape of man dressed in the finest clothes, sitting upon a throne.

§6 The image of Mars is the shape of a man riding upon a lion and holding a huge lance in his hand.

§7 The image of the Sun is the shape of a clean-shaven man, handsome, with a crown on his head and a lance in his hand, with an image before him that has a human head and [98] hands, with the rest of the body like a horse with four feet, lying upside down (that is, with hands and feet elevated).

§8 The image of Venus is the shape of a beautiful, young girl with her hair untied, with a comb in one hand and an apple in the other.

§9 The image of Mercury is the shape of a naked man writing while riding on an eagle.

§10 The image of the Moon is the shape of a man riding on a rabbit.

§11 Mercurius warned Alexander that when he wished to do something with any of the planets, he should work with a body congruent in nature to the planet itself. If you wish to accomplish anything, consider the nature of the ascendant at the time you wish to operate, and dress yourself in clothes suited to the rising sign. Make the ascendant itself fortunate by the fortunate planets, and make the seventh house unfortunate by the unfortunate planets since the ascendant pertains to the querent (therefore, it must deservingly be fortunate so that it may progress more forcefully); the seventh house, however, is attributed to the thing desired (therefore, it must appropriately be unfortunate so that—by its weakness—it may be set out more gently toward the effect). Here follow the colors of the clothes or vestments of the planets. The color of Saturn's vestments is all black, and they are best made of wool. The color of Jupiter is green and is best made of silk. The color of Mars is like the flame of a fire and is best made of silk. The color of the Sun is golden yellow and is best made of silk or golden yellow. The color of Venus is like pink and is best made of silk. The color of Mercury is a mixture of many colors and it is best made of silk. The color of the Moon's garments is shining white, and silk or linen is most preferable. Now, let us discuss the suffumigations of the planets. The suffumigation of Saturn comprises all foul-smelling things, like asafoetida, gum, bdellium, hemlock, and the like.[10] The suffumigation of Jupiter comprises all good and balanced scents, such as amber, aloewood, and the like. The suffumigation of Mars comprises everything hot, like pepper and ginger. The suffumigation of the Sun comprises all things with a balanced and good scent, like musk, amber, and similar things. The suffumigation of Venus comprises everything that smells balanced, like the rose, the violet, the green myrtle, and the likes. The suffumigation of Mercury comprises everything with composite odors, such as narcissus, violets, myrtle, and similar things. The suffumigation of the Moon comprises all the cold scents, like camphor, lily, and so on. Heed all these things in your rituals.

§12 Here follow in order the colors of the signs' faces:

§13 The color of the first face of Aries is red and is made thus: take one part each of green gall, gum, and orpiment.[11] Grind them up separately, then mix them together. When you desire to write or paint anything with it, combine it with egg whites. The color of the second face is yellow of a golden hue, and it is made thus: take equal parts of blue vitriol[12] and talc. Grind them up separately, and mix them with [99] honey. Distill this into a little gum, and set it aside for the ritual. The tincture of the third face is white and is made thus: take equal parts of white lead and talc.

§14 The first face of Taurus is a tawny and smoky color, and it is made thus: take soot, and mix it with gum, and keep it for use. The second face is white, which is composed thus: take equal parts of white lead and talc, and keep it for use. The third face is black and is made from burnt wool.

§15 The first face of Gemini is a yellow color similar to gold in hue, and it is composed thus: crush up gall,[13] and take the black parts that are inside. Soften these in water but only in enough to cover them. In another container of water, do the same thing with lac resin. Then mix these liquids with a little gum, and keep the mixture for use. The second face of Gemini is red, and it is made thus: take some arsenic and cinnabar; mix them together. Distill them, and add a sufficient amount of gum, then set it aside for use. The third face is red, and it is made as we have said above.

§16 The first face of Cancer is the color yellow, and it is made as we have said above. The second face is yellow, and it is made as we have said above. The third face is black, and it is made from orpiment and gall in equal parts with a little bit of gum.

§17 The first face of Leo is tawny, and it is made as we have said before. The second face of Leo is yellow similar to gold, and it is made as we have said above. The third face of Leo is red akin to the color of pomegranates, and it is made thus: take cinnabar, and wash it many times. Then soften the powders, and mix them with green gall in water, then add a small amount of gum and lac tree resin, and set it aside for use.

§18 The first face of Virgo is a red color fading to gold, and it is made thus: take very well pulverized saffron, and dilute it with the water of green gall, mix well, and put it aside for some time undisturbed; then add a small amount of gum. From this you will be able to write at a time suitable for the operation of the abovementioned face. The second face is tawny, whose composition is as we have described above. The third face is yellow fading toward red, and it is made thus: take orpiment, and pulverize it very well into saffron water with a small amount of gum, and set it aside for use.

§19 The first face of Libra is tawny and should be made as we have described above. The second face is black and is made as we have said above. The third face is white and is made as we have described above.

§20 The first face of Scorpio is black, the second is yellow, and the third is tawny; all made as we have said above.

§21 The first face of Sagittarius is red and is made as we have said above. The second face is yellow made thus: take yellow orpiment, and leave it over a fire overnight. Then mix it with a small [100] amount of very well-pulverized white lead. Add a small amount of gum afterward, then write with it. The third face is tawny and is made as we have said above.

§22 The first face of Capricorn governs the color green, which is made out of green with gum. The second face is red and is made with cinnabar and gum. The third face is black and is made as we have said above.

§23 The first face of Aquarius governs a red color fading to indigo, which is made from the blood of a snake with a small amount of gum. The second face is black and is made thus: take one dram of gall, gum, and arsenic, and a half dram of parchment. Grind them up separately, then mix them together, and dilute with egg white. Make pills, and let them dry. When you want to write, dilute one of these with water, and write with it. The third face is green and is made with the gall of any animal and with a small amount of gum.

§24 The first face of Pisces has a muted red color, made from powdered white lead with a small amount of cinnabar and gum. The second face is tawny and is made from the bark of burned tamarisk with a small amount of gum. The third face is red, and is made as we have said above.

§25 The colors of the faces discussed are those most necessary in magical procedures. We have also related much concerning the effect of the planets upon things, all of which are most necessary to those procedures. Everything mentioned was related according to the view of the wise Mercurius.[14] He willed the spirit of each planet to befriend him in order that they might serve him, and that he might use the ordering and positioning of all the things that are of the same nature as a planet. These are things suitable to the spirit of that planet in eating, drinking, dressing, suffumigating, teaching, timing, tinctures, prayers, sacrifices, stones, figures, images, and constellations. When all these things flow together in the ritual, celestial power descends upon these worldly operations. They are united as one, and the effect is brought about perfectly and completely. If something were missing from any of these, the desired outcome would be impeded.

§26 One must know the cities and their latitudes since the planetary powers are different among them. We see this in things produced at one latitude that are not found in another, such as minerals, stones, metals, trees, and plants.

Even characteristics of people are found in one particular place but not in others. For example, it appears in a certain land called Thebith that those who travel there are possessed by constant laughter without seeing anything funny; there, laughter is caused by the place's own nature.[15] Similarly, those from a land called Burgum do not live according to seasons unless they leave their country and spend some time elsewhere.[16] This results from the property of the place itself. The same is true of the Western sea, where silk, storax, and mastic gum are made, or in the land of Yemen, where absinth is found. There, a mountain stands from whose peak water flows down through the parts of the mountain itself [101] before it reaches the surrounding plain where it coagulates and is converted into white alum.

§27 Aloewood is found on a single island in India called Cabria, which is next to a certain island called Camer, five days' journey away.[17] On the island Camer there is a high quality type of aloewood called *cameri*. Close to it (by about three days) is another island called Azanif, and the aloewood found there is called *azanifi*.[18] It is much better than the *cameri* wood because it does not sink in water due to its quality and lightness. Aloewood is not found anywhere else in the world except on these three islands.

§28 In the city called Mecca and in Tripoli, nobody dies, and there are no lepers. In the city Haybar, fevers often erupt.[19] In a place called the Two Seas, ailments of the spleen are frequent, and abscesses erupt in the anus.[20] One finds plague in Jerusalem.

§29 Onyx is found in Yemen and China, the best of which is found in Yemen. Whoever carries this stone on a ring will always be gloomy in his gait, melancholy, and contemplative. They will envision wicked and deceitful dreams and have quarrels and discord with others. If you place it over a boy, froth will flow from his mouth. This arises only by magical effect, on account of which the qualities of things are altered by the powers of the celestial bodies, and the effects of evil are shattered and destroyed.

§30 In parts of India and in the land of Tin is found calamine; sometimes it is found in parts of Spain. It is a leaden stone, weighty and white, which—if cooked with red bronze—becomes yellow.

§31 Next to Armenia and Lorca, one finds lapis lazuli. On a mountain close to Lisbon is found the garnet. Next to Malaga in a field called Montemayor is found the red jacinth. In parts of Tadmir diamonds are found. In parts of Córdoba hematite is found. In the mountains of Ubede is found the Jewish stone that shatters kidney stones. The gold marcasite there is better than all the rest in the world. In parts of Barcelona there are pearls. In the Grenada river gold is collected. Quicksilver is collected on the mountain of Hermes. In

Bathea (namely in the town named Piterna) is found better calamine than all other places for making brass. On the mountains of Córdoba is found the source of alcohol. In parts of Nebila is found the best agate. In the city of Alahavez, there was found some man without color, but he had constant fevers.[21] Over this city stands a mountain upon which dwells an infinity of vipers. In the homes of this city are many spiders, worms, and murderous beasts. In Sedauran, which is in a part of Africa, there is a stone produced [102] in the holes of mastic tree wood, which, when rain falls on it, is coagulated and made black and light, similar in taste to gall. Many other wonders are found in one place and not in others. This happens on account of planetary powers and the images of the heavens which are more dominant there than elsewhere.

§32 According to Hippocrates, the forms of human bodies are shaped according to the qualities and properties of the places where they were born and raised.

§33 From this, the necessity of knowing the qualities of cities, their latitudes, and the planetary influences upon them is quite clear. Now let us move on to the planetary properties upon the lesser things of the world. First regarding the Moon, whose property is growth: she grows and withers plants and crops. She is the cause of eggs and precious stones, and the ebbing and flowing of rivers and seas. On the one hand, the Moon gathers and binds the planetary powers and the heavenly spirits to the lesser things of this world. Thus, she appears atop every tree, which grows and is strengthened by her power, then is destroyed by the power of the other planets. On the other hand, the Moon plays a role in some things (such as figs) that the Sun's power generates and strengthens but that the Moon destroys. While the Moon plays a role in maritime animals and plants that grow by her power, she harms terrestrial animals by her cold gaze, when they go uncovered at night. Jupiter is the author of life and the sciences. Laws, treaties, and judgments proceed from him. Venus, however, is the author of games, instruments, sounds, and songs; in all her desires and knowledge, there are no rules as there ought to be; it is she who governs power and discretion. Mercury is the author of eloquence, rational intellect, and sense perception; from him proceeds the understanding of subtle and profound things. Saturn is the author of deceptions, plowing the soil, and workhouses; from him proceeds the understanding of deep time and of ancient laws. The Sun gives light to all the other planets since every darkness flees from him. The spirit rejoices and expands thanks to him, and through him the fruit of every tree is ripened and dried. The generation of all vegetation proceeds from him. Commonly, we say that he is the light and candle of the universe.

Chapter 4

On Why Only Those Trained in This Knowledge Can Understand Its Secrets

§1 The ancient sages who wrote in their books about mystical knowledge and magic did so as obscurely as possible such that few or none [103] might benefit from them except for the wise and those who study and work with them assiduously. This part is placed here more or less frivolously since it does little to advance our purpose.

Chapter 5

On the Intrinsic Qualities of Animals and the Notable Necessities to This Science, and How the Planetary Spirits Are Attracted by Figures and Suffumigations

§1 After the properties of each planet were described in three lower categories (namely, animals, plants, and minerals), it follows that we should say something about these. Among them, the animals are the most excellent, and from these, humankind is recognized as the noblest because it exists with a more elevated self-awareness. There are animals with a single sense, like seashells, mollusks, and the like; others have two, three, four, five, and ten senses. Humans have ten manifest senses and five hidden ones, which we will discuss now. The forms of animals are diverse, as is apparent by running down through all the animals. As a human is an animal intermediate between discrete celestial spirits and beasts, thus fish are in the middle between birds and beasts. Conches are intermediate between animals with and without senses since they have only two senses—this is because their terrestrial nature overtakes them and makes them similar in nature to plants. Thus, it is clear that the more animals participate in any element, by that much more do they share in the nature of that element. Humans are the most excellent of the animals on account of the mutual balance of elements in their bodies (as they ought to be); because of this, humans are the most balanced in complexion among the other animals. Each and every element governs its own animal, which can never be separated from it: birds are never separate from air nor fish from water nor the diabolical spirits called "infernal" from perpetual flame. The fire that is felt and perceived by the senses is appropriately assigned to an animal called the salamander, a creature in the shape of a mouse made of fire. Weighty animals, on account of their heaviness, are never separate from earth. (Let us now respond to a certain implicit question, namely how devils exist in fire. I say that humans are called microcosms, reflections of the macrocosm, since everything contained in the greater is essentially contained in the lesser. Therefore, if the devils exist in the macrocosm, it is fitting that they be found by their effect in some way in the microcosm. This is what happens: when a wrathful intent is set alight in humankind, it is immoderately inflamed, and they become furious and enraged in the utmost. At that moment, a devil is produced in every action. We can say through a certain analogy that [104] devils exist in fire—that is, in the ignition of the fire of human wrath from which devils bring about their effects. Vice versa, when the human will is one's own in due temperament, virtue, and reason, it is as if angels are produced. Therefore, we can very well say that devils exist in the microcosm, as in the macrocosm.)

§2 Now, however, I return to the proposed topic. The aforesaid division of three categories in these sciences concerning the planets and their effects exists—according to the Copts, the Nabataeans, the Egyptians, the Greeks, the Turks, and the Indians—by mixing parts of those categories together and working them into suffumigations, clothing, foods, and incenses. This is how they produce very great miracles, as we surely learn in their books. They make compounds that, when conjoined to the power of the stars, are released into the air and then mingle with the powers of fire until reaching this world. Then the effect or request is fulfilled. Air is a body without which other bodies are incapable of life since it is the medium for receiving bodies, influences, or the planetary effects, by the agent's will arranged through a combination of his own air with the air in general. It takes effect through suffumigations placed according to the limbs of the human body, and these suffumigations are composed from plants and other kinds of things. These suffumigations move the spirits of men toward their desires. The works of magic have many wonders and manifest effects.

§3 I myself have seen a book entitled *The Division of Sciences and Revealer of Secrets*, wherein one particular sage wrote this:[22]

> A certain trustworthy man said to me that he had run into another man from the land of Khorasan who had just visited the land of the Indians and was initiated into this knowledge. When the first man debated with himself regarding certain points, he had his doubts about this knowledge. The traveler said that he proved it clearly. There was in that country a certain young woman believed by everyone to be the most beautiful.[23] The man said that he would make her come to my abode. I asked him myself if he would fulfill this promise to me, and this I did for two reasons: one,

certainly, for the love of knowledge; the other, for the use of the girl. He did this work in my sight; by immediately lifting up an astrolabe and finding the altitude of the Sun, he determined the ascendant and also set out the twelve houses. He found Aries in the ascendant, whose ruler Mars was rising, and Libra, whose ruler Venus was in the seventh house. I asked what these things meant. He responded: "The ascendant and seventh house are fundamental to the petition that you seek." Mars and Venus calculated thus, he placed them on a chart just as they were, saying: "When they face each other in a trine aspect, which is the aspect of love and friendship, the intent will be accomplished." He discovered [105] that this aspect would be perfected in forty days. He claimed that on the fortieth day from the day when the petition was done, he would reach his intent. Then picking up a small piece of diamond stone, he pulverized it very thoroughly and combined it with an equal amount of ammoniac gum. From the compound, he shaped an image in my likeness. Afterward, he took dried mulberries and pulverized them very well and then mixed them with wax. Next, he shaped an image out of this compound in the likeness of that young woman and dressed her with clothes similar to her own. Then he took one new jug into which he placed seven staves or sticks (namely, sticks of myrtle, willow, pomegranate, apple, cotton, mulberry, and laurel), and he placed these in the shape of a cross in the middle of the jug—four on the bottom and three on top. Then he placed the image made in my name into this jug. Next, he placed the image of the girl into the same jug. Before doing this, he waited for Venus to be in opposition to Mars and Mars to be strengthened by the fortunate planets. He shut the jug and opened it every day on the hour in which he had placed the things in it. At the end of those forty days, when the lord of the ascendant was facing the lord of the seventh house in a trine aspect, he opened the jug and placed those images facing one another, that is, face to face. Then he sealed the jug and ordered me to bury it under a hearth wherein a small fire was lit. While burying it in a little bit of gravel, he told me to say one word from India, which he translated and showed me (and I shall state later). When the task was completed as above, he dug up and opened the container and removed the images from it. Right then and there, we saw the abovementioned young woman entering my house through the door; she stayed there continually for ten days. At the end of those ten days, however, the operator said to me: "Since I have fulfilled my promises to you, I think it best that we release the young woman that she be restored to her prior freedom." I agreed that this was for the good. Taking the aforesaid two images, he placed them back where he had buried them.

> After taking ground chastetree and combining it with wax, he made a candle out of it and burned it in the fireplace. Once burned up, he extracted the images from their burial, dividing them from each other, throwing one this way and the other that way, speaking other words that he revealed to me afterwards. He did this whole thing to make manifest to me his entire body of knowledge. When this was done, we at once saw that young woman sighing as if surprised from sleep, and she stood up. She spoke this: "State what you want from me!" Then she left the house in flight.

This was one of the great wonders that I have seen in this science during my life. I have only reported these things so that you may heed the wonders of this knowledge and the magnitude of its effects. This work is wrought while observing the planets and their positions, aspects, ascensions, departures from houses, the materials for assembling images, suffumigations, and everything else suited to these tasks. [106] You could do the same in your own rituals so long as you seek out all the required, suitable, and congruent things to your conclusion. Thus, you will be able to attain the desired end just as the wise men have written.

§4 Now let us discuss those things promised in regard to the operations of the planetary spirits, the commingling of the stars, and the fulfillment of necessities for image-making to receive the planetary powers (e.g., from which suffumigations and foods one must abstain during a ritual such that the effect may be brought about easily). I say to you, dearest friend, that I have composed this book with great effort and study, encompassing as large a number of books of ancient sages as possible, observing and contemplating the opinions of certain men, and writing down true conclusions and proven effects, to the extent that I had studied 224 books of wise ancient predecessors word by word. With all these, I composed this book like a flower or a lily of sorts, working on everything tirelessly for six years.

§5 Before we make a statement about the above, I shall put forward a notable aphorism that one should observe very well. The reception of the planetary spirits according to the opinion of the ancients, however, is as related below. First, it behooves you to know about the planet's nature you desire to use for the reception of its powers and spirits and to gather their powers into the chosen figure or image, as well as the natures of things connected to a specific planet, as was touched upon above (namely, on colors, foods, incenses, and suffumigations). Then ensure that the color of the surface of the image's body be a similar color to that of the chosen planet; the incense to the incenses; and the color of the image's clothes—and those of the operator—must also be suited to the color of the chosen planet; so too should the suffumigations belong to the incenses suited to that planet. The inner body of the operator should belong to the nature of that planet, that is, one should eat foods assigned to the chosen planet as much as one should for that operator's body to sustain a complexion of humors suited to the chosen planet. If by chance such food was contrary to your own nature, eat only a little and moderately at first. Eating little by little, you temper the stomach until it is used to such things. As you eat these foods, you increase your appetite for them until the body is mastered and nourished. When the body is thus mastered, observe where the planet stands in the Zodiac of signs and that its rays be projected in straight lines toward the Earth and not intersected by the rays of other contrary planets. Let the rays be poured down into the Earth directly with every obstacle removed. Then take some metals suited to the chosen planet from which you should smelt a cross; do this in the appropriate constellation, and make it two feet high. Combine it with one of the aforementioned figures or images matching with your petition and that planet's spirit. For example: if you wish to create [107] an image for fighting and crushing or terrifying enemies, place the cross over an image of a lion or snake. If you wish to operate for fleeing and evading, place the cross over the image of a bird. If your work involved increasing wealth, power, honor, and social standing, place the cross over an image of a man sitting on a throne. Make all your petitions according to these kinds of examples by placing the cross over a figure suited to your petition. If you desire for anyone to obey you and not transgress your orders, make an image of the person on a stone appropriate to the planet's nature that has the greatest power in the root of their nativity and ascendant. Make the image in that planet's hour, and the planet ruling their nativity should be neither in opposition nor in the same sign nor in any aspect with any planet contrary to it. Once you have done these things perfectly, place the image such that it may be the one propping up the other principal figure.[24] The reason this figure is made in the shape of a cross has been explained (i.e., because everything gathers its own powers from the figures relative to their respective qualities, and everything avoids its contraries). We seek the powers of the planetary spirits so that they might join their own figures, but we do not comprehend the form of spirit, nor could we understand it by experience except in the form of a human, animal, or another thing. We thus conclude that every power of the planets manifests most powerfully in images. We see that all the figures and forms of trees and plants are diverse in their shapes, as are likewise the forms of animals and minerals. Since we could never fully comprehend the forms of the planetary spirits, the ancient sages of this art chose the cross as a universal figure. This is because all bodies have a surface, and the surface of an image has a longitude and latitude (and the cross is the appropriate image for longitude and latitude). Therefore we have said that this image is the universal tool in these rituals and the receptacle of the planetary spirits' powers because they work well with other images. This is one of the secrets of this art. Furthermore, all humans have a place beneath the seven circles of the planets. When the power of a planetary spirit is joined with the shape of a cross, then the ritual has strength and power over whatever other image is with it. Were it made in the image of a human, its power would pour out onto humankind, and it is likewise with the images of other animals. When you will have made these images thus, make a censer out of the same material as the cross such that it is completely enclosed except at the top where a hole should allow smoke [108] to exit. The smoke of burning substances should not escape elsewhere. Moreover, have a building set aside into which only those involved in your ritual may enter (if at all possible) and only at the time of performance. This building should have a place exposed to the heavens. It should be decked in the herbs of that ritual's ruling planet alone—there ought to be nothing in it other than those herbs. Then inhale the suffumigations according to the chosen planet's nature—burn it in the fire of that censer. Place the cross above the censer in such a way that the smoke exiting from the censer may enter through the lower parts of the cross and flow to the upper parts. All these things should occur in an appropriately selected hour with the ritual's ruling planet being as mentioned. These orders having been fulfilled carefully, the smoke of this suffumigation ought to reach the sphere of the signs in a straight line. It should not be intersected by the rays of other planets contrary to the elected planet. If your ritual involved those things of the lesser world, the planetary spirit should be harnessed, and its power should descend through its own rays down to the Earth into the ritual. Then the thing sought will be fulfilled.

§6 Whoever intends to work with this knowledge should first recognize and understand that each of the planets have powers (with both general and particular implications, with one power overcoming another). So in this matter, the nature of the ritual is that you should observe the planet with general power and not conjoin it to another planet with a particular power. You should operate with the spirit and influence of a planet with general power. Furthermore, if that planet with general power were perchance the ruler of the operator's nativity or the *almuten* ruling therein, then the ritual would be more effective. One sage said this is the only method to unite incorporeal spirits to corporeal ones; this is a secret of this art. Whoever performs this without error will be able to achieve their desire. The wise Aaron said that when one works according to this knowledge with one's own nativity in mind, one can discern the hour when the conjunction of one's own spirit and body came together and consequently the ruling planet in one's nativity. By understanding this, one knows the planet that effected the union of spirit and body during one's own birth. If that planet were unfortunate, however, that individual would be made unfortunate. On the contrary, if it were fortunate, they would be made fortunate.

Chapter 6

On the Craft of Attracting the Planetary Spirits with Natural Things; On What an Image Is, and How It Can Have Power

§1 None can be perfected in this science unless they are so inclined by their own nature, and by the power and disposition of the planets. This is what Aristotle says in [109] his *Book of Aztimehec*,[25] wherein he says this: "A Perfect Nature fortifies the philosopher and strengthens both his wisdom and understanding so that he may accomplish all his works with greater ease." The sages concealed everything belonging to this science as much as possible according to their achievements, and never did they wish to clarify it to anyone but philosophers. They themselves taught all knowledge and philosophical subtleties to their disciples in addition to the works of the spirits of nature. They would call those spirits of "Perfect Nature" with these four names: MEEGIUS, BETZAHUECH, VACDEZ, and NUFENEGUEDIZ. These are the names of the four parts of that spirit of "Perfect Nature." When those sages were defective in that "Perfect Nature," they invoked them by those four names, which signify the power of a "Perfect Nature." Hermes, however, said:

> When I myself desired to understand and extract the secret workings of the world and its quality, I positioned myself above a certain pit, a very deep and dark one, out of which blew a furious wind; I was unable to see anything within it on account of the darkness. When I dropped a burning candle into it, at once it was extinguished by the wind. In my dreams appeared a handsome man with an imperious authority, who said: "Take a burning candle, and place it in a glass lantern so that it is not extinguished by the fury of the wind, and thus you will be able to hold the light there. Drop it into the pit, in the middle of which you should dig. There, you should pull out an image that, when it is extracted, will extinguish the wind of that pit. Thus you will be able to hold a light there. Then dig in the four corners of the pit, from which you should extract the secrets of the world, a Perfect Nature, its qualities, and the origins of all things." I asked him who he was. He then responded to me: "I am Perfect Nature; and when you desire to speak with me, call me by my appropriate name,

and I shall respond to you." I asked him what his name was, then he responded: "I am named and called by the four names, MEEGIUS, BETZAHUECH, VACDEZ, and NUFENEGUEDIZ, by which I shall respond when you call." I asked him again when I should invoke him and how I should act while invoking. He then said: "When the Moon is in the first degree of Aries, by night or day, whenever you desire, enter a clean and resplendent house in the corner of which you should place a table raised from the ground on its eastern side. Take four containers (each of them should have one pound of capacity), one of which you should fill with cow's butter, another with nut oil, another with almond oil, and the fourth with sesame oil. Afterward, take four other containers made the same size, and fill them with wine. Make a blend from the nut oil, butter, honey, and sugar. Take those eight containers, this mixture you have made, and one glass vase. Place the vase in the middle of the table and atop it the mixture that you have made. Place those four containers filled with wine on the four corners of the table distributed in this way: the first container in the eastern part, the second in [110] the western, the third in the southern, and the fourth in the northern part. Take the other four containers, and first place the one filled with almond oil eastward next to the container of wine; place the one filled with nut oil westward; the one filled with butter southward; and the one filled with the oil of this mixture northward. Take a burning wax candle, and place it in the middle of the table. Take two censers filled with burning coals, in one of which you should place incense and mastic gum, in the other you should place aloewood. After doing these things, stand on your feet facing east, and invoke the four aforementioned names seven times. After invoking them seven times, say this: 'I call you out—O strong spirits, high and powerful, since the knowledge of the wise and the understanding of those who understand proceed from you, and by your power also are fulfilled the requests of philosophers—that you may respond to me and be with me; that you may unite me with yourselves, your potencies, and powers; that you may strengthen me with your knowledge so that I may comprehend those things that I do not fathom; that I may recognize the things I overlook, that I might see the things I do not see; that you may remove blindness, disgrace, forgetfulness, and disease from me; that you may make me climb to the level of the ancient sages (those with hearts filled with knowledge, wisdom, and understanding); and that you may imprint these things upon my heart that it may become like the hearts of the ancient sages.'" Afterward, he said: "Once you have accomplished this task in this way, you shall *see* me."

This ritual is taught in a book called *Astimequem*.[26] The ancient sages would perform this ritual once a year to benefit their own spirits such that they might set their Perfect Natures in order. After this was done, they ate whatever was set on the table together with their friends.

§2 Aristotle said that each and every sage has a personal virtue poured into him by the lofty spirits, by whose powers the enclosed senses and mind were opened up and the sciences made clear. This virtue was bound with the virtue of the planet governing the root of the nativity such that the virtue thus cocreated in him strengthened him and gave him intelligence. Ancient sages and kings would do this ritual, and with the four aforementioned names, they would utter this prayer by which they empowered themselves in their knowledge and reasoning and in the advancement of their businesses and affairs. With these they protected themselves from the plots of enemies and did many other wonders.

§3 Aristotle claimed that the first man who worked with images and the one to whom the spirits first appeared was Caraphzebiz.[27] He was the first to discover the magical art. The spirits were first manifest to him performing wondrous things. They unveiled a "Perfect Nature" in regard to science, causing him to understand the secrets of nature and knowledge. Thus spoke the familiar spirit: "Hold me with you, but reveal me to no one except to those who invoke me and sacrifice in my name." [111] This sage, who was made wise working through the spirits, benefited himself by their powers and actions in magical rituals. Between this wise Caraphzebiz and another sage named Amenus (this Amenus was the second one to work on spirits and magical operations), 1,260 years passed. In Amenus's teaching, he warned that any sage who wishes to perform a magical ritual and protect himself from the power of the spirits must cut himself off from all inner anxieties and every body of knowledge other than this one. All the senses, the mind, and the thoughts that are turned toward something exclusively are capable of acquiring it more easily. Although contemplation is most regularly suited to this magical science, it is appropriate that the one occupied by it not be involved in any other affairs.

§4 Tintinz the Greek claimed the same thing in the beginning of his book, that whoever desires to perform this ritual must prune their thoughts and desires toward other matters since the source and foundation of all this work consists in thought. Aristotle claimed that an image is called an image because the powers of spirits are joined to it. Thought is enclosed in the thing wherein the spirit's hidden virtue rests. The powers of the spirits are fourfold: sense perception, which exists as a composite in the world; the spirit of an object, by which a spirit is attracted; the spirit of thought, which is perfect, pure, and inviolate; and the spirit of operations wrought by hand. These three spirits existing in matter, in will, and in ritual are united to the perception of perfected thought, which we have said is a composite in the world. A magical image attracts rays and brings them together in the things that it intends to bring together (like a mirror that, when raised to the light of the Sun, reflect his rays into a nearby shadow). The image receives the rays of the Sun by his light and projects them to a shaded place. The shaded place is illuminated and made shining without ever diminishing the Sun's light. This is how the three above-mentioned spirits function. When the spirits of motion and rest are joined to the perception of the upper world, the powers of the spirit are attracted and poured into matter. This is the origin of the image and its designation.

§5 Socrates claimed that a "Perfect Nature" is the sage's very Sun and the source of his light. Some questioned the wise Hermes, asking: "What do science and philosophy have in common?" He answered: "Perfect Nature." Then they asked him more directly: "What is the key to both science and philosophy?" He answered: "Perfect Nature." Then they inquired: "What is a Perfect Nature?" He answered: "A Perfect Nature is the spirit of the philosopher or sage in harmony with the planet governing him. It is that which unlocks the knowledge that is otherwise impenetrable and from which the effects of nature [112] proceed directly, in both sleeping and waking." Thus, a "Perfect Nature," considered as such in the sage or philosopher, is just as the teacher is to his pupil, instructing him principally in fundamentals and easy things, then gradually proceeding to greater and more difficult things until the pupil is perfected in his knowledge. Therefore, a "Perfect Nature" is appropriately put into effect by its own power and influence by disposing the mind of the philosopher according to his natural inclination. Understand that these things are necessary to commit to memory. Hence, it should be concluded that it is impossible for anyone to be interested in this science unless they were naturally inclined to it, as much by their own virtue as by the disposition of the planets ruling their nativity.

Chapter 7

On the Attraction of Planetary Powers; How We May Speak with Them; How an Effect Is Divided Between the Planets, Images, Sacrifices, Prayers, Suffumigations, and Words; and the Conditions of Heaven Necessary to Each of the Planets

§1 A certain sage named al-Ṭabarī claimed this concerning the rituals of sages for receiving the planetary powers according to observations from ancient books of magical rituals:

When you wish to speak with any of the planets or to request something necessary to you, first and foremost, purify your will and your belief in God. Take particular care lest you believe in anything else. Rid your body and your clothes of all impurity. Observe the nature of the planet to which your petition corresponds. When you wish to invoke the right planet for your petition, dress yourself in clothes dyed with the colors of that planet, suffumigate yourself with its suffumigations, and pray with its prayer. Do all this when the chosen planet is positioned in its own dignities and the aforementioned dispositions—after these are observed, what you desire will ensue.

§2 Now let us briefly recite the requests suited to each of the planets. Seek Saturn in petitions concerning the elderly, generous men, elders, kings of cities, hermits, those who work the lands, returns to cities, inheritances, exceptional men, farmers, builders of buildings, slaves, thieves, fathers, grandfathers, and great-grandfathers. If you were caught up in deep thought and grief, in melancholy or grievous illness, in all these things or affairs, seek petitions from Saturn, and request things assigned to his nature. Seek those things from him as we say below, and aid yourself with Jupiter in your request. Fundamental to all these requests is that you never seek anything from a planet unless it is attributed to its dominion. [113]

§3 Seek from Jupiter all that belongs to his division, such as requests concerning noblemen, individuals with power, prelates, sages, speakers of the law, judges, good men, interpreters of dreams, hermits, philosophers, kings and their sons and the children of their sons, soldiers, first cousins, and petitions of peace and goods. Everything similar to this, seek from Jupiter.

§4 Seek from Mars those things that rest upon his nature, such as requests against soldiers, officials, fighters, and those getting themselves involved in armed conflict; also on account of kings' alliances, those destroying homes and cities, those doing evil to men, murderers, executioners, those who work with fire or in stables, litigators, shepherds, thieves, guardians of roads, the deceitful, traitors, and brothers. Similarly, seek him concerning illnesses in the body below the groin and also on account of bloodletting, bloating, and similar things. In these petitions you may aid yourself with Venus because the nature of Venus dissolves what is suited to Mars and restores what he damages.

§5 Seek from the Sun those petitions suited to him, such as petitions against kings, the sons of soldiers and kings, high-class men who delight in justice and truth, abhor deceit and violence, desire a good reputation, and aspire to be praised by men, officials, clerics, physicians, philosophers, humble noblemen, individuals with good sense, the magnanimous, great brothers, fathers, and similar things.

§6 Seek from Venus things pertaining to her, as are the petitions of women, boys, girls, sons, things pertaining universally to the love of women and carnal sex with them, paintings, singing and playing instruments, making jokes, all individuals devoted to worldly delights, individuals indulging vices, slaves, and maidservants, husbands, mothers, friends, sisters, and all things similar to these. In such petitions you will aid yourself with Mars.

§7 Seek from Mercury petitions appropriate to notaries, scribes, arithmeticians, geometricians, astrologers, grammarians, public speakers, philosophers, rhetoricians, poets, sons of kings and their secretaries, toll keepers, merchants, ministers, lawyers, slaves, boys, girls, younger brothers, painters, designers, and the like.

§8 Seek from the Moon all the things pertaining to her and attributed to her nature, such as petitions toward kings, tenants of cities or villages, toll keepers, messengers undertaking journeys over land and sea, individuals who work and plow the land, geometricians, mayors, portrait painters, mariners and all those working by means of maritime skills, the peoples of nations, geomancers, divorced women, wives of kings, mothers, beardless boys, and similar things. [114]

§9 Next I decided to write down the natures of each and every one of the planets, the things appropriate to each of them, and what each of them signifies. This begins with Saturn, as before. Saturn is cold and dry, an unfortunate planet, damaging, author of bad and foul odors, proud and treacherous—when he promises anything, he brings about treachery. His symbols are farmers, streams, those working the land, controversies, great and long journeys, great and persistent enemies, evil deeds, battles, things done unwillingly and by force, and physical labor. Truthful words, hope, blackness, old age, buildings, fear, great contemplation, worry, fits of anger, treachery, pain, difficulty, death, inheritances, orphans, ancient places, estimates, keen elocution, the knowledge of secrets, and the secret and profound perceptions of science: he signifies all these things as long as he is direct in his motion. While retrograde, he signifies unfortunate things, weakness or illness, prisons, and a long-lasting evil in all things. If he were in the aspect of any other planet, he weakens and damages it in its qualities. If he were retrograde and you were about to seek something from him, the thing sought will be fulfilled through trouble, misery, and great toil. If he were retrograde in any of his own dignities, his curses are augmented and grow; but if he has potency or dignity on the ascendant, then he will be more harmonious and kindly disposed.

§10 Jupiter is hot and humid, temperate, and a fortunate planet (he is called the "Great Fortune") and follows Saturn in the order of the planets. He symbolizes things done with subtlety, the bodies of animals, inceptions, the growth of animals, correct judgments, courtesy and fairness in all things, sense perception, clemency, truthful statements, truth, good belief, faithfulness, chastity, honor, gratitude, skill, the sustenance of good words, good perception and intellect, knowledge, philosophy, teaching, things obtained from well-directed reasoning and peace, honor from men, improving all business endeavors, the completion of petitions, the will of kings, a lover of riches and their accumulation, gentleness, liberality, sacrifices, a help to humankind in all things and all their works, delighting in crowds and all populated places, benefactors of men, piety, following and upholding the law in all things, delighting in places of faith, men of honest words, decent decorations, beauty, joy, laughter and many discussions, speaking well and with joy, benign aspects, also lovers of good and individuals abhorring evils, individuals preaching good words, and individuals who perform all good acts and avoid evil ones. [115]

§11 Mars is hot and dry, an unfortunate planet, destructive, and the author of evil things. He symbolizes doom, evil deeds, the depopulation of homes and cities, dryness and the inhibition of rain, fire, combustion, differences, blood, spontaneous violent mental urges, bad and biased judgments, oppression, pain, the deaths of men and the damnation of all things, destruction, quarrels, war, battle, terror, disagreement between men, anxiety or misery, penalties, wounds, prisons, depression, flight, litigation, stupidity, treasonous acts, and all things cursed without rhyme or reason—quasi-happiness, lies, ungratefulness, a mediocre life, shame, interruptions on roads, burial, the lack of comforts, discord, sharpness and wrath, doing things prohibited by laws, fear, quasi-legality, acts of treason, false oaths and assessments in all works, evil deeds during sex with women in a prohibited fashion (such as do those who desire beasts, other animals, and foreign women), killing sons and condemning creatures, killing fetuses in a mother's womb, depredations, acts of treason and deception, all manner of fraud, having misery, plots, thefts of clothes and shoes, attacks on the road, nighttime break-and-entry, opening doors, all manner of wicked deeds, and all things remote from truth and lawfulness.

§12 The Sun is hot and dry, mixed with good and evil in his makeup. He rectifies and condemns, doing both good and evil—a fortunate and an unfortunate planet. He symbolizes and provides the senses and the mind, exaltations and high honors, yet without fear, and even easily he makes one gain at the expense of enemies and easily inflicts violent deaths. He illuminates those who give gifts to friends (to those appropriate and deserving of it). He condemns those who plead many things and those who attack collectively. He grants goods and sometimes does both good and evil. He governs those who observe the law and who keep their promises. For all humankind he provides benefit and delight, great eloquence, and quick answers in all things. He increases the appetite for accumulating riches, seeking the good, speaking well of individuals, having heights and honors above mankind, and doing all things lawfully and well. The Sun's quality is especially necessary for kings and nobles in the land and the ways of life they require, as well as the works of noble and ornate minerals for making the crowns of kings and noblemen and those who do great deeds with honesty.

§13 Venus is cold, humid, and a fortunate planet. She signifies cleanliness, neatness, reward, puns, delight in song, joy, illustrations, laughter, pictures, beauty, shapeliness, the beat of wind and string instruments, loving one's bride, [116] and seeking spices and things that smell good. She delivers dreams and provokes games of chess and dice. She desires to sleep with women, to strengthen love with them, and she longs for faithfulness from them. She governs the desire to appear beautiful, to love freedom, nobility of heart, and joy. She abhors anger, quarrels, vengeance, and lawsuits. She wishes to guard the desire for friends and has a focus on the opinions of the world. She welcomes false oaths and is inclined toward desire. She desires to drink excessively. She incessantly desires abundant sex in filthy ways and to do it in inappropriate places, such as some women are accustomed to doing with others. She governs loving in animals and children and making good things for them, exerting fairness in things, delighting in merchants and living with them, being loved by women, being loved by men, being a good host, involving oneself in the manufacture of crowns, making stable things, operating from stones, having a sweet skill, looking down on the world with no fear of it, holding back humankind from anger, quarrel, or discord; she demonstrates a soft heart and will toward litigation, and she denotes weakness in battles. She signifies the desire for all beautiful well arranged things that conform to her will. She governs making tinctures and working diligently in the skills pertaining to them, selling merchandise, shows, and speeches, observers of law, and being bound to the desires that inhibit science and philosophy.

§14 Mercury is changeable, permuting himself from one nature to another. He receives the nature of the other planets—the good from the good, the bad from the bad. He signifies sense perception and the rational mind, good eloquence, a strong and profound understanding of matters, good intellect, good memory, good apprehension, the quick mind suited to acquiring knowledge, scientists and philosophers, an understanding of history, arithmetic, geometry, astrology, geomancy, ceremonial magic, auguries, scribes, grammar, smooth rhetoricians, an effortless understanding of the questions of sages, individuals working through the sciences who seek exaltation from that knowledge, books, poetry, individuals desiring to make rhythms, writers of books, charts, and the sciences, individuals desiring to know the secrets of sages, expounders of philosophy, the mercy of men, clemency, individuals who love sensation and pleasure, spendthrifts, squanderers of riches, merchandise, individuals who buy and sell things, those who partake in judgment and reasoning, the astute and deceptive, individuals who contemplate evil in their wills and keep it hidden, liars, individuals who assemble false documents, the cowardly before enemies, the lighthearted in all endeavors, the unstable in matters relating to diverse skills, individuals who get involved in everything, individuals who are daring in everything that comes about through subtlety, individuals who work with great appetite, profiteers, supporters of friends and individuals, and their guide away from all illicit things. [117]

§15 The Moon is cold and humid. She symbolizes the beginning of works, great contemplations of things, good sense and motives, the best wording in advice, boasting of speaking well, daring in all things, necessities in life that the fortunate desire, and good manners in society. She is gracious, quick, and neat in all acts, moving lightly toward what she desires, with a healthy and clear will among humankind, a great appetite for eating, and a small one for sex and womanly delights. She signifies the forsaking of evil, a desire for a good reputation, a love of joy and beautiful things, an investigator of noble sciences and those worth the cost like astrology, magic, and other arcana, one who desires marriage, to generate sons and grandsons, and to make a home for a group of them, and good things for their relatives. She symbolizes love and honor from humankind, abhors iniquity, and is fair in all her works. On account of one of her own qualities, she signifies forgetfulness and necessity.

§16 *How one can speak with Saturn.*[28] When you desire to speak with Saturn and you want to ask something from him, it is proper that you wait until he enters a favorable position. The best of these is in Libra (his exaltation), then in Aquarius, which is the house of his joy, and last in Capricorn, which is his second house. If you cannot have him in any of these three locations, place him eastward on any of his boundaries, triplicities, or in any of his angles (among these, the best is mid-heaven) or subsequent locations, direct in his course, and in the masculine quadrant east of mid-heaven. Beware of the harm he causes and his unfortunate aspects, the worst of which is his fourth aspect toward Mars. Do not have him descending. A fundamental (which you should heed carefully) is to ensure that the planet himself be in a favorable position and quality, removed from unfortunate aspects. Positioned thus, Saturn is like a well-meaning individual with a courageous heart and a great mighty will, who can hardly deny whatever is sought from him. When this planet is retrograde in motion or falling from the angles, he is like a man filled with anger and ill will, who quickly denies everything sought from him. When Saturn is in a favorable position, as touched upon above, and you wish to speak with him and pray to him, dress yourself in black clothes—that is, let all the clothes on your body be black—with a black cape tailored in the manner of a professor. Wear black shoes. Go to a place assigned to such a task, remote from mankind and humbly chosen. Walk there with a humble will, in the fashion of a Jew, for Saturn was the lord of their Sabbath. Hold an iron ring in your hand and carry an iron censer. In it, place burning charcoal upon which you should set the suffumigating mixture whose [118] recipe is this: take equal parts of opium, storax (which is an herb), saffron, seed of laurel, carob, wormwood, lanolin, colocynth, and the head of a black cat. Grind them up, and mix everything together with the urine of a black she-goat in equal parts. Make tablets out of it. When you want to operate, place one of these on the burning coals of the censer. Keep the others aside. Then turn your face toward the part wherever Saturn stands at that time. While smoke rises from the censer, say this prayer:

> O lord on high whose name is great and stands firm in a place above all the heavens' planets, he whom God placed sublime and lofty! You are lord Saturn, cold and dry, dark, author of good, honest in your friendship, true in your promises, enduring and persevering in your amity and hatred. Your perception is far and deep; honest in your words and promises, alone, lonely, removed from others in your works, with sadness and pain, removed from rejoicing and festivities. You are old, ancient, wise, and the despoiler of good intellect. You are a doer of good and of evil. Wretched and sad is he who is cursed by your misfortunes. The man who attains your fortunes is blessed indeed. In you God placed power and strength and a spirit that does both good and evil. I ask you, father and lord, by your splendid names and wondrous acts, that you should do such-and-such a thing for me.

Then speak the request you desire, and throw yourself to the ground with your face always toward Saturn with humility, sadness, and gentleness. Your will should be pure and firm. Repeat these words many times. Do these things on Saturday in his hour. Know that your request will be fulfilled with effect.

§17 There are other sages who used to pray to Saturn with other prayers and suffumigations, whose recipe is this: Take equal parts of southern wormwood, *bericus* seed,[29] juniper root, nut, old dates, and thistle. Grind them up, and mix them with a good wine aged for many years. Fashion pills, and set them aside for use. When you wish to operate, do as we have said above: place some of this suffumigation in a censer while having your face toward Saturn. While the smoke is rising, say:

> In the name of God and HEYLIL, who is the angel to whom God assigned the strength and power of Saturn for perfecting actions toward the cold! Indeed, you stand in the seventh heaven. I invoke you by all your names, which are in Arabic, *Zohal*; in Latin, *Saturnus*; in the Phoenician language, *Keyhven*; in Roman, *Koronez*; in Greek, *Hacoronoz*; in Indian, *Sacas*.[30] I invoke and call out to you by all those names. I conjure you by the name of God on high, who gives you potency and spirit so that you may accept me and take up my prayer through the obedience with which you obey God and His dominion so that you may do such-and-such for me.

State your request, the suffumigation always sitting atop the censer's coals. After you have said these things once, throw yourself onto the ground toward him, just where he stands in his nature. Reiterate these words many times, then make this [119] sacrifice to him: decapitate a black goat. Gather and keep its blood. Take out its liver, and burn it whole. Store the blood. By doing this, what you seek will come to pass.

§18 *When you wish to speak with Jupiter.* If you wish to speak with Jupiter, place him in a favorable position just as we have said regarding Saturn. Then dress yourself in yellow and white clothes. Go to a place set aside for these works, humbly and gently, as in the fashion of hermits and Christians. Have a ring of crystal on your finger, upon which is a cross, and a belt around your waist. Dress yourself in a white cape. Take a censer made out of the metal of Jupiter.[31] In it light a fire. Add the suffumigation. Take equal parts of *classe*,[32] storax gum, columbine, peony, aromatic calamus, pine resin, and hellebore seeds. Grind them up, and mix them with pure, old wine aged for many years. Make pills from these. When you wish to operate, do as we have said, and throw one of these pills in the censer's fire. After turning toward the part of the heavens where Jupiter resides, say:

> God salutes you, O blessed lord, the Greater Fortune, hot and humid, fair in all your works, courteous, comely, wise, truthful, lord of truth and fairness, removed from all evil, righteous, a lover of those who uphold divine laws, contemptuous of worldly affairs and their vices, a lover of divine law and its servants, noble in your will, a doer of good, free in your nature, exalted and honored in your sphere, lawful in your promises, and honest in all your friendships. I conjure you, first through the names of

> God on high, who gives you power and spirit, then through your goodwill and beautiful effects and through your excellent and precious nature that you may do such-and-such for me (here name your request). You belong to the Good and the source of goodness. You are the maker of all good things. You perceive all requests that are formed in the Good.

§19 There are similarly other sages who pray to Jupiter with other prayers and suffumigations, whose recipe is this: Take equal parts of fleabane, incense, and hackberry; three parts of myrrh; and two parts of skinned grapes. Grind these things up, and mix them with a wine aged for many years. Make pills, and set them aside for use. When it is time to operate, place one of these in the censer as said above regarding Saturn. Dress yourself in the fashion of a friar or a monk. Place around your neck one of the books of the law. Go humbly and gently to the place where you will be operating. Turn your face toward the heavens, toward Jupiter, and say:

> O angel RAUCAYEHIL, whom God set beside Jupiter! You, O Jupiter, are the Greater Fortune, perfect, the maker of good and all completed things. You are indeed discerning, wise, and intelligent, remote from evil works, from all malice and [120] sin. I invoke you and call you by all your names, which are in Arabic, *Misteri*; in Latin, *Iupiter*; in Phoenician, *Bargis*; in Roman, *Dermiz*; in Greek, *Raus*; and in Indian *Huazfat*. I conjure you by the spirit and the powers that God has placed in you, by the obedience with which you obey God, and through your goodness and wondrous effects and through your good nature, shining and pure, that you may do such-and-such for me.

Speak your request. Then take a white lamb, decapitate it, burn it whole, and eat its liver. Then what you asked shall be.

§20 There are, however, others who pray to Jupiter without suffumigation so that by his power they might be saved from a storm at sea. Rasis[33] said in his book of metaphysics:

> For evading danger at sea, turn yourself toward Jupiter sitting in mid-heaven, and speak: "God hails you, O noble planet, splendid, precious, and honored star! In you God placed power and spirits for doing good, giving form to the bodies of the universe that themselves enter into divine law and life, helping those who sail at sea and saving their lives. I ask you through the strength that God has placed in you that you grant me your light and spirit by which I will be saved. Wash and purify the

> sins of my nature such that my senses and my spirit be enlightened that I may know and understand."

If your work is done accordingly, you should see the appearance of a burning candle before you. If you do not see it, know that your work was done incorrectly. Repeat it until you see this burning candle, and then what you seek shall be.

§21 Most sages agree that you should turn yourself toward Jupiter and say:

> God hails you, O Jupiter, planet of complete and noble nature, splendid, honored, appreciated and benign lord, hot and humid, likened to air in your nature, fair in your works, wise, truthful, a lover of divine law and those who believe and guard it, wise and learned, a truthful lord of truth and law, the Greater Fortune, shining, complete, direct, fair, just in your judgments, righteous, splendid, honored, a disdainer of the knowledge of this world, lofty in your will! You are, by your nature and power, a real lover of the sublime, lawful in your speech and promises, truthful in your friendships, complete in your goodness, and removed from all malice and obscenity. You are shining and God-fearing, a giver of spiritual fortitude and a lord of good and true laws, far from all evil works and speech (since your thought and opinion is to sustain the law with sense, mercy, intellect, and acuity); a lover of the wise and of wisdom, an interpreter of dreams; a lover of those upholding divine laws; a supporter of friends and those who adhere to Him; a steadfast victor for truth; [121] a lover of kings, noblemen, soldiers, and rulers; a collector and accumulator of riches that might be granted to the people and to the services of God and to those who please him well; a benefactor for individuals who do good and observe God's laws and mandates; an official observer of promises and statements, < . . . > peoples, populated countries, and places; a lover of humankind, righteous; a helper of population; a guardian of oaths; a lover of ritual dances, words, beautiful affections, jokes, laughter, speaking assiduously, good sensible manners, sex with women in a good way (and according to the law); a hater of all evil works and of those opposed to the law; a subscriber to good deeds so that we may be capable of attaining them. You order that one abhor evil deeds and stay away from them. God hails you, O planet helped by God. God has given you goodness and righteousness. To the pure spirits who operate with God and live for His service, you grant good things and guard them from all evil and worldly worries. You are potent in the waves of the sea, a helper of those who pray to God. I ask you by these virtues that you enlighten us, our sons, and our friends, whom you deign to help by your brightness and your splendid

powers and honored spirit that God placed within you. We ask that with this spirit, we be able to save our bodies, our business, and grow our riches, and remove from ourselves evil thoughts, sadness, and misery, lest we have melancholy or anxiety in this world; that we should live a good life with great and perfect abundance; that we should do works pleasing to the Lord our God; that by your powers and spirit you should fortify our bodies in such a way that they be healthy and free of any illness or pain, just as our life should be protected; and that all sickness and bad circumstances be removed from us. Pour down upon us the power of your sublime, excellent, and splendid spirit through which we should gain honor from everyone such that they should fear, respect, and please us, and so that we are able to take land back from them and also from those who seek to harm us so that neither their words nor actions might harm us. Let us be removed from every evil affair of man or beast. Let us have your divine grace and love, which opens us up with your spirit and power and defends us with a good and beautiful shelter. He looks upon us with a positive aspect, and with him we are defended from all worldly things. Let those cursing and speaking wickedness be far removed from us, and let their eyes be darkened such that they cannot see our plots and deceptions nor speak evil of us nor seek evil things for us nor be able to blame us for any evil word or deed. May we be defended and revealed by the excellent power and splendor of your spirit. Look upon humanity's heart and will so that all those seeing us be terrified by our appearance and be ashamed, whereas we be illuminated and honored by them like solar rays on high, sublime and honored above all things of this world. Grant us the assistance [122] of your strength and spirit, from which we may have the perception and intellect to understand divine law and be able to keep it and be saved by it and so that we follow the things that are pleasing to God and urged in His service, as we ought to. Cover us with the strength of your spirit so that we may be saved and secured by it; that we may reach the divine knowledge of the Lord our God; that we may enter into His grace; and may He protect and defend us from this land of malediction and spare us from worldly desires. May our senses be purified from the superfluities of nature so that they might be joined to the natural senses and that we may be able to reach the knowledge and grace of that sublime and splendid God. Direct us with your spirit to good and straight paths. Lead us this way until our spirits are purified and purged from all vain and sinful impurities; may they become illuminated. May their hearts remain unharmed from every worldly evil desire, sin, and impurity. May they be covered by your power and spirit so that the spirit and the senses may reach the lofty source. May they remain with the spirits of angels into eternity in divine grace in His service. Through you our acts of will are withdrawn from all corruptible things, and we reach eternal things. God pardons and remits our sins, deeds, and curses through His mercy until our spirit is united with things similar to Him and divided from His contraries such that we can understand our own nature and our shapes and figures and also our own true names without any changes until we may rest our spirit from all miseries. Cleanse our spirits from every distraction in nature, and may you demonstrate by what means we can attain the good things of this world and of the other! Amen. I invoke you by all your names: namely, in Arabic, *Misteri*; in Phoenician, *Bargis*; in Latin, *Jupiter*; in Roman, *Harmiz*; in Greek, *Biuz*; so that you may recall my prayer and recall my statements and that you may deem my requests completely worthy. I conjure you by the name RAUBEIL, who is the angel whom God placed with you for carrying out the powers and potencies of the spirit, and your effects; and by the names DERYES, AHATYZ, MAHATY, DARQUIZ, THEMIZ, CARUEYIZ, DEHEDEYZ, CARNADUYZ, DEME; and by the oldest rituals in the world, ancient and splendid above all things, which lack beginning and end, the principle of all things. I conjure you by all these names so that you may hear the spoken prayer and my entreaties and that you may fulfill my petition that I have made to you and that you may purify my will toward you. I ask you with small and modest capability and with the fragility of my nature and actions. I myself run back to you and to your spirit in all my dealings, you who purifies and purges my will toward you and disposes me toward asking you with humility and good will, toward serving your name and spirit. I myself know and recognize your dominion and power and am obedient to it. Hear my prayer, my words, and all my requests with kindness, as they were made by me without fault! May you deign also to fulfill those things that have been forgotten in the request! In your goodness and [123] excellence, may you concede your part, and may you cover us with the spirit and light of your sublime and honored will so that we may have power from it, by which we may be able to rectify our dealings and attain riches. May we draw away the human desires from ourselves and our abilities from which we may acquire the love of humankind until our business is well received and that all might obey our judgments and mandates! May we acquire the favor and esteem of kings and that of exceptional and inimical men! May we be thought of as upright and truthful in all our acts and words! May we secure our hearts from worldly pleasures and vices! May it be pleasing to fulfill all these requests for us

> through your strength and invoked spirit, excellent and splendid, which God placed in you for doing good, respecting creatures, and granting life to the people of the world. I beseech you by your righteousness, your great honored excellence, your noble and precious deeds, and the light that you receive from our God, who is Lord of the universe, so that you may heed my prayer and that you may turn toward it. May you pay attention to what I conceal in my heart and will, although I do not express it with my mouth! May you grant me power and intellect by your powers and spirit, by which I might secure my petition that you have benevolently taken up! May you set out to help us with your piety and cut off from us worries and sadness! May you grant us a durable fortune from your fortune that may last with us through all time! I conjure you by your names and your piety, goodness, and excellence so that you may be an advocate for me before our Lord God, precious, and Lord of the entire universe so that He may fulfill my request with effect. May I easily, effortlessly, and joyfully reach what I seek! May I have the favor of kings and lords of the land, of the powerful, and of all rational and irrational creatures! I conjure you through our Lord God, who is the only God in the world as much in past as in future, so that I may beseech you and your noble powers. I seek in my prayer that you may have complete salutations always from the Lord of the universe and His piety and grace through the infinity of time. Amen!

To a pure and redeemed will toward our Lord God, amen.

§22 The sages who operate with this knowledge have claimed that whoever performs this ritual—by saying all these things to Jupiter—all their requests in the world will be fulfilled on account of Jupiter's spirit's power reaching out to them. They will be safe and sound in body through the entire cycle of the year, without detriment and illness. Everyone will obey them. Everything they propose will be completed easily, with effect, and diligently. They will be well received by everyone, especially if Jupiter has power in their nativity. Know that the more humbly and gently you act while you perform this ritual, the better it will be so long as you have a pure and clear will, [124] removed from all worldly things. Do not think about or occupy yourself with worldly things except for the proposed ritual. Throw yourself onto the ground, speak your prayer humbly while dragging your forehead on the ground, since you will have a great helper for completing your request in everything.

§23 *When you wish to pray to Mars.* When you wish to beseech Mars, to speak with and honor him, place him in a favorable position as above concerning Saturn. Dress yourself in red clothes, place on your head a red linen or silk cloth and a red ceremonial hat. Carry a sword on your neck, and equip yourself with all the weaponry that you can bear. Tuck up your clothes in the fashion of a man going to court or of a soldier, and upon your finger place a bronze ring. Take a bronze censer with burning coals, and place this suffumigation upon it. Take equal parts of wormwood, aloe, squinancywort, spurge, large pepper, and watercress. Grind them all up, and mix them with human blood. Make pills out of this, and set them aside for use. When you wish to begin the ritual, place one of these in the censer, which you will carry with you to a remote place chosen especially for this operation. Once you have reached it, stand upright and say secretly, daringly, and without fear, facing south when Mars is fortunate and in a favorable position (as we discussed concerning the other planets), looking toward him continuously while the smoke rises:

> O Mars, you who are honored lord, hot and dry, capable, weighty, robust at heart, the spiller of blood and giver of infirmity itself! You are strong, powerful, sharp, daring, shining, agile, and the lord of battle, punishment, misery, wounds, prison, sorrow, and mixed and discrete things. You who have neither fear nor concern for anything! You are sole helper in investigating your effects, strong in your judgments and willful acts toward conquering and making petitioners fortunate, an actor of lawsuits and battle, a performer of evils on the weak and the strong, a lover of the children of battles, an avenger of wicked and harmful people in the world. I conjure and ask you by your names and qualities present in the heavens, by your conquests, and by your requests to the Lord God who placed in you power and strength, gathering them for you and separating them from the other planets so that you might have strength and power, victory above all, and great vigor.
>
> **§24** I beseech you by all your names: in Arabic, *Marech*; in Latin, *Mars*; in Phoenician, *Baharam*; in Roman, *Bariz*; in Greek, *Hahuez*; and in Indian, *Bahaze*. I conjure you by the high God of the universe that you hear my prayer, heed my request, see my humility, and fulfill my petition. I ask that you do such-and-such for me.

Here state your request, whatever it may be; then say: "I conjure you by [125] RAUCAHEHIL, who is the angel whom God placed with you for fulfilling your affairs and effects." While you say these things, smoke should always rise from the censer. Repeat these things many times, and ask what you desire. Then if you can get a male leopard—if not, a mouse—decapitate it, burn it, and eat its liver as we have said regarding the others. Your wish will be fulfilled.

§25 When you wish to locate things stolen by an enemy or if someone did you harm and you want revenge, equip yourself with weapons, and dress yourself as above. Come to the place above carrying a censer and a suffumigation. While the smoke rises, say:

> O Mars, you who are of the nature of blazing fire; an author of wars and toils; a crusher of noblemen and deposer of their offices and ranks; an igniter of fury, ire, and wicked will in the hearts of evil men; a bringer of death, people killing one another, bloodshed, and the rape of women; a cause of class division, the elevation of one over another, and of attacking and defending! Now I seek from you that you protect and defend me, who is joined with you in all this. You are strong, hot, and potent in your works and do not withdraw from whoever seeks and entreats you. I beg you by all your names, manners, works, motions, and the paths present in your sphere, by your light and by the power of your domination and rule that you pay attention to me and heed my petition. I come to you with bitter complaints about someone who acts to seek me out with pride and a bigoted ill will. You are commander of those with recourse to you. You act and fulfill the request of those asking. I beseech you by the light, fortitude, and potency that God, Lord of the whole world, has placed in you that you might send over one of your furies onto such an enemy of mine that they be kept away from me, may not remember me, nor think about me. Send them some kind of penalty and misery so that they might receive a heavier and worse retribution than the damages they did to me. May I sever their hands and feet! May you bring every evil and misery to them through me, as well as the ire and fury of a king. Through me, may both thieves and bandits be poured out upon that person and their riches! May they endure ulcers on their body, fevers, blindness of the eyes, and deafness of the ears. May all their senses be damned until they are blinded, deafened, muted, and paralyzed in every limb! Have them pay the penalty, and give them prolonged misery, spoil all their food, drink, and flavor. May they be deprived of life! Bring them all manner of misery and punishments. Bring vengeance upon their body, riches, community, and sons. Pour the ire and the fury of a king and the hatred of their neighbors and kin onto them. Send thieves to their property and lands or wherever they may go by land or sea. May these things be implemented at once with effect! May you carry them away from honor and status! You are the famous mighty one, performer of fury and evil works. I conjure you by your strength, [126] evil, and powerful effects through

> the things that alter, change, and corrupt generation, that act against travelers at sea, that do evil things to people, and that put effort into your works. I conjure you so that you may heed my request, and I ask that you be capable of fulfilling it and that you take pity on me and the evil works that that person does to me, on account of which I am pouring out prayers to you. I conjure you by RAUBEYL, who is the angel whom the God of the universe has placed with you for executing all your effects and powers. I conjure you by your spirit, namely the one that condemns those sailing by sea, and by the power that you pour into the hearts of the furious, the warmongers, and the murderers since they involve themselves in arduous affairs and the most difficult conflicts. With all this, I conjure you that you might hear my prayer. Take note of my affairs, and grant me the fortitude of your spirit, by which I may distinguish my prayer that you have heard. May you receive full honor from God, the universal Lord of the world. You are a commander of the excellent and of things happening to excellent people. You are a giver and distributor of penalties and miseries for those who commit evil, just as they deserve. Amen, amen. Again I conjure you by the names DAYADEBUZ, HEYAYDEZ, HANDABUZ, MAHARAZ, ARDAUZ, BEYDEHYDIZ, MAHYDEBYZ, and DEHEYDEMIZ! With all these I conjure you so that you may fulfill my request, take note of my petitions, have pity in my lamentations and tears, heal my burdens, and protect and defend me from the evils and plots of that individual and others who seek evil. I conjure you by the high God of the entire firmament, of great power and dominion, the Lord of names that are prayed to, and the Lord of good things, giver of life to the entire world, who created life and death, boundaries and durations. He is the one who remains and lasts through the infinite cycles of ages, without a beginning or end; by this God, I conjure you so that you may fulfill my request at this hour and moment. Amen, amen.

While always speaking these things over the smoke of the censer, repeat these words many times, and you shall fulfill the intent. If you decapitate one of Mars's animals, burn it on a fire, and do with it as you did with the others. Thus, you shall be more certain that your request will be fulfilled.

§26 *For avenging yourself against an enemy.* Ancient sages would do things suited to a kind of vengeance with the stars present next to the pole, namely Benethnays, a star that stands in the constellation of Ursa Major. The sages established the prayers in this way. When an enemy is harming you or quarrelling with you and you wish to send them punishment and misery such that they may have no thought against you in order to avenge yourself from that deed, enter the house that you will have built for this task, and turn your face toward where Benethnays will be at that time. Throw onto the lit coals of the censer some of that suffumigation that is described below. While smoke rises, say:

> May God bless thee, O greater BENETHNAYS, you who are splendid and beautiful in your position in the firmament! I ask and conjure you by the power that God, founder of all things, has placed in you [127] that you might send such an individual a spirit to enter his body to bind and tie it in knots such that all his limbs be cursed and all his senses be reduced to nothing (sight, hearing, and the other senses, the ability to walk, speak, eat, drink, and delight in anything, and that he be overall devoid of life). I pray that you, stars of Benethnays, might strew him out to die and pour into him every kind of misery from every direction. May his eyes behold toil and sadness, anger, the fury of kings, the victory of enemies and that of wild, savage beasts! May you command him to come into the ill will of neighbors and kin! May you hastily make bitter and manifest vindication over him throughout the universe! Ruin his body and his household, and cast him down headlong from high places. Make his eyes pop out, shatter his hands and feet, and curse all his limbs. Bring him as strong and extreme a misery and as potent a punishment as is possible to befall anyone. Divert him from the mercy and piety of God. Do not receive any piety from him, nor cure his impediments. I ask that you act swiftly against him. My will acts and seeks you openly on account of the great misery that I endure through him and the evils done to me without any reasonable cause. You are the stars that accomplish with effect the requests and supplications done toward you. You defend and equip the one who has recourse to you. I ask you that you pour into this individual your power and spirit with great fury and anger, that you swiftly transmit to him all these penalties because he deserves loss, misery, great pain, to be treated poorly by everyone around, that he be despised, that you shower great infirmities and pains upon all his limbs. Inflict these upon him, the penalties and miseries that I am saying. I conjure you by your power and spirit that you may remember my request. Take pity upon my tears, and grant me the power and intellect of your spirit that I may perceive your fulfillment of my request. I conjure you by the God of the great firmament and exalted power, and by Him, namely the One who has dominion and power over all the creatures of heaven and the world, who indeed is God Himself, so that you may fulfill my request. Now I ask that you act punctually through the names of that exalted Lord who is God to

> fulfill this request of mine through His power and His virtue. Look upon my prayers and words closely.

Once you have spoken all these words thus, prostrate yourself on the ground. While saying these things, repeat them many times with the smoke always rising from a suffumigation created this way: take 1 oz. each of storax gum, incense of nutmeg, holly, and aloewood with 3 oz. each of spikenard and mastic. Grind them all up, and mix them with the best wine, and make pills. Set them aside for use when you want to operate through those polar stars. [128]

§27 *When you wish to pray to the Sun.* When you wish to pray to the Sun and request something from him, such as a petition of grace from a king, the love of lords, lordship, and how to acquire it, let the Sun be fortunate and in the ascendant, both in his day and in his hour. Dress yourself in regal clothes, yellow silk mixed with gold, place upon your head a golden crown, and wear a gold ring on your finger. Prepare yourself in the appearance of noble Chaldean men because the Sun is lord to their ascendant. Enter a sequestered house chosen for the task. Place your right hand above your left, and look at the Sun with a respectful and humble gaze like that of a fearful and modest person. Take a golden censer and a good-looking cock with a handsome neck. On top of the censer, place a small burning wax candle on a piece of wood the size of your palm. Place the suffumigation described below in the fire of the censer. While the Sun is rising, turn the cock toward him; indeed, with the smoke ascending continuously from the censer, say:

> You who are the root of heaven and are above all the stars and planets, holy and honored, I ask that you heed my request and grant me the grace and love of such-and-such a king and other kings too. I conjure you by the one who granted you light and life. You are the light of the world. I invoke you by all your names: in Arabic, *Yazemiz*; in Latin, *Sol*; in Phoenician, *Maher*; in Roman, *Lehuz*; in Indian, *Araz*. You are the light of the world and its brightness; you exist in the middle of the planets. You are the cause of generation in the world, by your power and heat made sublime in your position. I ask by your splendor and power that you deign to help me in such a way that such-and-such a king and the rest of the earth place me in a noble and sublime position so that I may have dominion and nobility in the same way that you are lord of the other planets and stars, since they receive their light and brightness from you. I ask you, who are the root of the entire firmament, that you have pity on me and note my prayers and requests.

While the smoke is rising, speak these words. The suffumigation necessary for this task is one we call "the suffumigation of hermits," and just as the ancient sages have claimed, it has great and wondrous effects. It is composed of thirty-one species, and this is its recipe: take 7 oz. each of common fleabane, bdellium, myrrh, labdanum, elecampane, and cicely; 3 oz. each of nettle tree, poley germander, and cleaned pine nuts; 5 oz. each of lily root, sonchus, cardamom, aromatic reed, incense, and nutmeg shell; 4 oz. each of dried roses, saffron, spikenard, root of caper, cinquefoil; 9 oz. each of clove, balsam seed, cuscuta; 1 oz. of squinancywort; 2 lbs. each of cucumber seed, amomum, terebinth, date powder, skinned grapes; and 5 lbs. of skimmed honey. Grind everything up, and mix it with the best wine. Make pills, and set them aside for the rituals of the Sun, with which you will suffumigate while uttering the Sun's prayer. When it is finished, decapitate the cock, and eat its liver. [129] Do everything as above regarding the other planets, and you will attain your objective.

§28 The suffumigation of the Sun and its prayer, however, are better done in this way. Dress yourself in the clothes mentioned above, prepare yourself in the fashion we described, and place this suffumigation on the fire in the censer. Take equal parts of saffron, storax gum, incense, nutmeg, litharge, pomegranate flower, aloewood, and saxifrage. Grind and mix them up. Make pills that you will set aside for use. When the ritual begins, place some of those on the lit coals of the censer. While the smoke is rising, speak:

> May God preserve you, O Sun, you who are lucky and the Greater Fortune, hot and dry, bright, resplendent, excellent, beautiful, splendid and honored king above all the stars and planets. The quality of beauty, subtlety, good disposition, truth, wisdom, knowledge, riches, which are acquired by means of your power, are strengthened in you. You are the lord of the six planets, who are steered by your motion, and you rule above them, and you have authority and dominion over them. They exist obedient to you, and they debase themselves in your aspect such that when they are conjoined with you by their motions, at once they are more obedient to you and overflow with your light. When conjoined to you physically, they are burned up by your rays and are altogether concealed from our sights. They all shine by your light, power, and splendor. You have powers over all. You are the king, and they the vassals. You give light and power to them all; from you they receive fortune and become fortunate when you favor them in good aspect. When you face them in a bad aspect, they lose their fortune and are rendered unfortunate. There is no one who can perceive all your blessings and noble characteristics, which are infinite to our intellects.

While speaking these things, throw yourself to the ground, and turn your face toward the Sun repeating these words many times. Make a sacrifice from some solar animal according to what was said above on the other planets, and you will attain your objective.

§29 Now another prayer of the Sun that sages claim is for kings, potentates, and high-class nobles who, when their powers and kingdoms have been dissolved, want to return to their former states. When you wish to operate for these or similar reasons, first place Scorpio in the ascendant with the Sun aspecting Mars. Take a golden censer, and place a fire from the coals of holm oak in it. Hold in your hand grains of amber the size of chickpeas, which you should throw on the censer's fire one after another in sequence. While smoke is rising toward the Sun (that is, while he is in mid-heaven), turn yourself toward him, and speak:

> O Sun, you who are the source of riches, the increase of strength, the honor of life, the source of splendor, and the beginning of all goodness! I entrust my entire will upon you, and with it place myself wholly in your hands. I entreat you on account of my depression, loss, the lessening of my power, and because others gloat over me and do not respect me according to my status. I conjure you by the Lord on high, who [130] is the mover of your motions and the giver of your power, through whom you accomplish your actions; by the obedience with which you obey that Lord; by the reason you have for helping and saving those who throw themselves at you and your will (that is, those who pray to you and supplicate you with a clear and pure intent); and by the dominion and capability that God granted you over the planets, turn yourself onto me and liberate my will! Carry it away from worried and sad contemplations, and lead me back into my power, station, and fortifications. Grant that that particular individual of this world comes to my obedience and dominion. May you deign to grant me the power and strength of your splendor and excellence, by which I may have fortune and influence in working upon everyone such that they obey me. I conjure you by your hidden and concealed noble qualities; by the influence you have in the order of motion; by the influence, power, strength, and the works you govern upon the generation of things in this world; by your piety, which reaches the meek; by your fortune, which reaches the great; by your fidelity and legality, which you have toward the Lord God, who granted competence to you; by the debt of assistance that you have for those fleeing to you and beseeching you; by the ways and paths of the heavens, which have no parallel upon the Earth

> so that you may heed my prayer, understand my request, pay attention to my words, and complete my petitions with effect. All those with a pure and untarnished will toward you should have complete salvation.

While you are saying those things, you should be dressed in the clothes we have mentioned above and be standing toward the Sun. Observe the rest of the things discussed here, and you will attain the objective.

§30 *When you wish to pray to Venus.* When you wish to pray to Venus and request something from the matters pertinent to her, let her be free from unfortunate planets, direct, not retrograde, and in a favorable position. Afterward, dress and adorn yourself with one of her two ornaments, the best of which is the clothing and ornaments of Arab noblemen. Dress yourself in white clothes, and on your head wear a white headdress, because it is her symbol. The other is an ornament like a woman's veil. Dress yourself in ample, precious, and beautiful silk clothes interwoven with gold. Place a crown on your head adorned with precious pearls and stones. Wear a gold ring on your hand decorated with a stone of pearl and golden bracelets on your arms. Take up a mirror in your right hand, and in the left carry a comb. Place a pitcher of wine before yourself and put aromatic powder, good-smelling spices, and nutmeg on your clothes, like women do. Take a censer made of gold and silver, then place lit coals in it. Throw upon them the suffumigation described below. While the smoke is rising, speak:

> May God preserve you, O Venus, who are mistress and fortune, cold and humid, fair in your effects and complexion, pure, beautiful, [131] pleasant-smelling, pretty, and decorated! You are the mistress of gold and silver jewelry; fond of love, joy, decorations, parties, elegance, songs, and instruments that resound with the voice and are sung from the heart, songs sung with a beat and pipe music, games and comforts, rest and love. You have stood firm in your effects. You love wines, rest, joy, and sex with women since all these stand as your natural effects. I myself invoke you by all your names: in Arabic, *Zohara*; in Latin, *Venus*; in Persian, *Anyhyt*;[34] in Roman, *Affludita*; in Greek, *Admenita*; in Indian, *Sarca*. I conjure you by the Lord God, Lord of the high firmament, and by the obedience that you render unto God, and by the power and dominion that He holds above you so that you may heed my prayer, remember my request, and do such-and-such for me (state your request here). I conjure you by BEYTEYL, who is that angel whom God placed with you for bringing about all your powers and effects.

While speaking these things, throw yourself to the ground while facing Venus, and say these things while prostrate, motionless on the ground. Get up, and repeat these things. When this is done, decapitate a dove and a turtledove, and eat their livers. Burn their bodies on the censer's fire. While doing this, the suffumigation should be constantly burning in the censer, the composition of which is this: Take equal parts of aloewood, sukk, costus, saffron, labdanum, mastic gum, poppy husks, willow leaves, and lily root. Grind everything up, and mix it in rosewater. Make tablets the size of chickpeas. Throw them in the censer's fire until your ritual is complete.

§31 *The prayer of Venus for love.* Perform the prayer of Venus for love between two individuals or between a husband and a wife in this way. Dress and adorn yourself as we described above, and observe the position of Venus and those things related above. Place this suffumigation in the fire. Take 5 oz. of sukk and peppered thistle[35]; and 2½ oz. each of grapes, frankincense, and mastic gum. Grind everything up, and mix it with rain water. Make tablets the size of chickpeas. Throw them into the fire one after another until the end of the ritual lest the smoke be lacking at any time during the operation. While the smoke is rising, speak:

> O Venus, you who are the spirit of love, builder of friendships, and the jewel of intimacy! From you proceeds the power of taste and love. From you flow good friendship and enjoyment between individuals. Through you the spirits seeking evil are clumped up and those seeking good overflow. You are the source of love's intimacy between men and women. You are the root of procreation. You attract the spirit of one toward the other, and through you, they are conjoined. Spirits are disposed toward loving one another by your power. O Venus, you who are beautiful, you who give the power [132] of love's intimacy to those calling upon you by your will! I beseech you by your names, by the name of God, sublime and on high, who created you and moves you in your sphere; by your light and by the firmament of your reign and potency so that you may heed my prayer and request on account of such-and-such an individual's ill will toward me and by the misery, toil, and sadness that exist because that person's enmity and will divert good things away from me—for that reason I am making a request. I ask and beg that you turn these things around for me regarding their love and friendship and that, out of all your spirits and powers, you pass over them, their spirit, the spirit of their essence and of their prayer. May all their spirits and acts of will toward me be rectified through you. By your motion and robust potency, may you move toward me like fire and violent wind. I conjure you and

> your spirits—you who are truthful in your friendships and loves, beautiful and steadfast in your social interactions—your spirits, who create loving relationships and sexual intercourse and move the power of delight and vice in the mind and bring about love—by all those things, I conjure you so that you heed and take note of my request and prayer. I conjure you by BEYTEYL, who is the angel whom the Lord our God placed with you for bringing about your powers and effects. I conjure you by your spirit, by whom you have powers and potencies in your works. I conjure you by your brightness and light, that you may pour the yearning for luxury, vice, and friendship into my heart and will. Heed my dealings so that you receive my request, fulfill my desire in what I seek, and transmit to me by your light, power, and love what I need to perceive how you receive my request regarding these things. You are the one who joins hearts together, who conjoins and unites love and acts of good will. May you bring about joy, comfort, and delight! May you receive complete and whole salutations forever! Amen.

Once you have spoken and done these things thus, sacrifice a white dove. Eat its liver. Burn up the remains, and set aside the ash. Give it to whoever you wish in food. This will delight you.

§32 *When you wish to pray to Mercury.* When you wish to pray to Mercury and seek something pertaining to him like the things relevant to scribes and kings' regents, dress like a notary or a scribe when the Moon is conjoined with Mercury. Behave like a scribe in all your actions, and place on your finger a ring of solidified mercury, since the wise Hermes had worked with such a ring. Sit on a throne similar to a magistrate's, and turn your face toward Mercury, holding a sheet in your hands pretending as if you wished to write upon it. Use the suffumigation appropriate to him in a censer of solidified mercury filled with fire; place it therein. While the smoke is rising, say:

> May God preserve you, [133] O good lord Mercury, you who are truthful, sensible, intelligent, and wise in all manner of writing, arithmetic, computation, and knowledge of the heavens and Earth, and the infuser of all these! You are the noble lord of modest enjoyment, riches, business dealings, and wealth. You are lord, sustainer, and subtle interpreter of deep perception. You govern the prophecies of prophets and their perceptions, reason, teaching, apprehending diverse sciences, subtlety, intellect, philosophy, geometry, knowledge of the heavens and Earth, divinations, geomancy, poetics, writing, eloquence, the sense of agility, depth in all crafts and skills, quickness, changing from one business deal to another,

lying, preparing yourself and maintaining purity and cleanliness, being helpful to others and behaving yourself well with them, piety, sense perception, tranquility, and the diversion of evils. You are the disposer and expounder of law to humankind and of the good law toward God. You have concealed yourself by means of your subtlety such that none can ever know your nature nor determine your effects. You are fortunate with the fortunate planets and unfortunate with the unfortunate planets. You are male with male planets but female with female ones; diurnal with diurnal planets and nocturnal with nocturnal ones. You harmonize with the planets in all their natures, conform with them in all their forms, transmuting yourself into all their qualities. Now I beseech and invoke you by all your names: in Arabic, *Hotarit*; in Latin, *Mercurius*; in Roman, *Haruz*; in Phoenician, *Tyr*; in Indian, *Meda*. I conjure you first by the Lord God on high, who is Lord of the firmament and of the elevated and great kingdom. I conjure you by Him so that you may receive my request and accomplish what I ask from you. May you pour onto me the powers of your spirit, by which I may be strengthened, that I may assist myself in accomplishing my request and that I may be suited and well-disposed for learning knowledge and wisdom. Make me beloved and well-received by kings and nobles. Make me exalted and honored by humankind. Give me the intimacy of kings so that they may grant me permission and effectively take up my words such that they need me and seek my knowledge and wisdom in accounting, arithmetic, astrology, and divination. Work in me, and dispose me such that I may profit and become rich. May I receive honors and excellence before kings, noblemen, and everyone. On account of this I conjure you by ARQUYL, who is the angel whom God placed with you for bringing about your acts and works, so that you may accomplish my request, heed my prayer, and fulfill my petition. I ask that you help and fortify me with your spirit and join me in love with kings by your spirit and power. May I reach knowledge and wisdom by your power. Thus, by your assistance, you will help me so that I may know those things I do not know and that I may understand the things I do not understand and that I may see the things that I do not see and that you may remove from me want, sickness, and what weakens the mind and increases forgetfulness. Do this until I may attain the level of the wise sublime ancients (those who had knowledge and [134] understanding by means of their spirits and acts of will). May you transmit to my spirit your potency and spirit, which elevates me and makes me reach the abovementioned state. Direct me in knowledge and wisdom and in all my acts so that I may have grace and power by serving kings

> and noblemen. Thus, may I acquire wealth and treasure! Fulfill this request for me quickly. I myself conjure you by the Lord God, Lord of the firmament on high and the kingdom of power, that you remember my request and effectively fulfill all the petitions I have made.

While you are saying all these things, throw yourself to the ground toward him, humbly and devoutly, repeating the above once. Afterward, raise your head, and behead a cock with a large crest, burn it up in the aforementioned way, and eat its liver. Suffumigate a suffumigation made this way: take equal parts of nutmeg, holm oak, cumin, dried cloves, myrtle branches, bitter almond husks, acacia, seeds of tamarisk, grapevine branches, and squinancywort. Grind them up, and incorporate them with pure and delicate wine. Make tablets, and set them aside for use.

§33 *When you wish to pray to the Moon.* When you wish to pray to the Moon and seek something pertaining to her, prepare yourself in the appearance of a boy. Have with you some good smelling things, and hold a silver ring in your hand. Be lighthearted in your gestures and actions, and speak lavishly, well, and pointedly. Have a silver censer in front of you. On the fourteenth day of the lunar month when the Moon is above the Earth and in aspect with the fortunate planets with favorable aspects, wash yourself, turn your face toward her, and speak:

> May God preserve you, O Moon, blessed lady, fortunate, cold and humid, proportional and beautiful. You are chief and key of all the other planets, swift in your movements with a shining brightness, lady of merriment and joy, of good words, good reputation, and a lucky kingdom. You are a lover of the law, contemplative of the matters of the world, subtle in your musings. You appreciate and love enjoyment, songs, and parties. You are the mistress of ambassadors, messengers, and revealer of secrets. You are free and precious, closer to us than the rest of the planets, larger and more luminous than them all. You are the connector of good and evil, you bring the planets together and carry down their brightness. By your goodness you reconcile whatever they might be. All are adorned by your decoration and condemned by your cursing. You are the beginning of all things; you are their end. You have excellence and honor above all planets. Through things of this kind I beseech you. I conjure you by CELAN, who is the angel whom God has placed with you for realizing all your effects, so that you may take pity on me and receive my request by the humility you have toward our Lord on high and toward His kingdom, so that you may hear me in the things sought and asked. I invoke you by all

> your names: in Arabic, *Camar*; in Latin, *Luna*; in Phoenician, *Mehe*; in Greek, *Zamahyl*; in Indian, *Cerim*; in Roman, *Celez*, that you may receive my petitions in this place.

Afterward, [135] throw yourself on the ground toward the Moon while repeating the above. While saying these words and doing these things, use the "suffumigation of hermits" composed of twenty-eight ingredients in this way. Take 1 oz. each of mastic gum, cardamom, savin, storax gum, and peppered thistle; 2 oz. each of elecampane, myrrh, squinancywort, *dar sessahal*,[36] spikenard, costus, frankincense, and saffron; 4 oz. each of cucumber and its seeds and henna root; 3 oz. each of lily root, Celtic nard,[37] Indian poley-germander, and shelled cleaned pine nuts; 2 lbs. each of St. John's Wort, labdanum, apple leaves, dried roses, and jelly; 2 lbs. of cleaned grapes; and 5 lbs. of dates. Mix them into as much of the subtlest wine as is sufficient to combine those things. Make tablets the size of chickpeas. When the task is at hand, take with you a bovine calf, decapitate it, and burn it in a large fire, as we have said above, such that its smoke rises in the air as discussed regarding the other sacrifices. If you have made your sacrifice from a sheep, burn it, and eat its liver (as said above regarding the other sacrifices). You will fulfill your request.

§34 The opinion of sages about the prayers and petitions suited to the planets is that each of the planets act on matters corresponding to its own nature (the fortunate to the good and the unfortunate to evil). When you wish to ask something from the planets, see to it that the chosen planet be aspected by the lord of the ascendant, that the *almuten* of the figure be in the east and also high in its epicycle in the fourth altitude in the east. Then the sages would make their petitions. The powers and effects of the planets are stronger and of greater influence at night. Beware lest you seek anything from any planet that is not from its own proper nature since it would be the downfall of such a request.

§35 The sages who made prayers and sacrifices to the planets in mosques did the abovementioned things. When the heavens moved by eight degrees, they made the sacrifice of one animal, and while it was setting by eight degrees, they made another sacrifice. They say that Hermes ordered them to do this in mosques or in their churches. Those sages have claimed regarding Hermes that he was the lord of three thriving roles, namely a king, a prophet, and a sage. They mandated that no sacrifices of any animal that is bicolored, black, with a broken bone, with a broken horn, with a sick eye, or with a blemish on its body be made in their mosques. While they were decapitating that animal, they would take out its liver right away. They examined it, and if they found any defect or stain on it, then they would claim that the lord of that place had a notable impediment. Then they would hash up this liver and give it to everyone present so that they might eat it.

§36 They would call Mars in their language *Mara Smyt*,[38] which means lord of malefactors. They say he is a malefactor because he is swift in his malign effects. According to their opinion, his form is the shape of a man holding a sword in his right hand and a burning flame in his left [136] while threatening in turn with blade and fire. For this reason, he was honored among them, and they made sacrifices out of fear of him and for preventing his evil. The sacrifices that they made to him they performed when the Sun is entering Aries because it is the house of Mars, and similarly when the Sun is entering Scorpio, they make another sacrifice of this kind.

§37 They have one experiment on children, which is in the month when the Sun is dwelling in Scorpio. They take a boy, lead him to a secret house prepared for this operation, and stand him on his feet. They bring up one handful of tamarisk and set it on fire in a tin censer. They speak words relevant to Mars over the boy and dress him in the clothes of Mars. If fire were to touch the boy's backside, they would judge him incapable, unsuitable, and untrained for this ritual. If the fire were to touch him in the front, they claim that he is suitable and apt for this operation. Then they lead him to the house of their prayers and inspect him to see whether his limbs are healthy. Then they lead him to another dark house with his eyes covered. A priest is prepared ahead of time and places one stick of red tamarisk upon the boy. They dress him in a hide, and the priest places a burning censer next to the boy's feet on the right-hand side. He places another censer with water on the left. The mother of the boy then comes with a cock in her hands and sits in the door of that house. Next, the priest takes up a bronze cooking pot full of burning coals in his hands. The priest summons the boy and binds him with the fetters of an oath that he never reveal his secrets. The boy is greatly terrified so as not to reveal this to anyone. They tell him that if he were to reveal anything to anyone about these things, he would die immediately. When the priest has finished these things, he should uncover and open the boy's eyes. His mother comes with the abovementioned cock, and the priest takes it with his hands and decapitates it above the boy's head. At once, the mother throws a red cloth on him and takes him out of the house. When the boy leaves the house, he immediately puts a ring on his finger with the image of a monkey on it.

§38 These men say that the first sacrifice pertaining to Saturn is made while he is in Taurus, and they sacrifice a single cow to him. They claim that its horns are set as a crown, that it is more beautiful and more suited for sacrifice than the other animals. They used to make this sacrifice once they had fattened up the cow by feeding it herbs gathered by virgin girls at sunrise. They would return home by paths other than the ones they used when they left home. Those men hold all the above as the greatest secret in their works. They would be attentive that this cow be totally unblemished, entirely [137] lacking white spots, no matter how insignificant. Over its eyes was placed a golden chain twirled around its horns. They say that the wise Hermes taught a ritual of this kind. When they wanted to decapitate it, however, they would prepare it for funerary rites and suffumigate it with the suffumigations of Saturn. They spoke in the manner of the Greeks. The priest decapitated it with a sharp sword on which there was to be found no tarnish or diminution; then he collected its blood in a dish. He then retrieved its tongue, ears, snout, and eyes; and the rest took their share. Afterward they would inspect the blood sitting in the saucer, and the froth rising from the blood. From that froth, they understood the dominion and motion of Saturn, which according to them is the first motion because in him motion begins and ends. They used to make this kind of sacrifice when Saturn entered the sign of Taurus.

§39 Those men used to wash their faces and bodies with wine and ground salt so that their skin or flesh would dry out and their blood would circulate throughout their bodies. They maintained that their operations were accomplished through these things.

§40 They had a locked house, which none entered, wherein there was a deep pit. When the Sun entered the first degree of Leo, they made a red ram enter from the land of *Canuiz*[39] and covered it with precious cloth. They led it to gardens and places filled with trees and flowers. Making great celebrations there, they gave it as much wine to drink as it could take. They led it to that house at night and threw it into the pit and there they washed it with sesame oil. Next, they took it out of the pit, and they gave it dried roses to eat, mustard, lentils, chickpeas, rice, honey, and wheat, all mixed together. At the end of the twenty-eight days after the entrance of the Sun into Leo (namely, that night), they led it out of the city or out of the populated area into the woods, and there they decapitated it. There, they made a hole and buried the ram in it. The head, however, they carried back to the house of the ritual and set it in front of their images. They claimed they could hear a feeble voice from it from which, allegedly, they learned their king's lifespan and the waxing and waning of their peoples. The man who discovered this operation or the one who taught us this secret was Barnac Elbarameny, who ended his final days in the land of the Indians; a certain class in India were called Brahmin after his own name.[40] Among those peoples, certain sages have many diverse operations of this kind that, if we wanted to cite them all, would prolong our book inordinately. Therefore, let us here return to our proposed topic. [138]

Chapter 8

On How the Nabataeans Used to Pray to the Sun and Saturn, and How They Would Speak with Them and Draw Down Their Spirits and Effects

§1 The Nabataean sages claimed that the powers and effects of the heavens and stars are simply from the Sun because they see and understand that the Moon helps him (that is, with respect to his effects), while the Sun does not require her nor the other planets.[41] Similarly, the other five planets follow the Sun in their effects and are obedient and subservient to him, and they persist in their effects according to the dispositions of the Sun. Likewise, the fixed stars are his handmaidens: they serve, obey, and are submissive to him. They help him in his effects, without him needing them. The Nabataean people are accustomed to make this prayer to the Sun:

> We pray, honor, and praise you, high lord Sun! For you give life to everything living in the world, and the world as a whole is illuminated by your light and governed by your power. You are seated in an exalted place. You have a great kingdom filled with light, perception, understanding, power, honor, and good. All things that can be generated are generated by your power. Through you the things that should be governed are governed. All plants live through you. All things persist in their strength through you. You stand excellent and honored in your effects, and powerful while remaining in your heaven. We salute, praise, honor, and pray to you in obedience and humility. We reveal all our intentions to you, and we ask and request all our necessities from you. You are our lord, and we beg you day and night that we obtain life and governance from your power. We disclose our intentions to you that you may both free us and defend us from our enemies and from all those seeking to do us harm. Let this also be done by the Moon, who is your handmaiden and is obedient to you—her light and brightness proceed from you and your power. You give power. You are the chosen lord in your heaven. The Moon and the rest of the planets are always servants to you. They obey you and never recede from your order. Thus, we praise you forever through the infinite ages of time. Amen.

§2 The sages of the *Chaldean Agriculture* claim that they used to pray to Saturn with this prayer, but they would first see to it that this lord not be descending in the circle nor west of the Sun nor under his rays nor in the midst of retrograde motion. When they found him free from all impediments and unaffected, they made the prayer written out below to him and made a suffumigation of old hides, fat, sweat, dead bats, and mice. Of these, fourteen bats are burned up and fourteen mice are likewise burned. They would take their ashes and place them on the head of their image. They threw themselves down around the image on a black stone or sandy floor. [139] From these efforts, they were defended from his Saturn's malice and evil, since every evil, cursed thing, and grief proceed from him. He is lord of all poverty, misery, pain, imprisonment, turpitude, and lamentation. He signifies these things while descending and unfortunate. When he is in a good disposition and in his exaltation, however, he signifies purity, lifespan, social standing, rejoicing, honor, riches, inheritance, and the durability of inheritance in sons and grandsons. His benevolence is when he is east of the Sun, in mid-heaven, direct in his movement, swift in motion, elevated in his circle, and in increase.

§3 Zeherit, the first of the three sages in the *Chaldean Agriculture*, said that because he made this prayer to Saturn and sought from him what he wished, a good disposition immediately overcame the magical image from which he wished to receive a response in these matters. The course of this prayer is as follows:

> We stand on our feet, we pray and honor you through obedience and humility. We stand on our feet before that splendid lord, alive and enduring, fixed in his potency and dominion, who is Saturn. He endures in his heaven, potent in his dominion, and united in his effects, heights, and magnificence. He encircles all things and has power in all visible and invisible things and in all things existing upon the Earth. Everything living on the Earth lives and persists by his power and durability. He begins them and causes them to endure by his power and ability, and by his permanence, everlastingness, and his resilience, he causes the Earth to abide. By his power, he makes the waters and rivers move down and flow. By living, he causes living things to move in order to live. He is cold just like his nature. The trees grow and rise up into loftiness by his reign, and the Earth is made weighty by the weight of his motions. If he so wished, he could transform beings into another type. He is wise, the power of things, and the maker of perception. His knowledge is manifest in all things. May you be blessed, you who are the lord of your heaven.

May your name be blessed, pure, and honored. We are obedient to you, we beg at your feet, and by your honor, we beseech you by your names, will, excellence, and honor that you may sharpen our senses, that they might endure within us throughout our life, that they might persist as they are at present. When they are severed from the life of our bodies, we beseech that you might have pity so that the worms and reptiles be withdrawn from our flesh. You are a precious and ancient lord, and none but you are able to repair what you have damaged. You are permanent in your statements and works and do not repent for your actions. You are slow and profound in your powers. You are so great a lord since there are none who can carry away that which you concede, and none can grant what you prohibit. You are lord, decorated in your works and unique in your reign. You are lord of the other planets, and the other stars moving in their circles fear the sound of your motion and [140] panic in terror from you. We ask and seek that you deign to remove your evil effects from us. By your purity, have pity on our people—through your good and excellent names and those who attain your pity, we pray that we may remove all your evil effects from ourselves by your power and that, by your power, you may have pity on us and our people. We beg and seek by all your names, by your exalted and excellent name—this name—that is, the one you prefer to all other names, that you might pour your piety toward us.

§4 Abenrasia wrote these words in the *Chaldean Agriculture*, which he translated from the Chaldean tongue.[42] We have included this prayer here solely for demonstrating the common agreement between the ancient sages concerning the planetary operations and the constant protection of their bodies by means of planetary natures. We include that prayer in this book such that nothing intelligible in this work of ancient sages be lacking. We pass along our book complete with what we promised when we began to write. Now, since this prayer is forbidden in our law, we included it here merely for uncovering the ancient sages' secrets, since they performed this ritual in ancient times before the law was given. For this reason, no one must reveal these things since, despite everything I have said about this and other rituals, I am and shall always be a teacher with good intentions. Ultimately, I ask that all those who see and hear this book never reveal it to fools. If it were necessary to reveal it to someone, do not do so except to good sages enlightened by intellect and leading their lives according to the laws of good conduct. I pray to God omnipotent: May He defend our work from the hands of fools and forgive me for everything mentioned here, for I have spoken everything above with good intentions.

Chapter 9

On How to Attract the Powers of Each Planet Separately and the Spirits of Their Powers, Naming Them According to Their Roles, and How to Operate These Names

§1 The spirit of Saturn called REDIMEZ is the one binding all his compound names and separate names and his parts below, above, and elsewhere. All this is according to the opinion of Aristotle in the book he wrote for Alexander called *Antimaquis*, wherein he discussed how the powers of the planets and their spirits ought to be attracted.[43] Their names, divided according to the opinion of Aristotle himself, are these. His spirit of above is called TOZ, the spirit below is COREZ, to the right DEYTYZ, to the left DERIUZ, to the front TALYZ, and to the rear DARUZ. His motion in his sphere, his progression in the signs, and his motion [141] in the spirits—all the above are joined together in this name: TAHAYTUC. All these names are contained in this first name, REDIMEZ, and this name is the root and source of all the names mentioned.

§2 The name binding Jupiter's spirits is DEMEHUZ; the spirit of above is called DERMEZ, below MATIZ, to the right MAZ, to the left DERIZ, in front TAMIZ, and behind is FORUZ. The spirit of motion through his own heaven and the division of his signs is DEHYDEZ. The name by which all these names are joined together, the name that is the root and source of all names, is the first name touched upon above, that is, DEMEHUZ.

§3 The name by which Mars's spirits are bound is DEHARAYUZ; the spirit of above is HEHEYDIZ, below HEYDEYUZ, to the right MAHARAZ, to the left ARDAUZ, in the front HONDEHOYUZ, and the rear MEHEYEDIZ. The spirit of his motion in the heavens, his advancement through signs, and the motion of his spirit is called DEHYDEMEZ. The name including all these names that is their root and source is named above, that is DEHARAYUZ.

§4 The name binding the Sun's spirits is BEYDELUZ. The name of his spirit above is DEHYMEZ, below EYDULEZ, to the right DEHEYFEZ, to the left AZUHAFEZ, in front MAHABEYUZ, and at the rear HADYZ. The spirit of his motion in the heavens, through the signs and his spirit, is called LETAHAYMERIZ. The name including and joining all these names, the root and source of them all, is the one mentioned above, that is BEYDELUZ.

§5 The name binding Venus's spirits is DEYDEZ. The spirit above is HEYLUZ, below CAHYLUZ, to the right DIRUEZ, to the left ABLEYMEZ, in front TEYLUZ, and in the rear ARZUZ. The spirit of her motions in the heavens, through the signs, is DEHATARYZ. The name including all these, the root and source of them all, is DEYDEZ mentioned above.

§6 The name binding Mercury's spirits is MERHUYEZ. His spirit above is AMIREZ, below is HYTYZ, to the right CEHUZ, to the left DERIZ, in front MAYLEZ, and at the rear DEHEDYZ. The spirit of his motions in the heavens, through the signs, is MEHENDIZ. The name including all the names mentioned above, the root and source of them all, is MERHUYEZ.

§7 The name including the Moon's spirits is HARNUZ. Her spirit above is HEDIZ, below is MARAYUZ, to the right MELETAZ, to the left TIMEZ, in front HUEYZ, and at the rear MEYNELUZ. The name of her spirit of motion in the heavens and her advancement through the signs is DAHANUZ. What joins and brings together all the names stated above, the root and source of them all, is HARNUZ.

§8 Aristotle talks about these things in the aforesaid book assigning these names to these spirits by asserting that they are the spirits of the parts of the world, which are the six parts in all the regions of the seven planets. The names of these spirits are those that individuals who pray to the planets are accustomed to using [142] and being intimate with in prayer to the planets. Heed these things diligently.

§9 The philosopher said that for this reason all the spirits' powers affecting the climes and generative things descend from those spirits. From these things, wondrous effects ensue through prayers—from these emanate wealth and poverty since they give, take away, and divert. They have bodies by which they are covered and made physical. In their own climes, each of them governs individuals into whom flow their powers and spirits. They grant these to be arranged in their systems of knowledge and to be used in affairs of their natures.

§10 Later, the same philosopher said: "When you want to draw forth some of the abovementioned planetary spirits in any clime, heed these fundamentals since each of the planetary effects works more strongly in its own clime."

§11 *A ritual of Saturn.* When you want to operate through Saturn, do this. With the Sun in Capricorn and the Moon in Sagittarius, make an image whose feet are made of iron, and dress it in green, black, and red-colored clothes. Afterward, go to a field, and step under a tree with no scent at all. Bring along with you your sacrifice (a cow or a calf) with a suffumigation made from the brain of a black cat, euphorbia, hemlock, myrrh, and St. John's Wort. You should say: "BEDIZEZ, TOZ, EDUZ, HAYZ, DERNIZ, TAYUZ, HUARUYZ, TALHIT,

NAYCAHUA, HUENADUL! Come, O spirits, be at hand for your sacrifice!" Say the prayer again and again while continually suffumigating. State your request, and it will be fulfilled. All these things Aristotle posited in his book.

§12 *A ritual of Jupiter.* When you wish to operate through Jupiter, perform on Thursday when the Sun is in Pisces or Sagittarius and the Moon is in the head of Aries (which is the exaltation of the Sun). Prepare a house suited to this ritual, clean and tidy, decorated with drapery, curtains, and the best textiles. In your hand hold a dish with this kind of mix or blend: honey, butter, oil of nuts, and sugar; make it liquid and moist. Then create one pie (that is, a tart) made most deliciously with flour, butter, milk, sugar, and saffron, and make as much as you can out of these. Place a large table on top of a robust tripod on that house's roof. Place a censer made of Jupiter's metal[44] in front of you. Place on the table nutmeg, camphor, aloewood, and other fragrant things (civet, and the like). Add one dose of mastic gum to the pie and the mixture you made with the wet and dry things. In the middle of the table, place a huge lit candle. Behind the candle, assemble four open baskets filled with pomegranates, cooked meats, and ram, chicken, and dove roasts with platters of cabbage. Place a jug and a clear vessel filled with wine on top of each basket. [143] On the table, place branches of myrtle. Once you have done this, suffumigate mastic gum and aloewood at the head of the table, and place another suffumigation of mastic in another part of the house. No one but you should be in the house. Say: "DEMEUZ, ARMEZ, CEYLEZ, MAHAZ, ERDAZ, TAMYZ, FERUZ, DYNDEZ, AFRAYUZ, TAYHACIEDEZ!" These are the names of Jupiter's spirits in all six parts of his heaven. The meaning of that name AFRIDUZ and the others is: "Come and step in, all you spirits of Jupiter, and smell those fragrances, eat these foods, and from them do what you please!" Repeat these things seven times. Afterward leave the house while uttering the prayer stated above. If you have done the work five times, while you are returning to the house a sixth time, utter the prayer stated above, and the spirits will come in beautiful forms, dressed in ornate clothes. They will undertake your petition, whatever it was. They will help you in knowledge and understanding. The power of the spirits will shield and cover you. After these things have been accomplished in this proper order, gather friends and associates, and eat these foods together, and drink the wine, smell those fragrances, and suffumigate everyone with those suffumigations. Roman sages used to make this prayer to the planets each year, especially to Jupiter.

§13 *A ritual of Mars.* When you wish to operate through Mars, do this on Tuesday with the Sun in Aries (which is the house of Mars) and with the Moon in the mansion *Cahadabula* (which is the exaltation of Mars).[45] Do this at the end of winter when the trees bear fruit. Take a cow or a sheep sacrifice; a censer filled with charcoals; a suffumigation made of myrrh, mustard, and sarcocolla;

a woven basket full of offerings (namely, the best you can make); and a pitcher filled with wine. Carrying all of the above with you, go to a field, and climb up a tree. Drop the sacrifice from your hands, and light a fire wherein you should place the suffumigation. Speak these words: "DAHAYDANUZ, HAHAYDIZ, HAYDAYUZ, MIHYRAZ, ARDAHUZ, HEYDAHEYDEZ, MEHENEDIZ, DEHYDEMEZ." This is the prayer to Mars. Once you have spoken these things, say: "This sacrifice is for you, spirits of Mars! Take and eat from it, and do what you will!" Afterward, bring that same sacrifice to some place away from the tree, and suffumigate yourself with the abovementioned suffumigation. Decapitate your sacrifice, flay it, and roast its liver. Take the offerings that you have brought with you, and lay them all out on the hide. Lay this sacrifice upon it, and speak the prayer. Then speak this: "O spirits of Mars, this is your sacrifice! Come, and smell this suffumigation, and make what you will from that sacrifice and those offerings." At that moment, a red spirit will descend like a tongue of flame. While passing over those offerings, it will consume some of them. Once you have seen it, ask what you wish. [144] It will assist you in all your operations. When that flame dies down, go to the offerings, and eat as much as possible. Likewise, drink as much wine as possible, then ask a request relevant to Mars. Know that Mars is a diverse planet, powerful in his nature and inconsistent in his reception and hearing. Therefore, once you have performed the ritual of Mars, even if he has not come at the abovementioned conjunction, do not lose hope. Return home once you have carefully completed these tasks.

§14 *A ritual of the Sun.* When you wish to operate through the Sun, do this on Sunday with the Sun in Leo and the Moon in the fifteenth or nineteenth degree of Aries. Prepare a suitable house, which is clean and tidy, and decorate it with the priciest cloth that you can get. Place seven golden images in it. If you cannot have them made of gold, at least have them made of wood. If you manage to get them made of gold, place assortments of jacinth stones, rubies, and pearls on them. If the images, however, were made of wood, cover them with red silk garments, and on these place assortments of gold, jacinth, and rubies.[46] Place those images in the middle of the house. Prepare a table in front of each of the images. On each of the tables, place pies made from refined flour, dry, and moist ingredients. In the middle of each of them place a pitcher of wine and near it a vessel filled with spices and fragrant things like musk, camphor, and amber. Place myrtle throughout the house. Light a large wax candle, position yourself seated upon something elevated facing the images, and say: "TEBDELUZ, DIHYMEZ, ANDULEZ, DEHYCAYZ, AGINAFEZ, MAHAGNUZ, AHADYZ, TUYMERYZ!" Once you have spoken this, state the request that you set out to ask. When this is done, gather some of your friends and associates, and eat with them this food, and drink the wine. Afterward, leave the house because the spirits of the Sun will grant you what you have sought and heed your request.

§15 *A ritual of Venus.* When you wish to operate through Venus, do it on Friday when the Sun is entering Pisces and the Moon is sitting in Cancer. Purify yourself, and enter a bath. Once you are clean and bathed, find and climb a fig or palm tree. Bring a ram with you. Say: "HUEYDEZ, HELYUZ, HEMYLUZ, DENERIZ, TEMEYZ, CEMLUZ, ARHUZ, MEYTARYZ!" Once you have spoken the above, ask what you wish. Beware not to ask any of the planets anything other than what is attributed to their respective natures.

§16 *A ritual of Mercury.* When you wish to operate through Mercury, do it on Wednesday with the Sun in Capricorn, because the Chaldean year begins at that time. [145] Sit on a golden throne in an empty house. Suffumigate yourself with aloewood, incense, myrrh, hemlock, and elecampane. Put a golden table before you. Place seven goats in a circle, which you will strike with a wooden stick to make them yelp. While the smoke of the suffumigation is rising, say: "BARHUREZ, EMIREZ, HAYTIZ, COCIZ, DERIZ, HENIZ, DEHERIZ, ZAHUDAZ!" Once you have said these things, decapitate the goats, and flay them. Cut them up into pieces in a circle around the table, continually suffumigating the suffumigation. While doing the above, cover your whole face completely except the eyes, suffumigating continually. Afterward, exit the house. Carry out all the meat cut in the manner described above. Cook it in a pot with vinegar. Find bread made from refined flour. While suitable, place all these things in a woven basket, and set it aside with preservation in mind. Ask your petition from the questions pertinent to Mercury.

§17 *A ritual of the Moon.* When you wish to operate through the Moon, do it when the Sun is in Cancer and the Moon is sitting in Aries (which is the exaltation of the Sun). Do this ritual on Monday night (namely, on Sunday, when the day is over).[47] Once the Sun sets, go to a field. After you have washed yourself and become well cleansed, bring a ram and a suffumigation made of frankincense, hemlock, elecampane, myrrh, and aloewood. Bring some of your friends and associates with you, and make each of them lead a ram and carry the suffumigation. Make them carry offerings in woven baskets. When this is done, they should light a large fire with wood. Place the woven baskets of food around the fire. The one to whom the request is of interest should rise up and sit on some source of water facing a fig tree around which he had led the ram. He should place the suffumigation that he carried in the fire. He should say: "HEDYUZ, DENEDIZ, MUBRYNAYZ, MILTAZ, TYMEZ, RABYZ, CELUZ, DEHENIZ, MERNIZ!" Once he has said the above, decapitate the ram. Each of the associates should let go of the ram that he led. Since all the rams will come to you, cut all their throats while speaking the words above during the decapitation of each one as you suffumigate the suffumigation. At this point, leave that place, and return to the place of the lit fire. Next, you yourself and all your associates should go to the place of the slaughtered rams. Skin them and bury their pelts, heads, feet, and all their inner organs in a pure place where no animal might eat them. Roast the rams. Once well roasted, put them back in the baskets of offerings around the fire. When sunrise is near, place cloths of different colors under that fig tree. While you are doing these things, suffumigate with the abovementioned suffumigation. Speak the prayer of the spirits three times, and state your requests. All will be fulfilled. [146]

Chapter 10

On the Demonstration of the Planetary Spirits' Compounds; Reducing Damage from Rituals and Effects; the Wonders of Magic and Foods, Suffumigations, Ointments, and Fragrances That the Operator of the Planetary Spirits Must Use; the Effects Proper to the Planets and the Effects That Operate Unseen

§1 In the aforesaid *Book of Antimaquis*, which he put together for King Alexander, Aristotle related the makeup of four stones that have powers and wondrous effects upon spirits. The first stone he named *Rayetanz*. Whoever carries this stone encrusted in a ring will be humbly obeyed by any human or animal with a spirit. If one were to use this stone to imprint the seal of a letter and send it to a king (or any other person), when that king (or another) sees it, they will at once tremble and obey it. Through the spirit, what is sought will be endlessly accomplished. Wicked men would do likewise if the letter were transmitted as above. This stone is red in color, and its composition is this: 2 oz. of ground rubies mixed in with a half dram of ground diamond with 1 oz. each of ground lead and magnesium; ½ oz. of sulfur; and 2 oz. of gold. Mix all these things in a crucible, and place them on a low fire, increasing it gradually until they fuse. The ruby is melted by the power of the diamond; the diamond is melted by the power of the magnesium; the magnesium is melted by the power of the sulfur; and the gold also fuses with them. When they have been well mixed, remove the crucible from the fire, and allow it to cool down. You will find one completely mixed body with a muddy color. Remove it. Take the brain of a lion, the fat of a leopard, and the blood of a wolf—equal parts of each. Liquefy the fat, and mix it with the brain. Throw the blood on it, and it will turn tawny in color. Beware not to touch it with your hands nor should you go near it with your clothing. Avoid its smell entirely because this is a deadly poison in all of its qualities on account of its particular shape (according to Cetras regarding dreams). When it has settled down, remove it. Take 10 oz. each of arsenic, saffron, and yellow and red sulfur. Pulverize and purify them, and throw them on top of this poison. At once, its toxicity is subdued and wholly dissolved. Once everything is liquefied and mixed together, place it in a small urn or vase that should be plugged with goldsmith's luting and put over a low fire. When the whole thing is liquefied like wax, lift it from the fire, and allow it to cool. Liquefy the first substance, gradually add the spirit until everything is blended and homogenous. Once this is done, take it out of the fire, and allow it to cool. From this make small, suitably sized, round pebbles [147] on a lathe, since Aristotle said this to Alexander: "O Alexander, know that this is a body that surpasses all wonders."

§2 The second stone is named *Helemetiz*. This stone is recommended against rain, hail, and snow. When any of these happen, raise this stone with your right hand toward the heavens, and you will be safe. This stone is tawny in color. Its composition is this: take 4 oz. of hellebore, and liquefy it in the fire with white wolfsbane. When it is liquefied, add 4 oz. of silver and 4 oz. of lead. When all things have been liquefied together, lift it from the fire, and work it with the powers of the spirits. Take bones from the hands and feet of a pig, which are well-cleaned from flesh and nerves, then cook them well in brine. Once sufficiently cooked, lift them from the fire, and let them dry. Pulverize and liquefy them with mandrake and chalk in an earthenware vase, well-sealed with goldsmith's luting—that is, place first in that vase one part of chalk and mandrake, then on top of it another portion of bone dust in turn until the vase is filled. Liquefy these over a dung fire for one night. Afterward, remove the vase from the fire, and allow it to cool. Grind these things into a powder. Toss a small amount of red and clear arsenic on top of it. Grind them up again with human blood sprinkled from a vein. Grind them up for an entire day, then set them aside for use. Once these things have been accomplished, melt the first substance upon which, little by little, should be thrown this latter substance until they are well-blended. When this is done, remove it from the fire, and allow it to cool because you will find it tawny in color. Work this stone into an appropriately-sized, spherical shape on a lathe. Subsequently, work with the words and operations that we have stated above on the works of "Perfect Nature."[48] If you see rain, snow, hail, and thunder anywhere and if you want to remove them from your area, speak those words that we have stated before, and raise your right hand holding the stone toward the heavens. Everything will settle. This is the stone composed from immaterial powers and spirits.

§3 The third stone is called *Astamatis*. Aristotle says that this stone is one of the wonders of the world because whoever carries it into a quarrel or battle will stand secure against harm, enemies, and deadly weapons (both themselves and their associates). The composition of this stone is this: take 10 oz. of iron liquefied in sulfur. Melt it over a fire, and place on it the white stone of magnesium and borax, all well-pulverized until fully blended. At first it will appear yellow, then white like silver but even more beautiful (and the substance will be smooth). Then take a measure of pig fat and brains. Liquefy [148] and mix them with the blood of a black crow. Allow the mixture to cool, and it will harden like a coagulate. Then take 4 oz. of magnesium; ½ oz. of burnt diamond; 2 oz. of red and clear arsenic; and 4 oz. of yellow sulfur. Grind and pulverize everything together. Throw the resulting powder over the coagulated substance. Place everything into a suitably sized earthenware vase. Its opening should be sealed in the best possible way with goldsmith's luting. Thus prepared, place it over a fire, and the entire thing should melt like wax. Then remove it from the fire, and allow it to cool. It will coagulate and take the shape of a stone. Put it aside. Next take 10 oz. of iron processed as above and 1 oz. each of gold, silver, and bronze. Place them on the fire, and melt them until they are very well mixed. When this is done, throw that substance that you have just made into it gradually until mixed. Let the mixture be purified over the fire. The substances' dross will be purged, and these things will fuse and become very sleek. Once this is done, remove them from the fire, and allow them to cool. You will find those substances combined into one and be somewhat smooth. From this, work small, round stones of a suitable size on a lathe for three days with the words that we discussed. Save this stone, and carry it with you into war. You will be safe from all your enemies' iron weapons—you and all those present with you, so long as you have this stone.

§4 The fourth stone is called *Handemotuz*. Aristotle said that this stone exists for removing the desire for women. For example, it is made for soldiers and warriors before battle, since if they were to have sex with women, their bodies would become weaker, and consequently they would be more easily vanquished. This stone is white in color. Its composition is this: take 10 oz. of lead; 1 oz. each of bronze and iron melted with white sulfur; and ½ oz. of silver. Melt the bronze, iron, and silver together, then add the lead on top. When everything has been mixed together, take ½ oz. each of magnesium, diamond, and yellow sulfur; and 2 oz. of red arsenic. Pulverize everything, and throw the powder on the mixed substances until everything is absorbed. Next, lift it from the fire, and set it aside. Then make a spirit in this way: take equal portions of gazelle fat with the marrow and brain of a horse. Melt the fat, and mix it with the brain or with the marrow. Throw sparrow blood on it until it is congealed. After, take 1 oz. of pig bone, and pulverize it thoroughly with a little bit of borax, ½ oz. of magnesium, 1 oz. of yellow sulfur, and 1½ oz. of red arsenic. Throw everything together in a heap atop the marrow and fat we already referred to. Place it over the fire until the whole thing melts. Next, lift it from the fire, and allow it to cool. After it has cooled, take the substances that you have made before, and liquefy them over the fire. Add to them gradually the said medicine until they absorb it all. Everything will become slippery. Next, lift the mixture from the fire, and [149] allow it to cool. A stone ensues, which you should make spherical and even upon a lathe. Afterward, work for three days using the words that we have mentioned. Next, make two images of bronze, one in the shape of a man and the other of a woman. Place the stone in the image of the man. Have those images placed with their shoulders touching. Take an iron needle, and speak over it three times the words that we have said. When this is done, press it into the chest of the woman's image until the whole image is pierced through the shoulder. Push the needle into the image of the man such that both images are stuck together. Place those images thus prepared into a well-shut iron chest. Speak over it the words that we have spoken above day and night. Hold it, and you, all your associates, and soldiers will be wholly liberated from the desire for women.

§5 Aristotle narrates all these things in the aforesaid *Book of Antimaquis*. The makeup of these stones is a deadly poison. Whoever performs these operations should take due care to avoid their touch and smell. Here is an antidote for this poison with which these operations can be performed without fear. Take 2 oz. each of aloewood, seeds of myrtle, mandrake seeds, seeds of moringa;[49] ½ oz. of nutmeg; and 1 oz. each of chastetree, skinless grapes, and white sandalwood. Mix everything together, grind them up thoroughly, and combine with myrtle sap. Make pills, and allow them to dry. Whoever wishes to fashion the aforesaid stones, which are deadly poisons, should take some of those tablets and place them in their nostrils, ears, and mouth. He should cover his entire face with a cloth while these things are being pulverized and worked. Next the operators require some remedy for protecting the hands, which is this: take equal parts of laurel seeds and the kernels of basil seeds, with four measures of balsam and hare's blood. Grind the things that can be ground up, and mix them with the balsam and the hare's blood. Always have this medicine with you in all operations of these stones, and wash the hands of the operator, and it will be worked safely and without hazard.

§6 Aristotle says in the abovementioned book that the spirits sometimes attack those working on the aforesaid stones by cursing their natures. When you wish to free the operators from this infirmity so that their natures may be returned to their normal states, give them to drink the medicine written out below. Take ½ oz. of human blood, and mix it with 4 oz. of sweet almond oil and 2 oz. of rabbit's marrow or brain, and mix them with 1 oz. of donkey urine. Combine these things, and give them to drink to the ones suffering (every day for nine days on an empty stomach). By this medicine they will be cured, and their natures will be made right. The seven evil planetary spirits, whatever kind they were, will be driven from them with their natural complexion remaining strong. [150]

§7 Aristotle said this in the book named *Malatiz*.[50] When Alexander inquired about Caynez, an Indian sage and master of this wondrous art, Aristotle wrote this book *Malatiz* based on Caynez's knowledge, wherein he recounted the miracles done by that Caynez, who was thought to be a spiritual man who had lived for 840 years. He existed at the time of King Aydeneruz, who was a powerful murderer. This sage performed great miracles by mixing the macrocosm and the microcosm. His words are made of the spirits that exist in the composite world. He attracted the will of the aforementioned king and of other kings whom he wanted. Moreover, he would perform miracles and various prayers, which I have decided to relate at present.

§8 *For acquiring the love of women.* He called this mixture *Deytuz*, whose composition is this: take ½ oz. each of gazelle marrow and cow fat. Melt them both together, and add ½ oz. portion of camphor and the brain of a hare. Place all these things in an iron vase over a fire until liquefied. Lastly, add powdered camphor to this. When everything has been mixed together, it should be pulled from the fire. Then make an image of fresh wax, which has never been used, and keep in mind that woman whom you desire. In the mouth of that image, make a hole leading all the way into its belly, through which the aforesaid liquid medicine should be poured. While pouring say: "DAHYELIZ, HANIMIDIZ, NAFFAYZ, DABRAYLEZ!" Next, place 2 oz. of white sugar into its mouth. Take a thin silver needle, and stick it into the chest of the image until it emerges between the shoulder blades. Once you have positioned the needle in this way, say: "HEDUREZ, TAMERUZ, HETAYTOZ, FEMUREZ!" After this is done, wrap the image in a white cloth and on top of it another silk cloth also white. Tie it with a silk thread. Fix it well under the chest, and let the two heads of string be joined together, which you will tie with seven knots. Upon each and every one of the knots, speak these words: "HAYRANUZ, HEDEFIUZ, FAYTAMUREZ, ARMINEZ!" Afterward, place the image into a small earthenware jar, which you will plug with goldsmith's luting. Dig a hole in the person's house on behalf of whom this operation is being conducted (in whatever house or place he would prefer). Bury the image there, head up, and cover it with soil. Afterward, take 2 oz. each of incense and galbanum, and throw them into the fire. While the smoke is rising, say: "BEHEYMEREZ, AUMAULIZ, MENEMEYDUZ, CAYNAUREZ! I move the spirit of this woman N. and her will toward this man through the power of these spirits and through the virtue and power of the spirits BEHEYDRAZ, METLUREZ, AULEYUZ, NANITAYNUZ!" Once you have done these things, return home. Know that all the spirits and the intentions of that woman for whom the operation was performed will be turned toward that [151] man for whom it was conducted. She will not be able to rest nor sleep nor do anything until she is obedient to the man on behalf of whom such toil is poured out—all this by the power of the abovementioned image's spirits. By the power of these things, that woman will be led to the house where this image lies buried.

§9 *Another mixture for the same purpose taken as food.* Take 2 oz. each of dried hare's blood and wolf's brain; three grains' worth of melted cattle fat; two grains each of amber and nutmeg; three grains of camphor; and 2 oz. of the blood of the person doing the ritual (that is, the person on whose behalf it is done). Place this blood in an iron container over the fire until heated. Once heated, toss the other medicines on top. Mix everything. Remove them from the fire, and mix with wine or honey, a dish of meat or fowl, or with whatever dish you please. While doing the above, keep your mind firmly on the woman who is the target of this ritual. Afterward, take a small amount of incense and an equal amount of galbanum gum, and throw them into the fire. While the smoke is rising, say: "YE DEYLUZ, MENYDEZ, CATRUDIZ, MEBDULIZ, HUENEHENILEZ! I move the spirit and desire of this woman N. by the power of those spirits and this mixture. I move her spirit and desire with a feeling of anxiety as much in her waking and sleeping as in her walking, standing, and sitting. May she have no rest until she obeys those spirits that we will name: HUEHEYULEZ, HEYEDIZ, CAYIMUZ, HENDELIZ!" Once you have done the above, give to eat the entire mixture to whomever you desire until nothing is left. While this medicine sits in the stomach of the consumer, she will be unable to rest—rather, she will be moved by a powerful emotion. Obeying it, she will go to the place you desire. If perchance, on account of difficulty, it happened that you could not get this chosen woman to eat or drink the mixture described above, use it, but instead of the adept's blood, use the blood of the one against whom the ritual is performed. Mix everything very well into one mass, stir it into food or drink, and place it in the cup of your hand. Take 2 oz. each of incense and galbanum, and suffumigate with them. While the smoke is rising, say: "ADYERUZ, METAYRUZ, BERYUDEZ, FARDARUZ! I move the spirit and desire of such a person toward such a person, and I move her by all her spirits, desires, and heart such that she may neither rest nor be calm while waking, sleeping, speaking, sitting, nor standing until she submits to such a person and fulfills his desire. I draw the spirits of her heart and move them toward such a man through the power of those spirits: VEMEDEYZ, AUDUREZ, MEYURNEYZ, SANDARUZ!" Then give this mixture to eat to that person (the one for whom the ritual is performed). When the man will have eaten and swallowed this mixture, order him to take 2 oz. each of incense and galbanum in his hand, and throw them into the fire. Let him be suffumigated. While the smoke is rising, say these names: "HAMUREZ, HEYDUREHIZ, HELDEMIZ, HERMENIZ!" When this has been spoken, have him say: "By these names, the desires of that woman for whom you have performed the ritual are attracted." She will come to you with great love and obedience [152] in order to fulfill your desire and command. Furthermore, the same sage said that if you are unable to obtain that woman's blood, find 2 oz. each of wolf and cow blood. Mix them in an iron vase over a fire as above. Throw upon them two grains of rabbit marrow; three grains of wolf marrow; and four grains of cow fat, all melted and mixed together. Add two grains each of nutmeg, camphor, and rabbit cheese. When all this is well mixed and melted, remove it from the fire. Give that mixture in drink or food, and suffumigate with incense and galbanum. While the smoke is rising, say these words: "ANIMUREZ, MAPHUELUZ, FENIZ, FADRULEZ! I move the heart, spirits, and desires of such-and-such toward such-and-such, and I move her spirit by preventing her sleep such that she may have no peace in waking, sleeping, standing, walking, or rising. I move her spirit and desire and lead her toward such-and-such a man by the power of the spirits written here: HUEYTAYROZ, BERYENUZ, AUNUHIZ, ANDULEZ!" Once you have spoken this and made the mixture above, give it to the man in food. While it sits in his stomach, take 2 oz. each of incense, galbanum, and the hairs of a wolf tail. Then suffumigate him with it. Teach him these names that are to be spoken just as they are: "HEYUDEZ, MAHERIMEYZ, TAYDUREZ, UMEYRUZ!" Once this is done, know that the spirit and nature of the woman for whom this ritual was performed will feel a great love and desire for that man. She will be unable to rest in any activity until she goes to that man humbly inclined.

§10 *Another mixture, that is, a suffumigation for love.* Take 2 oz. each of a wolf's vulva and rabbit's penis; 1 oz. of male white cat's eyes; 2 oz. each of white dog's fat, incense, and galbanum. Melt a quantity of cow fat equal to the weight of all these in an iron vessel. Throw all these things on top. When everything is mixed together, take ½ oz. of camphor; 1 oz. each of white sandalwood and aloewood; ½ oz. of amber; and ¼ oz. of nutmeg. Grind them up, throw them onto the aforesaid mixture, and mix them very well. When this is done, the result should be divided into seven equal parts. Find seven censers filled with lit charcoals. Place them before you in a single straight line, and place a portion of the mixture in each of them. While the smoke of these censers is rising, say: "AHAYUARAZ, YETAYDEZ, AHARIZ, AHARYULEZ! I move the heart, spirit, and nature of such-and-such a woman toward such-and-such a man. I move the spirits of her own heart with love and desire toward that man by preventing her any sleep or rest. May she have no calm in sleeping, walking, sitting, or in any other activity until she submits to him, well performing his pleasures and commands. I myself attract and draw her spirits toward him by the power of those spiritual spirits: ALHUERIZ, HEYEMIZ, HUETUDIZ, TAUEDUZ!" Once this is done, return to your house. That woman will come to him and submit thoroughly to his pleasures and commands. [153]

§11 *Another suffumigation for the same purpose, to be inhaled.* Find two grains of rabbit cheese and one grain of goat liver. Throw powdered incense over them. Place it all on the fire, and roast it until all its moisture escapes. Afterward, take it with iron tongs, and divide it into many parts with a knife. Compress it into a jar until all the water escapes, and set this water aside in a glass vessel. When you wish to perform the ritual, take two grains of this water, three grains of nutmeg, and four grains of amber. Place all these over a fire of coals in an iron vase until they are liquefied and mix. Remove them from the fire, and transfer them into a glass vessel. When you wish to operate with it, take 1 oz. of the finest pure oil of amber, and place in an iron vessel over a fire. Place upon it a single grain of the mixture from the glass vessel, which you should liquefy so that they are mixed and homogenous. When this is done, take 2 oz. each of incense and galbanum, and suffumigate with them. While the smoke is rising, say: "YETAYROZ, MAHARAHETYM, FAYTOLIZ, ANDARARUZ! I move the heart of such-and-such a woman, her spirits, and her desires toward such-and-such a man, and I move the spirits of her heart toward this man with love and desire by preventing her sleep, rest, and tranquility. May she have peace neither in sleep, nor waking, sitting, nor standing! I attract and draw her spirits and desires toward that man by the power of those spiritual spirits: HUEYQUITAROZ, HEDILEZ, MENHUERIZ, MEYEFUREZ!" Once you have said these things, take some of the abovementioned oil, and with it anoint the woman for whom the ritual is being performed (if you can). If you cannot, place it on something people smell from, and make the woman for whom the ritual was done smell it. Once she is anointed with it or smells it, her spirits and desires will be moved immediately by a powerful feeling, a great love and desire toward the man for whom the ritual has been performed. She will have peace neither in sleep nor in waking, nor any rest whatsoever until she goes to him, obedient and tame. If perhaps you were unable to give it to her to smell, make a wax image in her likeness. Send it to her that she might hold it in her hands. Suffumigate it with incense and galbanum for three days continually. Do this at the rising of the Sun while speaking the words above, suffumigating with the suffumigation, and anointing yourself with the oil. Once this is done, her spirits and desires will be moved toward him with affection.

§12 If you want to work the image in another way, take a branch of myrtle or some other fragrant plant, good or bad, and anoint it with two grains' worth of the abovementioned medicine. Then suffumigate the image with incense and galbanum. While the suffumigation is rising, say this: "NEFORUZ, HEMIRULIZ, ARMULEZ, FEYMERIZ! I myself move the heart of such-and-such a woman and her spirits and desires toward such-and-such a man. I move [154] her spirit and nature toward him with affection and desire. I remove from her sleep, wakefulness, and peace in sleeping, waking, getting up, and sitting down. I attract her and draw her forth with the power of those spiritual spirits: VENEHULEZ, MANTAYRIZ, FEYMELUZ, BERHUNEZ!" Then make the woman you want (namely the woman for whom it was done) smell it. When she has smelled it, at once her spirits and desires will be moved by a powerful feeling and a great love and desire. Thus, she will be able neither to sit still nor to rest in any way until she goes obediently to the place of that man to fulfill all his wishes. If you cannot give her the aroma, make the wax image we mentioned above. The agent (namely, that man who ordered this work to be done) should hold it in his hands, and he should take 2 oz. each of incense and galbanum, which he should throw into a fire with his own hands. Teach him to say these words: "HEYDINEZ, BEYDURIZ, AFFIHUZ, DERIYENUZ!" Then make that man on whose behalf this ritual is done smell these things. At once, the spirits and desires of the target woman and her heart will be moved with great affection and desire. She will be unable to rest in any kind of peacefulness or tranquility until she goes obediently, prepared for the will of the querent, so that she may fulfill his every wish.

§13 Thus, Decaytus named these four composite images that we have mentioned (the ones that the sage Caynez cited for the joining of men and women).

§14 *For acquiring the love of a king.* When you wish the love of a king and to attract his benevolence toward the people, take fresh wax, and make an image in the name of that king whom you have selected to influence. Find ½ oz. of gazelle brain; 1 oz. of rabbit brain; and 2 oz. of human blood. Mix everything together in an iron vessel, and place it over a fire until everything is blended. Then throw upon that mixture 1 oz. each of powdered camphor and amber with ¼ oz. of nutmeg. This should be thrown atop the first medicine. Distribute these things until everything melts and is mixed together. Next, make a hole in the head of the image through which the medicine should be poured into its belly. Plug that hole very well with wax. Afterward, take 4 oz. each of human blood, the blood of a white cock, and the brain of a horse; ½ oz. each of nutmeg and camphor; and 2 oz. of liquefied cow fat. Add all these, and keep them all over the fire. Make a hole in the throat of the image through which you should pour those things, and allow them to cool down. Then shut that hole with wax. Next take a thin silver needle, a new one that has never been used, and stick it into the chest of the image in such a way that it does not go through to the other side. While you are sticking it in, say: "ACRIUZ, FENDEYUZ, NEPHALEZ, FEYEDUZ!" Then place the image into an earthenware vessel, the outside [155] sealed with luting. Then take 1 oz. each of incense, powdered galbanum, and the eyes of a white cock, and mix them all together. Afterward, take the image, this suffumigation, and a single censer, and climb up a tall mountain from which you can see a city. There, make a hole the size of the image, and bury it head or face downward. Place a stone or a brick upon the mouth of the container or vessel, and throw soil upon it until everything is covered. When this is done, throw the suffumigation into the fire. While the smoke is rising, say: "ACDERUZ, MADUREZ, FEYLEUZ, HUERYRELIZ!" Then say: "I turn the heart of such-and-such a king with love, friendship, goodwill, and mercy toward such-and-such a man or such-and-such a people by the strength and power of those spiritual spirits: HUEYFEDUEZ, AFFIMUZ, BEEFINEZ, MEDARIUZ!" Know that this king will esteem that man or people, extending them his grace.

§15 *For generating enmities.* He says: a mixture for generating enmity, which is given to eat, is the following.

§16 Take ½ oz. each of black cat's gallbladder and pig brain; 2 oz. of black dog's fat; and two grains of sweet myrrh. This mixture, once eaten, attracts the spirits of enmity and malevolence.

§17 *For the same.* Take 2 oz. of black cat's brain; 1 oz. each of pig gallbladder and brain; ½ oz. each of black dog's penis, sweet myrrh, and ammoniac. Make a suffumigation with all these things mixed together, and it will be as above.

§18 *For the same.* Take three grains of black dog's gallbladder; 2 oz. each of pig brain, black cat's gallbladder, pig grease, sulfur, sweet myrrh, black cat's eyes, and oil of *caubac*[51]; two grains of arsenic; 4 oz. of black cat's brain; and 1 oz. of hairs from its tail. If a suffumigation is made from all these mixed together, it will generate malevolence and enmity. A certain sage has worked these confections, and he claimed to have found them to work.

§19 *So that a man may have no desire for a woman.* When you want to do this, take ½ oz. each of black cat's brain and mandrake seeds. Mix those two things together, and blend them very well. Next make a wax image with a hole on top of its head through which you should throw the abovementioned mixture. Next make an iron needle, and press that needle into the image (that is, in the place where the delight of a woman is).

§20 Next, take 4 oz. of pig blood; 2 oz. each of rabbit cheese and swallow's brain; and 1 lb. each of cow milk and myrtle sap. Mix all of these things together, and serve it in a drink to that man from whom you wish to strip the desire for a woman. Suffumigate him with 2 oz. each of mixed incense and galbanum. What you wish shall ensue. [156]

Chapter 11

On the Effects of an Image upon Various Things; On the Alterations of Sight, to See Things Other Than How They Are; Also, on How to Sleep and Wake, Make Poisons, and Their Remedies

§1 I have discovered these compounds in books of this art's sages, none of which are found in the words of Caynez.

To bind tongues lest they speak evil of you. When you want to bind tongues lest they speak evil, put together this mixture. Take the tongues of everything listed here: a crow, an eagle, a toad, a water snake, a white dove, a white cock, and a hoopoe. Grind up all these tongues, and gather them together as one. Afterward, take one grain of pearl; ½ oz. each of gold, silver, camphor, borax, and aloe. Pulverize everything, and mix them together. Then add them with the powder mentioned above, and mix the whole thing with honey. Next, put them in a white silk cloth. Then take two eyelashes from a hawk, two eyelashes from a peacock, the liver of a hoopoe, the liver of a cock, two wing bones of a dove, and two wing bones of a hoopoe. Pulverize all those things, mix them with milk, and place them in the white silk cloth mentioned above with the mixture. Afterward, make a white wax image, which you will name after yourself. Write your name and the symbol of the Sun on its head. On its chest, write your name and the symbol of the Moon. Next, wrap the image in another white silk cloth, and put it wrapped up in the middle of the abovementioned mixture. Then bind the whole thing with silk thread. Whoever carries an image thus prepared will behold wonders nor will anyone speak evil of them. They will be loved and esteemed by all.

§2 *For love.* Take 5 oz. of gazelle brain; 1 oz. of leopard blood; and 2 oz. of rabbit cheese. Mix everything together, and blend them very well. Give this mixture to whomever you desire in food or drink, and they will fall in love with you.

§3 *For the same.* Take 2 oz. of white dog's blood and just as much of its brain; and 4 oz. each of gazelle brain and human blood. Suffumigate whomever you wish with those things blended and mixed together. That person's spirit will feel love toward you.

§4 *For the same.* Take 4 oz. each of chicken blood and brains, rabbit blood, gazelle blood, and human blood. Mix and blend everything together. To these add 2 oz. of mandrake seeds. If you have suffumigated someone with these things, you will see great wonders.

§5 *For the same.* Take 2 oz. each of a white dove's brain and blood and eagle blood; 1 oz. of rabbit cheese; and ½ oz. of hawk brain. Mix everything into one mass, and blend it well. Give this mixture to whomever you desire as food, and you will be loved by him.

§6 *For the same.* Take 1 oz. each of cock blood, leopard blood, rabbit cheese; and 2 oz. of human blood. Mix everything together, and add 1 oz. of euphorbia. [157] Whoever you suffumigate with that compound will esteem you. Their spirit and desires will be moved toward you.

§7 *For the same.* Take 2 oz. each of sparrow blood and brain; 1 oz. each of female cat blood and brain; 4 oz. of human blood; and ⅓ oz. of euphorbia. Mix them, and give the mixture in a drink to whomever you wish.

§8 *For the same.* Take a measure of black cat's brain and human urine. Mix them, and give it as food to whomever you wish. Their spirits and desires will be moved in love toward you.

§9 *For the same.* Take 4 oz. each of a red dog's blood and brain; 2 oz. each of rabbit cheese, dove blood, cock blood; and 1 oz. of euphorbia. Mix everything, and suffumigate whoever you wish with it.

§10 *For the same.* Take 8 oz. of donkey blood and 1 oz. each of fox blood and hedgehog blood. Mix everything, and add 2 oz. of euphorbia to the mixture. With this you will suffumigate whomever you desire.

§11 *For generating discord and enmity.* These compounds are put together for enmity and malevolence.

§12 Take 4 oz. of black cat's blood; 2 oz. each of pig blood and brain; and 1 oz. of donkey brain. Mix everything together, and blend it well. Whoever you have given this medicine to in food or drink will hate you.

§13 *For the same.* Take 4 oz. each of black cat's blood and of chastetree; 2 oz. each of kite brain and blood and fox blood; and 4 oz. of chastetree. Pulverize the chastetree, then mix everything together. If you suffumigate someone with this, their love will be purged, and their desire and spirit will fall away from love.

§14 *For the same.* Take 2 oz. each of fox blood and monkey blood; and 1 oz. each of cat blood, wolf blood, monkey brain, and pig brain. Once everything is mixed and blended together, if you give it to someone as food, the same as above will happen.

§15 *For the same.* Take 2 oz. each of toad and crane brain; 4 oz. each of a red dog and black cat's blood; and 1 oz. of pig grease and the brain of a red dog. Mix everything together, and add 4 oz. of cinquefoil. With this, suffumigate that individual by whom you wish to be hated.

§16 *For the same.* Take 4 oz. each of human and donkey blood; and 1 oz. of leopard blood. Mix everything together, and give it to whomever you want in food. The same as above will happen.

§17 *For the same.* Take 4 oz. each of black cat's blood and eagle blood; and 1 oz. of donkey blood. Warm those things up, and with them mix 3 oz. of chastetree. Make a suffumigation from this mixture for that man in whom you wish to elicit hatred.

§18 *These are the four suffumigations made for enmity, division, and massacres.*

§19 *The first of these.* Take equal parts of black cat's blood, a red dog's brain, and fox blood. Mix everything, and add 2 oz. each of St. John's Wort and chastetree. Suffumigate whomever you wish with this. [158]

§20 *The second for the same.* Take 4 oz. each of pig cheese and fat and female cat's blood; and 1 oz. of Egyptian vulture brain.[52] Mix everything, and add to it St. John's Wort and cinquefoil, each in equal portion to everything mentioned above. Pulverize everything together. Suffumigate whomever you wish with it.

§21 *A third one for the same.* Take 8 oz. each of crane brain and kite blood; 1 oz. each of rabbit cheese and blood; 1 oz. of donkey fat. Mix everything, and add chastetree in a portion equal to all the rest in weight. For whomever you suffumigate with these things, it will happen as above.

§22 *A fourth one for the same.* Take 1 oz. each of crow and vulture blood; and 4 oz. each of donkey fat and blood. Mix everything, and add chastetree to it in an amount equal to the weight of it all. Whomever you suffumigate with these things, the same as above will happen.

§23 *For the same.* Take 4 oz. of black cat's brains. Grind them up, and mix them with an equal amount of dried and ground human excrement. Give it as food to whomever you wish. To be sure, that individual will hate.

§24 Aristotle said: "A learned individual is one who understands the spirits' separations, unions, and natures—the layout of the macrocosm and microcosm. They know and understand the mutual separation and union of all things, both spiritual and material."

§25 *These are the seven mixtures that are given as food to men to prevent sex with women.*

§26 *The first of these.* Take 2 oz. each of horse brain, pig fat, and black cat's blood. Mix everything with 1 oz. of pulverized colocynth, give a little of this mixture to whomever you wish as food.

§27 *A second for the same.* Take equal parts of horse brain, pig fat, and wolf blood. Mix everything, and give half a dram as food to whomever you wish, and it will be as above.

§28 *A third for the same.* Take equal parts of monkey blood and brain; ostrich fat; and the eyes, hooves, and horn of a deer. Grind everything up, and mix it together. Give ½ oz. as food to whomever you wish.

§29 *A fourth for the same.* Take 4 oz. of donkey brain; 1 oz. of pig grease; and 2 oz. of horse blood. Mix everything, and give 8 oz. as food to whomever you want.

§30 *A fifth for the same.* Take 4 oz. of powdered pig bones; 2 oz. of peach leaves; 2 oz. each of burnt wolf fur, black cat's eyes, and donkey brain. Mix everything together. Give 8 oz. as food to whomever you wish.

§31 *A sixth for the same.* Take equal parts of black cat's blood and water buffalo brain. Mix them, and give 8 oz. as food to whomever you wish. [159]

§32 *Here are seven soporific mixtures that put all the spirits of the body to sleep—they are thought to be deadly.*

§33 *The first of these is this.* Take equal parts of pig brain and *chami* brain (an animal similar to a deer); add mandrake seed to a weight equal to the above-mentioned things. Give ½ oz. in a drink or as food to whomever you wish.

§34 *A second for the same.* Take 4 oz. of woodland black poppy seeds; and 1 oz. each of fox brain, human brain, and pig gallbladder. Mix them. Give a little to whomever you wish as food.

§35 *A third for the same.* Take equal parts of human sweat and black cat's blood; add mandrake seed of an equal weight to the mixture. Mix everything, and give 8 oz. to whomever you wish as food.

§36 *A fourth for the same.* Take 8 oz. each of pig brain and black cat's blood. Mix them, and give some to whomever you wish as food.

§37 *A fifth for the same.* Take equal parts of dove brain, pig blood, and the fat of a snake called the "deaf asp." Mix them, and give 8 oz. to whomever you wish as food.

§38 *A sixth for the same.* Take 4 oz. of cat urine; 2 oz. of horse sweat; and 1 oz. of colocynth. Mix everything, and give ¾ oz. to whomever you wish as food.

§39 *A seventh for the same.* Take equal parts of forest rue sap, human sweat, and pig brain. Mix everything together, and give 8 oz. to whomever you wish as food. This mixture kills through the power of its own spirits.

§40 *These are the ten mixtures that cause sleep and death.*

§41 In the *[Met]hedeytoz Book* are found ten mixtures that cause sleep and death.[53]

§42 *The first is this.* Take 2 oz. of coagulated black cat's urine; and 1 oz. each of mouse and *chami* brain.[54] Give 8 oz. to whomever you wish as food.

§43 *A second for the same.* Take equal parts of pig brain and sweat[55] and the salt of human urine. Mix them together, and give it to whomever you wish as food.

§44 *A third for the same.* Take 2 oz. each of monkey grease, dog brain, and the blood of *racanus* or *lagarius* (that is, any large green lizard). Mix them together, and give ½ oz. to whomever you wish as food.

§45 *A fourth for the same.* Take equal parts of donkey brain and human sweat. Mix them together, and give ½ oz. to whomever you wish as food, and the above will come about.

§46 *A fifth for the same.* Take equal parts of human semen and gazelle brain, and add animal sweat to the weight of these things. Mix them together, and give ½ oz. to whomever you wish as food.

§47 *A sixth for the same.* Take equal parts of human semen and gazelle brain. Mix them together, and give ¼ dram to whomever you wish as food. [160]

§48 *A seventh for the same.* Take equal parts of black cat's brain, bat brain, and wolf fat. Mix everything, and give 1 oz. to whomever you wish as food.

§49 *An eighth for the same.* Take equal parts of mouse brain and black crow's blood; add ¼ the weight of these things of colocynth. Mix everything, and give 1 oz. to whomever you want as food.

§50 *A ninth for the same.* Take 2 oz. of bear gallbladder and brain; 1 oz. each of mouse blood and black cat's grease. Mix everything together, and give 1 oz. to whomever you wish as food.

§51 *A tenth for the same.* Take equal parts of monkey and human brain. Mix them together, and give 1 oz. to whomever you wish as food.

§52 These ten mixtures have qualities and powers from the planets and the fixed stars along with the qualities of the things from which they were composed. Out from this mixture emerges a single spiritual power. The above-mentioned things are found in a book that is called *Hedeytoz*, compiled by the wise Hermes.

§53 In this book, he tells of a kind of mixture for performing miracles, and it is for lifting all curses from people (namely, those carrying this mixture on themselves).

Against the curses or enchantments of men. Take a frog's head and spine, and grind them together. Next, place in a silk cloth 1 oz. each of Berber's *aloaxac*,[56] donkey brain, and peony—all dried. Whoever fears curses should carry it on their person, and they will be safe from these things. Galen made this mixture for a certain king who ruled during his lifetime.

§54 *Miracles that arise from the properties of humankind.* In the book just discussed, Hermes said that the human body possesses many marvels pertaining to magical operations when one performs rituals with them (as did the sages who discovered this knowledge). From among these Hermes wrote of a wondrous mixture that produces many miracles, and it was made as follows. He took the whole head of a man who recently died and placed it in a large container. He added 8 oz. each of fresh opium, human blood, and sesame oil until the head was covered by them. He then shut the opening of the container very well with luting and placed it over a tame charcoal fire for a whole twenty-four hours. Then he removed it from the fire and let it cool down. He covered his face and strained these things, having found everything liquefied like oil. Then he put it aside. He said that there are many wonders in this oil. First of these is that it permits one to see those things one wishes to see. If you light a light with the oil or anoint something with it, or if you give a little of it to someone in food, you will see whatever you wish.

§55 *For appearing in the form of any animal you wish.* Take the head and fat of any animal you wish with datura seeds, using as much as necessary.[57] Cover them in a container with oil, and place them over a low fire, day and night, until all its oils run. Once cooled, strain the mixture very well. If you light a lamp with it and [161] anoint someone's face with it, that person will appear in the shape of that animal to witnesses. This mixture can be made from the heads of various animals, and thus that person would have the appearance of various animals.

§56 *For ruining the senses and thoughts.* Take a recently severed human head, and place it in a large container. Place with it that person's spleen, heart, and liver. Next, place in the same container the heads of the following animals: a cat, a fox, a monkey, a cock, a hoopoe, a crow, a kite, a bat, a gander, a swallow, a turtle, and an owl. Cover everything in oil in a container whose mouth should be very well shut with luting. Place it over a low fire where it should sit for three days and nights. Then remove it from the fire, and allow it to cool. Strain these things with a covered face. Set it aside in a container. Take the bones of these heads, and burn them in some other container until reduced to a powder. Mix this powder with seeds of black henbane and datura. Set it aside for use. When you wish to operate the aforesaid things, give some of that powder to whom you wish in food or drink, and light three lamps with that oil. You will see the things you have strived after. [*For making wonders appear on your figure.*] Take some of the oil mentioned above, and anoint your face with it. Enter the house lit with the said lamps, and you will appear monstrous in nature to witnesses.

§57 *For erasing the senses and memory.* Take 2 oz. each of hawk, mouse, and black cat's brain; and ½ oz. each of sulfur and myrrh. Mix everything, and set it aside until it rots. When you wish to operate, take 8 oz. of it and an equal amount of crane excrement. Blend them together, and place it over a fire until smoke rises up. Whoever breathes in that smoke through the nostrils will be turned into a demon. They will lose both perception and memory and be unable to recognize where they are.

§58 There are many other wonders arising from the human body. In one book published by the wise Geber, I found many wonders arising from the human body. He said this:[58] "I, Geber, observed that the elements do what they do when combined. Alone they can do nothing because they are self-contained.

When joined together such that all four are united, I saw how they create and cause generation, growth, and life. When one of these four is lacking, I saw how they cause death, withering, and corruption. Here I begin with humankind, starting with the head.

§59 The brain is good to eat for those who have lost their memory.

§60 Burnt skull drunk with squill extract for nine days cures epileptics. [162]

§61 Whoever carries a human eye bound with a wolf eye cannot be hindered by an evil eye nor a wicked tongue.

§62 Burnt and powdered human hair mixed with labdanum warms the brain.

§63 A fasting person's saliva heals scabies if the area is moistened often.

§64 If the saliva of a fasting man or woman is placed on a snake's head or mouth, it will die quickly.

§65 A woman's tongue helps those who wish to utter falsehoods or incantations.

§66 If one wishes to steal or carry off something, one should carry the tongues of both a human and a kite.

§67 Blood water absorbed into sublimated arsenic allows it to penetrate bronze melted over a fire.

§68 Ear wax causes the Moon or the Sun to melt or solidify.[59] With it one can solidify as quickly as with borax.

§69 Ear wax mixed with opium is a strong soporific.

§70 Brain fluid drunk with a mixture of brain heals the insane.

§71 Clip fingernails and toenails with a red bronze knife when the Moon is in conjunction with Jupiter, then burn them when she is conjoined with the Sun. Give that powder in a drink to whomever you wish, sprinkle the powder on their clothes, and they will fall in love with you.

§72 Give the patient burnt and powdered human foreskin to eat so that new leprosy or scabies (which is a kind of leprosy) may not grow. It shall spread no more.

§73 Human urine burns everything in its path. If someone has scabies, they should wash themselves in it, and they will quickly be cured.

§74 Human excrement dried in the Sun, powdered, and thrown onto a gold-iron alloy will corrode the iron, destroy it, and refine the gold.

§75 The oil in excrement softens the Sun and the Moon and increases their color.[60]

§76 Whoever has a deadly illness on the legs should wash them with excrement water distilled three times and on top should sprinkle the powder of that same burnt excrement. They will be cured quickly.

§77 One suffering from an acute fever should wash their head with human blood water. They will be cured.

§78 Wash a wound with blood water, and sprinkle the lime of the same blood onto the wound. It will be healed.

§79 Any burn, whether from fire or boiling water, if first cleaned with excrement water and then covered with its burnt powder will be healed.

§80 If you see a sick person who cannot recover through any medicine, wash them with blood water, and they will improve.

§81 Whoever has a great dryness within their body, give them blood water to drink, and he will be healed. [163]

§82 If someone is suffering from diarrhea, give them morsels of any blood you want, and they will be healed.

§83 If someone has quartan fever, take some human arm bone and some bone from the tip of a hawk's wing. People with fever should carry it with them, and they will be cured.

§84 Anyone with nightmares during sleep should be washed with excrement water, and they will be cured.

§85 The oil from excrement distilled three times and imbibed with an amalgam of the Sun and green silver water with dissolved cinnabar water tints the Moon and other metals.

§86 An eye salve made from human gallbladder heals tearing and cloudy eyes.

§87 Whoever has a canker sore or a fistula should burn blood, make lime from it, and throw it up in the air. First, however, wash the area with water distilled from blood.

§88 All human excrement dried in the Sun is very strong and sharp. It cured rheumatism and diseases from horses and other animals. It helps the eyes and removes cloudiness from the eyes of animals.

§89 A woman's menstrual fluid given to anyone will cause leprosy. If anyone bathes in it, they will die quickly.

§90 *The cure.* Take human sperm, and give it to them to drink. They will be cured. Similarly, they will be cured if they were given some evil *amreps* herbs.[61]

§91 Make a pouch with a human heart, and fill it with the blood of three other people, and warm it over a fire. Call the demons, and they shall respond.

§92 Collect your own sweat in a well-cleaned and beautiful bowl, then place it in a glass vessel. Place some shavings from your feet with a little bit of your own sun-dried excrement and the root of an herb called *fu* in Arabic but *valerian* in Latin. Give it to whomever you want to drink. They will fall in love with you.

§93 I, Geber, have tried this out, and it is most effective. Women, however, add the water with which they washed their behinds while pointing them eastward.

§94 All burned human meat and bones generate and provoke goodwill.

§95 Three measures of dead humans—that is, measure out a human corpse three times: measure out the length of the arm from the elbow to the middle finger, from the shoulder to the same finger, and finally from the head to the feet. There will be ruin and retrogradation.

§96 Blood extracted from a left-hand finger provokes enjoyment when the Moon is conjoined with the Sun or when the Moon is with Venus and given when the Moon is in opposition to the Sun. This is an experiment of the Egyptians. I myself have seen many men test and discover its power.

§97 Excrement water and snail water dissolve tartar. Quench bronze lamellae in it, and they will whiten. Throw into feather alum some dissolved glass, and it will improve. [164]

§98 Take the skin from a woman's vulva in a ring such that it retains its hole shape. Whatever you look at through it will be a sign of death. This is a matter requiring great purity. Likewise, it causes illness. This was taken from those Greeks called the Ephesians.

§99 Skin a man's penis, then tan and soften it like leather with salt and flour. Know that with it you can bind and release.

§100 The testicles of a man, dried, pulverized, and eaten with incense, mastic gum, cinnamon, and cloves, makes a man truly younger and gives him an exceptionally good color.

§101 A person's eyes bound up in a snakeskin cause whoever sees you to admire you and get out of your way. Rather, they will be good to you.

§102 Whoever is feverish or suffering from a headache should anoint their head with the milk of a woman, and it will remove the pain.

§103 The milk of a woman with opium causes the feverish and insomniacs to fall asleep.

§104 If you wish to go on a safe journey, make a pill from your semen and ear wax, and hang it from your neck. You will go safely. Certain sages would carry it around, saying there were a great many properties in it. Some of them believed there were seventy-two, to each of which they assigned a cause that none could deny.

§105 The umbilical cord of a newborn boy wrapped in a red silk cloth with the tongue of a green frog from a fig tree—whoever carries these will be honored by their lord (and others too).

§106 Whoever has bad pustules or bad scabies should anoint themselves in the hot Sun with blood oil distilled three times, then apply the dregs of the blood to the wounds. They will be cured. They should do this seven times or more. This we have demonstrated already in the book *On Properties*.

§107 A human right arm with the head of a greyhound in anyone's house is effective against lies.

§108 The distillate of human gall with a cat's eye helps and sharpens light. Whoever makes this does so in order to see wonders that seem to be demons.

§109 Take human blood, and mix it with magnetite and deadly nightshade, which is called the "herb of light."[62] From this make a clump, and carry it in a small gold or silver vessel. You will have power over all incantations, tricks, and illusions, especially if you collect the plant with your own hands and the blood is from your own body.

§110 Someone from Baldach told me that the herb that is called *fu* in Arabic (*valerian* in Latin; *amantilla* in Greek) has a similar power. He also told me that this mixture caused goodwill when eaten or given as a drink.[63]

§111 Take the vulva of a woman (that is, the skin), and carry it in a yellow cloth with the tongue of a snake bound to it. You will be powerful in making factions and friendships. A woman's pubic hair does the same. [If you wish to destroy a horse, take the herb that is called *tarsia*, crush it with the grease of a hog, and add some powdered human excrement. Anoint the horse between the armpits. Then its testicles will become swollen to the size of plates. When you want to cure that horse, take strong vinegar and smear its testicles. It will be healed. If you wish that those around you might appear to have the heads of beasts to one another, take the semen of any given beast while it is having sex, and mix it with wax. Set it on fire. They will appear with the head of that beast. The saliva of a fasting woman sprinkled onto plants dries them out, but the menstrual fluid of a woman does this more.][64] [165]

§112 I found all these things in a certain book published by the wise Geber.[65] The experiments written out below, however, I found in the [*Met*]*hedeytoz* book.

§113 *For blinding by suffumigation.* Take the blood of a dog, an ass, a cat, a goat, and a cow in equal parts. Mix all these bloods, and place them over a low fire until they are blended. Afterwards, add ground arsenic and an equal part of sublimated mercury. Then mix them all, and throw them into a single container. Seal it very well with luting, and place it in dung until it rots. Next, take it out and beware of its odor. If you place ½ oz. of this mixture in a fire, whoever ingests the smoke will have their vision blotted out by darkness such that they will never see light again. *The cure*: Take fennel sap and green coriander. Mix them, and place them over the eyes. From that moment they will be cured of blindness.

§114 *For rendering mute.* Take 2 oz. each of cock and bear gall; 4 oz. of bat blood; ½ oz. each of lettuce seed, black poppy seed, and mandrake root. Liquefy the blood, and mix it with the other things. Mix them very well, and let them dry. Afterward, grind them up with a well-aged, old wine, and make pills to the weight of ½ lb. If you give one of these to anyone in food or drink, they will swallow their tongues and be unable to speak at all. *The cure*: Fill the mouth of the afflicted person with oil or butter while holding it closed.

§115 *For rendering deaf.* Take equal parts of mandrake, cow gallbladder, and goat gallbladder. Mix and grind everything together. Allow the mixture to putrefy. Give ½ oz. of it in food to whomever you wish, and they will totally lose their sense of hearing. *The cure*: Put the sap of rue into the afflicted person's ears, and they will be cured.

§116 *For generating discord and enmity.* Take the heads of a lizard and a snake with equal parts of dog and black cat's hair. Mix them together, and burn them in a container until they can be ground up. If you were to throw some of this anywhere between people, enmity and conflict would arise between them until they killed each other. *The cure*: take 4 oz. of mallow seed and 2 oz. each of the blood of a white dove and a cat. Grind everything up, and mix it with the blood over a fire. Make tablets of ½ oz. in weight. When you want to remove such a discord, grind up one of these tablets, and throw the dust in that place (namely, where you threw the other powder). At once, the spirit of discord and enmity will depart.

§117 *A soporific mixture.* Take ½ oz. each of opium and black henbane seed; then ⅙ oz. of nutmeg, sukk,[66] and fresh aloewood. Grind them up, and blend them into a single mixture with the sap of green coriander; allow this to putrefy in a jar such that its complexions and spirits are mixed with each other. Next take it out of the jar, and give ½ oz. in a drink to whomever you wish. They will sleep for a great span of time, unable to be awoken. [166]

§118 *For the same.* Take 4 oz. each of datura, red arsenic, mandrake seed or husk, and black poppy; 6 oz. of saffron; and 2 oz. of henbane seed. Mix everything together, and put it away for three days to rot. Once this time has passed, remove it, and give ½ oz. mixed with wine to drink to whomever you wish.

§119 *For the same.* Take equal parts of opium, mandrake husk, lettuce seed, branches of datura, sap of *arcole*,[67] black hellebore, and black poppy seeds. Grind everything up, mix together, and blend with a quantity of well-aged wine to the weight of all of the above combined. Put this aside to rot for seven days. Afterward, remove it, and give ½ oz. in food to whomever you wish.

§120 *For the same.* Take equal parts of sap from henbane, mandrake, green coriander, lettuce, datura, and white henbane; and a tenth part of all the said ingredients of opium. Mix everything together. Next, take jelly made from figs milled four times in a wine press where grapes are crushed. Take as much jelly as of the other ingredients combined. Mix everything together. Put it aside to rot until all its complexions and spirits are blended into one. Do not give any more than ¼ oz. of this mixture as a dose on account of its excessive strength from the spirits in its ingredients.

[*A deadly spiritual poison.* Take one toad. Stretch it out on its stomach over a post. Affix each foot with a nail. Then hit it with a long stick. Little by little, it will swell up while getting angry, and it will spew forth a triple venom with a triple color. Place a dish under it and catch it. Finally, get rid of the toad. Letters, food, and other such things are deadly when anointed with this. When you set the venom to ferment in a lead vase, it becomes stronger. If you distill the fermented venom, it will penetrate more. If you extract the essence from it, it will be suited to your work. If someone puts a drop in hot water, it will work wondrously. After all the venom from innumerable animals and plants has been fermented and you give a drop in hot water or in simple poisons, then it will activate quickly. The most powerful poisons are made from toad. Through this, a famous monk killed Pope Julius through the Sun's rays. Poisons can be made to ferment with hot water, and afterward, one drop can be given in a glass of wine.][68]

§121 *A deadly poison.* Take equal parts of dried scorpion, datura, black poppy, and colocynth. Blend them into one, ground up, and put it aside to rot. Beware of that stuff for your own sake, because ¼ oz. of it is lethal.

[If you trap an owl with a viper in a glass container during summertime, they will fight and sweat. A drop of this sweat given in wine kills within an hour.][69]

§122 *For the same.* Take equal parts of wolfsbane,[70] *ariole*,[71] and fresh euphorbia. Blend them together, and set the mixture to rot with adder gall equal in weight to all the above in a container suited to this. Leave it aside until it rots. Afterward, remove it. Be careful since it damages and destroys the blood of the heart on account of its excessive heat and abundant sharpness, and it can quickly kill a man. [Similarly, there was that venom with which that woman from Florence pricked an ox with a needle. It died that night.][72]

§123 *For the same.* Take as many frogs as you can catch, and place them on a spit divided as you wish (that is, as many on their own spit as you wish) by piercing them through the mouth and out the anus. Then place them standing with their mouths toward the ground. Afterward, take a lead vase, and collect the oil leaking from their mouths. Know that the oil that comes out last is much more effective than the oil that comes out first. Set it aside for use. Oil of this kind harms and kills most powerfully on account of the damage it causes to the organs. The first man who discovered this deadly poison was Rufus. He tested it and discovered in it great wonders.[73]

§124 *A wondrous stone fashioned against poisons.* Kings of India used to have this stone made as described below on account of its miracles. The stone stood among all those splendid things they had at their disposal for defending against and warding off the dangers of poisons. The composition of this stone is this:

take ten deer eyes [167] and ten eyes of vipers or venomous snakes. If you are unable to obtain the vipers, determine a weight equivalent to the weight of those ten. As much as the weight of one of those eyes, take that much of toad face. Dry and clean everything very thoroughly, and grind it all up very finely. Then sift it as well as you can with a fine clean cloth. Next, mix them together, and grind thoroughly again. Then, place them in a glass container with a very narrow opening. Afterward, take ½ oz. each of wine made bitter with cedar and radish sap; and 1 oz. each of white, clean spider webs and mastic. Spin these spider webs most finely, and put them with the mastic into the two abovementioned saps. Allow them to remain there for two days and nights. Next, strain it gently and evenly, and combine it with the abovementioned powders in the container. When this is done, plug the opening of the container very thoroughly, and bury it in burning straw, leaving it there until everything is dissolved and reduced to a sort of oil. Afterward, mix the oil with water, and put it back again into the same burning straw until all the water has been evaporated. Then turn it over in such a way that it becomes blended. When this is done, remove it, and empty it into an eggshell so that it is made round. Place another eggshell on top, and seal it very well, then place it again in the same burnt straw. Leave it aside until it solidifies a little. Afterward, draw it out through a hole, wrap it in a silk cloth, and place it in dough to cook in an oven. When this is done, remove it, and put it into the stomach of some bird. Once inside, roast the bird. Next, take it out of the bird's stomach. If you find it to be well solidified in the form of a stone, that is good. Otherwise, put it back into the stomach of another bird. Roast as above, and proceed in so doing until it becomes a stone, which you should thread with a string and attach around the loins. Kings of India used to make this stone and carried it around their loins at all times. Its effect is that if anything poisonous is placed before the stone in food or drink or in any other thing, it will shake and sweat greatly. This is very well-known among them and is one of the great wonders they possessed.

§125 The first to fashion this stone on his own was King Behentater, one of the kings of India, a great sage.[74] He himself built the city of Memphis, in which he erected great buildings and set up in those buildings images that could speak. This was the man who discovered the calculations of love through number, which is a very wondrous thing among his people. When these numbers are given to two individuals in food or drink (or in any other manner), they become united by the best friendship and greatly delight in each other. If these numbers were carved into a piece of wood and with it you were to inscribe bread or something edible and then give it to someone to eat, they would fall deeply in love with you. If you inscribed those numbers on your clothes, they could not be [168] stolen from you. If you wrote them on clothes that were to be brought to market for sale, the same effect would happen. The lesser number of these is 220, but the greater is 284.[75] The operation with these numbers is this: write the lesser and the greater number in the symbols of al-Khwarizmi.[76] Give the lesser in food to whomever you wish while you yourself eat the greater. That person will become obedient to you just as the lesser is obedient to the greater. They will esteem you on account of the wondrous property and power of those numbers. In fact, these calculations can be done similarly with grape seeds, pomegranate seeds, or with whatever edible fruit you wish. This occurs through the number and not through the symbols. I myself have tested these calculations many times, and I have found truth in them just as written above.

§126 King Behentater made twelve pastures for the people of Egypt in twelve months—that is, one per month. Furthermore, he made a house wholly surrounded by images that in fact cured every illness. On each image's head he illustrated the illness assigned to each. For a long time, the people of that land were often cured from illness by those images in the following way. They would come to those images demanding health from them. They would show their illness to the image assigned to their infirmity, and at once, they were cured. Afterward, King Behentater made an image in the form of a laughing man, and it had this power. Whoever was sad or depressed by melancholy would stare at the image, and at once, he would be cheerful and laughing, his worries carried off to oblivion. The effect of this image was so great among the Egyptians that they came to worship it like a god. This same king fashioned a bronze image in his city with two outstretched wings, which he gilded entirely. Then he erected it somewhere in the city. The image's power was such that whoever passed by it—whether man or woman—if they had committed adultery, it would reveal their nature. They would be unable to avoid that image without bringing attention to themselves. The king built this image so that his people could be alerted to fornication. Whoever this image exposed as a fornicator or a fornicatrix was brought before the king. For his or her crime, the culprit was fully exposed and punished deservingly in accordance with the Egyptians' laws. For this reason, the king's subjects, both men and women, avoided that ungodly practice.

§127 Furthermore, King Behentater made an earthenware vase that he filled with water. His whole army could drink from it, and its contents never diminished. That king lived in the time of Alexander the Great, and it is said that King Behentater presented this container to Alexander with some other wondrous things. This vase had been fashioned with the disciplinary techniques of science, the properties of nature, and the knowledge of planetary spirits' strengths and of the fixed stars. Likewise, [169] Acaym, a king of India, fashioned a pillar atop the gate of a Nubian city.[77] It was made of black marble and completely filled with water. No matter how much was carried away from it, it never lacked water. This happened because it would attract the humidity of the air thanks to the skill of its fabrication. He built this work for the restoration of the people on account of that city's distance from the Nile and its proximity to saltwater. The Sun's rays caused thick and humid vapors to arise from the seawater; the subtler parts were purified of their saltiness in the air. Drop by drop, by means of the most clever geometric skill and the science of magic, the water would drip into that pillar from the air. Thus, the city was never lacking water on account of attraction, which arises just like when a bloodstone attracts whatever is placed around it.

§128 These Indians have other great wonders aside from these, some of which I will relate at present.

For preventing any bodily motion. Take the penis of a man, slice it into pieces, and mix in the powder of opium, datura, and a little bit of arsenic. Put it into a lead container to ferment, and be careful with it. Once you have extracted it from the dross, you will find it liquefied and reduced to a sort of oil. If you were to give a little bit of that oil in drink or food to whomever you wish, all their senses, movements, and spirits would be shut down and stupefied. They would be unable to use any limb. The Indians would make many miracles with this oil (with other things mixed in), and by giving it in food, they would reveal the extraordinary things they desired. They would give it in food to whomever they wanted, and by this they would reveal what they desired from among untold things. They would even change a person into whichever shape or form they wished.

§129 *To appear in the shape of any animal you wish.* Take the sperm of a man in possession of all his limbs, place it in an egg (that is, in an earthenware container), and mix it together with the sperm of the animal you wish. Afterward, close the container well, and put it to rot in warm excrement for three days. When this is finished, remove it and you will find the likeness of the animal in the container. Take it out, and put it into sesame oil, which you will leave aside for three days. That animal will absorb this oil for three days. While it is still alive, grind it up into that oil. If you light a lamp and anoint someone's face with it, they will appear in the shape of the animal whose semen you used. This is held as a noble secret among the Indians since they revealed it to none but those disposed to these things.

§130 *To prevent a person from leaving a city.* Take the sperm of a man and a little of his blood, which should be cooked up with twice as much honey until all the sperm has dissolved in it. Next, cook this honey until it is [170] good and black. Give some of it in food to whomever you wish (namely, whoever intends to undertake the long trip). Whoever eats it will be unable to leave the city on that day; rather, he or she will remain there, ravaged and senseless.

§131 *The great wonders of magic.* The Indians used to make another mixture with which they performed great wonders of magic. Its composition is this. They would take one sow and shut it in an empty house. In one corner, they would firmly fit the house with iron bars such that the sow could not leave the house. Inside, next to the sow, they would place a male pig prepared in the same way as she was. Thus prepared, they would leave them there for twenty-four days. They began this work when the Sun was entering the first degree of Capricorn. Every day they would give them a piece of wheat bread softened in milk to eat, as much as they wanted. At the end of those twenty-four days, the sow would be moved by an extremely powerful urge to mate with the male pig. Through such great excitement, the male pig projected a great amount of sperm that looked like pieces of coagulated blood. Those Indians had great techniques to collect this sperm. They would store it in a lead container, seal the opening very well, then put it to rot in dung for twenty-four days. Subsequently, they would remove it, open the container in a cold place, and discover an animal that was moving therein. They would feed it for three days with nuts and milk as we have said above regarding the sow. After three days, they plunged it to its death in oil, which they used to accomplish great miracles of magic by giving it in food, by lighting a lamp with it, by anointing faces and bodies with it, and many other wonders unworthy of mentioning on account of length. We request that performers of these rituals hold them as utmost secrets and not reveal them except to a person experienced in these things.

Chapter 12

On the Rules Necessary to This Science

§1 Whoever intends to be involved in this science must know that it is through works and experiments in this world that the depths and secrets of science become known. Through works and experiments, doubts are resolved. This is because doubt is dissolved when one achieves one's desire. You yourself, however, should be hungry for everything we have taught so far. Have faith in those works, the ways of the wise, and do not cease to observe the manners of the ancients who worked in this body of knowledge. Withdraw, as much as you can, from illicit foods and delights. Seriously consider, as much as you can, the salvation of your soul and the love of God since desire and love attract the spirit and move it to [171] pursue spiritual effects and to carry out and reveal all its properties toward a desired outcome. If one's inclination were toward God, who is the beginning and end of all, the perpetual and eternal Lord of lords, then such a love would be durable and complete. If such a love and desire were focused on material things, it would be unstable, corruptible, and terminal. Desire is divided into parts since the love that accompanies health and honor is a love fixed in God, sublime and splendid, like the love of a father, a teacher, or a holy man. It is a love of piety and a love of sons. It is the love of the beneficial and the helpful, of men who esteem one another for the sake of free mutual advantage. When desire is very acute, it is called love. So as long as we place anything ahead of God, it must rightly be called a corruptible love. We pour out our prayers to God so that He Himself may illuminate your heart and spirit such that His profound knowledge may be revealed to you, so that He may protect you from treachery or harmful individuals, and that He may guard you from revealing your secrets to the ignorant since they would become the murderers of holy men and prophets.

§2 The properties and examples written in the books of this science of the prophets would seem fraudulent were you to apply them to a ritual half-heartedly; moreover, you would never achieve their application toward the promised effect. Were you to understand them as they were meant (that is, by understanding the credible things and the causes of their effects with a true and steady inclination), then they would seem excellent, splendid, and precious, unattainable by their nature to brutish folk. If we must rightfully repay the debt owed to our fathers who gave us life and being, by how much more must we hold fast to the prophets and holy men who gave us models such as the rules by which our souls might be saved and led to an eternal life? In our bodies there are reasons for the perfection of material elements: a durable power is found for a time that guards and governs bodies in their figures and effects; this is not separate from a body's own particular duration. This is what the prophets called nature. They call it "nature" since a power of the sort is the cause of the governing of bodies through a defined period of time for each and every being relative to their own natural lifespan. Thus, it is called "nature," and nature is the first natural principle of all plants and animals. For example: no matter how a stone is thrown, it naturally falls back down. This is not inasmuch as it is a body, since other bodies (inasmuch as they are bodies) are not similar to it, but rather they produce its effects through an opposite, like fire that naturally rises is still a body; this is understood to be the origin of that kind of motion, and it is called "nature." Moreover, they call that motion "nature," saying that the nature of an element is its form and [172] natural appearance. Physicians, however, use this word "nature" in referring to complexion through natural heat, to the forms and appearances of bodies, and to the motions and the spirit; according to each, a sense is given. In truth, this word "nature" is ambiguous because it applies to every body, to each particular thing, to the elements of the heavens, to the power God provided that causes generation and corruption, motion and rest in everything that can move or rest. For this reason, the earliest sages thus defined the word "nature" as the beginning and end of motion and rest. Plato defined it thus: nature is a body, perfect for creating beings. Galen, however, said: nature is an innate heat that helps bodies and removes damage and corruption from them as much as possible. When the power of the body works in tandem with it, it makes the body apt for government, order, and other things. Empedocles said: it is a simple body with a single form and shape; in it dwell power and life, though it itself is the form of life (as it appears in children whom nature gave certain life skills, like nursing, sleeping, and so on; once they are taught the crafts, they then become masters). I have not written these things except to brighten the light of your intellect since everything you have been instructed and taught regarding origins and considerations of all kinds has proven manifest in the universe. Thus you will possess a well-prepared intellect through the union of the potential intellect with the agent. Thus it is finished.

The third book of Picatrix ends; the fourth book follows. [173]

BOOK 4

The Fourth Book Begins Here. In It Are Revealed the Properties of the Spirits, the Necessities of This Art, and How the Spirits Are Empowered by Images, Suffumigations, and Other Things [174]

Chapter 1

Through What Strength and Power the Spirits Appear, and on the Properties of Sense Perception, Mind, Spirit, Body, and Soul (and the Differences Between Them)

§1 Truly, the ancient sages agreed on this: that God laid out and ordered five things into degrees, placing the noblest at the top—that is, the *Prima Materia* and the First Form, which is the principal source of everything, so to speak; the second thing is sense perception or mind, the third is spirit, the fourth is the nature of the heavens, and the fifth is the elements and their compounds. The First Form, however, He placed in the height of His own heaven where no other god nor lord but Him could endure. He ordained that the First Form should emanate light outward. That virtue emanates the knowledge and the excellence of power upon the things disposed to them; to other things, it bestows these by force. He then placed sense perception and mind in the first circle stretching downward from there like light. Next, the knowledge and the excellence of power that are suited to Him emanated from Him forcefully. He then placed the spirit circle below, which likewise emanated from the first light above. He poured forth His knowledge and excellence to the things disposed to them (namely, that which emanated from the circle of spirit and the circles above). Beneath spirit, He then placed nature, which likewise emanated from the First Form. By His power the excellence disposed to it was generated within it. Therefore, it is clear that the First Form is greater and subtler than the senses in every way; the senses more than spirit; and spirit more than nature; and nature more than the elements. He arranged each and every one of these circles one above another in suitable degrees, ordered as if He meant the first to be absolute, pure in itself, and cleansed from all gross nature; while the second has within itself still a little more gross nature or matter than the preceding but less than the third circle; and thus descending by degrees to the elements or elemental compounds. This is such that the primal essence shines more radiantly within itself, and the others lacking in purity cascade to their proper endpoint (just as species do, namely by running down through more specific types to the most general types since each receives excellence from those above it and pours its power forth unto those below it). He then created the heavens and the forms and placed the circle of the spirits in the midst of four heavens: the two above, those of primal essence and intellect, are luminous and clear; and the two below, those of nature and the elements, are dark and obscure. The circle of the spirit, as a subordinate circle, receives the knowledge and excellence suitable to it from its superiors and pours it down upon its inferiors. According to this, it is the spirit that finally binds and illuminates the two heavens above, receiving from them its light, knowledge, and excellence. The spirit itself was well-formed since it stretches up on high and dwells in the region where it was made and created, whence it receives fortune, goodness, and light; this place is called paradise. The spirit governing the two heavens below, however, is a dark spirit—wretched and unfortunate; he descends to the lowest circle and dwells in the region where he was captured and where [175] he may find no rest; this place is called hell. God Himself created the spirits of the animals, the plants, and the solid bodies. Those things, however, do not receive sense perception and knowledge from the First Form. He pours forth very little into those things because they were not predisposed to Him. Rather, they overtake the two lower heavens (namely, nature and the elements) and dwell upon the Earth where they exist, endure, and where they were created. Nevertheless, all these things appear by means of divine power and strength.

§2 Here follows an example: trees growing in the ground—their foundation is their roots, but their ends are the branches, leaves, and fruit growing upon them. Their roots attract their vegetative power from the humors of the earth while the branches attract it from the air. Therefore, when terrestrial matter overcomes the air in their nature, their roots become longer than their branches; and on the contrary, if air prevails over the earth, their branches will be made longer than the roots. Hence, to confirm the above, we see with the senses that trees and other plants growing in the earth have longer roots than branches and vice versa. Furthermore, we see the same thing in birds, wherein the more a terrestrial nature they possess, by that much more will they have difficulty flying, and when they are more similar in nature to air, they fly that much more easily. It is the same for humans, who the more their nature is composed of subtle elements (the more they are purified from the gross and fed on subtle foods), the more they will become subtle, spiritual, and skilled at understanding the spiritual. On the contrary, it occurs that such humans composed of terrestrial and gross elements and nourished on gross foods are unable to attain the subtleties of spirits since they are naturally inclined toward perceiving gross and corporeal things. From this, it is clear that evil proceeds from matter, while good proceeds from spirit.

§3 Matter is divided into two parts, namely, spiritual and corporeal. In fact, the spiritual is *Prima Materia*, which is the higher realm and the First Form—the first spiritual element (namely, sense, soul, nature, element, and all principles of the first genus stripped of matter) and the first unity, which remains indivisible like a unit, a point and the like that cannot be divided in time (like the beginning of a line, which is a point). Corporeal matter, however, is what exists composed out of the elements, like animals, trees, and the like. Moreover, matter is both simple and composite. Simple matter is everything above the heavens, while composite matter is everything below the heavens and thus may be perceived by sight and by experiment. The wise Empedocles said that all matter perceived by the five bodily senses is corporeal matter, entirely composite, and when it is in this condition, it is corrupted and altered—placed, though lacking place. All matter that cannot be perceived by the five bodily senses is called simple, pure, spiritual, luminous, [176] durable, and noble. All matter discerned by only one of the five senses is intermediary between simple and spiritual matter and between composite and corporeal matter. Thus, the corporeal matter pertains to the corporeal things, and with these it passes through changes of season and color. Spiritual matter remains with light and the lofty spirits, and it endures with these through infinite eras. You who propose to study this book, however, consider how you might lead your soul back to the degree and perception of blessed spirits. Indeed, you will succeed at this if you try to follow the spiritual part in everything you do. By understanding it, you will distinguish yourself from beasts.

§4 The wise are in disagreement concerning the properties of sense perception and its divisions. They express this word—"sense" or "mind"—as four separate things. The first of these is called "reason," by which humankind is distinguished from the other animals that lack sense and discretion. Reason is disposed toward receiving knowledge and the secret pursuits of the masters. The property of this sense is that it is disposed toward the acquisition of knowledge. Clearly, reason is a divine light poured into the heart by God, by which it will be disposed toward seeing and understanding beings as they are. This is the opinion of one faction of sages who discuss such matters. This is why Sesudalis said this word "human" is ambiguous, because it refers to both humans who thrive by intellect and humans who lack it.

§5 *The second opinion.* "Sense" is that which is discerned by knowledge and evident to sense perception, just as in children who can perceive very few of nature's secrets but who are granted perception by nature as if they innately understood (as is the case with numbers through which they determine what two plus one is; that two bodies cannot exist together in the same place; or that it is impossible for one body to exist in different places at the same time). The one faction of sages who spoke about these things asserted that this opinion was obvious to those who denied it.

§6 *A third opinion.* "Sense," according to another faction of ancient sages, consists of what is proven through extensive experience. Those lacking such perception or sense should deservingly be called imbeciles, idiots, blind men, and fools.

§7 *A fourth opinion.* "Sense," according to others, consists of an innate contemplation through which the depth of eternal things is understood in the rejection of worldly corruptible things. When this is discovered in anyone, we call such a person "sensible" because they overcame and conquered their bestial nature and were assimilated to the spiritual and the eternal. This is the property by which humans are distinguished from other animals. Therefore, the two former opinions are natural, and the two latter are acquired by study and science. A wise man said this: "I perceive that sense is twofold: the innate and the acquired. The acquired cannot be possessed [177] except by means of something innate, just as solar light is of little use for one with a naturally defective eye."

§8 Let us now move on to another higher distinction of "sense." The ancient sages divided "sense" into six parts, which can indeed be understood by two words—namely, in a "general sense" and a "universal sense," as we have said regarding the natural and the universal spirit. Those who hold this opinion do so because all things are divided into three parts—that is, the body, natural sense perception, and the spirits of intelligences (or the angels who move the heavens). Of these, the body occupies a baser place than the other two; the second we judge the noblest of all; and the third we reckon to be in the middle between them. The reason we say the second is the noblest is because it is free from all material dependencies. Those distinct intelligences (or angels who move the spheres), however, are intermediates between these since it is they who move the heavens. The "active senses" apply themselves to the heavens' movements. The "general sense," however, is as we have said above concerning the divisions of "sense" abstracted from form and matter because when we speak of humankind in general, it is understood we mean the reason of a rational human (or the reason that is fitting to all humans), by which humans are distinguished from all other animals. This the sages have called the "general sense."

§9 "Universal sense," however, is expressed with two definitions, one of which is more consistent with the term since the genus of the entire universe is understood through it. The idea that is understood because of the explanation of this term is itself a type of property removed from matter and all its parts, possessing movement neither naturally nor by accident. The highest degree of this genus is the active sense perception that is delegated to the human spirit and to higher knowledge. This genus is the beginning of all things after the First Principle; and the First Principle initiates all things. The whole, according to the second definition, is the ninth sphere that circles around everything once per day and night while enveloping the other spheres. On account of its size and capacity—which encapsulates all other bodies—it is called the body of the universe. Sensation of the universe, according to this opinion, is a homogenous substance, isolated from matter. It is the source of its own motion, desiring to assimilate motion to itself. Its motion was discovered to be the beginning of all things. The Founder of the Law spoke thus: sense perception was first created by God who exalted motion with a divine aspiration. Spirit in general, however, is called many different things, and each term exists according to that thing's purpose. Each and every one of the terms is a spirit delegated to its own individual body. The sense perception of the universe is its spirit. Therefore, all completely embodied substances overflow in moving celestial bodies, and this is on account of the stillness of sense perception. Thus, the proper relation of the spirit of all to the sense perception of all governs itself [178] in the same way that our spirits do in relation to active sense perception. The spirit or intellect of the universe is the principle around which occurs the perception of natural bodies. Its degrees in receiving perception follow the degrees of sense perception in all things; sense perception discovers itself. These are the laws that have been discovered concerning sense perception.

§10 Aristotle said that the senses of a sensible spirit are received from the thing being sensed. If anyone were to ask what kind of spirit has understanding, the response would be that a rational spirit discerns sensory perceptions through light when it desires to know something. When it receives that light, it rejoices in it and achieves its objective. Its light pours onto all perceptible things as evidenced in sleep (during which the spirits are cut off from the intellect), when all the spirits that provide sensation are stunned and in remission. If someone were to object, saying "who knows what the spirit perceives while sleeping?," the response to this is that some trace remains in the spirit just as some heat remains in a hearth after it was extinguished. On account of its unity with the body, the spirit can be determined (contrary to the opinion of one faction of sages).

§11 Empedocles said that sense perception cannot be determined since it is a simple substance. A simple substance has neither classification nor differentiation because it is not divided into parts. Definitions cannot be established except through classifications and divisions. Empedocles said that sense perception has two parts. The first, a "general sense," contains all things within its power and is inexhaustible (it has all things within itself by its own substance and exists with time, which does not precede it even by a mere instant). The other, however, is noble and elect; it suffers and is refined—it is found in the human body alone and only when this sense perception is refined by its purity and tested by its pain. It is the light of the "general sense's" light.

§12 The soul is the spirit of divine intelligence. Divine intelligence created it and placed it within the body without any intermediary. It planted the soul in those bodies that exist according to the Sun's light, itself existing through the one who touches those bodies through his rays. Bodies are organized in natural forms according to their effects; through the Sun come perception, judgment or thought, imagination, meditation, memory, and similar things.

§13 One faction of ancient sages reckoned this: nature is an enduring motion with which exists the perfection or completion of an acting body in living potency.

Chapter 2

How the Strength of the Moon's Spirit Is Attracted to the Things Below, and Out of Which Substances the Suffumigations of the Seven Planets Must Be Made

§1 Know that one faction of the Chaldean and Egyptian sages said that the Moon pours and transmits the influences of the planets into this composite world. For this reason, they created rituals, sacrifices, and prayers to the Moon herself on [179] each and every sign's entrance. I have already explained to you the works of other nations concerning these things. Everything we have said about this was translated from the Arabic language.[1]

§2 *How one can speak with the spirits of the Moon, first, when she is in Aries.* When you wish to draw upon the strength and power of the Moon while she is sitting in the sign of Aries at the hour when she ascends full and complete (since she is better and more useful for your request at that time); in that hour, crown yourself, and go to a green and boggy place, flat and close to a river or to running water. Take with you a cock with its crest cut off. Decapitate it with a bone since you should never touch it with iron. Turn your face toward the Moon because this is truly a great secret among the Chaldeans and Egyptians. Place in front of you two iron censers filled with burning coals. One after another, throw grains of incense until smoke rises from them. Then raise yourself up between the censers while looking at the Moon herself, and say: "You, O Moon, luminous, honored, beautiful, who break the darkness by your light, you rise in your ascent and fill all horizons with your light and beauty. I humbly come to you seeking recompense, seeking from you such-and-such a thing in humility." State your request here. Then walk ahead ten paces, always looking at the Moon while again saying the words above. Place one of the censers in front of you in which you should throw 4 oz. of storax gum. Next, burn your sacrifice, and inscribe on a page made of cannabis with the ash of the sacrifice and a little bit of saffron the figures written out below:

Burn this page in the fire. As soon as the smoke rises, you will see on the other side the shape of a handsome man dressed in the best clothes standing next to the censer. State your request to him, and it will be fulfilled. Anytime after this, when you wish to ask something of this man, repeat this ritual, and the shape will appear to you ready to answer your questions.

§3 *When the Moon is in Taurus.* When the Moon is in Taurus and you wish to draw upon her strength and power, know first that the Moon has diverse effects and powers in each and every sign. When you wish to perform this ritual, go to the same place we mentioned concerning the previous sign, and bring a cock and a censer with fire. Dress yourself in linen garments dyed with dyer's weed or pomegranate husks, and wear a hood on your head. Have one cooking pot full of water. Boil nut wood in it. Then take the water with your right hand, and sprinkle it over the left one. Then wash your hands, arms, and face. Be cautious that the hood not lift from your head. Lastly, wash your feet with that water. Take with you a mat or new carpet upon which no foot [180] has trod. Surround the entire carpet in a green linen cloth with a red decor. Jump over the carpet from where you were standing or from the linen cloth, throw yourself onto the carpet with your feet, and say: "RIBHARIM RIBHARIM CAYPHARIM CAYPHARIM DYAFORIM DYAFORIM!" Say these names twenty times. Afterward, get up, go back to the pot of water, and wash your hands. Then decapitate your sacrifice, and burn it while speaking the words mentioned above. Continually, while you are doing this ritual, suffumigate with frankincense and mastic gum. You will then see the shape of a man to whom you should state your request. What you desire will be fulfilled. Someone who was involved in this work told me that he had had a friend who lost everything and was reduced to great poverty. He said that the lord of the ascendant was Saturn. It was this very Saturn who brought about his misfortune and poverty. He showed his friend the prayer of the Moon while she sits in Taurus. He performed the whole ritual, and it revealed to him the aforesaid shape of a man to whom he stated his request and told him about his poverty. Then it seemed to him that that man took him by the hand, led him to a certain ditch, and told him to dig there. He did, and there he found a treasure that made him rich.

§4 *When the Moon is in Gemini.* When the Moon is in Gemini and you wish to draw upon her strength and power, go to an elevated place where it is windy. Bring a cock, the aforesaid suffumigation, a yellow tin pipe three cubits long, and a censer of the same tin. In it, light a fire by kindling it with the pipe. Then, in the center of the fire, place a pound of storax gum. Place one end of the pipe over the fire (namely, where the smoke is rising) and place the other end toward the Moon in such a way that the smoke may rise directly toward the Moon. Afterward, throw ½ oz. of incense and a little bit of amber into the fire, and make smoke with the pipe as we have said. Then sit by the censer's fire, take the pipe in your hands, and make a circle with it such that you yourself are the center of that circle. Next, take seven handfuls of bean straw, and place them in seven spots around the circumference of the circle. Then set out seven pieces of your sacrifice, and place each of them on one of the seven parts of straw. When this is done, kindle a fire with the pipe in the straw until the sacrifice is burned up. Then stand up in the middle of the circle, and say: "You, O Moon, resplendent and luminous, honored in your reign, placed and positioned in the degree of your exaltation because you govern this world by your power and spirit—I ask and I beseech from your spiritual powers that you do such-and-such a thing for me!" Then explain your request. When supplicating and praying, prostrate yourself on the ground, and say: "ABRUTIM ABRUTIM GEBRUTIM GEBRUTIM" twenty times. Next, lift your head from the ground, and you will see the shape mentioned above to whom you will relate your request. It will be fulfilled with effect. [181]

§5 *When the Moon is in Cancer.* When the Moon is in Cancer and you wish to draw upon her strength and power, climb to an elevated place above a wide plain. Look to your right and to your left, listening in front and behind with a turtledove in your hand. Decapitate it, and take four feathers from its right wing and the same number from its left. Amputate its beak, which you will burn completely. Next, take these feathers, and add to them 2 oz. of colocynth and 4 oz. of storax gum. Put everything in a cloth. Afterward, take 2 oz. of white iris,[2] which are to be mixed with the ash of the sacrifice and blended with the sap of birthwort, out of which you should make the shape of a man riding upon a lion. Once this is done, stand up with the image before you. Light a fire in which you should place your suffumigation, and say: "You, O Moon, who are filled with light, goodwill, and replete with beauty and well-proportioned in your altitude, I pour out my prayers to you, and I send my request." Once this is done, make a circle on the ground. In its center, place the image you made, then write the name of the man you wish to avoid in it. Next, return to speaking those words, and prostrate yourself on the ground. Afterward, get up, take 6 oz. of vinegar, and dissolve that whole image in it. Add to it one grain of nutmeg, a ¼ oz. of amber, 4 oz. of sukk,[3] and ½ lb. of storax gum; put them over a fire until they are boiling well. Then make 1 oz. tablets from this, and suffumigate the Moon with them for seven nights (that is, one tablet for each night). Set the others aside. The sages who worked on this ritual said, however, that if you suffumigate anyone you wish with this suffumigation and they inhale it, whether a man or a woman, the person will in no way be able to contradict your orders. Many who practiced this knowledge while setting out on journeys in which there were lions, bears, snakes, scorpions, and other harmful animals were spared from harm by using this suffumigation.

§6 *When the Moon is in Leo.* When the Moon is in Leo and you wish to draw upon her strength and power, go to an uninhabited place. Take with you seven censers and place them on the ground in a circle with one cubit of distance between each of them. Always have your face turned toward the Moon. Between each censer, place a goose egg on which is inscribed these figures:

Then take a thick yellow tin needle three palms long. Hold it in your right hand. Always keep a woolen yellow cloth on your head in the Arab fashion, and dress in a woolen yellow shirt. In the middle of the circle of censers, as we have said regarding the sign of Aries, decapitate a cock with a cut-off crest. Next, burn the pieces of that cock in the censers. Take some of its blood with the head of the needle, and drip it on all the censers and eggs. Once this is done, by counting two censers [182] from the censer in front of you, distance yourself by that much, and take the egg after the second censer, and place in front of you. Pierce through it completely with the needle while suffumigating with frankincense and yellow sandalwood, and saying "HENDEB HENDEB" fifteen times. Then the shape of a man mentioned above will come. State your request to him, and at once it will be fulfilled with effect.

§7 *When the Moon is in Virgo.* When the Moon is in Virgo and you wish to draw upon her strength and power, take thirty thrushes, decapitate them, and cook them until well done. Afterward, remove them once their feathers fall off, and salt them a little bit. Set them aside for use. Do this for thirty days before the Moon enters Virgo. Then, on each day, eat one of them after it has been suffumigated with four drams of saffron. After you have consumed one, eat nothing else for six hours. Do this every day until the thirtieth day, during which time you will abstain from wine completely. At the end of this period, wash yourself in the water of an eastward-flowing spring, and put a pound of that spring water into a medium-sized container (which should be made while the Sun is crossing the fourth degree and the Moon is sitting in the seventh degree of Aquarius). Plug the mouth of that container well with wax never touched by fire. Once this is done, go to an open location, put before you a censer with ¼ oz. each of incense and saffron. Say: "You, O Moon, who are beautiful, positioned in an aspect, copious in giving, great, and splendid. By your light, the darkness shines and the spirits go forth; hearts are rejoiced by your beauty. I beseech you and confide such a matter in you." Afterward, take up the container in your left hand and say: "HAPHOT HAPHOT." Then dig the ground with your right hand. Always while digging, repeat this word continually. Do this until the hole is one cubit deep. Place the container into the hole with the opening facing south. Next, fill the hole with dirt until leveled. While doing this, repeat the word continually. Inscribe the figure that you wish on a thin sheet of lead with a golden needle, and bury it atop the hole just mentioned. Once all of this is done, your request will be fulfilled immediately.

§8 *When the Moon is in Libra.* When the Moon is in Libra and you wish to draw upon her strength and power, gird yourself with a thong made from aquatic reeds. Go to the eastern bank of a river, and burn your sacrifice while running upstream along the bank, looking continually at the Moon while holding in your hand a bronze bow (which should be made while Venus is retrograde in Taurus, and Mercury is in Aries). Do these things five times, coming and going on the riverbank. Once this is done, hit the water of the river with the bow. Once the sacrifice has been burned, say: "You, O Moon, excellent and honored! To you I pour out and send this sacrifice. I have done this for obtaining your grace since you have the power to grant my request and fulfill my desire." Afterward, light a fire with wild olive wood, and [183] throw storax gum on it. Then run in a circle around the fire, maintaining as much speed as you can. Next, prepare yourself where you have made the fire. There, make a line on the ground from your feet to the fire, and write this name on it: "GANEYTANIA GANEYTANIA." Take the soil on which this name was written, and mix it with undisturbed earth and water. Make two images from this mixture, one in your image and another in the form of whoever else you desire. Have the images embrace each other, especially if your operation is for love. If it were for another purpose, however, do it in the same manner. The ritual of this image (or these images) should be performed in the hour of the Moon as quickly as possible, and what you desire will be fulfilled.

§9 *When the Moon is in Scorpio.* When the Moon is in Scorpio and you wish to draw upon her strength and power, rise up when the Moon is in the thirteenth degree of Scorpio, and go to a place where there are many thick trees and bodies of water. Make a square figure on the ground, and cover it with the leaves of nut, lemon, and pine trees. Moisten the whole thing with rosewater. Next, place before you nine silver censers. In each of them, place as much aloewood, storax gum, and incense as you can. Next, dress yourself in the whitest clothes into which no color was mixed. Once this is done, place before you two earthenware censers filled with water. Take a small earthenware jar with which you will pour the water of one censer into the other, and throw some of that water with it onto your ribs. Make your sacrifice out of animals pertinent to it. When these things have been completed, raise yourself onto your feet, and prostrate yourself onto the ground four times. During each prostration, say: "SERAPHIE SERAPHIE." Then sit back down and throw aloewood and incense into the fire. Then place storax gum on each of the nine censers. Prostrate yourself four more times as before. Then a man will come to you in a perfect and pleasing form, to whom you should ask whatever you desire. It will be very well fulfilled.

§10 *When the Moon is in Sagittarius.* While the Moon is in Sagittarius and you wish to draw upon her strength and power (since great sages once judged this work to be a powerful and perfect ritual and in many instances, performed the ritual of Sagittarius for finding treasures)—when you wish to carry out these things, do this ritual while Mercury is in the fourth degree of Cancer. Then pour 10 lbs. of tin from which you will make five images in the shape of dragons. Make these while Mercury sits in the degrees of the same sign. When the images have been completed, go to a clear flowing river, and divert some of the water from that river through five small channels. Make each run down in its own path separately. Place into each of those channels one of the five dragon-shaped images made above such that water enters through their tails and exits through their mouths. Next, take five jugs, and affix them to the mouth of every dragon such that the water enter these jugs. [184] Leave them there for an hour. Next, the jugs should be taken away from the mouths of the dragons. Let the water run from those dragons onto the ground for the following hour. Return the said jugs to the original place (that is, each one placed to its image as before), and let the water flowing through the mouths of the dragons fall into them for another hour. At the end of that hour, carry them off as before. Proceed with the same order until they are filled. Once filled, back up twenty palms from the river while holding them. Once this path has been traced, place those jugs on the ground there. Pierce each of them with a needle. Dig a trench in a circle around them into which the water emerging can enter, and place beside each of them one of the dragons. Once this is done, get up, and come running to the shore of the river while continually looking at the Moon. Take some water from the river in your mouth, as much as you can hold. Then, holding that water, turn back to the location of the aforementioned jugs, and spit that water onto the jugs and the dragons. Place a silver censer filled with lit coals next to each dragon into which you should throw amber and aloewood. Their smoke should not be extinguished while the water is coming out of the jugs. When all the water has come out, put the dragons back into the jugs, and bury them in the aforesaid hole. Cover them up in the ground. When these things have been accomplished, stand over that place, and decapitate your sacrifice in front of a straight line of fifteen trees. Raise your head toward each of those trees, and each time, say: "HARMUM HARMUM." Say these words five times for each tree. Then your request will be fulfilled such that a well-disposed man of comely appearance will appear to you immediately and lead you back to any place you desire from the four corners of the Earth.

§11 Truly I say to you that I once had a friend who performed the ritual above. When he completed it, a man appeared to him asking about his request. He responded that his request was to give him an image for finding hidden treasures. It seemed to him that the man had taken him by the hand and led him to some place where he handed over the image of a bronze elephant. In its hands and feet, it held an iron key. It seemed to him that the man said: "Take the elephant. Wherever you go, he will take you with him. Wherever the key falls from his feet, know that there is treasure there." He took the elephant in his hands. Moving with it the distance of four cubits, the key dropped from the hands of the elephant. At once, he stopped there and dug a hole wherein he discovered stairs. Going down them, he found a large dwelling filled with gold and silver and precious stones. He took as much as he could and led the elephant back with him while carrying treasure of this kind. [185]

§12 *When the Moon is in Capricorn.* When the Moon is in Capricorn and you wish to draw upon her strength and power—when the Sun is sitting in the sign of Cancer, enter a house that can only fit two individuals, and cover it for seven days with odoriferous branches (that is, on each day, renew the covering with fresh branches). On each and every one of those seven days, suffumigate the house with aloewood and incense. After these seven days, enter the house dressed in the most beautiful red clothes. See to it that the house be covered with a board or something similar. Whenever you wish, uncover it and say: "HEYERIM HEYERIM FALSARI FALSARI TIFRAT TIFRAT." Afterward, leave the house, and walk around it seventy times. Then suffumigate the house for one hour with 2 oz. of aloewood in a silver censer. Next, go outside, and go around the house again seventy times as before. Once finished, make your sacrifice with the cock that we have often mentioned above, then enter the house again. There, you will find a seated man to whom you should say: "I conjure you by the beautiful and luminous Moon, ornate and honored, so that you may speak to me." Once that man addresses you, state to him your desire, and it will be accomplished with effect.

§13 All rituals described in this chapter are, for the most part, designed for acquiring love. Some close friend of mine told me that he himself had had a certain servant girl whom he sold. After selling her, he realized he loved her. He asked the man to whom he had sold her that he give her back; the man refused to make this restitution. Seeing that he was not able to have her in this way, he performed the aforesaid ritual as above. Immediately, the man who owned her started to hate her. He sent asking that my friend purchase her back for the same established price as he wanted. Seeing that he hated her, my friend got her back for a modest price. Fundamental to this ritual and others of its kind is that the operator be inherently inclined toward good works and effects and uninvolved in evil works. The operator must be holy, pure, and as removed from temptation as possible.

§14 Here I propose to relate a story that happened recently to someone who wished to draw upon the power of the Moon. He performed this ritual urged by necessity and so did it on some night totally irrelevant to the ritual. Then one night, while he was actually operating, a man appeared to him with something in his hand that he placed in the practitioner's mouth. He closed his mouth immediately, and it appeared as if he never even had a mouth. He remained filled with the greatest terror for forty hours, at the end of which he was completely ruined.

§15 *When the Moon is in Aquarius.* When the Moon is in Aquarius and you wish to draw upon her strength and power—know first that all the ancient sages agreed on this: that the rules of those rituals are found to be more useful than the rituals themselves. For that reason, the theoretical and the practical together [186] have the most effective results in reaching the desired end. When the theory is not joined to the practical, the utmost danger to spirit and body arises. Those who do not know how to properly perform rituals bring about the greatest perils and utmost terrors, which for my part are too awful to tell. I say this to you to teach and chastise since none should dare to familiarize themselves with this work except those who possess good memory and good character.

§16 When you wish to operate with the Moon in that sign, take three heads of male geese. Put them over a fire in the oldest wine possible until they are cooked very well. Afterward, reduce all of them, and grind them well in an iron or lead mortar until they become a single mass. This must occur when the Moon is in Cancer. Next, take ½ lb. of cinnamon, 2 oz. of sandalwood, ½ lb. of dried storax gum, 4 oz. of incense, and an equal amount of goat's-thorn. Mix everything together with the wine in which the heads were cooked, and out of this make forty tablets. Place these over a fire in an iron frying pan until desiccated. Once you have done these things at night, go to a field when the full Moon is in Aquarius. In front of you, place fifteen censers made partly of bronze, partly of silver (they are reckoned to be better if they are golden), and full of burning coals. Into each of them, throw one of these tablets. Sacrifice the cock. While smoke is rising, a man will appear to you who will often waver between visibility and invisibility. Next, take three of the tablets, throw them on the fire, and say: "HANTARACERET HANTARACERET." Repeat these words ten times. Then you will see that man completely to whom you should state your petition. It will be fulfilled with effect.

§17 *When the Moon is in Pisces.* When the Moon is in Pisces and you wish to draw upon her strength and power, take 1⅕ lbs. of cannabis resin and the same amount of plane tree resin, and mix them together. Extract these resins while the Sun is in Virgo and Mercury is luminous and advancing directly. Grind them up in a marble mortar. When this is done, add 4 oz. of mastic gum; 2 oz. each of amber and camphor; 1 oz. of sukk;[4] and 10 oz. of sarcocolla. Blend everything very well, to which you should add ½ lb. of the blood of a stag decapitated with a bronze knife. When everything has been blended together, place it in a glass container. Go to a running spring, and position the glass vessel on its outer lip. Next, take a censer, and set it on a stone in the middle of the spring's waters such that the censer be entirely surrounded by water. Then light a fire in it. Once it is lit, open the mouth of the glass container, and empty out the container into the fire little by little [187] until the whole thing has poured out into the fire. Next, make your sacrifice. The servant of the Moon will appear to you, to whom you should state your request. It will be led to its effect.

§18 Great wonders and great effects exist among the Indians in suffumigations that they call *calcitarat.* With these, the Indians work the effects on the seven planets. These suffumigations must correspond to the nature of the planet to which the request is made.

§19 *First, regarding Saturn.* When you wish to operate through Saturn, fast for seven days beginning on Sunday. On the seventh day, namely the day of the Sabbath, decapitate a black crow, and say: "In the name of ANZIL who is positioned with Saturn. You, O ANZIL, who are the angel of Saturn! I conjure you by the lord of the high firmament so that you may fulfill my request and my desire." Then operate with *calcitarat* toward the things you wish. The figures of Saturn are these:

§20 When you wish to operate through Jupiter, fast for seven days as above, beginning on Friday. At the end of those days, that is on Thursday, decapitate a lamb, eat its liver, and say: "You, O ROQUIEL, angel who is placed with fortunate and good Jupiter and in the Greater Fortune, perfect and beautiful! By the lord of the high firmament, I conjure you so that you may receive my prayer and my request and that you deign to bring about what I ask." Then operate with *calcitarat* toward the things you wish. The figures of Jupiter are these:

§21 When you wish to operate through Mars, fast for seven days beginning on Wednesday. At the end of those seven days, that is on Tuesday, decapitate a tawny cat, and say: "You, O ZEMEYEL, angel of Mars, are mighty and strong in arms-bearing and quarrels, a lord of burning fire! I conjure you by the lord of the high firmament so that you may receive my request and that you make such-and-such a thing have effect for me." Here state your request, and operate with *calcitarat* toward the things you seek. These are his figures:

§22 When you wish to operate through the Sun, fast for seven days as above, beginning on Monday. On the last day, namely on Sunday, decapitate a small bovine calf, eat its liver, and say: "You, O YEBIL, angel of the Sun, of that luminous one who is the goodness of the world, lord of light and luminosity; O perfect fortune and author of misfortune and harm! I conjure you by the lord of the high firmament so that you may do such-and-such for me and [188] accomplish this request of mine." Ask what you want, and operate with *calcitarat* toward the things you seek. These are his figures:

§23 When you wish to operate through Venus, fast beginning on the day of the Sabbath all the way to Friday. On Friday, decapitate a white dove; however, you must eat its liver on the fourth day, and say: "You, O ANBETAYL, angel of Venus, fortunate and beautiful! I conjure you by the lord of the high firmament so that you may do for me such-and-such a thing and fulfill this request." Ask what you wish, and operate with *calcitarat* toward those things you seek. These are her figures:

§24 When you wish to operate through Mercury, as above, fast for seven days beginning on Thursday. On the last day, namely Wednesday, decapitate a black and white cock, eat its liver and say: "You, O ARQUIL, angel of Mercury, noble lord and of a good sort! I conjure you by the lord of the high firmament so that you may do and fulfill such-and-such a thing for me." Here state your request, and operate with *calicarat*. These are his figures:

§25 When you want to operate with the Moon, fast for seven days beginning on Tuesday. On the last day, namely Monday, decapitate an ox, eat its liver, and say: "You, O CAHIL, angel of the Moon who is the key of goodness whose principle is speed! I conjure you by the lord of the high firmament so that you may do such-and-such a thing for me and fulfill such a request for me." State your request, and operate with *calcitarat* toward the things that you seek. These are her figures:

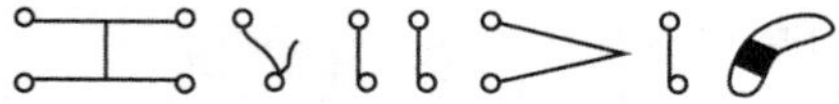

§26 All the above about this ritual was discovered by ancient sages. In these rituals, there are many effects emerging from magical works, that is, from wondrous suffumigations and images. The Chaldeans, who dwelt in the Promised Land and who were at one time called the *Capti*, were very skilled in these works. Much is found concerning their works in the book *On Chaldean Agriculture*. Abenvasia, who translated the book, named all their works. We ourselves intend to discuss some of these things in our book.

Chapter 3

In Which Are Discussed the Chaldeans' Beliefs Concerning the Depths and Secrets of This Science, and What They Have Said About These Things

§1 The Chaldeans who initiated themselves into this work and science are magi. These men are considered most competent in this science. The magi claim that Hermes [189] was the first to build a kind of house of statues. With these statues, he would measure the length of the Nile all the way to the Mountain of the Moon.[5] Here, he built the house of the Sun.[6] Moreover, he occulted himself from humankind such that none in his presence could see him. It was Hermes indeed who built the eastern city of Egypt twelve miles long, wherein he erected a tower with four gates on its four sides. At the eastern gate, he placed the statue of an eagle, on the western gate that of a bull, on the southern gate that of a lion, and on the northern one that of a dog.[7] Hermes caused loud-voiced spiritual entities to enter them.[8] Nobody could enter that tower's gates without the entities' permission. There, he also planted certain kinds of trees, in the middle of which stood a great tree that bore every type of fruit. At the summit of that tower, he built a kind of turret thirty cubits in height, on the top of which he placed a round orb whose color would change according to each of the seven days. At the end of the seven days, however, the cycle began anew. Every day, that city was covered by the color of that orb, and thus it glowed differently each day.[9] Around the turret, there was abundant water where plenty of fish dwelled. He set up various statues of every kind around the city, and by their power the inhabitants were made virtuous, free from sin and wicked idleness. This city was called Adocentyn.[10] These people had been taught in the knowledge of the ancients, their depths, and secrets, along with the science of astronomy.

§2 I myself have seen a kind of mixture for invisibility made in this way. When you want to make it, take a rabbit on the twenty-fourth night of the month of the Arabs, which you will decapitate while continually looking toward the Moon. Suffumigate with the suffumigations of the Moon while speaking the words of the Moon, and say: "I ask you, angel of the spirit of magic and the arcane, you who were called SALNAQUIL! Through she who grants you the power, potency, and fortitude in this ritual, I beseech you so that you may deign to grant me what I ask from those things attributed to your powers." Once you have said these things, take the blood of the rabbit, and mix it with its bile. Bury its body such that no one sees it. If you bury it and it is discovered the next day (that is, when the Sun has risen above it), the spirit of the Moon will kill you. Carry it with you, and set the blood that you have mixed with bile aside for use. When [190] you want to conceal yourself and be seen by none, take some of its blood mixed with bile in the hour of the Moon and anoint your face with it. Speak these words of the Moon loudly because while reciting them, you will be made completely invisible and thus accomplish your goal. When you wish to become visible, cease reciting the words, wash your face, then anoint it with the brain of the rabbit, and say: "You, O spirit of the Moon, uncover me, and make me appear to all." Then all will see you. This stands as one ritual of the Moon and is considered to be among the great secrets and complexities of this science.

Chapter 4

On Images and Theories That Greatly Improve This Science

§1 Everything recited so far in our book was extracted from the sayings of the ancient sages and their books concerning that science and craft. Whoever reads this book, examines it perfectly, and understands the things we have said so far will understand and thoroughly recognize the effort we invested in compiling sayings from a variety of books on that body of knowledge that are the bases of these rituals. We have discovered one complete volume of those books composed by Mercurius, the sage of Babylon. In it there was a book of aphorisms called *The Secret of Secrets*. From it we have selected forty-five aphorisms reckoned to be quite useful in this science and craft.

§2 (i) If you work from things pertinent to a planet (and use these things liberally) and the nature of your ritual is also pertinent to the nature of that planet, then truly you will have the greatest assistance in attracting the fortitude, power, and potency of that planet.

§3 (ii) Entreat the Sun that you may be feared and have glory, the leadership of armies, a splendid heart, the rule of nobles, the destruction of kings, the lighting of fire, and the power to bring light into the darkness.

§4 (iii) Entreat the Moon for agility of movement, the flow of waters, the power of revealing secrets, the extinguishing of fire, the lessening of burdens to be overcome, and the separating of united opinions.

§5 (iv) Entreat Saturn for delaying movement, concealing purity, destroying cities, humbling hearts, and calming waters.

§6 (v) Entreat Jupiter for the accumulation of wealth, the enhancement of dreams, the pleasure of escaping sadness, the leaving behind of toil and quarrel, and safe journeys by land or sea. [191]

§7 (vi) Entreat Mars for conquering of enemies, emboldening of hearts, tracking and hunting harmful animals, setting fires, war planning, and conquest over enemies.

§8 (vii) Entreat Venus for the union of desires, the power of causing joy and friendship, driving out idleness and grief, for invigorating the appetite, augmenting procreation, multiplying sons, extinguishing fires, and remaining secure from animals.

§9 (viii) Make many suffumigations, maintain perfect belief, fast frequently, utter many prayers, pick worthy places for the ritual, look to the aspects of the planets. These are the fundamentals of magic works.

§10 (ix) Your request will be easily fulfilled if the planet to which the request is made is the lord of your nativity; if not, it will be difficult to bring your request to its deserved end.

§11 (x) The power of the planets lies in the spirits that strengthen effects, that modulate qualities (improving them or lessening and weakening them), and that spread out their powers.

§12 (xi) If the ascendant differs from the nature of the request, the petition will never be fulfilled nor will the prayer ever achieve what is sought.

§13 (xii) Images of fixed stars are thought to be more enduring than images of planets with retrograde motions.

§14 (xiii) If you perform your ritual with a planet assisted by some fixed stars of the same nature, it will be more complete and perfect since it will have the strength of the planet and the durability of the fixed stars.

§15 (xiv) When the ascendant, the petition, and the planet stand in a single nature and you serve yourself with the fixed stars therein (and you have belief and firm will), your request will be fulfilled easily and be strengthened by the power of the planet.

§16 (xv) Know that you will be helped in setting things in motion when the stars of Aquila are rising, and when these stars are falling, you will likewise be aided in effects for putting an end to motion.

§17 (xvi) Inspect the conjunctions of the planets diligently since this ritual is suitably augmented by them.

§18 (xvii) Fundamental to the images are their aspects and conjunctions with the planets.

§19 (xviii) Place the signifier in mid-heaven, in its own house and exaltation, and make sure it is strong in the ascendant.

§20 (xix) Use the Sun when you wish to conquer and overcome someone since then your request will be fulfilled and flourish more easily. [192]

§21 (xx) Use the Moon when you wish to keep something; then your request will be fulfilled and flourish more easily.

§22 (xxi) Use Saturn when you wish to ruin someone and bring about evil; then your request will be fulfilled and flourish more easily.

§23 (xxii) Use Jupiter when you wish to ascend to the good; then your petition will flourish and be fulfilled more easily.

§24 (xxiii) Use Mars when you wish to win in peace and in war; then your request will be fulfilled and flourish more easily.

§25 (xxiv) Use Venus when you wish to seek love and friendship; then your request will be fulfilled and flourish more easily.

§26 (xxv) Use Mercury when you wish to know, understand, and expel distraction; then your request will be fulfilled and flourish more easily.

§27 (xxvi) Delays in the results of your request come from an error made in your ritual, your inadequate belief, or a poor setup for the ritual.

§28 (xxvii) Rituals performed with suffumigations and prayers are more effective than those in which suffumigations are lacking or the will is divided.

§29 (xxviii) The light of the Sun and the projection of rays hide the spirits of the nocturnal planets.

§30 (xxix) The darkness of night and the stillness of motion hide the spirits of the diurnal planets. Thus, serve each planet according to its appropriate hour.

§31 (xxx) A weighty planet with its slowness has more powerful effects than a lighter planet, although it is quicker in its effects.

§32 (xxxi) Do not seek union from Mars nor separation from Venus. Do not seek to make any planet deviate from its nature and path.

§33 (xxxii) Work with comets in the things pertinent to them, as you would with the fixed stars.

§34 (xxxiii) Seek Mercury when he is in a pure sign; work with the Moon along with it. These produce two qualities.

§35 (xxxiv) Work with Mercury for infirmities of the head according to their diverse qualities.

§36 (xxxv) Among the works of Mercury, seek swiftness of tongue when he sits in his own house.

§37 (xxxvi) Sometimes it occurs that the things pertaining to Mars are received by the Sun, and inversely, the things pertaining to the Sun are received by Mars.

§38 (xxxvii) Sometimes it occurs that the things pertaining to the Moon are received by Venus, and the things pertaining to Venus are received by the Moon.

§39 (xxxviii) The Sun abhors the things pertaining to Saturn, and Saturn abhors the things pertaining to Venus.

§40 (xxxix) Venus receives the things pertaining to Jupiter, and Jupiter receives the things pertaining to Venus.

§41 (xl) The Moon abhors the things pertaining to Mars, and Mars abhors the things pertaining to the Moon. [193]

§42 (xli) Jupiter abhors the things pertaining to Mars, and Mars abhors the things pertaining to Jupiter.

§43 (xlii) Mars abhors the things pertaining to Venus, and Venus abhors the things pertaining to Mars.

§44 (xliii) Mercury abhors the things pertaining to Jupiter, and Jupiter abhors the things pertaining to Mercury.

§45 (xliv) It appears from the opinions of the sages that two unfortunate planets are made enemies on account of the diversity and discord they have in their respective natural essences. Know and understand all of this perfectly. We selected these aphorisms from the words of the aforesaid sage.

§46 Now we present these ten aphorisms from the book of Ptolomy called *The Centiloquium*.

§47 (i) The astrologer can withdraw and deflect the many impacts of the stars' effects and natures if he knows them, their works, and their effects. This occurs because the effect of the stars reaches the astrologer before it reaches the target.

§48 (ii) The magician's spirit enhances the celestial effects in the same way natural harvests are supported by plowing and land cultivation.

§49 (iii) The forms of this composite world obey the celestial forms. Thus, when the sages of the magical art wished to understand this knowledge, they mandated that these shapes be inscribed when the planets are residing in those celestial forms.

§50 (iv) Work with the unfortunate planets, and with them assist yourself in your desires, just as physicians are aided by a correct dosage of drugs.

§51 (v) The combination of two substances into one takes up both of their nativities. If there were a similarly in them, they would have a bond between them; and whichever one among them remained in a more powerful rank would obtain rule and lordship; what is weaker in rank would be subordinate and passive.

§52 (vi) Friendship and enmity arise from movements of the Sun and Moon, their origin, and the harmony and dispersal of the ascendant of friendship and of enmity. Obeying the sign is stronger in friendship.

§53 (vii) Make use of the fixed stars in the construction of cities, and work with the planets in the construction of homes. Whoever lives in a city built when Mars or another star of his nature sits in mid-heaven will violently die by the sword.

§54 (viii) Existence and effects upon this world (namely, what arises from generation and corruption) ensue from the 120 conjunctions made by the seven planets. Observe in every effect that being is a form of reception since it produces effects from its own form.

§55 (ix) The Sun is the substance of animal power, the Moon is that of natural power, Saturn of retentive power, Jupiter of the power of increase, Mercury the power of thought, Mars the power of perception and wrath, and of course Venus is the source of desire's power. [194]

§56 (x) Mars, Mercury, and Venus in nativities signify the wills and manners of that nativity, and they demonstrate its works and realms of knowledge.

§57 *The sayings of Plato.* In the philosophical books published by Plato, we have found that none but Jupiter reveals truth. Elsewhere, he says that at the beginning of generation, just as blood, yellow bile, black bile, and phlegm are the elements of the body, correspondingly the powers of those elements proceed from the planets (and thus the action of one humor upon another and the reception of one by another comes from the planets). Elsewhere, Plato says that when the science of astrology seems false or entirely a sham, this arises purely from a mistake or error on the astrologer's behalf. Thus, the claims of astrology are different from those of divinations and auguries (since, according to their claims, they reveal the future). Thus, things happen and come about whether predicted or not.

§58 *The sayings of Hippocrates.* In the philosophical books of Hippocrates, we found that when Jupiter is the lord of the solar year, there will be little illness, great health, and animals will multiply a lot in that year.

§59 *The sayings of Aristotle.* We found in the books of Aristotle that rule is attributed to Saturn, justice to Jupiter, cheerfulness to Venus, judgment to Mercury, accomplishments to the Moon, and pride to Mars.

§60 Know that I have not recited all this except for you to know and understand what only these sages studied in observing the depths and secrets of this work so that they thus may be reconciled. In this way, they were able to reach a desired end.

§61 *Concerning Johannitius.*[11] Johannitius, the son of Isaac, translated a certain book by Aristotle, the teacher of the Greeks, which I myself have seen. Since you can understand the words of the wise, the depth of their intuition, and the conclusions of their minds, I propose to convey them here. I have already made reference to certain things in a volume from his first book, from which I shall quote selections here. Some sages, while speaking therein, said: "All works and all realms of knowledge have a door through which one can enter for understanding. Each have ladders by which individuals may prevail in climbing toward their desire." And this: "None can attain their desire without order and rules." And: "In what is sought, peril is generated." All wise philosophers said this science was given by God and by the celestial powers.

What they said, they said such that only those enlightened in this science could understand them on account of their complexity and depth. This work and knowledge, however, is completely revealed to the wise on the right path who delve into it deeply in all respects. The basis of this science is knowing the figures of heaven's ascending stars, which figures are depicted through them, which figures are determined to be apart from the others, and which figures are not depicted through those stars nor completed without the addition of a part from another figure. Once you have learned these figures and their natures, you will be able to work according to their natures upon the terrestrial things pertaining to these figures' natures [195] (namely, upon the figures of living beings according to their harmony and proportion with the celestial figures). If you heed the right harmony and harmoniously join and prepare the figures, that will be the building blocks and foundation of this work. With an image made thus, its effects will be lasting and complete because were an image not made this way, its effects would be lost according to the damnation of earthly matter and the degradation of its composition. Its durability hinges upon a fixed star. An image's nature and effect are better if they come about through the planets. The effect is more lasting when a planet is faced by a fortunate planet that assists it in the strength and power for drawing spiritual things from the heavens down to Earth. Therefore, there are among the names of God some words that cause spirits to descend from the heavens to the Earth. Were one who works with those names and words not wise and learned in the natures of spiritual matters, the power of the descending spirit would kill them. None but the wise may have the grace of working with those names. Among magical rituals are found words that also work in this manner. These, however, are not accomplished by words and magical names unless they are joined with the power, command, and grace of God. Then, celestial things above will be joined with terrestrial matter, descending all the way to the center of the Earth.

§62 An image is first ordered to be made according to the natural substance for which it was made; it cannot be made without powerful, magical words. Whenever you can, be diligent lest there be antagonism and discord between the natures and figures in the components of the ritual. For example: A master who makes the image of a lion must be strong and have a brave heart. They should fear no animal of that nature. Indeed, one must have once seen a lion, know and understand its nature and the things that anger it, and acknowledge its malicious will. On this the ancient sages are in great agreement. When these things have been done as outlined, they will produce a desired end.

§63 Likewise, when you wish to craft some image, make it at a time when the animal is active, and its nature is strengthened. Thus, the power of that image is reinforced. In the same way, beware lest you make it at a time when some accident arises. For example, concerning the lion: Do not make the image of a lion at a time when fevers are about since the image's ritual would be weakened in its power. All heavenly motions are moved in that earthly image by the power of God. Therefore, observe the motion of that star from which you want a lasting power for the image so that it is not impeded until the final product of the image is assembled. Observe two figures, that is, the degree of the planet's sign that governs the figure's ritual and its motion so that it not be hindered by anything. When the planets move freely in their heavens, the powers of the image are similarly moved by coming, going, ascending, and descending. Similarly, pay very close attention to the conjunctions, oppositions, and aspects in constructing an image for its figure is manifest in the heavens and its [196] contraries are hidden. Know that if you have not observed the aforesaid in constructing the image, its effects will not be fulfilled.

§64 Geber Abenhayen,[12] speaking on this topic, said:

> The work of an image is similar to the effect of nature. This cannot be done except by knowing the things pertaining to the stars from among the animals, trees, and stones; by understanding the aspects of the planets, fixed stars, and signs pertaining to earthly places; the heavens' motions in the science of astronomy; the planets' houses and exaltations; their longitudes and latitudes; the mansions of the Moon; the natures of the Earth's regions and its waters, lands, rains, snows, geography, seas, and seasons; how far they are away from the equator; what kinds of animals thrive there; when the effects of certain creatures, whether reptiles or others, last longer; and the times when these effects are and are not generated in such creatures. In the construction of these images, the task will be easy for the wise since nothing is difficult for them. In the composition of these natures (i.e., in the work of the images), the images are reckoned more durable in stones than in plants and animals because plants burn easily and animals rot. The effects of animals are twofold: one is for acquiring and attracting them and the other is for casting them out and driving them off. These have two times and two motions—namely, a time of acquiring and attracting them and a time for casting them out and driving them off. This is described in the chapters on the opposition of degrees. A certain great secret lurks in stones: when some animal—one you wish to drive off—is hot in nature, the stone must be cold; if the animal is moist, the stone should be dry; and vice versa. From this it is understood that if you wish to drive off vipers and wasps, it is ordered that the work be made of carnelian stone, diamond, or the like. If the creatures are cold in their natures like scorpions, bedbugs, flies,

> lice, and similar things, use a hot stone like the malachite, crystal, bronze, gold, or similar things. Do this in rituals to drive off creatures. Perform the rituals for acquiring and attracting creatures using those things suited and pertaining to them, just like with operations concerning vipers where you craft an image of gold or bronze and the like. All this occurs on account of the balance of complexions, the directions of motions, and the diversity of conjunctions and of motions of conjoined things and of the substance's motions. Fashion the figures and forms in the shape of that animal for which it is made (the image of a mouse is made in the shape of a mouse, the image of a snake is in the shape of a snake, and the image of a scorpion is in the shape of a scorpion). This I say to you, if the amount of stone used to make the image is large (that is, between one ounce and one pound), its strength and power stretches out a hundred leagues away. This occurs because a thing composed in [197] its natural form has no intrinsic motion or effect other than to demarcate its location, but this is not according to substances and natural bodies. Spirits inhabit vaster places than bodies with few spirits.

§65 Plato said this: "Bodies are opposed to spirits since only the life of one depends on the sustenance of the other." He adds: "You yourselves must suffer the death of your bodies on account of your spirits' lives for bodies are the handmaidens of the spirit and should serve the spirit in all their works and deeds. Never allow your spirits to serve your bodies nor destroy the dead on account of the life of the living nor kill the living out of a love for the dead."
§66 Then they asked Plato: "How are spirits rejoiced by the vibration of strings?" To them he answered:

> Since nature, by its powers, moves the rational and animal spirits on account of the obvious similarities of that nature that belongs to the body, thus the order of harmony, love, and victory belongs to the spirit. Sometimes, nature unites divided parts, and at other times, it divides united parts. When nature is moved by a unifying motion (I mean to say, one toward the gathering of parts), then two spirits are unified in a spiritual love of their own. They are united with the rational intellect. The spiritual is first because it perceives its world; thus, it is made pure and simple. When it is moved by a scattering motion, it attracts to itself the animal spirit and acquires a corporeal partnership. Thus, the rational spirit rejoices in a victorious end and leads on account of its similarity to the subtle, which arises from a part of the rational order. Similarly, the animal spirit rejoices on account of parts and strings divided according

> to a similarity distinguished from the parts of nature. This is because spirit has wondrous forms within itself, which the spirit is unable to attract toward nature. Next, the motion of nature assists in the substance of its own body (I mean to say, the bodies of the strings and their heaviness), and at that point, the spirit rejoices by the motion of these forms that cannot be attracted by reason. Spirit attracted them through images, subtle motions, and visions of the eye and of the body's other organs.

You, however, who propose to work in this science should fix your spirit and thoughts upon the matters that those men practiced and strive in spirit until you achieve what the wise achieved. Ancient sages who taught about the spirit in waking and in sleep said this: "Accustom your spirits to visions because they may happen to you often, and by them you may attain in sleep what you have never been able to attain while waking." This is understood: at a time when the manifest senses are awake, the hidden senses are weakened and are incapable of bringing about their effects. When the manifest senses are at rest and inactive, however, then the hidden senses [198] function according to the power of thought, imagination, memory, and the intuition of the spirit. Then the strength of intuition is simple and unhindered by any impediment. Then the heat lies hidden. So long as it is hidden, the excesses of the body dissolve. You yourself, who are thoroughly researching this knowledge, should know that when you accustom your spirit to these things, they will be revealed to you at a moment of vision, and in the things sought, you will understand what is necessary.

Chapter 5

The Ten Sciences Necessary for This Art, How This Science Is Assisted by Them, and the Origin of the Science of Magic

§1 The ancient sages who discovered this knowledge did not reach it except while seeking with incessant effort and probing everything, in waking and sleeping, toward what they desired. By following this path, they knew and understood two conclusions: the first of these is that you must know the ten arts, five of which are concerned with the laws, the other five with the philosophy the sages reckoned to be necessary.

§2 The first of these arts is agriculture, sea travel, and governing people since these are the primary skills in the rule of cities and kingdoms. These cannot be performed except through the ancient knowledge that is found in very many books.

§3 After this is the art of leading soldiers, commanding armies, waging skirmishes and battles, calling animals and birds, and deceiving them. Very many books are also found on these topics.

§4 After these are the civilized arts by which humankind is sustained. Among these are grammar, the division of languages, legal jurisprudence, devising explanations, understanding laws and those who follow them (like scribal work with its pertinent affairs), buying and selling, and so on. Very many books are found on these things.

§5 Then follows arithmetic and all the books through which numbers and the like are known. After these follows geometry, which consists of the theoretical and the practical; from this comes the art of measuring land, lifting heavy weights, making discoveries, directing water flow, and constructing aerial instruments and incendiary mirrors (and their reflections). Next follows astronomy, through which the paths of the planets and the judgments of the stars are known. After this, music must be learned, through which singing, playing, and notation are understood.

§6 After that is dialectic, which is divided into eight books, that the wise Aristotle taught us to enter.[13]

§7 After this is medicine, which is divided into two parts, namely the theoretical and the practical. [199]

§8 After that follows natural philosophy, which Aristotle and other wise philosophers laid out. On this a great many books are known, which require many glosses and explanations. The first of these is called *Oydus the Natural*;[14] the second, *On Heaven and Earth*; the third, *On Generation and Corruption*; the fourth, *On Signs Appearing in the Heavens*; the fifth, *On Minerals*; the sixth, *On Plants*; the seventh, *On the Motion of Animals* (namely, from one place to another).

§9 Next follows *On Metaphysics*, which Aristotle wrote in thirteen books. Whoever understands and knows these well will be a perfect and complete sage and will reach out to touch the fulfillment of his desires.

§10 After all this, the two conclusions we mentioned rightly follow from these ten arts. Whoever ignores them will never attain the said conclusions. Keep in mind what we have said so far and strive out of necessity to learn all these disciplines. When you work, having mastered these disciplines, you will achieve what the ancient sages achieved and understand the works of the wise and the spiritual sciences. You will perform those things that they themselves once did. You will acquire grace from the Highest according to what work you do upon your spirit and your animal drives. This is understood from the secret statements of the prophets.

§11 After this follows love, for the greatest power exists in love. Note, however, that love is twofold: namely love acquired by virtue and love steeped in vice. The love acquired by virtue is what we speak of here, and you should seek to acquire nothing else. The love steeped in vice is a love of bodily lusts and material forms.[15] Therefore, flee as far as possible from this love. It is said in the books of the wise that the binding of spirits with harmonies and appropriate substances consists primarily in love. The human spirit is divided into three parts, namely the animal spirit, the natural spirit, and the rational spirit. When the human natural spirit overcomes others, the person will be a lover of things, like eating, drinking, and nothing else. If the animal spirit overcomes the others, the person will be a lover of nothing but conquering and overcoming others. If the rational spirit prevails, the person will be a lover of intelligence, goodness, and knowledge.[16] All this occurs purely because one of the planets presided over that person's nativity, and this planet is called the lord of the nativity. Know that if the Moon or Venus were the lord of anyone's nativity, such a person would be a lover of women and of a jolly disposition. If the Sun or Mars were lord of the nativity, such a person would be a lover of victory and conquest. If it were Jupiter or Mercury, that person would be a lover of knowledge, learning, understanding values, [200] goodness, and justice. On account of this, whatever stands out in a person appears as much in their nature as in their passion. A love that dwells upon earthly things is acquired by sight, and by using such a sight, it grows continually, just as wheat grows in the ground from its seed, as a tree when planted, or as the sperm of an animal when received by a womb. In this, sight is like matter since sight stands at the root of such a love. Thus, when a thing is loved, that love grows and is augmented by using and receiving the object by sight. When that object is united with the lover, their spirit is made one. This is a bodily love between two spirits in whom love is found through harmonious friendship. If this love exists in the rational spirit, however, it will delight in what is from its own kind (that is, wisdom, knowledge, goodness, stable virtues, and endless eternal things). This love of goodness, excellence, and splendor is deservingly called the rational spirit. The other loves that we have mentioned are evil and should rightly be relinquished because they contain maliciousness of spirit. The object of sight is corrupted and ruined on account of such a friendship and union of spirits and their persistence.

§12 In the book *On the Soul*, Plato said this: "Dry and melancholic complexions and dry sources of sickness and corruption are factors worth examining and contemplating. When these arise, individuals become like dry animals from hot and dry lands or mountains. Such places harm and corrupt whoever approaches or dwells in them, and this occurs very quickly. These places also harm and corrupt through the aspect they face. Therefore, whoever examines their own complexion and spirit with an ill will harms and corrupts what they behold."

Chapter 6

How Suffumigations of the Stars Must Be Made and a Demonstration of a Certain Compound Necessary for This Science

§1 Some Indian sage who had been very well taught in this body of knowledge combined compound suffumigations and terrestrial natures with celestial natures. The Indians used to operate with suffumigations in all their works and effects and thereby attract the spirits of the planets and make them enter whatever they wished. Thus, the sages accomplished whatever they desired. This work is not designed for one single objective; rather, it is useful in its single effect or product to the rituals of each and every planet, as we have often said in this book. Thus, rituals are conjoined with suffumigations.

§2 *The suffumigation of Saturn.* Take 100 oz. each of mandrake fruits and dried olive leaves; 10 oz. each of black myrobalan seeds and dried black chickpeas; [201] 30 oz. each of black crow's brains and dried crane brains; 40 oz. each of pig blood and dried monkey blood. Grind, and blend everything well. From this, make 8 oz. tablets. In making them, operate with the spiritual power of Saturn, namely with the thing that we have discussed in book 3, chapter six of this volume.[17] Next, compress them, and set them aside for use.

§3 *The suffumigation of Jupiter.* Take 10 oz. each of balsam and myrtle flowers, all of them dried; 14 oz. of frankincense; 4 oz. each of shelled nuts and shelled, dried hazelnuts; 40 oz. each of cock, dove, and goose brains, all dried; 20 oz. each of peacock and camel blood, dried; 8 oz. each of nutmeg and camphor. Ensure the bloods we mention in this suffumigation not be extracted from the heart of the animal. Blend everything together after grinding well, as described above; do everything as we have said above regarding the suffumigation of Saturn.

§4 *The suffumigation of Mars.* Take 40 grains each of red asafoetida, mustard, and terebinth; 4 oz. each of pine resin and red orpiment; 20 oz. each of sparrow and dried scorpion brains; 40 oz. of leopard blood; and 10 oz. of red snake grease. Blend everything together once well ground. Do everything as said above with the other suffumigations.

§5 *The suffumigation of the Sun.* Take 10 oz. each of spikenard flowers and yellow and red sandalwood; 6 oz. each of sedge, thyme, and red cinnamon bark; 2 oz. of costus; 20 oz. each of eagle brain and blood and cat brain and blood. Dry them out. Do everything in the same order as you did above with the other suffumigations.

§6 *The suffumigation of Venus.* Take 8 oz. of laurel berries, nut kernels, and frankincense grains; 20 oz. each of mastic gum and henbane stalks; 4 oz. each of poley germander stalks and storax gum; 2 oz. of borax; 16 oz. each of sparrow brain and dried hawk brain; and 40 oz. of dried horse blood. Blend everything together once well ground. Do everything as you have done with the other suffumigations.

§7 *The suffumigation of Mercury.* Take 20 oz. each of henbane flowers, indigo leaves, and hazelwort; 4 oz. each of amber and toad testicles; 2 oz. of red ammonia; 20 oz. each of crow, hoopoe, and tortoise brains; and 40 oz. of donkey blood. Mix and blend everything together once well dried and ground up. Do everything as you have done in the other suffumigations.

§8 *The suffumigation of the Moon.* Take 100 oz. each of peach tree and cinnamon leaves; 20 oz. each of iris and dried storax gum; 10 oz. of cumin; 4 oz. of white snake grease; 20 oz. each of dried white rabbit's and black cat's brains; and 40 oz. of fox blood. Blend everything together once well ground. Do everything in the same order as done in the other suffumigations above. Remember that the compounds of each planet must be blended with whipped honey. Make pills as was described regarding Saturn.

§9 Whenever doing those things, work with the power of the planet for which the compound is made (that is, with the spiritual power just as was touched upon in [202] book 3, chapter six). While performing this work, do not be silent: speak the words and prayers of that planet continuously. Be on guard lest anyone see these suffumigations and that neither the Sun's nor the Moon's rays touch them in any way. Set them aside in a chosen place, and tuck them away in a metal container. Make this case from the mineral of the planet to which the ritual pertains. If you do not do those things as described, the ritual will be ruined—know that destruction will come to the operator. After all these things, I will provide you the remedies in order that you not be ruined by that ritual.

§10 This Indian sage discovered a certain wondrous property that I wish to report to you from a book of his. It belongs to the works of Mercury and to the depths and secrets of the spirit (namely, the spirits of knowing, understanding, and learning). Know that this is taken from among the Indians' wondrous knowledge, secrets, and deep understandings. When any one of India's sages wished to preach to the people, he anointed himself and his companions with this mixture, and in doing so, the power of the spirit abounded in him, granting him grace, power, and strength above all others. Thereafter, the people were obedient to him. Its composition is this: take 40 oz. each of crow grease, sea crab fat, sheep grease, and the dried blood of a hoopoe; 20 oz. of amber; 10 oz. of each of dried pomegranate leaves and lemon seeds; and 50 oz. of costus. Grind and blend everything together very well. While working on these things, attract the spirit of Mercury to them by speaking continuously the prayer of the angel of Mercury we cited in our book.[18] Once finished, set it aside in a box made of solidified quicksilver. It is effective for the aforesaid things while anointing and suffumigating. These are among the wonders and secrets of this work. When the Indian sages wished to preach to the nations, they would smear themselves and their associates with this ointment; by this anointing they increased their spiritual intellectual power. Their words were devoutly received by all, and the people became obedient to their words.

§11 This confection relevant to the spirit of Saturn is put together in this way: take 40 oz. each of pig and bear grease; 20 oz. each of cinnamon and lupine seeds; and 10 oz. of myrobalan seeds and dried elephant's blood. Grind everything up well, and blend it together. Do everything in the order said above. While making it, attract the spiritual and celestial power to it, namely by uttering the prayer of the angel of Saturn as described in this book.[19] They used to offer up that compound before the spirit such that others not be heeded and that the operators be obeyed. I wish to teach you a ritual without which the planetary suffumigations and anointments above cannot be completed. Do this ritual so that the attraction of the planet's spiritual power might be completed most perfectly. This is held to be the greatest and deepest secret. When you wish to gather the blood or brains in these suffumigations and anointments, [203] decapitate the animals, and make these a sacrifice because the attraction of the spirits occurs more swiftly through sacrifice and suffumigation.[20] When you wish to make such a sacrifice, place the planet whose spirit you wish to attract in its exaltation and free from the unfortunate planets. Let no one see this confection, and set it aside in a lead box.

§12 This compound guards and protects those who make suffumigations from the harm caused by the planetary spirits. The strength and power of this compound is universal to all the planets' rituals and communication with their spirits. It is also very powerful against poisons since it protects and guards the operators so that they might not be harmed by these spirits. Its composition is this: take 6 oz. of scorpion brain; 4 oz. of white dog's brain; 8 oz. each of peacock and quail brain; 4 oz. of sparrow brain; 2 oz. of hawk brain; 6 oz. of male hedgehog's blood; and 20 oz. each of donkey and hoopoe brain. Mix and allow all of these brains to dry. Afterwards, grind them up, and add to them 4 oz.

each of white and yellow sandalwood, saffron, cinnamon, and spikenard; 1 oz. of pine resin; 20 oz. of amber; 6 oz. of ammoniac; 10 oz. of frankincense; 4 oz. of nutmeg; 2 oz. of camphor; 16 oz. of *quia* (a certain kind of gum); and 4 oz. of mandrake. Mix everything together once well ground, and blend with well-made moringa oil.[21] Make seven round pills from these, and dry them in the shade. While you are making these planetary compounds, utter their prayers and those of their angels continuously. Once the pills are made as described, set them aside in a box made from the seven metals of the seven planets so that the spirits of the planets abide in them continuously. One who wishes to perform one of the rituals of the seven planets or the celestial operations should carry one of those capsules, and they will not be harmed by the planetary spirits. The ancient sages would protect themselves from the harmful effects of those spirits with this mixture. Know that this is an utmost and very useful secret, so guard and hide it most well.

§13 The ointment that follows was discovered in the books of the wise. It is called the ointment of the Sun, and its power is receiving grace, honor, splendor, and the love of kings, soldiers, and nobles. Take a glass vial, and place in it very good, pure, and clean rose oil. On a Tuesday, rise to your feet facing toward the Sun in the sign of Aries or Leo in an ascending degree with the Moon facing him with a friendly aspect. Then take the vial in your right hand, holding your face toward the Sun, say:

> God bless you, O planet, filled by your light and goodness! O how beautiful and good you are in your origin and honored in your spirit! You are the Sun who governs the universe by your light, spirit, and strength. You are candle of the heavens, brightness of the universe, maker of all generable things. [204] This power was poured into you by God. You are the Sun who gazes through the four corners of the world while spinning in your heavens. Light and beauty have been granted to you by divine power. You grant without concealment a luminous life or light to the Moon from her beginning unto her end. Therefore, I ask that you grant me friendship, benevolence, and an amicable reception through this oil such that my friendship and will might overflow into the hearts of everyone, through which I might have the love and grace of kings, nobles, and lowly men. I myself am such a man. I beseech and conjure you by your rule that my friendship and love may be found in their hearts, their tongues, their places of delight, and their thrones everywhere, that they might rejoice at my sight and friendship in the delights they are accustomed to enjoying. Noting my presence there, let them honor me and be glad. I conjure you, lord, by the angel ANCORA, who

> resides in the fourth heaven, and by ANEHUTYORA, ACTARIE, AHUDEMEMORA, BEHARTYON, ACTARIE, AHUDEMEMORA that in this oil, which I hold in my hand, you should place the love and benevolence of kings', lords', and noblemen's hearts that they might enthusiastically take a liking to me and that I should not have an enemy in the universe. Let all men esteem and love me with obedience. Let there be no transgressor of my orders but rather seekers of my grace. I conjure you by BEHIBILYON and CELYUBERON, who dwell in the fifth heaven, so that you may open their hearts and bind their tongues such that they might be unable to speak ill of me and incapable of gossip. Ensure this binding for now and forevermore. I conjure you, lord, by ZAUCEB, angel of the sixth heaven, so that you may stop up the mouths of my enemies; rather, pour the love and delight of me into their hearts. I conjure you, lord, by BARHAOT, who resides in the seventh heaven, that you may grant to me the love, goodwill, good reputation, and good reception before the hearts of everyone in the universe and grant me, by your spirit and grace, the good reception and complete love of all men by day or night. I conjure you by the name that kindles love and friendship and that unites and brings together the hearts of lovers so that you may pour my love and benevolence into their hearts, enduring now and forever. Amen.

Utter this prayer twelve times having observed the conditions mentioned before. Afterward, guard this oil very carefully. When you wish to enter the presence of kings, lords, or noblemen, anoint your face with this oil. You should achieve what you desire and see wonders in being amicably received by these men. This ritual I found as above in the books of the Indians. It is still in use among them in all matters. [205]

Chapter 7

On What Is Found Concerning the Art of Magic in the "Chaldean Agriculture," Which Abubaer Abenvaxie Translated from the Chaldean Language into Arabic

§1 In the *Chaldean Agriculture*, which Abubaer Abenvaxie translated into Arabic from the tongue of the Chaldeans, we have found many writings on the art of magic and very numerous things of that sort, which we will now relate here.[22] On one page of that book, it is said that a certain gardener, while sleeping at night in a garden beneath a laurel tree, heard the tree speaking. It said:

"O human, look in this garden of yours to see if you find a tree that exceeds my beauty and quality; for indeed none can say that they have found a better, more beautiful, more honorable, and more precious tree than I." To this the gardener responded: "Why do you say such things? Explain to me what they mean." The tree responded: "I say such things to you so that you may acknowledge and honor me above the other trees. Know that I am honored and appreciated by Jupiter, who esteems and respects me. Therefore, I say that you should honor me above the other trees and adore me at the appropriate time. I shall reveal to you a wondrous ritual that is suitable for the future (wherein you will find the greatest uses). Therefore, arise in the middle of the night carrying acorn oil in your hands. Anoint your face with it. Next, lift your head up toward the heavens, look to Jupiter and say: 'O Jupiter, fortune of fortunes! I ask you, by the praise and honor that this laurel tree has toward you, that you may grant me life for the following fifteen years to come.' Once this is done, you will remain secure until the allotted lifespan is spent. In truth I say to you that if you have done the work, you will find it true, not deficient. Thus, you will benefit yourself. With this ritual, you will be able to perceive the honor and love that I share with Jupiter and how he esteems and appreciates me."

§2 In the aforesaid book concerning the properties of this tree, it said this:

> The prophet Adam said to take fourteen seeds of laurel tree fruits, then dry and pulverize them very well. Place the resulting powder with wine vinegar in a very clean pot. Strike it with the stick of a fig tree—whoever you wish to become demonically possessed, give them some of this powder in a drink. That person will seem profoundly vexed by a demon that nobody else will be able to see. The cure: give the person three medium-sized radishes with all their leaves such that not a single leaf remains. Once they have entered the stomach and remain there a while, the person will be released from the demon.

§3 In the same section regarding this laurel tree, it is proven that if you take some of the leaves of that laurel, throw them up with your hands, and before they touch the ground, [206] put them behind your ears, then for as long as they remain there, you will never become drunk nor have a hangover no matter how much unmixed wine you drank.

§4 In the same book, regarding this tree, it says: "Take some laurel leaves and one pound of either lime or blue vitriol. Pulverize them well, and mix with strong vinegar. Anoint your hands thoroughly with this. Once this is done, you will be able to hold glowing hot iron in your hands without injury."

§5 Again in the aforesaid book, it says: "If someone takes some of the branches of the ash tree and cooks its leaves, all the bedbugs in the area will gather to it."

§6 Abenvasia also recounts that wise magicians have said how if one works with words and rituals, the sap, fat, and oil of trees (all these exist in each and every tree) rapidly receive the power of the spirit and its effects. The sap is more disposed in reception than anything else. This is why some process the tree sap with words and rituals and give that sap, altered by words, to someone in a drink so as to destroy and ruin the hearts and bodies of the wise.

§7 Some sages have claimed that myrtle has the power to augment magical works once mixed with other things. Chaldean sages claim that those who work with this tree's roots craft varying images of animals where myrtle trees grow. Those sages claim that this is assuredly a magical root since effects and the spirit of an individual are manifest while gazing upon this root so similar to a human in form, figure, and likeness. Moreover, the sages claimed that they take myrtle tree branches on someone's nativity and fashion the image of a man or a woman from them while inscribing the image with the name of the target. They craft other figures from these branches (namely of lions, snakes, scorpions, or any other kind of venomous animal) combined with or placed upon the other image. They do this at a determined and appropriate time (when the planets and the fixed stars are properly placed for executing these works). The target for whom the images were crafted will immediately be struck with illness and seem cruelly afflicted by some demon while losing their mind and suffering various other ailments.

§8 In the *Chaldean Agriculture*, one finds that this tree commends itself above other trees, saying:

> I am the golden tree and such is my color—through me, humankind is healed and cured from forty-eight illnesses. My oil fortifies the heart and cleans the gums. Through it the spirit is gladdened; no other oil does this but mine. I am the blessed tree. [207] Whoever takes of my branches, leaves, or fruits and places them in their house will never suffer a wicked misfortune or sad thoughts. Throughout the whole cycle of that year, such people will live high-spirited and cheerful alongside their entire community. I am the tree blessed above all. Whoever gazes upon me in the morning with the rising Sun and carries me in their hand, on that day they will be gladdened and rejoice. I am the tree of Saturn, the heavy planet. I am a tree of greater fame and great Saturn. I am the tree through whom the troubled rejoice. I am the one who removes misfortune from

> the unfortunate. I am the one who populates desert regions. Through me the region of Phoenicia and the region of the Blacks are made fertile. Mine is the first among days, the highest and most honored among the planets, the oldest of cities, the strongest and most durable of forts, the greatest and longest of rivers, the coldest of winds, the most famous of regions, the highest of heavens, the tallest of trees, and I maintain the most excellent qualities and the finest among all the rest.

§9 Concerning this a certain sage named Zeherith, who was one of the three men assembling the *Chaldean Agriculture*, said:

> On the first day of the lunar month and in the first hour of that day, take olive branches with green and not yellow leaves, carry them home, set them aside until the beginning of the next Moon. Then, at the beginning of the subsequent Moon, take other branches home as before, carrying them as before and setting them aside in the place where the first ones are. Then take the first ones, and burn them, warming yourself with the heat of the embers. That person will be protected and totally free from all the evils and impediments of Saturn. They will become continuously cheerful in spirit and character. Rejoicing, they will never be sad nor mournful. They will profit in their works and stand in good fortune. They will be virtuous and not die until old age.

Moreover, he says: "If someone mixes palm tree branches with these olive tree branches while operating as before, all those dwelling in that house will enjoy healthy bodies until death. All cold illnesses will recede from them. The brightness and sight of their eyes will increase every day; all this by gazing upon these branches."

§10 Whoever takes nine olive pits, cleans them from all flesh, pierces them, and by threading them with a strong black silk thread, suspends them from the neck of any animal, that animal will fear nothing at night even when wandering alone. It will be cheerful and become docile to humans. If anyone would be afraid while wearing this around their neck, the fear would recede from them. If they would be boisterous, the boisterousness would be carried off and replaced by goodwill. If they would have wicked thoughts, these would flee from them and be replaced by persistent good thoughts. [208]

§11 If someone takes nine of these olive pits, cleaned from all extraneous juice and oil, and holding these in their hands, they face the Sun when he is rising in the morning and throw them one after another at the Sun's face, and while doing this, they say: "O Sun! Behold my piety and free me from this illness that I suffer"—if they do this seven times with forty-nine of these pits, they will be completely cured of that illness, even if it were a persistent one.

§12 If you wish to lift the ire of an angry person toward you, take (1)17[23] of these olive pits, well-cleaned as above, and wash them very well with hot water and, after a little while, with cold water. Dry them off completely with a clean and elegant cloth. Anoint the pits with olive oil. Next, put them up your left sleeve. Set yourself up over a flowing river, observing the water, and say: "O you running water that stands contrary to burning fire! Cool the anger of such a person toward me. Remove their ill will toward me, and pacify them until they love and esteem me unconditionally." Once this is done, throw one of the pits into the middle of the running waters, and speak these words (1)17 times, throwing one of the pits with each repetition. Once this is done, that person's anger directed against you will recede. Even if it were the anger of a great king or some other great lord, it will be pacified. He will delight in you and receive you honorably.

§13 If someone on a completely empty stomach takes any crystal container or one made of clear white glass and filling it with good clarified olive oil, places it in the morning Sun, continuously watching their own shadow and that oil, their sight will be sharpened; all the ocular ailments will recede; they will be gladdened in heart and mind; they will be loved and very well received by everyone around.

§14 If someone buries the flowering herb mallow while continually circling around it and observing its flowers, sadness, ill will, and wicked thoughts will be lifted from their heart. They will be very well received.

§15 If you wish that a source of running water regenerate itself once it dries up, do the following. Send a small and pretty virgin girl to this source carrying a drum. Standing above the water's course, she should begin to strike the drum gently; let her go on drumming for three hours. In the beginning of the fourth hour, however, have another beautiful and lovely virgin come to the same place carrying a tambourine that, while drumming, she should go along with the first girl making a similar beat as the drum with her tambourine. Make them do this for six hours (so nine hours in total), at the end of which the water in that source will be increased. Then on that same day or at least three days after, that source will be usable.

§16 Moreover, he adds:

> Pretty virgin girls dressed in clothes of various colors and carrying diverse instruments (whatever they have) should go on playing and drumming before the mouth of the spring. Afterward, [209] make them go on playing similarly two cubits from the mouth of the spring. Then,

one after another, make them recede to a distance of twenty-one cubits while drumming and return while singing. Then, make them go back around the mouth of the spring as before. Make them perform the ritual by coming and going to the spring, drumming, and singing as above. Once all this is done, the water of that spring will be increased on that day or the following one.

§17 If someone takes well-ground mallow leaves, mixes them with olive oil, and anoints their hands and body, when they place their hands amid bees or wasps, the insects will neither sting nor harm nor cause any pain.

§18 If someone wants to exterminate fleas, they should take white lead, quicklime, and bitter cucumber roots, grind them well, and add a little asafoetida. Blend everything with water, and mix in a little salt. If you sprinkle a house with this mixture, all the fleas living in that area will be exterminated.

§19 *For making wine drinkable.* Take chickpeas, and anoint them with olive oil, cook them, then grind them very well, and throw a half pound of them into wine turning bitter. That taste will recede in one day from the now normal wine.

§20 *For removing sadness.* Take chickpeas, place them in the light of the waxing Moon at night. The next day before the Sun rises, anoint them with olive oil, and put them in water to soften for two hours. Then cook them. Whoever you give some of these to eat, they will see sadness, ill will, troubled thoughts, and every kind of melancholy recede. Their heart will rejoice in the power of the Almighty, and they will always become joyous and cheerful.

§21 When clouds approach looking like they might carry hail and one wishes to defend crops from the hailstorm, assemble many associates, some of whom should carry silk in their hands and some should go to the field carrying nothing. Make them throw the silk bit by bit toward the clouds, and make the others who are without silk walk around clapping their hands and palms. Make everyone keep shouting in a loud voice like farmers do when they want to drive off birds and evil beasts. Make them do this many times. Make sure that those associates be even in number; the more numerous they are, the better. This has been tested and found to be very true.

§22 Take some pure steel (which is Andanican iron),[24] and make a very well-polished mirror out of it. Go toward the cloud, carrying the mirror in your hands, and raising it toward the cloud, shout in a powerful voice. The storm will recede from that area.

§23 In a book published by the wise Geber, I found this written for producing a storm and very many other things.[25] Make a mirror out of gold or gilded silver, [210] and suffumigate it with hair from a woman's comb, and anoint it with your semen. Next, suffumigate it with hairs from her clothes. After having bathed, look into the mirror, and in it have her likeness appear, then yours immediately (or yours first, then hers). This was tested by a man called Ptolomy of Babylon. Three Indian sages found it in Egypt and proved that such a mirror must be made when the Moon is conjoined with Jupiter and gilded or polished while the Moon is with Venus. I wish to reveal to you how to make this mirror and how to use and guard it (because it affects all humankind). Temper the mirror with living and natural blood, suffumigate it, then write the names of the seven stars, their seven figures, and the names of the seven angels and the seven winds upon it. The names of the seven stars are these: "ZOHAL, MUSTERI, MARRECH, XEMZ, ZOHARA, HOTARID, and ALCHAMAR." These symbols should be drawn in a circle around the outer edge:

These are in a circle. Next, write the names of these seven angels on the inside of the polished and gilded circle: "CAPTIEL, SATQUIEL, SAMAEL, RAPHAEL, ANAEL, MICHAEL, and GABRIEL." When this is done, write the names of the seven winds on the unpolished part; these are the winds of power, whose names are: "BARCHIA, BETHEL ALMODA, HAMAR BENABIS, ZOBAA MARRACH, FIDE ARRACH, and SAMORES MAYMON ACZABI." Then suspend the mirror in silk for seven days above water, and suffumigate it. Suspend it from a bramble branch. Suffumigate it for three nights with pleasant incenses (better yet with the ones found in the book of Moses). If you gaze into that mirror and guard it well, know that through it you will bring together men, winds, spirits, demons, the living, and the dead. All shall be obedient to you and heed your command. Proceed such that there is some of each of man's seven properties in the suffumigation (namely, blood, semen, saliva, ear wax, tears of the eyes, excrement, and urine). Suffumigate with those things, and instruct the winds of your desires; they shall enact your will. Guard this, and heed everything I have said. You will thereby have power over winds, humans, and demons, and you will do what you wish. When you are washed and clean, call them; they will come to you obediently. Do this above a basin or any clean vessel full of water. There you will behold the fulfillment of what you sought.

§24 A sage whom we have named elsewhere (namely Zeherith) cites the nineteen experiments written out below. The first is for defending vines from poor weather. Take a marble or wooden tablet, and inscribe images of vines and grapes upon it—do this between the twenty-second day of October and the fourth of December (that is, any day out of these); place this tablet thus prepared in the middle of the vines. This image is proven to defend vines from bad weather. [211]

§25 *For driving off animals that harm vines.* Take equal parts of black dog's and wolf's excrement. Mix them with human urine, and allow them to sit for seven days, after which you should sprinkle the vine you want with it. No harmful animals (like bears, wolves, foxes, snakes, and the like) will go there. Do these things continuously for three successive days. For driving off snakes, take euphorbia wood, and suffumigate the place where snakes gather with it; at once, they will flee that area.

§26 *For driving off snakes.* Take 1 oz. each of ammonia, asafoetida gum, and the strongest wine vinegar. Boil them over a fire, and while boiling, liquefy these gums until well mixed. Then sprinkle the powder from the horn of a stag over it; mix everything very well until blended together. Then take it out, and make tablets, which you will set aside for use in a glass container. When you wish to drive off snakes, whatever kind they are, suffumigate the place that you want to purify with these or any similar tablets. You will achieve your intent.

§27 *For driving off reptiles and mice.* Take mustard, stag horn, *axenus*,[26] and the claw of a leopard. Pulverize everything and mix it with the strongest wine vinegar. Blend and cook everything together until similar in thickness to oxymel. Next, mix the powder of pomegranate leaves with it. Make pills from this, and set aside for use in a glass container. When needed, suffumigate the area with the pills, and it will be rid of those pests.

§28 *For killing mice.* Take equal parts of litharge and white lead. Grind everything up, and add a quarter part of the said powders. Blend everything together with a bit of oil. Make pills that you should entirely cover with well-aged, good-smelling cheese. Put those in a place where mice gather; all those that eat any will die shortly.

§29 *For the same.* Take a bronze vessel. In it place the dregs of oil into which black hellebore was mixed. Place the container in a house where mice gather. They will assemble there because of the smell of the oil, and after they consume a little, they will immediately fall down as if intoxicated.

§30 *For killing scorpions.* Take radish leaves, and place them on top of scorpions. They will sting themselves until they die.

§31 *So that a lover may forget his beloved.* Take beans while the Moon is sitting in any of Saturn's houses, and soften them in wine for a single day and night. Then cook them in the same wine. Once cooked, give them to the lover to eat, and he will forget his beloved. [212]

§32 *So that wasps or bees do not sting you.* Take dried and ground asparagus roots, and mix them with sesame oil. Anoint your hands and feet with this, and you will be safe to enter a place since you will be free from their harm.

§33 *A deadly poison.* Take the sap of a plant that is found in parts of Armenia whose leaves are similar to palm leaves, except thinner. If you anoint the tips of lances or any other weapon with the sap and then strike someone to wound them, they will die on that very day or the next. *The cure.* Take fresh or dried human excrement. If you take it fresh, give the victim 2 oz. in a drink mixed with rose oil, violet oil, or both mixed. The only way they can avoid harm is with this drink. If you take the excrement dried, however, give them 4 oz. in a drink with the same amount of dried roses. As I recall, I believe that this herb is wolfsbane because its sap is a deadly poison when used on a sword to shed blood by wounding.[27]

§34 *Another deadly poison.* If someone takes one grain's worth of wolfsbane, they will die within four hours despite every remedy given afterwards (except fresh human excrement taken in a drink). Know that human excrement, fresh or dried, is generally good for curing all poisons except for the stings of the deaf adder, which it alone cannot heal. Rather, a bandage of very well-crushed radishes must be placed on the bite, and the pain will subside.

§35 *A panacea for every venom.* Take 3 oz. of laurel wood; 7 oz. of its leaves; and 2 oz. of its fruit. Dry and grind them very well. Add to this 6 oz. of human excrement. Mix and blend everything with honey and wax. Avoid having more of the latter mixture than the weight of the former. Keep this compound in a gold or silver container. It is a universal panacea for all venoms. Furthermore, it prevents grey hair. Place a laurel bough in a house where an upset infant is being nursed; the infant will be calmed when you place the bough above its cradle.

§36 If you plant a laurel tree in any house you wish, fear will depart from it, and its inhabitants will be happy, cheerful, and well-disposed through the quality of this tree.

§37 Darnel seed damages the brain, darkens the eyes, strips vision, and causes sleep. Some wicked men take equal parts of darnel seed, saffron, frankincense, and wine dregs. If anyone drinks that mixture, they will fall asleep, their tongues will dry out such that they will be unable to speak or even stand. If another four things are added to those [213] (mandrake, wild lettuce seed, black poppy, and the seed of henbane), whoever you give some of this blend will be intoxicated, senseless, and completely out of their mind. Abenvasia, speaking of this, recommended that this mixture be kept secret and not revealed to any wicked man.

§38 In the *Chaldean Agriculture* while speaking about that herb, Abenvasia claimed that there are many wondrous properties in it—that is, if you put a handful of it into a bowl and then toss snakes into it, they will rise up on their tails as if trying to jump. If you place this herb next to a mirror standing in the Sun, it will catch fire.

§39 *For healing leprosy.* When the Sun is rising at the beginning of the illness, take as many beans as you can in your hand, and say: "I beseech you, Sun, precious and high lord, that you carry this leprosy away from me, and make it vanish from my body, my chest, or wherever it is." After you have said this, throw the beans over your shoulder. Repeat these things, and throw them as above until the beans have all been thrown. Do this seven days in a row while the Moon is waning.

§40 *For catching birds.* Take beans and darnel, moisten them in wine for a single day and night. Then take them out, and put them in the migratory paths of cranes, crows, and other birds so that they can eat some of them. While eating some of them, they will fall to the ground as if dead.

§41 *For removing leeks.* Count the number of leeks, and take that number of chickpeas. While the Moon is conjoined to the Sun according to true motion, heat those chickpeas a little bit over a fire. Next, place one of them on each and every leek, leaving them there a while. Afterward, remove them, and place them in a black cloth tied with a string. Stand upon an elevated area, and throw those chickpeas behind your back. Return home without turning back or looking at the chickpeas.

§42 *For separating two from each other.* The seeds of some tree called *sebestan*[28] have many properties in magical rituals. Some of these are performed for separating two individuals from one another and sowing discord and enmity between them. The seed also has the property of separating friendships and altering the will of another toward inflicting evil upon others. This tree is similar to the laurel. The wise Zeherith has spoken up to this point.

§43 Abenvasia recounts how all the Chaldeans (nobles and commoners, men and women) used to place this under their [214] pillows on the first night of March: one piece of cheese, four dates, seven grape seeds, and a little salt fastened inside a cloth. They claimed that some old woman called "the handmaiden of Venus" would go looking for everyone in their beds on that night to stroke their bellies and look beneath their heads. If she found their bellies empty and did not find those things beneath their heads (namely, that portion of cheese, dates, and grapes), she would immediately pray to Venus that such a person be struck ill for that whole year and that they sustain a setback in all their endeavors from that point on to the subsequent year. All the Babylonians used to do these things without fail.

§44 He also claimed that the powers of Saturn and Mars are united in a certain fruit similar to a melon, which is called "watermelon." Those who work in mathematical operations use it. Again, he says: "If someone places some watermelon seeds in a human skull, buries it, and covers it very well with earth and waters it, from it will grow little melons. Whoever eats these little melons will have improved energy, memory, and intellect. If you place this seed in a donkey skull, bury it, and moisten it with water as above, little melons will grow there. If someone eats them, they will become ignorant, foolish, and lose their strength, daring, and intellect." In the same book, it is held that the Chaldeans use the roots of that herb for one purpose, the leaves for another, the twigs for another, the seeds for another, and the whole plant all together is used for yet another purpose. In these parts reside the magical art's wondrous and beautiful effects. This occurs because of the herb's sudden attraction and swift reception of those things placed around it. When mixed with human brain, whoever eats it performs wonders. The same book says that if this seed were placed in the head and stomach of any animal and either were buried in the ground, little melons would grow there that have wondrous effects. The effects of these would be similar to those of the animal into whose head or stomach the seed had been placed. Whoever eats some of them, causing them to become mixed with that person's nature, those seeds will do wondrous things in that person's body.

§45 In the same book it is held that if someone takes one mandrake root and buries it somewhere together with those watermelon seeds, they will perform many wonders there, which I omit at present on account of their tedious length; nevertheless, the wonders are fully contained in that book.

§46 One ancient sage, a forerunner in philosophy, recounted twelve miraculous rituals, which I have decided to describe here. The first one is that if someone places a human skull in a seeded area, seeds watermelon there, and covers the area with soil—if the seed were tossed onto ground primed for it and watered every day with human blood mixed with warm water, [215] little melons would grow there. If anyone eats some, they will behold terrifying things and many other wonders.

§47 And again he said:

> If someone takes an onion stalk in their hand while watching the Moon on the night in which she is rising during the first hour of the night, while standing upright facing the Moon, speaking the words and prayers of the Moon that we have mentioned in this book, and while uttering this subsequent conjuration: "I swear by you, O Moon, that if you remove from me the pain and infection of my teeth, I shall never eat an onion again!"

Then, they should heat the onion they hold and eat it. Whoever does this every month with the position of the Moon as mentioned above will be defended from all dental problems.

§48 *So that a cock may follow you.* Take the leaves of a garden onion, and fold them one upon the other. Give it to eat to the cock you desire for three days in a row—that is, three lumps on each day. Begin this task on a Wednesday. The cock will take a liking to you and follow.

§49 *So that all hard bodies be softened.* Take 10 lbs. each of alkali salt and galbanum. Put them in a container with three times the amount of pure water as both of those combined. Let it sit there for seven days, at the end of which you must strain the water with a cloth. Afterward, take hot water, and throw as much of the alkali and galbanum into it as you did before. Let it sit for another seven days, then strain it as above. Take hot water and for each 10 pounds of water, put a half pound of ammonia salt and 2 oz. of ink. Next, place everything over a gentle fire or in the very hot Sun. Leave it there for ten days, and cook it for one whole day. Then strain it, and it is done. If you place bones, horns, stones, or any hard metallic substance in it and allow it to stand there warming up in the Sun while covered in lead sheets, they will be softened like dough.

For the same. Take the bitter of cedars, and mix with bitter red wine. Mix them thoroughly until blended as one. For each pound of that mix, add 3 oz. each of ammonia salt and powdered sea salt. Mix them very well, and place them in the Sun for three days, stirring every day. Once this is done, place any hard body you want in it, and it will become so soft you can work it as you please.

For the same. This sage also claimed that sulfur softens metallic bodies and that its effect on all stones and metals is amazing.

§50 *For inducing copious laughter.* Give 10 oz. of powdered saffron in a drink to anyone you wish. At once, they will catch a pernicious laughter that will ultimately kill them.

§51 Broomrape harms all the plants and herbs living around it. Neither plant nor herb can grow where broomrape grows. [216] Nobody can uproot it except in this way: make a virgin girl go to it carrying in her hands a white cock with its crest cut off. She must circle the place where this herb is found, then make the cock strike the plant with its wings. Such a strike will dry out this herb.

§52 If some cat approaches an area where there is spikenard, after smelling that spice's odor, it will not leave, but instead it will seek out the spice there as often as it can while crying out loudly—this is one of the manifest wonders of herbs and their habitats.

§53 A good many regions have diverse properties, that is, there are plants and animals specifically attributed to them that are hardly found anywhere else, as is the case with balsam found only in Egypt; or ebony from the island of Huac and nowhere else; or the so-called "Tree of the Blacks" found only in the land of the Blacks; or the frankincense tree found in the field of Hamen;[29] or the tree of the muse that is only found in the West; or a great number of other things that exist in some places and not others, that is, precisely because they are suited to those places. The property of lands and places arises from the balance of water and air. The primary cause of all these is the line of heaven that crosses over that place and the power of the stars that dwell therein. The production of animals and plants there arises from the power and nature of the stars that occupy that line, a production that cannot occur elsewhere.

§54 In the western sea is a certain island called Cadiz where an herb grows in the springtime. Herds on that island eat that herb. If anyone drinks the milk of those herds, they will be drunk as if the milk were wine.

§55 In France there is a kind of tree that, if someone stands beneath it for half an hour, they will die. If someone touches it or takes some of it, they will die immediately.

§56 In the southern part of France, there is a small plant the size of a cabbage with leaves similar to rue leaves. If anyone takes the root, branches, and leaves of that plant, places them in cold water, and leaves them there for an hour, that water will be heated as if it had sat over a fire. Once lifted from there, it will immediately become cold as before.

§57 A certain tree is found in the lands of India that cannot in any way be burned by fire. Another tree is found there that moves like a snake if you take a branch from it and put it on the ground.[30]

§58 Another tree is found there around which are heard emanating human voices in spring and autumn. Its roots appear in the shape of a human. [217]

§59 In the land of Bequien, there exists a certain tree that shines at night like a candle.

§60 Moreover, this sage claimed that the costus found in the lands of India smells stronger than all other kinds; this is the suffumigation they made to the images in their ritual houses. The Chaldeans say that this is the very best suffumigation to sacrifice and suffumigate before images of Venus; they often use it on her images. In the *Chaldean Agriculture*, the wise Zeherith found this plant. He claimed that one group of Chaldeans would mix this herb with nutmeg, holm oak, fresh and dried storax gum, rose and myrtle flowers, and frankincense too. They then mixed everything with saffron. On their sacred days, they used to suffumigate their clothes, images, and faces with these ingredients, claiming that the odor of this smoke is harmful to all diseases and wards off their pains.

§61 They claimed that a suffumigation of the myrrh tree or its branches hinders epidemics. They claimed they used to make a suffumigation from the wood of this tree and its gum, which they enhanced by mixing incense, nutmeg, holm oak, and storax gum, believing that this suffumigation was graciously taken up by Venus. When they burned this suffumigation with the sacrifices of Venus—in the presence of her scripture and image, and with her prayers and conjurations, as mentioned in this book—they struck instruments, uttered the conjurations of Venus, and asked whatever they desired from her. This ritual would be received by Venus, and she would accomplish all their requests. They did not perform this ritual, however, unless Venus was free from the other planets and in such power and strength that she might not be impeded, especially from the aspects and conjunction of Mercury, since among the other impediments of Venus, the conjunction or aspect of Mercury takes precedence. The wise Zeherith states that adding saffron and costus increases the power of the aforesaid suffumigation, and the work is concluded easily.

§62 Moreover, we have here decided to describe the wondrous properties of vegetation because plants are one part of this elemental microcosm, subject to generation and corruption. Generation and corruption are divided into three parts, that is, into animals, plants, and minerals. Plants are in the middle between animals and minerals since they correspond with animals in living, growing, and reproducing while corresponding with minerals in their corporeal nature and lack of sense perception. Plants are more useful to human life than animals or minerals. The parts from plants useful to human life and health are the seeds, roots, branches, bark, leaves, flowers, and fruits. Minerals are also beneficial for humans who use their salts, alums, stones, and metals. Humans use the flesh, fat, bones, blood, and other ingredients from the bodies [218] of animals. It is therefore obvious that plants are situated closer to men than minerals. Among them are the trees that exceed the others in value, smell, quality, yield, or any other thing. The same is clear regarding minerals (that is, regarding precious stones reckoned to be more valuable than other ones) and the same regarding metals (among which gold prevails). Ultimately, the most excellent and valued of all corruptible things is the rational animal, namely humankind, to whom by sense and industry all things are made subject as if toward a purpose. The elemental world exists through the elements; the elements exist through nature; nature exists through spirit; spirit exists through mind; and mind exists through God Himself upon whom all heaven and nature depend. Let Him be praised through the infinite cycle of ages. Amen.

Chapter 8

On the Qualities of Other Things That Nature Produces by Her Own Properties

§1 Here we shall recount the wondrous properties of simple things, such as plants, animals, and minerals.
§2 First regarding the emerald, which, when seen by weasel-headed adders, causes them suddenly to go blind. If the afflicted adders turn their eyes toward fennel, they are healed immediately. Eagles carry this hard stone to their off-springs' birthplace so that their chicks may be protected from snakes. If a bear sees the eyes of a mouse, it will flee from there suddenly.
§3 When the bones of a hoopoe are thrown into hot water, some of them sink to the bottom and others stay at the surface.
§4 When an owl dies, one of its eyes remains open while the other stays shut. If you place the closed eye on someone, they will sleep and never be awakened while it remains on them. If, however, you place the open eye on someone, they will never sleep until it is removed. If arthritics place vulture feet upon themselves, they will be healed from their gout (that is, like this: if the gout is on the right side, they should place the right foot of the vulture upon themselves and do likewise for the left).
§5 In the land of Khorasan is found a very white stone named *assiffe* that cannot be filed.[31] When this stone is placed over anyone's stomach, it heals stomach illnesses of any sort.
§6 In the river Algeriche are formed white, grey, black, and mixed stones.[32] If rubbed together, they provoke rain into that river persisting as long as they are rubbed together. Consequently, no one can enter that river or walk on surrounding pebbles at night because of the rubbing of the stones, the [219] friction of which causes rain (one cannot see the stones at night).
§7 The aetite stone rattles on the inside when shaken as if there were another stone enclosed within. When it is shattered, however, nothing is found inside and each of its fragments rattles as above. This stone is red in color like the soil on Cyprus. Its wondrous power is in giving birth: if a woman about to give birth takes it, she will deliver immediately without danger and with little pain.
§8 There is a certain animal the size of a fox and similar to a cat in shape and appearance. This animal extinguishes fire by its coldness, and fire cannot harm nor burn it. The beak of an ostrich cannot be burned by fire nor can its stomach, into which a hot iron can be placed. Indeed, the iron is digested in its stomach, and it receives no harm from it—it is even nourished thereby. If you take all the feathers from any bird and make a big pile, then rub that pile on any

cloth or hand, any small object you touch will be attracted to it and float above the ground.

§9 There exists a stone named *behet* whose color is like that of marcasite, but it shines beautifully. If anyone sees it once, they will remain in permanent laughter until they die. There is no remedy for this laughter. Atop the stone is found a bird named *alphersit*. It is the size of a sparrow and black but has a red neck and legs. When this bird climbs atop the stone, the stone loses its power. Afterward, if someone sees it, the stone will do no harm.

§10 The peony plant produces a thick bough, and it is found to be sturdy when one tries to break it. If you place this bough on a possessed person, they will be freed from the demon. It will depart on account of that bough's odor.

§11 If you burn a stag's horn in front of snakes, they will die from the odor. Ants die from the odor of cumin. Scorpions flee from the odor of saffron and never stay in a place where it is. Fleas flee the odor of chalk and also from hot salt when placed in a house. If you suffumigate with fleabane, bedbugs flee at once.

§12 In pools of water there exists an algae that does not burn. This herb is similar to a green plant, but it is not one. It is called the swamp lentil. When a branch of jujube tree is burned, it neither glows nor makes a flame.

§13 The vulture carries the leaves of wormwood[33] to its nest so that the chicks may be guarded from harmful animals.

§14 The *atarac* stone is made from inseparable things and is never shattered whether large or small. If you place obols of a certain stone called amethyst in a container of wine and someone drinks from that container, they will never [220] be intoxicated and the wine will not harm them. If you place obols of a certain stone called *atambari* in a vessel,[34] anything that sits in that vessel will intoxicate the one drinking it. They will lose their minds and senses and become anxious and depressed. The magnet attracts iron. If you anoint it with garlic, however, it loses its power. Subsequently, if you place it in ram's blood, it recovers its power.

§15 In the river Cerich is found a certain species of snake.[35] If anyone sees one, that person will die. If the snake sees itself, it will also die.

§16 If you put a pig on top of a donkey and the donkey urinates by accident, the pig will die immediately.

§17 When hail appears, if a menstruating woman throws herself onto the ground completely naked, raising her legs toward the cloud, the hail will not fall around her on that field or harvest.

§18 If a dog climbs up a mountain or an elevated place and a hyena crosses its path and both shadows encounter each other, the dog will die since that animal will kill it.

§19 If someone afflicted with quartan fever sits on a wolf pelt, they will be cured from the fever.

§20 If you place the "fifteen square" on a woman giving birth, she will deliver easily and without danger.[36] If you place nutmeg on the neck of someone suffering from quartan fever, they will be healed.

§21 If you place elephant dung in a tree, that tree will not produce fruit so long as the dung remains there. If you place this dung upon a woman, she will never be impregnated.

§22 The stone that draws yellow fluid from a person with edema loses its power and is destroyed after it drains a person.

§23 With the stone called *ligia*,[37] quicksilver is congealed and becomes a solid.

§24 If you place a spider's web upon one suffering from quartan fever, it heals them in in a short time. If you mix beetles with that web, the afflicted will be healed completely.

§25 Snakes and adders flee when they hear the cry of an ostrich.

§26 When you mix < . . . > with silver extracted and purified from bronze and with these you strike the dwellings of birds, the birds will be paralyzed and easily captured.

§27 If you touch any meat with the forehead of a sea hare, it will be totally curdled into small lumps as if it had been ground up. If gold is placed in mouse droppings, it will be burned as if with lead. When it is thus burned and rendered to dust, if you place it in cat excrement, it will retransform and return to its pristine state. When gold is mixed with any [221] matter, it is wasted. Only melting gold with marcasite and sulfur purifies and refines it.

§28 Malachite softens gold. If you melt it with gold, it prevents the gold's combustion. If you place borax with it, its effect will be better. If gold is quenched in the sap of henna leaves, it will be subject to change many times in succession, losing its initial imperfection. Salt increases its redness. When you place silver over the smoke of sulfur, it will turn black. When you place it in salt, it loses that blackness and becomes white.

§29 Sal ammoniac has the property of drawing out all the moisture from every body, inside and out. Niter cleanses all bodies from their moisture and clears their surfaces. If you mix lapis lazuli with gold, the gold is enhanced in its beauty and clarity. If you place it over a fire, the lapis lazuli is burned away and disappears. It is also given for illnesses of the eyes. When marcasite is burned in sulfur, it enters into the Great Work.[38] From this comes the Great Work's raw material. Magnesium has a mix of lead in its body, and without it, glasswork could not be performed. Calamine tints red bronze golden and also draws moisture away from the eyes and cures them of every moist illness. White calamine is best of all. When you rub your teeth and gums with crystal dust, the teeth are strengthened, and the gums are freed from corrosion.

§30 The ash from burned sea crabs removes eye pain and fortifies sight. If a dog eats the spleen of a camel, it will die immediately. If you place the feces of a dog that ate bones upon an abscess of the throat, it dissolves the abscess, which will be healed at once. If you place the shell of a female tortoise over a pot, the pot will never boil.

§31 There are two kinds of milkvetch plant, that is, male and female. If you give 5 oz. to drink of the female plant to a woman, she will have a great appetite for sex with a man. A man will do likewise if you give him just as much of the male plant in drink or food. He will be highly irritated and unable to escape the irritation until you give him 2 oz. of oxide of bronze in a drink. If you give the flower of that plant to anyone in wine, they will sleep for three days. If you wish to awaken this person, give them hot water with olive oil to drink. If the leaves of this plant are ground up and distempered with sulfur water, it would heal wounds in a single day if placed upon them.

§32 If a snake or a scorpion is bound with the skin of this plant, it will die immediately. [222]

§33 Salt is good for the stings of scorpions, wasps, or snakes. Purslane eaten on consecutive days restricts the blood and immediately heals a sting by chewing it raw or cooked.

§34 If a ram encounters a lion, it will at once die a natural death right there.

§35 A tarantula dies when it encounters a scorpion, and a snake dies when it encounters an owl.

§36 If someone takes a steel or a carnelian ring on which they write these twenty-six figures and wear it on their finger when visiting a king or nobleman, they will be well received in the best possible way. Whatever is sought from this king or nobleman will be accomplished with effect. Pay very close attention that you make no mistake in any way in these figures, for if anything is lacking in them, nothing will arise from the effect. This is one among the miracles of this art. These are the figures:

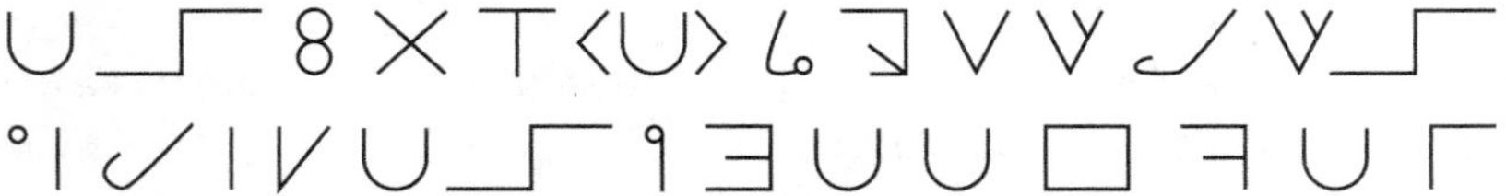

Moreover, these figures have been found in the book of Queen Cleopatra.

§37 If you put this ring on a tarantula bite and afterward wash it with human spit, at once, it will be healed. If you rub a tarantula bite with the leaves of an herb called *yembut*,[39] one side after another, it will be healed immediately. Tar mixed with salt heals a snake wound. If a man anoints his penis with tar and has sex with a woman, she will not conceive. Eating hazelnuts heals the sting of a tarantula. As long as someone carries hazelnuts, they will not be harmed by a tarantula's sting. If someone is bitten by a rabid dog and places chewed up bitter almonds upon the wound and eats some of them, they will be freed from the bite. If you place the herb called southern wormwood upon an adder's sting, it will be healed instantly. If the sap is sprinkled throughout a dwelling, fleas will go mad; if they fall into this sap, they will die.

§38 If you burn up tarantulas, mix their ash with bread, and give it to one suffering from a stone-related ailment, the stone will be shattered, and they will be healed. Flour of the seed of the herb called vetch mixed with milk heals a rabid dog's bite, if placed upon it.

Chapter 9

On the Images with Wondrous Powers That Were Discovered in a Book Found in the Church of Córdoba and in the Book of Queen Cleopatra; It Mentions Some Necessary Rules in the Use of Images

§1 In the book discovered in Queen Cleopatra's chamber, we found composite images that would produce wondrous effects and miraculous works by means of their properties and [223] powers. We here propose to mention these images in order that this science may lack nothing.

For healing reptile bites. Take shade-dried kite gall, mix a little fennel juice with it, and place it in a glass container. This powder applied to the eyes cures and heals them from the bites of tarantulas, vipers, wasps, snakes, and other reptiles. If the bite were on the right, place this powder on the left. If the bite were on the left, place the powder on the right. When you wish to do this, add a little water, and repeat three times.

§2 *That snakes may exit from their holes.* Take a shard of glass and shavings of yellow bronze. Pour them into a crucible, and add to them red arsenic and red magnesium. Next, remove them from the fire, and make small pieces. Then take the head of a kite and its bones (find this kite in Egypt), and mix them with black galbanum. Melt those things over a fire, and add that second medicine. When this is done, remove it from the fire. Make out of it a "sistrum," which we call a rattle, and place in it a grain of diamond found in Egypt. Once you have done this, rattle it at the mouths of the holes of adders, serpents, and other reptiles. Those among the serpents who hear this rattling sistrum will flee their holes immediately without posing any danger to the individual using the sistrum. One property of this bird (that is, the kite) is that when it calls and snakes hear it, they flee their holes and are killed by its voice.

§3 *For gathering mice.* Take the sap of white grape leaves, squill sap, borax, henbane, and red Indian calamine. The borax and calamine must be powdered and mixed with the aforementioned juices. From these, make tablets the size of a chickpea, and let them dry in the shade. When you wish gather mice, place one of these tablets upon the coals of a fire. When the mice perceive the smoke, all will assemble there. Do with them what you wish.

§4 *For gathering fish into one place.* Take millet, and set it to rot. Once rotten, mix it with tallow, pulverized beans, and cattle blood. Mix them well until rendered to a single substance. Next, put the substance into a reed, and thread the reed with hemp string. Then toss the reed into a place where there are fish. All the fish dwelling there will assemble around that reed, and you will be able to catch them with nets as you wish. [224]

§5 *For catching birds sleeping in trees.* Take equal parts of land tortoise fat, lily seeds, sweet myrrh, and gypsophila. Pulverize and grind them together well. Make a lump out of them with donkey urine, and make tablets the size of a chickpea, which you should let dry in the shade. When it is time to work, take a lidded earthenware pot filled with burning coals, and toss in one of these tablets to suffumigate the area where the birds are. Plug your nostrils with silk lest you inhale the smoke. All birds who ingest this smoke will fall to the ground as if dead. Take them as you wish. If you wish to heal them, wash their feet with hot water, and they will be free.

§6 *For the same.* Take mandrake and ammonia. Blend them with fresh hemlock sap. Then make tablets from this, and allow them to dry. Make a suffumigation from these under trees where there are birds. Do this while the weather is calm and without wind. All birds who inhale the smoke will fall to the ground as if dead.

§7 *For sharpening vision.* Make a crown out of the branches of a tree named *catlam*, which I reckon is sorbus, and place it on your head. While wearing it, your vision will be strengthened such that you will be able to see the smallest thing from far away. When you take it off your head, your vision will return to its original state. By anointing with the sap of this tree's leaves mixed with wine vinegar, scabies will be healed immediately.

§8 *To prevent intoxication.* Make a container out of brass as thin as you can, then take equal parts of wine vinegar (distilled through an alembic), cabbage juice, and sedge sap. Mix everything together. Once this is done, dip the container into this mixture many times until you have a pound of it. Then raise this container. When you wish to drink, however, anoint this container with the oil of bitter almonds, drink as much as you desire, and you will never be intoxicated.

§9 *That flies not approach the dinner table.* Take fresh wolfsbane, yellow orpiment, and basket-dried earth. Grind everything to a fine powder, and mix it with squill sap. Cover this in oil, and also anoint your own hands with the oil. Make an image in the shape of a fly with the aforesaid mixture, and place it upon the table. As long as it stays there, no fly will remain.

§10 *For expelling snakes and reptiles.* Take the skin of a leopard, which is tanned and softened into a hide. From it make a blanket. No venomous creature will abide there.

§11 *For evading adders.* Take round birthwort, and mix it with the meat of a *racanus*, which is a large green lizard. [225] Grind these together very thoroughly, and add to them lion gall. Make tablets from this. When you wish to use them, distemper one of these pills with water from sal ammoniac. With it write whatever you want on paper or parchment. Then wrap it in a cloth. Whoever carries this cloth will evade all adders. If any adder touches this cloth, it will die immediately.

§12 *That vapors may rise like fire.* Take the root of an herb called common corn-cockle (this herb shines at night as if it were a candle).[40] Grind this root very thoroughly with stag brain and ox gall. Make capsules out of this. If you place one of these into a dung fire, wondrous smoke will arise that will redden the entire sky, and vapors will rise that appear like a fire's flames. All who behold this will be afraid. This must not be performed except in cloudy and dense weather.

§13 *If this light is before you, you will see nothing; if behind you, you will see everything in the house.* Take dolphin fat, and anoint a wick thoroughly with ground arsenic and verdigris. Then put the fat in a bronze crucible, and place that wick in it. Set it alight, and it should make light that if someone holds it in their hands, they will see nothing; anyone holding it behind themselves will see everything that is in the house.

§14 *That a woman may not conceive.* Make the image of a monkey out of bronze, perforate its spine, and fill it with scammony. When you want to have sex with a woman, bind this image to your legs, and the woman will not conceive.

§15 *That dogs may not bark at you.* Take well-ground mandrake root, and blend it with the milk of a female dog. With these, make the image of a dog, and carry it with you. Dogs will not bark at you, but rather, they will flee.

§16 *That iron may be turned into water.* Take equal parts of the herb called *camesir*,[41] squill, and the husk of green pomegranates. Grind everything up, mix, and temper with white vinegar. Then distill through an alembic. Quench the iron many times in the vinegar, and it will be converted into water. Let it stand for an hour and a half, then drain the vinegar. You will find the iron shining, flowing, and pooling together.

§17 *That a cloth may be burned without fire.* Take golden marcasite, grind it up very thoroughly, and mix it with the strongest wine vinegar. Make it trickle down through an alembic into a glass container, and place it under a dung heap, leaving it there for fourteen days. Afterward, remove it, and put it in wheat chaff for the same number of days. Then take it out, and anoint whatever cloth you want with it. That cloth will burn as if on fire.

§18 *Water that burns and appears entirely red.* Take Cyprian blue vitriol,[42] roast it in a well-heated oven, and leave it there for one night. [226] The next morning, take it out, and you will find it completely red. If you do not, let it remain there for another night until it becomes red. Once red, take it out. Grind it very well, and sprinkle upon it distilled wine vinegar (five times as much as there was of the blue vitriol). Next, place it in a glass container, and leave it there for three days, mixing it three times per day. Then put it to boil, and froth very well. A reddish water like the color of ruby will emerge. Put this water in a crucible with a lit wick. This water will burn. From its light an entire house will appear red in color (that is, in the color of ruby). The entire house will shine like a ruby.

§19 *For making green tarantulas whose stings kill.* When you want to do this, fast for the entire day until nighttime. At night, take some of the herb called forest basil, mash it up well, and put that mash in a glass tube whose opening you will seal very thoroughly. Place it in a dark house where neither the Sun nor any other light shines. There, allow it to sit for forty days. Afterward, remove it. In it you will find green tarantulas that if they bite anyone, that person will die. These tarantulas have a property: if you place them in olive oil in the Sun and let them sit there for twenty-one days (or some such a span of time), they die and dissolve in the oil. If you anoint tarantula bites with that oil, they will heal. If a drop of it falls upon a tarantula, it will die instantly.

§20 *For making red snakes.* Take the web of large spiders, and place it with donkey milk into a glass tube. Let them sit there for three days, after which have them removed. Add tortoise fat, and grind those things very well until they have turned to the consistency of brains. Place everything in a red linen cloth, and bury it in manure for seven days. After this, you will find a red snake. If you place it around frogs or spiders, the serpent will take the form of a dragon, for the tarantulas in the land of Egypt are inimical to the dragon. When they see dragons, they bite them and wound them to death.

§21 *For repelling bedbugs.* Take one hair from the neck of a virgin mare—take it when a stallion is joined to her for the first time. Next, make images of bedbugs, as many as you can from the hair, laying them out in the shape of grape clusters. Afterward, take these clusters, and put them in a yellow bronze container. Seal its opening very well. Bury this in the middle of the house. Bedbugs will never enter that house as long as these things remain there.

§22 *That light may destroy whatever wood you want.* Take seadog fat, mix it with laurel oil, soap, and a little sulfur until [227] they are blended. If you smear the mixture on any wood you wish, a light will set ablaze like a candle. It will not be extinguished until the wood is consumed. This operation is among the ones done in Antioch.

§23 *For repelling wolves and all harmful animals.* Do this ritual with a drum specially made for it, crafted thus: take a sea urchin, decapitate it, and remove some of its spines. Skin it. Prepare and anoint the skin as done with other hides. Afterward, take the hide, and stretch it very well over a drum or a bronze naker. Set it aside for use. When you wish to repel the aforementioned beasts, strike the drum or naker at night since all harmful beasts will flee at its sound, and all reptiles hearing it will die.

§24 *To remove frogs from cisterns.* Take crocodile fat, and mix it with wax. Make candles from this with a wick. Burn the candle wherever you want. The croaking of frogs will be totally muted.

§25 *The capture of tarantulas.* Take chastetree and white thistle; shake them together thoroughly. Add red galbanum and a very well-ground bezoar stone. Blend everything with blackberry juice. Make the image of a tarantula from this mass. Make capsules from the residue of the preparations, and dry them out in the shade. Afterward, place the image before yourself, and toss some of those capsules in a fire for suffumigating. All the tarantulas there will gather together before the image. I believe that in this ritual, it is the power of the suffumigation that has a greater influence than the image.

§26 We have taken all the aforesaid images and mixtures from the *Chaldean Agriculture*, which we have decided to put here so that this book of ours may be more complete. You who intend to read this book should hold this as secretly as possible. Reveal it to none but the worthy, apt, and predisposed to this art. Those people are few in number. May you fail to reveal these secrets to anyone but yourself.

§27 Always remember the rules and lessons that the wise Socrates taught to his disciples at the end of his life.[43]

First: Direct and order your natures that they may be congruent, in and of themselves, to a perfect understanding of the things pertaining to this art. With these you will gain the greatest benefit in magic.

Second: Never reveal your secrets and holiness except to your own heart when circumstances are grim. Just as evil and tortuous times are set upon you through change, so too will change set forthright and good things upon you.

Third: Do not ignore the things that happen to you after having been exposed to receiving augment and ascension, and do not think those things as trifles. [228]

Fourth: Consult your friends, and build friendships bit-by-bit, in the way a child is reared. Do not reveal them your love and benevolence too suddenly but little by little. If your friends want something from you and get it all at once, their friendship will not last (rather, they will become enemies).

Fifth: Avoid and flee from twisted and shameful things as much as possible. Excellence is degraded, and goodness is corrupted by these things.

Sixth: Take care of your friends, and do not ask from them everything simply because it is justly yours. Heeding this rule, you maintain a good friendship.

Seventh: Do not incessantly criticize your friends' habits since you yourself will be criticized for similar things.

Eighth: Do not respond to those who seek something from you with contempt, since in God's eyes this is a distinct sign of the meager value of the goods granted to you by His grace. Fulfill the requests of the needy as much as possible while observing the expected customs. In doing so, give incessant thanks to God for putting you in such a station that you are able to provide for the needy. So long as this is the case, it proves that prosperity and an upright and praiseworthy intent belong to God.

Ninth: Recognize and appreciate the value and nature of things for their strengths—in this your own value will be recognized. Others will esteem you in some way or another.

The wise Socrates taught these precepts to his disciples at the end of his life. They are the useful fundamentals of magic.

§28 Here, I shall explain the seven rules that Pythagoras approved.

First: Balance burdens proportionally, and keep them in due order.

Second: Rectify your friendships and loves—act so as to keep them healthy.

Third: Do not set a fire in a green place cut by a blade.

Fourth: Steer your desires and appetites—measure them correctly according to the weight of their consequences. Keep your body in good health.

Fifth: Always spend time with the honest and fair; thus, the love and friendship of people toward you will increase.

Sixth: Observe custom, and act according to the word of lords and judges while observing the necessities for maintaining life in the world.

Seventh: Do not harm nor contaminate your spirit and body. Rather, pay respect to due temperance such that you can always act soberly at a time of necessity.

§29 *According to Plinio, these are the twenty-eight mansions of the Moon.*[44] The first of these is for destroying and depopulating, and this mansion is called *Alnath*. While the Moon is wandering in this mansion, make the image of a black man wrapped and cloaked in a garment of hair, standing on his feet, with a spear in his right hand in the manner of a warrior. Make this image on [229] an iron ring, and suffumigate it with liquid storax. Make a seal with the ring in black wax while saying: "You, O GERIZ, kill such-and-such son of such-and-such woman swiftly and soon; destroy them!" Once this process has been observed, what you desire shall be. Know that GERIZ is the name of the lord of that mansion.

§30 The second mansion is *Albotayn*, and it is for removing anger. When the Moon is travelling through this mansion, take white wax and mastic gum, and blend them together over a fire. Next, remove this mixture from the fire, and make from it the image of a crowned king. Suffumigate it with aloewood, and say: "You, O ENEDIL, cast away the anger of such-and-such from me, reconcile him toward me, and implement my requests toward him." Keep the image with you, and what you desire will ensue. Know that ENEDIL is the name of the lord of this mansion.

§31 The third mansion is *Azoraye* (that is, the Pleiades), and it is for acquiring every good. When the Moon is in this mansion, make the figure of a seated woman holding her right hand above her head and dressed in clothes. Suffumigate it with musk, camphor, mastic gum, and aromatic hooves. Say: "O ANNUNCIA, do such-and-such"; then state whatever request toward the good you desire. Make this figure on a silver ring whose flat part should be square. Then place it on your finger. Once you have done these things in this manner, what you wish will ensue, and your request will be implemented with effect. Know that ANNUNCIA is the name of the lord of that mansion.

§32 The fourth mansion is *Aldebaran*, and it is for creating enmity. When the Moon is crossing this mansion, take red wax, and make from it the image of a military man riding upon a horse, holding a snake in his right hand. Suffumigate this with red myrrh and storax. Say: "You, O ASSAREZ, make it so for me, and fulfill my request," then ask for animosity, division, and ill will from the pertinent people. Everything you have requested will happen. Know that ASSAREZ is the name of the lord of that mansion.

§33 The fifth mansion is *Almizen*, and it allows you to be well received by kings and officials. When the Moon is crossing this mansion, make a silver sigil on which should be sculpted the head of a man without a body. Write on this head the name of the lord of this mansion, and write your request on the sigil—whatever it is. Then suffumigate it with sandalwood, and say: "You, O CABIL, make it so for me, and fulfill my request—namely, that kings and nobles should receive me well and in the best possible manner." Once you have done this, carry that sigil around with you and your request will be fulfilled. When you wish to see something in your sleep at night, place this sigil under your head when you go to sleep, always contemplating your desire in mind. You will receive the answer you sought. Know that CABIL is the name of the lord of that mansion.

§34 The sixth mansion is *Achaya*, and it is for creating love between two people. When the Moon is in this mansion, make two white wax images [230] embracing each other, and wrap them in a white silk cloth. Suffumigate them with aloewood and amber, and say: "You, O NEDEYRAHE, join such-and-such and such-and-such, and place between them friendship and love." From this your desire will be accomplished. Know that NEDEYRAHE is the name of the lord of that mansion.

§35 The seventh mansion is *Aldira*, and it is for acquiring every good. When the Moon is crossing this mansion, make a silver sigil onto which you will sculpt the image of a man dressed in his clothes, stretching his hands toward the heavens in the manner of a man praying and supplicating. Write on his chest the name of this mansion's lord. Suffumigate it with good-smelling things, and say: "You, O SIELY, do such-and-such a thing, and fulfill my request." Request what you wish from among the things pertaining to the good. Carry the sigil around with you, and what you seek will ensue. Know that SELEHE is the name of the lord of that mansion.

§36 The eighth mansion is *Annathra*, and it is for acquiring victory. When the Moon is wandering through that mansion, make a tin image of a man with the face of an eagle. Write on his chest the name of this mansion's lord. Suffumigate it with sulfur, and say: "You, O ANNEDIEX, do such a thing for me, and fulfill such a request for me." Once you have made the image thus, hold it before an army. You will conquer and achieve victory. Know that ANNEDIEX is the name of the lord of that mansion.

§37 The ninth mansion is *Atarfa*, and it is for causing sickness. When the Moon is crossing this mansion, make a lead image of a man without a penis, holding his hands over his eyes. Write on his neck the name of the lord of this mansion. Suffumigate with pine resin, and say: "You, O RAUBEL, make such-and-such, daughter of such-and-such, fall ill, or make her blood flow." Ask for the one among these two you wish. What you choose will be fulfilled if you have done these things correctly. Know that RAUBEL is the name of the lord of this mansion.

§38 The tenth mansion is *Algebha*, and it is for healing the sick and making a woman give birth easily. When the Moon is travelling in this mansion, make a gold or brass image of a lion head. Write on it the name of this mansion's lord. Suffumigate it with amber and say: "You, O AREDAFIR, lift the pains, sufferings, and illnesses from my body and the body of anyone who drinks or consumes the liquid in which this sigil has been washed." Suffumigate it on any day, and give the sigil to the sick man to carry with him, or wash it in any liquid you will give to drink or ingest to the sick man or the woman feeling the pains of childbirth. Know that AREDAFIR is the name of the lord of that mansion.

§39 The eleventh mansion is *Azobra*, and it is so that you may be feared and well-received. When the Moon is in this mansion, make the image of a man riding upon a lion on a golden tablet, holding a spear in his right hand and holding his left hand over [231] the ear of the lion. Write the name of this mansion in a straight line on the image. Say: "You, O NECOL, grant me glory so that I may be feared by men and that everyone may tremble when beholding me. Placate the hearts of kings, lords, and noblemen, that they may receive me well and honor me." Carry this tablet around, and what you have sought will be. Know that NECOL is the name of the lord of that mansion.

§40 The twelfth mansion is *Azarfa*, and it is for separating two lovers from one another. When the Moon is crossing this mansion, make a black lead image of a dragon fighting with a man. Write the name of the lord of this mansion in a straight line on that image. Suffumigate this with lion fur mixed with asafoetida, and say: "You, O ABDIZU, disjoin and separate such-and-such from such-and-such." Bury this image in the place you want, and what you desire will be. Know that ABDIZU is the name of the lord of that mansion.

§41 The thirteenth mansion is *Alahue*, and it is for relaxing a man who is unable to spend time with a woman and for putting love between man and woman. When the Moon is crossing this mansion, make a red wax image of a man with an erection and a white wax image of a woman. Join both of these images embracing one another, and suffumigate them with aloewood and amber. Wrap them in a white silk cloth after having bathed them in rosewater. Write on either image the name of that man whom you want. If a woman carries these images, she will appear very attractive to that man named on the image (that is, when he sees her). If anyone is under the effect of a binding spell and is unable to spend time with a woman, he should carry these images. Thus, he will relax and able be to have sex with the woman. Know that AZERUT is the name of the lord of that mansion.

§42 The fourteenth mansion is *Azimech* and is for separating man from woman. When the Moon is crossing this mansion, make a red bronze image of a dog catching its own tail in its mouth. Suffumigate this with dog and cat hair and say: "You, O ERDEGEL, disjoin and divide such-and-such a man from such-and-such a woman through enmity and ill will." Name those persons you wish, and bury the image wherever you wish. Know that ERDEGEL is the name of the lord of that mansion.

§43 The fifteenth mansion is *Algafra*, and it is for gaining friendship and goodwill. When the Moon is in that mansion, make an image out of *enque*[45] on which you should draw the figure of a seated man holding a paper in his hand as if he were reading it. Suffumigate it with incense and nutmeg, and say: "You, O ACHALICH, do such-and-such a thing for me, and fulfill such-and-such request for me." Ask for those things that pertain to the joining of friendship, love, and also goodwill. Carry this image around. Know that ACHALICH is the name of the lord of that mansion. [232]

§44 The sixteenth mansion is *Azebene*, and it is for profiting in business (namely, in buying and selling). When the Moon is wandering through this mansion, make the figure of a man sitting upon a throne and holding scales in his hands on a silver lamella. Suffumigate this with odorous things, and show it to the stars every night until the seventh night while saying: "You, O AZERUCH, do such-and-such a thing for me, and fulfill such-and-such a request for me." Ask for things pertaining to the buying and selling of merchandise. Know that AZERUCH is the name of the lord of that mansion.

§45 The seventeenth mansion is *Alichil*, and it is for preventing a thief from breaking into a house in order to steal anything therein. When the Moon is sitting in that mansion, make the image of a monkey on an iron sigil with his hand above his shoulder. Suffumigate it with the hairs of a monkey and the hairs of a female mouse, and wrap it in the monkey's pelt. Afterward, bury it in your house, and say: "You, O ADRIEB, guard all my things and everything present in that house lest any thief enter it." Once finished, no thief nor evil will be able to enter that house. Know that ADRIEB is the name of the lord of that mansion.

§46 The eighteenth mansion is *Alcab*, and it is for removing fever and abdominal pain. When the Moon is crossing this mansion, make a bronze image of an adder holding its tail above its head. Suffumigate it with the horn of a stag, and say: "You, O EGRIBEL, guard this house of mine so that neither adder nor any other harmful beast may enter it." Place the image in a vase, and bury it under your house. Once finished, no serpent or any other harmful creature will be able to enter. If someone is suffering from a fever or abdominal pain, they should carry this image around. They will be healed immediately. Know that EGRIBEL is the name of the lord of this mansion.

§47 The nineteenth mansion is *Axaula*, and it is for prompting menstruation. When the Moon is crossing this mansion, make a sigil out of zinc (which is a kind of bronze) on which you will sculpt the shape of a woman holding her hand in front of her face. Suffumigate this with liquid storax, and say: "You, O

ANNUCEL, make the blood of such-and-such a woman flow" while naming her name. Then what you request will ensue. If the woman holds this image tied to her rear, she will give birth easily and without danger. Know that ANNUCEL is the name of the lord of that mansion.

§48 The twentieth mansion is *Alnaym*, and is for hunting on land. When the Moon is in this mansion, make on a tin tablet an image with the head and hands of a man, the body of a horse with four feet, having a tail, and holding a bow in his hands. Suffumigate this with fox hair, and say: "You, O QUEYHUC, grant me all the game of the land and that it comes to me immediately." Carrying this image, you will easily catch all the venison of the land. Know that QUEYHUC is the name of the lord of that mansion. [233]

§49 The twenty-first mansion is *Albelda*, and it is for destroying. When the Moon is crossing this mansion, make the image of a man with two faces, that is, one in front and the other facing backward. Suffumigate this with sulfur and carob, and say: "You, O BECTUE, desolate the place of such-and-such, and destroy him." Place this image in a small bronze container. With it, place sulfur and carob and some hairs, and bury it wherever you desire. What you have asked for will ensue. Know that BECTUE is the name of the lord of that mansion.

§50 The twenty-second mansion is < . . . > [*Sadahaca*, and it is for binding the tongues of men lest they curse you. When the Moon is in this mansion, make an iron ring on which the shape of a man with winged feet wearing a helmet on his head is sculpted. Suffumigate with quicksilver. Inscribe with this image made of iron for the safety of those fleeing. Say: "You, O GELIEL, bind the tongue of such-and-such lest they curse me, and make that they (named) may escape safely from their enemies." Wear this ring when fleeing, and inscribe black wax with the ring when binding tongues.][46] Know that GELIEL is the name of that mansion.

§51 The twenty-third mansion is *Zaadebola*, and it is for destroying and devastating. When the Moon is crossing in that mansion, make an iron sigil in the image of a cat with a dog's head. Suffumigate this with dog hair, and say: "You, O ZEQUEBIN, desolate such-and-such a place, destroy, and devastate it." Show this sigil to the stars when this mansion is in the ascendant. On the subsequent night, bury the sigil in the place you wish to destroy. What you seek will happen. Know that ZEQUEBIN is the name of the lord of that mansion.

§52 The twenty-fourth mansion is *Caadazod*, and it is for increasing herds. When the Moon is in this mansion, take a well-cleaned and most suitable horn of a castrated ram. On it, make a figure of a woman holding and nursing her son in her arms. Suffumigate it with the stuff you have taken off the horn while cleaning it, and say: "You, O ABRINE, improve and guide the herd of such-and-such." Then affix this image upon the neck of a ram in that herd. If you have done this for a herd of cows, make those things from a bovine horn, and affix it upon the neck of a bull. These herds will be increased, and mortality will not overcome them. Know that ABRINE is the name of the lord of that mansion.

§53 The twenty-fifth mansion is *Zaadalahbia*, and it is for protecting vegetation and harvests from unfortunate circumstances. When the Moon is in this mansion, make a fig wood sigil. On it, carve the likeness of a man planting trees. Suffumigate it with the flowers of these trees, and say: "You, O AZIEL, guard my harvests and my trees so that they may not be damaged or suffer any unfortunate circumstance." Place this image with a tree in the place you want protected. As long as the image thus prepared remains there, no harm will occur there. Know that AZIEL is the name of the lord of that mansion.

§54 The twenty-sixth mansion is the first *Alfarg*, and it is for generating love. When the Moon is sitting in this mansion, take white wax and mastic gum, and melt them together. From this make an image of a woman with her hair untied, holding before herself a container (as if she wanted to put her hair in it). Suffumigate this with odorous things, and say: "You, O TAGRIEL, draw me to the love and friendship of such-and-such a woman." Place this [234] in a small container, and place with it some of the things that smell very good, and carry it around. What you have sought will be accomplished. Know that TAGRIEL is the name of the lord of that mansion.

§55 The twenty-seventh mansion is the latter *Alfarg*, and it is for destroying a bath. When the Moon is in it, take red soil from which you should make the image of a man with wings holding an empty and pierced vessel in his hands while raising it to his mouth. Afterward, place the whole thing over a fire until it is cooked. Then put into this vessel asafoetida and liquid storax, and say: "You, O ABLIEMEL, destroy such-and-such bath of such-and-such man," and name the desired individual. Bury the image in the same bath. Thus, the bath will be cursed because none will come to it for bathing. Know that ABLIEMEL is the name of the lord of that mansion.

§56 The twenty-eighth mansion is *Arrexe*, and it is for gathering fish in one place. When the Moon is in this mansion, make a sigil out of zinc (which is a kind of bronze) on which you will sculpt the image of a fish with a colored spine. On its side, write the name of that mansion. Suffumigate it with the skin of a sea fish, then bind it with string and throw it in water (namely, in the place where you want fish to gather). Thus, all the fish will gather in that area, and you will catch them at will. Know that ANUXI is the name of the lord of that mansion.

§57 Know that on all these images you should write the name of the lord of the mansion and with it your request. In all those rituals toward the good (for assembling, uniting, generating friendship, and love), write on the chest of the image. In rituals that occur for disjoining, separating, generating enmities and ill will, write behind the shoulder blades (namely, on the spine of the image). All the rituals that occur for acquiring glory, honor, and social standing, write upon the head of the image. Thus it is finished.

§58 *The prayer of Saturn*:[47] "QUERMIEX, TOS, HERUS, QUEMIS, DIUS, TAMINES, TAHYTOS, MACADER, QUEHINEN; SATURN! Come quickly with your spirits."

§59 *The prayer of Jupiter*: "BETHNIEHUS, DARMEXIM, MACIEM, MAXAR, DERIX, TAHIX, TAYROS, DEHEYDEX, MEBGUEDEX; JUPITER, BARGIS! Come quickly with your spirits!"

§60 *The prayer of Mars*: "GUEBDEMIS, HEGNEYDIZ, GUEYDENUZ, MAGRAS, HERDEHUS, HEBDEGABDIS, MEHYRAS, DEHYDEMES; RED MARS, BAHARAM! Come quickly with your spirits!"

§61 *The prayer of the Sun*: "BEYDELUZ, DEMEYMES, ADULEX, METNEGAYN, ATMEFEX, NAQUIRUS, GADIX; SUN! Come quickly with your spirits."

§62 *The prayer of Venus*: "DEYDEX, GUEYLUS, MEYLUS, DEMERIX, ALBIMEX, CENTUS, ANGARAS, DEHETARIX; VENUS, NEYRGAT! Come quickly with your spirits." [235]

§63 *The prayer of Mercury*: "BARHUYEX, EMIREX, HAMERIX, SEHIX, DERYX, MEYER, DEHERIX, BAIX, FAURIX; scribe MERCURY! Come quickly with your spirits!"

§64 *The prayer of the Moon*: "GUERNUS, HEDUS, MARANUS, MILTAS, TAYMEX, RANIX, MEHYELUS, DEGAYUS; MOON! Come quickly with your spirits!"

§65 "LEYEQUIN, LEYELGANE, LEYEQUIR, LEYEQUERICH, LEYERIC, LEYERUS, LEYEXERIS." Write these names on a sleeve that you should burn. While it is aflame, read these names. From this, love and friendship will arise.

Thus ends the book of the wise Picatrix on astrological matters.

NOTES

INTRODUCTION

1. References internal to the text of our translation of the *Picatrix* stand alone as trinomials, referring respectively to the book, chapter, and paragraph numbers.

2. The concept of Platonic Orientalism has some overlap with, but is not coterminous with, Edward Said's Orientalism. See Hanegraaff, *Esotericism*, 12–17.

3. For an extensive summary of the issues surrounding Platonic Orientalism, see Tommasi, "Some Reflections," 20–29; on Hellenism and the *Ghāyat al-Ḥakīm*, see Saif, "From *Ġāyat al-ḥakīm*," 316–17.

4. Saif provides an extensive discussion on the intellectual background of the *Picatrix*'s original Arabic version (*Arabic Influences*, 30–36; and "From *Ġāyat al-ḥakīm*," 299–309).

5. Saif, "From *Ġāyat al-ḥakīm*," 312 and 344; Adamson, *Arabic Plotinus*, 6–8.

6. Though there already exists a good English translation of Pingree's Latin *Picatrix*, translated and edited by the respectable duo John Michael Greer and Christopher Warnock, their edition appears to be directed toward practicing "students of medieval and Renaissance magic" or "students of the occult" rather than toward an audience of historians. See Greer and Warnock, *Picatrix*, 19.

7. Fierro, "Bāṭinism in Al-Andalus," 87–112; and Saif, *Arabic Influences*, 37–38.

8. De Callataÿ and Moureau, "Again on Maslama," 330–31. On al-Qurṭubī's travels, see de Callataÿ and Moureau, "Milestone in the History of Andalusī Bāṭinism," 85–116, as cited in Boudet and Coulon, "Version arabe," 68 n. 8.

9. Ritter and Plessner, *Picatrix*, xxii.

10. Bakhouche, Fauquier, and Pérez-Jean, *Picatrix*, 22.

11. Kahane, Kahane, and Pietrangeli, "Picatrix and the Talismans," 574–93; cited by Bakhouche, Fauquier, and Pérez-Jean, *Picatrix*, 22–23.

12. Thomann, "Name Picatrix," 290.

13. Pingree, "Between the *Ghāya* and *Picatrix* I," 27.

14. Pingree, "Between the *Ghāya* and *Picatrix* I," 36. See also Boudet, Caiozzo, and Weill-Parot, "*Picatrix*, au carrefour," 13.

15. Regarding passages concerned with homosexual relations omitted from the Latin, see Boudet, "Amour et les rituels," 149–62; regarding passages from the Qur'an omitted from the Latin, see Boudet and Coulon, "Version arabe," 83–85.

16. Pingree, "Between the *Ghāya* and *Picatrix* I," 27–28; and Boudet and Coulon, "Version arabe," 77. Yehudā ben Moshē is known to have translated the *Lapidario* of Alfonso in 1250, a work notably similar in style to certain portions of the *Picatrix*.

17. The Spanish version of the *Picatrix* survives in a thirty-six-folio manuscript fragment that has been edited as part of two unpublished Ph.D. dissertations: Darby, "Astrological Manuscript"; and, more recently, Díez, "Alfonso X the Learned." It is also discussed in Perrone Compagni, "Picatrix Latinus," 237–337. Pingree additionally quotes lengthy sections of the Spanish version juxtaposed with the corresponding passages from the Latin text in order

to demonstrate the source of the latter in the former (see "Between the *Ghāya* and *Picatrix* I," 38–56).

18. Boudet and Coulon, "Version arabe," 81; and Burnett, "Magic in the Court of Alfonso," 37–52.

19. Weill-Parot, *"Images astrologiques,"* 477–88. For further arguments on the timing and placement of the Latin translation among circles of Jewish scholars in Montpellier around 1300, see Dumas, *Santé et société,* 443–63.

20. Pingree, "Between the *Ghāya* and *Picatrix* I," 36.

21. The most significant of these interpolations are found at 1.5.26–27; 2.12.1–59; 3.11.58–112; and 4.9.29–56. For further discussion, see Bakhouche, Fauquier, and Pérez-Jean, *Picatrix,* 27–28.

22. The oldest dated Latin manuscript is MS 793 from the Jagiellonian Library in Kraków, which was copied in 1458–59. For a full analysis of this manuscript, see Láng, *Unlocked Books,* 83–104. According to d'Agostino, the oldest manuscript fragment featuring text from the Latin *Picatrix* dates to the thirteenth century (*Astromagia,* 28 n. 51, as cited in Láng, *Unlocked Books,* 96 n. 41). Pingree indicates that the oldest such fragment dates to the fourteenth century (*Picatrix,* li). The first known explicit reference to the *Picatrix* was made circa 1456 by Johannes Hartlieb in his index of books concerning the forbidden arts. For an English translation, see Hartlieb, *Buch aller verbotenen Künste,* chapters 35, 48, and 49; and Kieckhefer, *Hazards,* 41. Page reports that the *Picatrix* was not among the numerous books pertaining to magic owned by the monks of St. Augustine's monastery at Canterbury (*Magic in the Cloister,* 19).

23. Saif, *Arabic Influences,* 96; and Pingree, *Picatrix,* xvi–xxiii.

24. MS Kraków, Biblioteka Jagiellońska, BJ Rkp. 793.

25. On Marzio's use of the *Picatrix,* see Perrone Compagni, "Magia cerimoniale," 303–9.

26. This text is the third part of Ficino's *De vita libri tres,* which is a self-help manual directed at an audience of fellow intellectuals. See Ficino, *De vita libri tres* L, fol. ii–Y, (fol. iv). The extent of Ficino's reliance on the *Picatrix* is explored by Perrone Compagni ("Magia cerimoniale," 285–302). His direct knowledge of the *Picatrix* is confirmed thanks to a letter he wrote to Michele Acciari in response to Filippo Valoris's request to borrow Ficino's copy, wherein he warns about the dangers of the work and claims to have only passed on what is good from it in *De vita libri tres,* leaving out everything illicit (Saif, *Arabic Influences,* 103, citing Branca, "Discepulo de Poliziano," 464–81).

27. Perrone Compagni, "Picatrix Latinus," 266–67.

28. This work is *De rerum praenotione,* according to Perrone Compagni, "Magia cerimoniale," 284; see also Yates, *Giordano Bruno,* 50.

29. Thorndike, *History of Magic,* 814; Saif, *Arabic Influences,* 73, as mentioned in Pingree, "Diffusion of Arabic Magical Texts," 102.

30. Rabelais, *Pantagruel* III, 23, cited by Yates, *Giordano Bruno,* 51; and Boudet, Caiozzo, and Weill-Parot, "*Picatrix,* au carrefour," 14.

31. Symphorien Champier, *Annotamenta, errata, et castigationes,* in *Petri Aponensis opera,* Petrus of Abano, *Conciliator controversiarum, quae inter philosophos et medicos versantur* (Venice, 1565), fol. 271v, col. 1G–H; also cited in Perrone Compagni, "*Picatrix,*" 359.

32. Nifo, *Ad Apotelesmata Ptolomaei eruditiones* V, fol. v; Naudé, *Naudeana et Patiniana,* II (*Patiniana*):59.

33. Perrone Compagni, "Magia cerimoniale," 318–23.

34. Ritter and Plessner, *Picatrix,* xx.

35. Pingree, *Picatrix,* xv n. 6.

36. Agrippa d'Aubigné, *Lettres touchant quelques poincts,* 435; see Yates, *Giordano Bruno,* 51.

37. Saxl, "Beiträge zu einer Geschichte," 151–77; see Burnett, "*Picatrix* à l'Institut Warburg," 26.

38. Solalinde, "Alfonso X astrólogo," 350–56.

39. Correspondence from Warburg to Saxl, June 25, 1928, cited in Burnett, "*Picatrix* à l'Institut Warburg," 30.

40. Brown, *Enquiry into the Life,* 183 n. 2.

41. Correspondence from Plessner to Saxl, February 9, 1929, cited in Burnett, "*Picatrix* à l'Institut Warburg," 30.

42. Correspondence from Ritter to Saxl, February 23, 1929, cited ibid.

43. Burnett, "*Picatrix* à l'Institut Warburg," 31.

44. Hartner relays an earlier version of this story relying solely on scholarly publications ("Notes on Picatrix," 438–40), whereas Burnett's more recent work draws upon archival materials (chiefly personal correspondence between the individual scholars) held at the Warburg Institute's archive (see "*Picatrix* à l'Institut Warburg," 26–32).

45. Burnett, "*Picatrix* à l'Institut Warburg," 32.

46. Plessner, "Medieval Definition," 358–59. The Hebrew versions of the *Picatrix* have not yet been published in a critical edition, although Leicht has promised one ("Chapitre II, 12 du *Picatrix*," 290 n. 9).

47. Pingree, *Picatrix,* xiii; Burnett, "*Picatrix* à l'Institut Warburg," 32.

48. Greer and Warnock, *Picatrix,* 17.

49. Saif, "From *Ġāyat al-ḥakīm*," 305–6.

50. Bakhouche, Fauquier, and Pérez-Jean, *Picatrix,* 6.

51. Pingree, "Some of the Sources," 13.

52. Porreca, "How Hidden Was God?," 143–45.

53. Pico della Mirandola, *Cabalistic Conclusions Confirming the Christian Religion,* Conclusion 13, as cited in Farmer, *Syncretism in the West,* 524–25. Regarding Azazel, see Leviticus 16:8–10; and Davidson, *Dictionary of Angels,* 63–64.

54. For example, in 4.9.5, the magician is warned to plug his nostrils with silk lest he inhale a smoke meant to kill birds. In 4.9.6, a suffumigation to kill birds made of mandrake, ammonia, and hemlock is to be burned under trees, but only while the weather is calm and without wind. These kinds of precautionary remarks, however, stand out as unusual in light of the rest of the text.

55. Burnett, "Talismans," 2–3.

56. Page, "Sacrifices d'animaux," 187–211.

57. Dumas, *Santé et société,* 450.

58. Pingree, "Some of the Sources," 1; Pingree is clear in distinguishing between the high, "more sophisticated forms of magic" in the *Picatrix* and baser demonological and necromantic practices.

59. For more information about the Sabeans of Harrān, see Chwolsohn, *Sabier und der Sabismus*; Marquet, "Sabéens et Iḫwān al-Ṣafā'"; Hjärpe, "Analyse critique"; Tardieu, "Sābiens coraniques et 'Sābiens' de Harrān"; Genequand, "Idolâtrie, astrolâtrie et sabéisme"; and Green, *City of the Moon God.*

60. Greer and Warnock, *Picatrix,* 12.

61. Bakhouche, Fauquier, and Pérez-Jean, *Picatrix,* 10.

62. It is noteworthy that Alan of Lille wrote an entire sermon around this statement but replaced the word "infinite" with "intelligible." For the Hermetic aphorism, see Hudry, *Liber viginti quattuor philosophorum,* 7; and d'Alverny, *Alain de Lille,* 298–99.

63. In the Gnostic and Hermetic texts, the eighth sphere is known as the *ogdoad* while the *Picatrix* usually refers to it as the *firmamentum* (firmament) or the *celum stellarum fixarum* (heaven of fixed stars).

64. For a detailed discussion of the philosophical underpinnings of the *Ghāyat al-Ḥakīm,* see Saif, *Arabic Influences,* 40–45.

65. Pingree claims: "The Neoplatonic theories of hypostases, that the author of the Ghāya uses as a framework within which he hopes to be able to operate magically without incurring the opprobrium of employing Satanic forces . . . [are] paralleled in Jābir's *Kitāb al-Khamsīn*" ("Some of the Sources," 3).

66. Bakhouche, Fauquier, and Pérez-Jean, *Picatrix,* 17.

67. Plotinus, *Enneads* 6.9.11.

68. Saif, "From *Ġāyat al-ḥakīm*," 300.

69. Saif, *Arabic Influences*, 40–45.

70. Ibid., 36.

71. Saif, "From *Ġāyat al-ḥakīm*," 305.

72. Saif, *Arabic Influence*, 25.

73. See Pasi, "Theses de Magia." In recent writings, Otto pushes back against this view he himself once espoused, noting that there is a "discourse of inclusion" revealed by growing research into works by self-professed magic users, "a fascinating and largely unexplored tradition of ritual texts and practices" that demands more attention than it has received ("Historicizing Western Learned Magic," 162).

74. Certain portions of this section have appeared in Attrell and Porreca, "Notes on the Picatrix," 1–6.

75. Boudet, "Amour et les rituels," 149–62.

76. Bever, *Realities of Witchcraft*, 11–39.

77. Véronèse, *"Ars notoria" au Moyen Âge*, 59.

78. This observation contrasts with the claims made by Boudet and Coulon, who state that both the *Ghāyat al-Ḥakīm* and the *Picatrix* "work themselves into the perspective of potential political and military use" ("Version arabe," 72).

79. The relationship between the *Ghāyat al-Ḥakīm* (*The goal of the sage*) with its sibling text, the *Rutbat al-Ḥakīm* (*The rank of the sage*)—a treatise dealing principally with alchemy—has been discussed in Hamès, "*Ghāyat al-Ḥakīm*," 216–18. For the manuscript transmission of the *Rutbat al-Ḥakīm*, see Catallaÿ and Moureau, "Towards the Critical Edition," 385–94.

80. Kieckhefer, *Magic in the Middle Ages*, 151–75.

81. Blake, "Marriage of Heaven and Hell," 253.

82. For information on some of the mildly psychoactive lesser ingredients, see Moussaieff et al., "Incensol Acetate," 3024–34; and Bendersky and Ferrence, "Therapy with Saffron," 199–226.

83. Sherratt, "Sacred and Profane Substances," 52; see also Merlin, "Archaeological Evidence," 296–313.

84. De Quincey, *Confessions*, 195.

85. The ritual in 3.11.54 describes an oil to be suffumigated, eaten, or used as an ointment made of eight ounces each of fresh opium, human blood, and sesame oil. After it is heated inside a decapitated human head for twenty-four hours, it is used for seeing "whatever you wish."

86. Panayotopoulos and Chisholm, "Hallucinogenic Effect of Nutmeg," 754; Shulgin, "Possible Implication," 380–84.

87. Franklin, *Prison Writing*, 150: "My cellmate was among at least a hundred nutmeg men who, for money or cigarettes, bought from kitchen worker inmates penny matchboxes full of stolen nutmeg. I grabbed a box as though it were a pound of heavy drugs. Stirred into a glass of cold water, a penny matchbox full of nutmeg had the kick of three or four reefers."

88. Panayotopoulos and Chisholm, "Hallucinogenic Effect of Nutmeg," 754.

89. Frank et al., "Ingestion of Poison Hemlock," 573–74; Bowman and Sanghvi, "Pharmacological Actions of Hemlock," 1–25. The alkaloids in poison hemlock affect the neuromuscular junction where they paralyze vital functions in the body. When death occurs from ingestion, it is usually caused by respiratory failure. The drying process greatly reduces the toxicity of hemlock, though does not eliminate it altogether. Unfortunately, no studies currently exist on the effects of smoked hemlock on humans, but we assume the predominant toxins coniine and γ-coniceine would retain their harmful qualities after combustion.

90. Greer and Warnock, *Picatrix*, 18.

91. The immediately following paragraph (3.9.14) describes a ritual to invoke the power of the Sun that also features the consumption of wine but in a way that is more convivial than stupor-inducing: the operator and an unspecified number of "friends and associates" are to drink the seven pitchers of wine used in the ritual. The size of the vessels is unspecified.

92. Bever, *Realities of Witchcraft*, 143. For an example of a suffumigation with mandrake seeds, see 3.11.4.

93. The group of rituals beginning on 3.11.32 contains ingredients (generally mandrake seeds mixed with animal brains) that are indicated as lethal in the section's heading ("they are thought to be deadly"). See also 3.11.56 for an example of a poison containing henbane (*iusquiami*), which serves "for ruining the senses and thoughts."

94. Saif (at the Warburg Institute) is preparing a new edition of the Arabic *Ghāyat al-Ḥakīm* with an accompanying English translation. We are grateful for her collaboration in reviewing the contents of this introduction and especially for her confirmation of al-Qurṭubī's authorship. Any mistakes, of course, remain entirely our own.

95. The critical apparatus in Pingree's edition—spanning a full 655 pages—was published as a set of microfiche that were included in a pocket attached to the back pastedown of the physical volume, rather than appearing along with the text on each page. When it is cited, the page numbers mentioned are those of the apparatus itself, not those of the physical volume containing the text.

PROLOGUE

1. Alfonso X, "The Wise," r. June 1, 1252–April 4, 1284, king of Castile. King Alfonso famously maintained an intellectually rich court culture, which lavishly sponsored occult pursuits and translation activities.

2. These dates do not perfectly match up with one another. See Pingree, "Between the *Ghayā* and the *Picatrix* I," 27.

3. The expression of thanks to God is part of the Hermetic tradition and as such can be found in *Asclepius* 41, in *Apulei Platonici Madaurensis*, 85. Such expressions of gratitude are also commonplace in the Islamic tradition.

4. Compare 1.7.1–4.

BOOK 1

1. "Generation and corruption" is a set of opposite terms used widely in antiquity, particularly in Aristotelian philosophy, to refer to the principles of growth and decay. In many ways, these are akin to modern conceptions of order and entropy, respectively.

2. By "knowledge," (*sciencia*) the author is referring to the seven liberal arts, which consist of the *trivium* (grammar [input], logic [processing], rhetoric [output]) and the *quadrivium* (arithmetic [number], geometry [number in space], astronomy [number in time], and music [number in space and time]).

3. As discussed in our introduction, the Latin word translated here as "magic" is *nigromancia,* literally "black magic," a term distinct in meaning from the Greek νεκρομαντεία (*nekromanteia*), which traditionally refers more precisely to divination using spirits of the dead or their body parts. The Latin word, in this context, might best be translated as "secret ceremonial magic."

4. All materials making up images must be made of substances that reflect the character of the planet whose spirits the magician is trying to invoke. This applies not only to metals but also to clothing, plants, animals, and many other things. E.g., see 3.1.3–9.

5. This refers to the "Philosopher's Stone," from the Arabic ألإكسير (*al-'iksīr*), which stems from the Ancient Greek ξήριον (*xēreion*, medicinal powder). This stone was the end goal of most alchemical operations, as it was believed to have the ability to turn base substances, such as lead, into gold.

6. This segment concerning the Elixir suggests that the compiler had some familiarity with the language of the *Emerald Tablet,* which first appeared in an Arabic context sometime between the sixth and eighth centuries and is often presumed (without evidence) to be much older. See Principe, *Secrets of Alchemy,* 30–33; and Greer and Warnock, *Picatrix,* 27–28.

7. The discussion of the Elixir in this paragraph of the *Picatrix* corresponds to the sibling volume by the same author, the *Rutbat al-Ḥakīm*, which was never translated into Latin during the Middle Ages. See Ritter and Plessner, *Picatrix*, 8–9.

8. Cf. Plato, *Stat.* 258e: "In this way then, divide all science into two arts, calling the one practical, and the other purely intellectual."

9. The attribution to Plato is apocryphal here.

10. This is the first reference in the *Picatrix* to the source known elsewhere as the *Chaldean Agriculture*. Here it is called *Liber Alfilaha*, from the Arabic *Kitāb al-Filahat al-Nabatiyya* (*On Nabataean Agriculture*), translated from Nabataean by ibn Waḥshīya (cf. 2.2.4; 3.8.2–4). Its sources were composed sometime between the third and ninth centuries C.E. and are made up mostly of older Babylonian information. Dealing with agriculture as well as occult sciences, it has long been considered among the most important works of Arabic occultism; it stands as one of the *Picatrix*'s most heavily quoted sources. See Pingree, "Some of the Sources," 1–15.

11. Greer and Warnock (*Picatrix*, 29) believe *yetelegehuz* to be an Arabic attempt at the Greek *entelechia* ("that which completes or manifests"), while Bakhouche, Fauquier, and Pérez-Jean (*Picatrix*, 50) simply follow Ritter and Plessner (*Picatrix*, 10), who translate the Arabic word as "syllogism."

12. This refers to the signs of the Zodiac.

13. It is worth noting that, within this context, there is no concrete distinction between the terms astronomy and astrology. The two words are used interchangeably, as evidenced in this very paragraph (*astrologia* from the books of *astronomia*).

14. Ritter and Plessner claim that this chapter is entirely derived from the works of Jābir ibn Ḥayyān (*Picatrix*, 12).

15. The link between perfection and the shape of a sphere is the central analogy in one of the definitions of God attributed to Hermes Trismegistus: "God is an infinite sphere whose center is everywhere and whose circumference is nowhere," which is aphorism 2 in Hudry, *Liber viginti quattuor philosophorum*, 7.

16. Henceforth, passages in square brackets represent text drawn from the appendices and excerpta. See Pingree, *Picatrix*, appendix 2, p. 237.

17. For a brief discussion of the *Picatrix*'s reliance upon the catarchic astrology of the *manāzil al-qamar* (i.e., the lunar mansions, *nakṣatrāṇi* in Sanskrit), see Pingree, "Some of the Sources," 8.

18. The "signs of direct ascent" are Capricorn, Aquarius, Pisces, Aries, Taurus, and Gemini, while the rest are considered signs of tortuous ascent. Greer and Warnock, *Picatrix*, 38.

19. The Head and Tail of the Dragon represent the northern and southern nodes of the Moon's orbit, respectively.

20. A "lord of the ascendant" designates a planet that governs an ascending sign.

21. The *Centiloquium* (*One Hundred Sayings*) is a collection of a hundred aphorisms about astrology traditionally attributed to the Greek astrologer Claudius Ptolomy. In Arabic, it was called the *Kitāb al-Tamara* (*Book of Fruit*) and was long considered one of the most important works in the practice of medieval astrology. Whether this book was actually written by Ptolomy, however, is highly dubious.

22. The "figures of al-Khwarizmi" are the so-called Arabic numerals that we employ today, all of which originate in India. Greer and Warnock suggest that 220 and 284 were considered "amicable numbers" in Pythagorean numerology since the factors of each add up to the other (*Picatrix*, 41).

23. Commanding signs: from Aries to Virgo; obedient signs: from Libra to Pisces.

24. In the cosmology of the *Picatrix*, the superior planets were those that were thought to dwell above the Sun (Saturn, Jupiter, and Mars). The inferior planets were those thought to dwell below (Venus, Mercury, and the Moon).

25. The Arabic "parts" (or lots) are imagined points derived from the mathematical calculations of three horoscopic entities like planets or angles. The distance between two points is

added to the position of the third (generally the ascendant) to figure out the location of the "part." The "Part of Fortune" is calculated from the positions of the ascendant, the Sun, and the Moon.

26. Al-Hanemi is a corrupted version of al-Khwarismi, according to Ritter and Plessner, *Picatrix,* 33.

27. This paragraph and the next one do not appear in the original Arabic version and thus are later interpolations inserted either when the text was translated into Castilian Spanish or when the latter was put into Latin.

28. This passage is reminiscent of the Maha Mantra originally found in the Kalisantarana Upanishad (see Greer and Warnock, *Picatrix,* 67). Note that the line divisions suggested here are our own and do not appear in Pingree's edition.

29. Solomon's seal (also known as the Star of David) is the symbol from the signet ring attributed to King Solomon in the medieval Jewish tradition and likewise in Islamic and Western occultism. It was this very ring that, according to tradition, gave Solomon goetic command over demons.

30. The *almutaz* (or *almuten figuris*) is the prevailing or ruling planet once all the essential dignities have been calculated. It comes from the Arabic *al-mateen*, which means "the firm/powerful one," though this concept existed in the pre-Islamic works of Ptolomy and other classical astrologers.

31. Bladder stones or gallstones could also be implied by this passage. The use of a golden image of a lion for healing kidney stones is discussed at length in Weill-Parot, *"Images astrologiques,"* 477–96; and in Dumas, *Santé et société,* 447–50.

32. Pingree, *Picatrix*, appendix 5, p. 238.

33. "Thebit ben Corat" is a corrupt transliteration of the name Thābit ibn Qurra (d. 901 C.E.), a Sabean mathematician, physician, and astronomer born in the last pagan city in Mesopotamia, Harrān. Living in Baghdad, he wrote a number of works on astrology and magic that reflect the *Picatrix* in style. According to Pingree ("Some of the Sources," 5), his *De imaginibus* has been "inadequately edited into two medieval Latin versions" by Carmody (*Astronomical Works,* 167–97).

34. Pingree traced the links between this Thoos in the *Picatrix* to the Toz/Tat/Thoth character from the Hermetic tradition ("Diffusion," 76–77).

35. From the Arabic *jawzahirr,* which is the point on the ecliptic that planets intersect when moving from a northern to a southern latitude (and vice versa); Bakhouche, Fauquier, and Pérez-Jean erroneously claim it is the planet's *domus* (house) (*Picatrix,* 78).

36. This refers to moral conscience or "the knowledge of good and evil."

37. Compare Plato, *Theaet.* 152a for Protagoras's "man is the measure of all things."

38. This refers to humankind's subtle spiritual nature.

39. Here we have left the ancient Greek concept of *Prima Materia* or Prime Matter (πρώτη ὕλη, *prṓtē húlē*) untranslated since it is more generally recognized by English speakers in its traditional medieval Latin form.

40. By implication, only God is considered as being outside the bounds of the intellect.

41. This statement captures the essence of what Plato has Socrates say in *Phaedrus* 275a–b.

42. This passage is inspired by Aristotle's hylomorphism. See Aristotle, *Physics* 2.2.194b 23–24.

43. This passage draws on Aristotle's discussion on the properties of the elements in *On the Heavens* 3.7.305a34–306b3.

BOOK 2

1. The materials and procedures described in this narrative correspond to the recipe described above in 1.5.25.

2. The *quadrivium* consists of arithmetic (number), geometry (number in space), astronomy (number in time), and music (number in space and time), in this order.

3. Bakhouche, Fauquier, and Pérez-Jean claim that this Rozuz is to be identified with Dorotheus of Sidon (*Picatrix*, 91). See 2.3.10 below.

4. The ostensible movement of the heavens can be determined in two ways: first, by means of the constellations (patterns made up of visible stars); second, by means of the signs and decans (divisions of the ecliptic). Zodiacal signs, despite being called constellations, are of the second category. Greer and Warnock, *Picatrix*, 63.

5. Abenoaxie is a one of many corrupt forms in the *Picatrix* for ibn Waḥshīya, the translator of the *Chaldean/Nabataean Agriculture*; cf. 1.2.4; 3.8.2–4.

6. Tymtym (Tumtum al-Hindi) was a legendary Indian alchemist among early medieval Arab intellectual circles, which attributed to him many works of astrology and geomancy. Greer and Warnock, *Picatrix*, 64.

7. Aristotle was literally known as "the Philosopher" in the medieval scholastic tradition. In Arabic, however, Aristotle was reverently called the "First Teacher." Most, if not all, references made to Aristotle in the *Picatrix* are drawn from pseudepigraphic material.

8. For a brief discussion on the history of the Egyptian decans (that is, the thirty-six equal arcs of ten degrees on the ecliptic that the Egyptians conceived of as daemons), see Pingree, "Some of the Sources," 6–7.

9. The falling (or cadent) houses are the third, sixth, ninth, and twelfth houses in a chart; the Moon is considered falling/cadent from the lord of her house when she is three, six, nine, or twelve houses or signs away from her lord. Greer and Warnock, *Picatrix*, 69.

10. The other two "mobile signs" are Cancer and Libra.

11. The "common signs" are Gemini, Virgo, Sagittarius, and Pisces.

12. The "fixed signs" are Taurus, Leo, Scorpio, and Aquarius.

13. Dorotheus of Sidon (ca. first century C.E.) was a Hellenistic astrologer who composed a poem on horoscopic astrology in five books called the *Pentateuch*. The *Pentateuch* has mainly come down to us from an Arabic translation (dated around 800 C.E.) of a Middle Persian translation. Very little is known about Dorotheus himself, although he likely wrote in Alexandria. According to Firmicus Maternus, Dorotheus was a native of Sidon (Firmicus, *Mathesis* 2.29.2). See Dorotheus of Sidon, *Carmen Astrologicum*.

14. "The lord of the house of the lord of the ascendant" is the planet governing the sign wherein the "lord of the ascendant" sits.

15. This refers to Jupiter.

16. This refers to Venus.

17. The "malign places" are the sixth, eighth and twelfth houses, which are traditionally considered unfortunate; see 2.3.10.

18. On the *almuten*, see note in 1.5.28.

19. Perrone Compagni links this passage to Surat 30.7 from the Qur'an ("*Picatrix*," 363). It is possible that this link is more evident in the Arabic version of the *Picatrix*, but in our view, it more broadly represents the expression of a deeply entrenched philosophical dualism that permeates all Abrahamic religions and so-called Gnostic schools of thought, which were deeply intertwined with mystical Platonic ideology. For other examples of such dualism, see 2.5.5 or 4.4.65–66.

20. The "four quarters" of heaven are determined according to the solstitial and equinoctial points.

21. Greer and Warnock point out how this particular chapter discusses the "theory of trepidation," as proposed by the Sabean astrologer Thābit ibn Qurra, which posits that the precession of equinoxes moved back and forth in an arc by eight degrees rather than spinning in a small circle that lasts 25,920 years (a cycle more commonly known as the "Great Platonic Year") (*Picatrix*, 77).

22. *Alquelquella* is *al-kankala* in Arabic. See Burnett, "European Knowledge," 10–11.

23. This may be a reference to divine draught of immortality called Soma, Amṛta, or Nektar in the Vedic Indo-Aryan tradition.

24. This is an example of a sort of medieval Arabic "Orientalism," whereby the Indians are thought to be an inherently more mystical people by virtue of being a distant (but not too distant) "Other."

25. The author intended "scripture" to imply the Qur'an, but a Christian audience would have assumed the Bible.

26. This figure represents a generic combination of stars that, once linked by the correct combination of lines, can represent constellations. Specific figures that, with some imagination, one can assimilate to patterns of prominent stars in relevant constellations appear below at 2.9.2–7. Cf. Ritter and Plessner, *Picatrix*, 111.

27. See 2.2.2 above for descriptions of the decans having bodies.

28. This reference to storms in the Sun (*turbine in Sole*) belongs among the early reports of sunspots, an idea that challenged the belief in the perfect and unchanging nature of the world above the lunar sphere.

29. It should seem ironic to a modern reader that a medieval text devoted to conjuring spirits would not blame entities such as succubi for a phenomenon like premature ejaculation.

30. We are using the modern psychological term "consciousness" to express the Latin *sensus communis*, which was believed to be the sum total of the five senses in Aristotelian psychology.

31. "Albunasar Alfarabi" is a transliteration of Abū Naṣr Muḥammad al-Fārābī (ca. 872–951), who was honored in the Arabic tradition as "the Second Teacher" after Aristotle on account of his prolificacy and breadth of knowledge regarding law, philosophy, metaphysics, mathematics, astronomy, and so forth.

32. The author implied "Founder of the Law" to mean Mohammed, though a Christian audience would liked assumed Moses.

33. This is another example of Aristotelian hylomorphism. See note in 1.7.2 above.

34. Ḥunayn ibn 'Isḥāq (ca. 809–873), known in the Latin West as Johannitius, was an Arab Christian scholar, physician, and translator of predominantly Greek medical works.

35. Potions made up of animal parts were called "theriacs" from the Greek θηριακός (*theriakos*, pertaining to beasts). They were in fact discussed extensively by the Roman physician Galen in two separate works, *De theriaca ad Pisonem* and *De usu thericae ad Pamphilianum*.

36. The First Mobile (*Primum Mobile*) was a concept used by Aristotle and developed by Ptolomy to account for the movement of the heavens around the Earth. It is the outermost sphere in the geocentric universe, and its motion is derived from its Empedoclean "love," which can never be consummated, for the Prime Mover situated just outside itself.

37. The *hayz* is a condition that symbolizes planetary empowerment on account of its suitable positioning vis-à-vis sign and sect; for a masculine planet, this is when the planet is above the Earth during daytime while sitting in a masculine sign; for a feminine planet, this occurs when the planet is below the Earth at nighttime while sitting in a feminine sign. Greer and Warnock, *Picatrix*, 90.

38. As opposed to "composite bodies."

39. The divisions described thus far in this paragraph conform to Aristotle's *Categories* 6, 4b20–24.

40. The Latin reads *astronomia*, which highlights the lack of distinction in the mind of the author between "astrology" and "astronomy."

41. Compare with the emblem of the Warburg Institute, which is described on its website as follows:

> The emblem . . . is taken from a woodcut in the edition of *De natura rerum* of Isidore of Seville (560–636) printed at Augsburg in 1472. In that work it accompanies a quotation

> from the *Hexameron* of St Ambrose (III.iv.18) describing the interrelation of the four elements of which the world is made, with their two pairs of opposing qualities: hot and cold, moist and dry. Earth is linked to water by the common quality of coldness, water to air by the quality of moisture, air to fire by heat, and fire to earth by dryness. Following a doctrine that can be traced back to Hippocratic physiology, the tetragram adds the four seasons of the year and the four humours of man to complete the image of cosmic harmonies that both inspired and retarded the further search for natural laws.

For the image, see https://warburg.sas.ac.uk/about-us/history-warburg-institute.

42. "By extension" can be understood as the addition of 1 + 2 + 3 + 4 + 5 + 6 + 7, which adds up to 28, the number of mansions of the Moon.

43. Ritter and Plessner speculate that the figures in the following paragraphs correspond to patterns of stars in their respective constellations (*Picatrix*, 111). See the comment above in 2.5.2.

44. As first pointed out by Greer and Warnock, this statement stands curiously at odds with the rest of the chapter (*Picatrix*, 100).

45. The word *premonada* is otherwise unknown in Latin; Ritter and Plessner report that the Arabic text reads "marcasite" here (*Picatrix*, 113).

46. Greer and Warnock (*Picatrix*, 101) claim that *azernec* is cupric oxide (CuO), whereas Bakhouche, Fauquier, and Pérez-Jean sometimes call it arsenic (*Picatrix*, 140) and sometimes orpiment (As_2S_3, *pigment d'or*; e.g., ibid., 267), which appears elsewhere in Latin as *auri pigmentum*. We believe *azernec* refers more broadly to arsenic, while *auri pigmentum* refers more specifically to the arsenic sulfides.

47. The word *azumbedich* is rendered as "céruse" (white lead) in Bakhouche, Fauquier, and Pérez-Jean (*Picatrix*, 141), while Rossi has "conrindone" (corundum) (*Picatrix*, 94). Ritter and Plessner have "Smirgel" (emery) here (*Picatrix*, 114).

48. We have rendered *Beylus* as Apollonius here and in the rest of this chapter (paragraphs 12, 15, 22, 26, 31, and 36 below). For more on Apollonius of Tyena in the Middle Ages, see Poneca, "Apollonius."

49. See Pingree, *Picatrix*, appendix 10, p. 239.

50. See Pingree, *Picatrix*, appendix 11, p. 239.

51. There appears to be no further discussion of such an image in the rest of the text.

52. See Pingree, *Picatrix*, appendix 12, p. 240.

53. This may refer to the image in 2.10.9 or to something else: the intent is not clear.

54. See Pingree, *Picatrix*, appendix 13, p. 240.

55. Pingree, *Picatrix*, appendix 14, p. 240.

56. These illustrations are absent from the Latin manuscripts.

57. Pingree, *Picatrix*, appendix 15, p. 240.

58. This word appears as *feyrizech* in Latin, a transliteration of the Persian word for turquoise. In Marsilio Ficino's *De vita libri tres*, the Latin reads *pheyriech* (Plessner and Klein-Franke, S, [fol. iii]), which is rendered as "sapphire" in the translation by Kaske and Clarke (*Three Books on Life*, 335).

59. On this point, see Bakhouche, Fauquier, and Pérez-Jean, *Picatrix*, 153.

60. The Spanish translator was unable to identify the Arabic word سلحفاة (*sulaḥfāh*) as "turtle" and thus rendered it as *celhafe* in an attempted transliteration.

61. *Adorugen* is a corrupt transliteration of the Arabic *durayjan* (decan), according to Greer and Warnock, *Picatrix*, 118.

62. The section 2.12.38–51 is an interpolation inserted into the Latin text at Montpellier around 1300, according to Dumas (*Santé et société*, 460), and is absent from the Arabic text.

63. Compare 2.12.39 above.

64. Al-Razi (also known in the West by his latinized names, Rhazes or Rasis), more specifically Abū Bakr Muhammad ibn Zakariyyā al-Rāzī (854–925), was a Persian natural phi-

losopher, physician, and polymath who composed over two hundred manuscripts, most of which are vital documents of the history of science and medicine.

65. Geber Abnehayen is the common Latin transliteration of Jābir ibn Ḥayyān, an enigmatic figure in the history of alchemy who may or may not have ever even existed but to whom has been attributed a great body of natural philosophical literature. See Principe, *Secrets of Alchemy*, 33–45.

66. According to Pingree, this passage is a quotation from the *Liber vaccae*, a compilation of magical recipes not unlike the *Picatrix*, with its Arabic origin in late ninth-century Spain ("Plato's Hermetic Book," 134–38). The links between this passage and the *Liber vaccae* have also been noted in van der Lugt, "'Abominable Mixtures,'" 233; and Page, *Magic in the Cloister*, 65.

BOOK 3

1. Bakhouche, Fauquier, and Pérez-Jean identify this bird as a "grand-duc," which is the Eurasian eagle-owl (*Bubo bubo*; *Picatrix*, 178). Rossi skips this word entirely (*Picatrix*, 123).

2. There is an inconsistency in the text here as 3.1.4 assigned Greek to Jupiter, and 3.1.8 below assigns the Turkish language to Mercury.

3. This refers to the Sabeans, or more broadly to pagans.

4. Litharge is one of the naturally occurring types of lead monoxide (PbO; lead [II] oxide).

5. *Arhenda* is an Arabic word for roses; see Bakhouche, Fauquier, and Pérez-Jean, *Picatrix*, 181.

6. Skeptics are probably implied by the categories "speculations on religion" and "those who love the philosophers' faiths," while "those faiths that exist according to sense perception" likely correspond to materialist beliefs, such as Democritean atomism and/or Epicureanism.

7. The Latin word is *azebias*, which Greer and Warnock render as "zebras" (*Picatrix*, 136).

8. "Alemannic" means Germanic.

9. "Rouncey," a term in the later Middle Ages referring to an all-purpose horse, translates the Latin *Picatrix*'s *runcus*, a word not otherwise attested with any meaning relating to animals; *runcinus*, however, is a type of horse. Rossi has *buoi* (oxen) here (*Picatrix*, 126).

10. Bdellium is a myrrh-like gummy resin extracted from *Commiphora wightii*, a flowering shrub found in northern Africa, central Asia, and India.

11. Orpiment, an elision of *auri pigmentum*, is a deep yellow-colored arsenic sulfide mineral (As_2S_3) found around volcanoes and hot springs. It is formed by sublimation as a by-product of the decay of another arsenic mineral, realgar (α-As_4S_4). It has long been used as a gold pigment base from ancient Rome to China.

12. Blue vitriol, also known as *calcanthum*, is a copper sulfate.

13. The Latin term *fel, fellis* (n.) can mean either bile or gallbladder. The meaning here is unclear.

14. Compare 3.3.3 above.

15. Bakhouche, Fauquier, and Pérez-Jean suggest that this Thebith is Tibet (*Picatrix*, 191). The description may well refer to the light-headedness induced by altitude sickness.

16. Ritter and Plessner report that this is the land of the Bulgarians on the Danube (*Picatrix*, 171). We believe the description suggests a location closer to or on the equator. Pingree's corresponding apparatus reports the following variant spellings: *burguz, burgutz, brugum, bugum* (Pingree, *Picatrix*, Apparatus Criticus, 287).

17. Bakhouche, Fauquier, and Pérez-Jean suggest that this *Camer* is Cambodia (Khmer), which, of course, is not an island but is more easily reached from India across the Bay of Bengal than over land (*Picatrix*, 192).

18. Bakhouche, Fauquier, and Pérez-Jean suggest that this *Azanif* is a region of central Vietnam known as Annam (*Picatrix*, 192).

19. Bakhouche, Fauquier, and Pérez-Jean suggest that this *Haybar* is the oasis of Hidjāz in northern Arabia (*Picatrix*, 192).

20. Bakhouche, Fauquier, and Pérez-Jean suggest that the Two Seas is Bahrain (*Picatrix*, 192).

21. Bakhouche, Fauquier, and Pérez-Jean suggest that this *Alahavez* is al-Hawaz (*Picatrix*, 193).

22. Bakhouche, Fauquier, and Pérez-Jean identify this sage as al-Rudbāri (*Picatrix*, 198).

23. In the original Arabic text, the "young woman" appears as a young man of servile condition (*ghulām*); see Boudet and Coulon, "Version arabe," 93–94. This entire episode is a prominent example of the Latin translator modifying the text to suit his Christian audience's cultural sensibilities. This is also the most elaborate example of predatory sex magic in the *Picatrix*.

24. This refers to the "cross" mentioned earlier in the paragraph.

25. This is a corrupt transliteration of the *Kitāb al-Istamāṭīs*; see Burnett "Hermann of Carinthia," 167–69.

26. See note above in 3.6.1.

27. Pingree's critical apparatus reports eleven distinct variants on this name, none of which help to clarify the identity of the character in question (Pingree, *Picatrix*, Apparatus Criticus, 316).

28. Pingree explains how the prayers in this section, 3.7.16–33, describe the private rituals of the Sabeans of Harrān, whose public planetary liturgies were informed by a number of Arabic writers ("Some of the Sources," 12). Saxl confirms their Harrānian origins ("Beiträge zu einer Geschichte," 151–77).

29. *Bericus* is unknown in Latin. The corresponding passage in Ritter and Plessner indicates that this ingredient is absent from the Arabic text (*Picatrix*, 215).

30. For the remainder of this series of prayers to the planets (3.7.17–33), the transliterations of "Phoenician" are to be understood as representing Syrian Aramaic, "Roman" as colloquial Byzantine Greek (note the distinctions made between "Latin" and "Roman"), and "Greek" as the contemporary Greek that was used by many Christians in the Islamic world. These names have all been thoroughly corrupted by the process of transliteration through numerous languages, though some familiar names may shine through (e.g., *Koronez* or *Hacoronoz* from Cronus/ὁ Κρόνος).

31. The "metal of Jupiter" is tin.

32. The Latin word means "small crystalline sheets," but the Arabic version specifies that it is sandarac gum. See Ritter and Plessner, *Picatrix*, 216.

33. This individual appears elsewhere as al-Razi; see 2.12.55.

34. This name corresponds to Anahita, the Avestan (ancient Persian) goddess of waters, associated with healing, fertility, and wisdom.

35. The Latin word *cardellum* (*-us*?; probably derived from the word for "thistle," *carduus*, *-i*) appears as "Storax" in Ritter and Plessner (*Picatrix*, 232); as "pissenlit poivré" in Bakhouche, Fauquier, and Pérez-Jean (*Picatrix*, 234); as "long pepper" in Greer and Warnock (*Picatrix*, 175); and as "cardo stellato" (amethyst eringo) in Rossi (*Picatrix*, 169).

36. Ritter and Plessner have "Stechginster" (gorse) here (*Picatrix*, 236), while Bakhouche, Fauquier, and Pérez-Jean have "herbe à chameaux" (camel grass) (*Picatrix*, 239), and Rossi has "ginestra" (*Cytisus scoparius*, Scotch broom) (*Picatrix*, 169). It could also be *Calicatome villosa*.

37. Greer and Warnock have "nettle tree" (*Picatrix*, 179); and Ritter and Plessner have "Greek nard" (*Picatrix*, 236).

38. This is a garbled transliteration of the Aramaic for "the Blind Master." See Ritter and Plessner, *Picatrix*, 238.

39. Ritter and Plessner suggest this *Canuiz* is Cyprus (*Picatrix*, 240), while Bakhouche, Fauquier, and Pérez-Jean suggest Canodj (Kannauj) in Northern India (*Picatrix*, 242).

40. Barnac Elbarameny or Bartim al-Brahmani is here allegedly the eponymous founder of India's priestly Brahmin caste, though it is certain that it is al-Brahmani who took his name from the Brahmin, contrary to what the text here would suggest.

41. Pingree, "Some of the Sources," 12. The following set of prayers to the Sun and Saturn are drawn from ibn Waḥshīya's *Chaldean/Nabataean Agriculture*; cf. 1.2.4; 2.2.4; and 3.8.4.

42. Abenrasia is another one of the *Picatrix*'s many corrupted forms of ibn Waḥshīya, the translator of the *Chaldean/Nabataean Agriculture*; compare 1.2.4; 2.2.4; and 3.8.2.

43. This *Antimaquis* book is a corruption of *Kitāb al-Isṭamākhis*, presented in the form of a letter from Aristotle to Alexander. According to this pseudo-Aristotelian Hermetic work, each planet has seven spirits, one for each side plus one that binds them all. In the *Kitāb al-Isṭamākhis*, there are special prayers accompanied by specific talismans, sacrifices, and incenses (to be performed at specific times) for each of these spirits. Pingree, "Some of the Sources," 12; Saif, "From *Ġāyat al-ḥakīm*," 307.

44. "Jupiter's metal" is tin; compare 3.7.18 above.

45. *Cahadabula* is Sa'ad al Bulah in Arabic. Compare 1.4.24, where the mansion is called *Caaddebolach*, and 4.9.53, where it is called *Zaadalahbia*. The mansion also appears in Firmicus Maternus, *Mathesis* II: 3, 5.

46. The word "assortment" in this sentence was rendered from the Latin term *scolarilia*, which seems unattested elsewhere and is translated as "couronnes" (crowns) by Bakhouche, Fauquier, and Pérez-Jean (*Picatrix*, 251); as "jewels" by Greer and Warnock (*Picatrix*, 190); and as "mescolanza" (mix) by Rossi (*Picatrix*, 179).

47. This sentence suggests that the following day was considered to begin at nightfall (i.e., Monday began when the sun set on Sunday evening).

48. See 3.6.1–5.

49. The word "moringa" translates the Latin *alben*. It appears as "Bennüsse" in Ritter and Plessner (*Picatrix*, 258); as "troène" (privet) in Bakhouche, Fauquier, and Pérez-Jean (*Picatrix*, 258); as "centaury" in Greer and Warnock (*Picatrix*, 196); and as "ligustro" (privet) in Rossi (*Picatrix*, 184).

50. Alternate name for the *Antimaquis* (*Kitāb al-Isṭamākhis*), see note in 3.9.1.

51. Bakhouche, Fauquier, and Pérez-Jean translate *caubac* as "jasmine" (*Picatrix*, 267); Rossi has *mercurio* in parentheses after *caubac* (*Picatrix*, 191).

52. Bakhouche, Fauquier, and Pérez-Jean translate Egyptian vulture (*arrahama*) as "pélican" (*Picatrix*, 272); Ritter and Plessner translate the Arabic as "Pelikan" (*Picatrix*, 275); Rossi has "avvoltoio" (vulture) here (*Picatrix*, 193).

53. A treatise attributed to Hermes below, 3.11.52; the Arabic transliterates as *al-Hâdîtûs* according to Bakhouche, Fauquier, and Pérez-Jean (*Picatrix*, 274). It is mentioned again in 3.11.112.

54. The word *chami* appears as "giftigen Reptils" (poisonous reptile) in Ritter and Plessner (*Picatrix*, 278), while Greer and Warnock translate it as "chamois" (*Picatrix*, 208).

55. Pigs possess a very limited number of sweat glands, which are essentially useless, hence the reason they love to sit in pools of water for regulating body temperature. This ingredient would therefore be singularly difficult to collect.

56. Bakhouche, Fauquier, and Pérez-Jean translate this as Berber "carob" (*Picatrix*, 276); Greer and Warnock have "barberry aloaxac" (*Picatrix*, 209).

57. Bakhouche, Fauquier, and Pérez-Jean identify the *nux scialte* as the datura plant, which we believe is the correct conjecture given the context of each of its appearances in recipes for psychotropic effects (*Picatrix*, 276). Greer and Warnock leave it untranslated (*Picatrix*, 209).

58. The following quotation attributed to Jābir ibn Ḥayyān runs from the next sentence down until 3.11.111 below and is an interpolation that is absent from the Arabic text (see Principe, *Secrets of Alchemy*, 33–45).

59. The Moon and the Sun are common cryptonyms (*Decknamen*) for silver and gold, respectively.

60. See note for 3.11.68 above.

61. Greer and Warnock have "male barberry" for the Latin *male amreps* (*Picatrix*, 212).

62. The term used in the Latin text is *lucula mortifera*, which is otherwise unattested. Our identification with deadly nightshade (*Atropa belladonna*) is conjectural based on the context. Rossi suggests "ortica bianca" (white nettle) here (*Picatrix*, 200).

63. According to Bakhouche, Fauquier, and Pérez-Jean, this *Baldach* is Baghdad (*Picatrix*, 281).

64. Pingree, *Picatrix*, appendix 37, p. 245.

65. On Jābir ibn Ḥayyān, see Principe, *Secrets of Alchemy*, 33–45.

66. Bakhouche, Fauquier, and Pérez-Jean render the Latin *gallie* as "civette" (chive) (*Picatrix*, 283); Ritter and Plessner have "Sukk" (date juice with gall-nuts mixed with Indian astringent drugs, often used as a perfume) (*Picatrix*, 282); Greer and Warnock have "lady's bedstraw" (*Picatrix*, 215); Rossi has "ambra (o muschio)" (amber [or moss]) (*Picatrix*, 202).

67. This may refer to sarcocolla gum: cf. 3.9.13 and 4.2.17. Ritter and Plessner suggest "Marienbaum" as an uncertain reading (*Picatrix*, 283); Rossi has "erba indovina" (diviner's herb) (*Picatrix*, 202); Bakhouche, Fauquier, and Pérez-Jean link the word to "hariola" and thereby to diviner's sage ("herbe de devineresse"—*Salvia divinorum*) (*Picatrix*, 283). Nevertheless, the latter plant is native to the New World and is therefore not relevant in this context.

68. See Pingree, *Picatrix*, appendix 38, p. 246.

69. See Pingree, *Picatrix*, appendix 39, p. 246.

70. Bakhouche, Fauquier, and Pérez-Jean identify this as incense ("encens") (*Picatrix*, 284); Greer and Warnock refer to it as "soapwort" (*Picatrix*, 215). We have identified this *condisi* (elsewhere *alcondiz*) as wolfsbane (aconite).

71. Manuscript variants in Pingree also suggest *arcolle* as a reading, thereby linking this word to the *arcole* that appeared above in 3.11.119. Again, this could refer to sarcocolla gum. Greer and Warnock leave the word as "ariole" (*Picatrix*, 215). The passage in Ritter and Plessner has "Seidelbast" (daphne) and "Niesgarbe" (sneezewort) as the two herbs aside from euphorbia (*Picatrix*, 283).

72. Pingree, *Picatrix*, appendix 40, p. 246.

73. Some frogs and toads—especially when traumatized—secrete bufotenine (5-HO-DMT), an indole-based tryptamine related to serotonin. It is similar in chemical structure to psilocin (4-HO-DMT), the active ingredient in many hallucinogenic mushrooms, and has somewhat similar psychotropic effects.

74. Boudet and Coulon discuss the identity of this king, who appears in the Arabic version of the text as Kankah ("Version arabe," 70); see also Ritter and Plessner, *Picatrix*, 285–86.

75. Compare 1.5.6 above.

76. By this, the text implies decimal Arabic/Indian numerals.

77. Ritter and Plessner identify this city as Dongola in the Sudan (*Picatrix*, 287).

BOOK 4

1. It is worth considering whether this comment implies that the following material was not read in Arabic.

2. Ritter and Plessner specify that it is the root of the plant that is needed (*Picatrix*, 312); Greer and Warnock leave the Latin term *behem* (*Picatrix*, 233); the identification with the iris is found in James, *Medicinal Dictionary*, s.v. "behem."

3. Ritter and Plessner have "Sukk" here (*Picatrix*, 312); Bakhouche, Fauquier, and Pérez-Jean have "noix de galle" (gall nut) (*Picatrix*, 305); Greer and Warnock have "gall-nut" (*Picatrix*, 234); and Rossi has "muschio" (moss) (*Picatrix*, 219); cf. note in 3.11.117.

4. Ritter and Plessner have "Sukk" here (*Picatrix*, 319); Bakhouche, Fauquier, and Pérez-Jean have "gali" (*Picatrix*, 312); Greer and Warnock have "alkali" (*Picatrix*, 240); and Rossi has "zibetto" (civet) (*Picatrix*, 224-225); cf. note in 3.9.12.

5. The Mountains of the Moon are mentioned in Ptolomy's *Geography* 4.9.3 as being one possible source for the Nile. See *Geographia Cl. Ptolemaei,* 152: "Hunc quidem sinum circumhabitant Aethiopes antropophagi. A quorum occidentali parte pertingit Lunae mons, à quo Nili paludes niues suscipiunt, et Lunae montis fines gradus habet 57 Australis 12 30 et 67 Australis 12 30." (Indeed, man-eating Ethiopians dwell around this bay; the mountain of the Moon, from where the snows feed the floodplain of the Nile, and the borders of the mountain of the Moon have these coordinates 57 Australis 12 30 et 67 Australis 12 30.) For the translation, see http://amshistorica.unibo.it/184. For the Greek text, see *Claudii Ptolemaei Geographia* 1:283.

6. For the biblical "House of the Sun" (*Beth Shemesh*) situated in Egypt, see Jeremiah 43:13; it is not clear how this locale relates to the ancient city of Heliopolis, situated on the southeastern end of the Nile delta.

7. Compare the figures in Ezekiel 1:10, but note the difference between the image of a dog here and the human face in Ezekiel.

8. The infusion of spirits into statues is a well-established practice in the Hermetic tradition, appearing in Hermes Trismegistus, *Asclepius* 23–24, in *Apulei Platonici Madaurensis,* 63–65; see also Porphyry, *On Statues,* in Smith, *Porphyry,* 407–35.

9. A consistent association of specific colors with each of the planets is attributed to Mercurius in 3.3.2 and 3.3.11, while a separate list links slightly different colors with the planets at 3.1.3–9.

10. The name *Adocentyn* is a corrupt transliteration of al-Ashmunain, which is the Arabic name for Hermopolis in Egypt, the city dedicated to Thoth-Hermes.

11. See note in 2.6.2.

12. This is a transliteration of Jābir ibn Ḥayyān; see Principe, *Secrets of Alchemy,* 33–45.

13. Aristotle's *Organon* is what is implied here.

14. This *Oydus the Natural* refers to Aristotle's *Physics.*

15. See Diotima's Ladder in Plato, *Symposium,* 201d–212c.

16. This tripartite division of the human soul can be found in Plato's *Republic,* 4.436a.

17. This internal cross-reference (and the one in 4.6.9 below) is slightly wrong in that the material referred to actually appears in 3.8.3.

18. Compare above 3.7.32.

19. Compare above 3.8.3.

20. This passage confirms the sacrificial nature of all the animal ingredient collection in the rituals of the planetary spirits, thereby linking all of these recipes and rituals to the Sabean/Hermetic traditions of Harrān, derived ultimately from the pagan religious practices of classical antiquity. See Page, "Sacrifices d'animaux," 187–211.

21. The word "moringa" appears as "Weihrauch (*kundur*)" (incense) in Ritter and Plessner (*Picatrix*, 364); as "troène" (privet) in Bakhouche, Fauquier, and Pérez-Jean (*Picatrix*, 337); as "centaury" in Greer and Warnock (*Picatrix*, 260); and as "ligustro" (privet) in Rossi (*Picatrix*, 242); cf. note in 3.10.5.

22. Abubaer Abenvaxie is yet another corrupt form of the name Abu Bakr ibn Waḥshīya, the translator of the *Nabataean/Chaldean Agriculture;* cf. 1.2.4; 2.2.4; and 3.8.2–4.

23. Some manuscripts have the number 17, and others have 117 here and below in the paragraph. We use "(1)17" to capture this variability and ambiguity.

24. According to Greer and Warnock, this refers to a formerly Greek town in Italy named Andanica, now Andorossa (*Picatrix,* 267). There is no such town in Italy, but there are two towns in Messenia in the Greek Peloponese that could correspond to the adjective in the *Picatrix:* Androusa or Andania.

25. This entire paragraph (4.7.23) is an interpolation absent from the Arabic.

26. According to Ritter and Plessner, the Arabic text has *galbanum* as the ingredient here (*Picatrix,* 382); Greer and Warnock left the Latin term *axenus* (*Picatrix,* 268); Bakhouche, Fauquier, and Pérez-Jean have the expression "gibelle de Damas" here, a substance unknown to us (*Picatrix,* 348); Rossi has "nepitella" (lesser calamint) (*Picatrix,* 250).

27. Here the deadly poison "wolfsbane," (also known by the folk name "monkshood," or "aconite" after the Latin name *Aconitum*) translates *alcondiz.*

28. Bakhouche, Fauquier, and Pérez-Jean translate this word as "jujubier," which is "ziziphus" in English (*Picatrix,* 351); Ritter and Plessner indicate that the Arabic text has the "Brustbeere" (chestnut tree) here (*Picatrix,* 388). This plant might be the Assyrian plum (*Cordia myxa*), among whose common names is "spistan." Rossi has "giuggiola" (jujube) (*Picatrix,* 252).

29. Hamen could just as well represent either Oman or Yemen.

30. Compare Exodus 7:10–15.

31. Ritter and Plessner suggest that *assiffe* is "Bimsstein" (pumice stone) (*Picatrix,* 404), while Rossi has "basalto" (basalt) (*Picatrix,* 257).

32. Based on the Arabic text, Ritter and Plessner suggest that this river is the Wâdi al-Harluh in Turkestan (*Picatrix,* 404).

33. Ritter and Plessner have "sycamore" for this word (*Picatrix,* 406).

34. Ritter and Plessner identify the stone as "Anbaristein" (*Picatrix,* 406); Bakhouche, Fauquier, and Pérez-Jean translate the word as "amber" (*Picatrix,* 359).

35. This Cerich river is likely the Algeriche mentioned in 4.8.6 above.

36. For further discussion of magical squares and their links with the seven planets, see Folkerts, "Zur Frühgeschichte," 313–38; Karpenko, "Between Magic and Science," 121–28; and Burnett, "*Picatrix* à l'Institut Warburg," 31–32. The "fifteen square" refers to a 3 by 3 pattern of digits in which each row, column, and diagonal adds up to 15. Such squares of digits were considered magical, and there was one corresponding to each of the planets. The square with the shared sum of 15 belongs to Saturn and looks like this:

4	9	2
3	5	7
8	1	6

37. According to Ritter and Plessner, the Arabic text has the herb "spurge" instead of a stone here (*Picatrix,* 408).

38. Here, the "Great Work" implies alchemy.

39. According to Ritter and Plessner, the Arabic text has *Anagyris foetida* here (*Picatrix,* 411).

40. Ritter and Plessner identify this plant (*cotrop*) as the wild lychnis. Another instance of a plant shining like a candle occurs above at 4.7.59 (*Picatrix,* 372).

41. Based on Ritter and Plessner, this ingredient is meant to be wild parsley resin (*Picatrix,* 417). Rossi identifies the plant as *Athamanta macedonica* (*Picatrix,* 263).

42. We have rendered the Latin *calcantum* as blue vitriol; Bakhouche, Fauquier, and Pérez-Jean (*Picatrix,* 367) and Greer and Warnock (*Picatrix,* 284) all say incorrectly that it is lime; cf. 3.3.13 and 4.7.4. In 4.7.4, lime and *calcantum* are mentioned as distinct ingredients.

43. Pingree reads "Zucrat" where we have provided Socrates (*Picatrix,* 227). If this is indeed Socrates, the following aphorisms are pseudepigraphical.

44. This Plinio is not to be mistaken for Pliny, the author of the *Historia Naturalis* (pace Greer and Warnock, *Picatrix,* 286). The twenty-eight mansions of the Moon appeared above in 1.4.2–29. In 1.4.1 and 1.4.30, the paragraphs that introduce and conclude the list of mansions of the Moon, the list is credited to "Indian sages," implying that Plinio is thus an Indian sage. The entire section 4.9.29–56 is an interpolation absent from the Arabic text.

45. The word *enque* could be "zinc" but remains unidentified otherwise.

46. A complete text for this paragraph is found only in three Latin manuscripts. Of these, the more elaborate version has been selected for inclusion here. See Pingree, *Picatrix,* appendix 65, p. 253.

47. The section 4.9.58–65 is an interpolation absent from the Arabic version of the *Picatrix.*

BIBLIOGRAPHY

PICATRIX EDITIONS AND TRANSLATIONS

Bakhouche, Béatrice, Frédéric Fauquier, and Brigitte Pérez-Jean. *Picatrix: Un traité de magie médiéval*. Turnhout: Brepols, 2003.

Greer, John Michael, and Christopher Warnock. *The Picatrix: Liber Rubeus Edition*. Phoenix, Ariz.: Adocentyn Press, 2011.

Pingree, David. *Picatrix: The Latin Version of the "Ghāyat Al-Ḥakīm."* London: Warburg Institute, 1986.

Ritter, Hellmut, and Martin Plessner. *"Picatrix": Das Ziel des Weisen von Pseudo-Mağrīṭī*. London: Warburg Institute, 1962.

Rossi, Paolo A., ed. *Picatrix: Dalla versione latina del "Ghāyat Al-Ḥakīm."* Milan: Mimesis, 1999.

WORKS CITED

Adamson, Peter. *The Arabic Plotinus: A Philosophical Study of the "Theology of Aristotle."* London: Duckworth, 2002.

Agostino, Alfonso d'. *Astromagia: Ms. Reg. lat. 1283a*. Naples: Liguori, 1992.

Agrippa, Heinrich Cornelius. *De occulta philosophia libri tres*. Edited by Vittoria Perrone Compagni. Leiden: Brill, 1992.

Agrippa d'Aubigné, Théodore. *Lettres touchant quelques poincts de diverses sciences, no. 5, à M. de la Rivière, premier médecin du roy*. In *Œuvres complètes*, edited by Eugène Réaume and François de Caussade, vol. 1, 433–37. Paris: Alphonse Lemerre, 1873.

Alverny, Marie-Thérèse d'. *Alain de Lille: Textes inédits, avec une introduction sur sa vie et ses oeuvres*. Paris: J. Vrin, 1965.

Alverny, Marie-Thérèse d', and Françoise Hudry. "Al-Kindi: *De radiis*." *Archives d'histoire doctrinale et littéraire du moyen âge* 41 (1974): 139–260.

Attrell, Daniel, and David Porreca. "Notes on the *Picatrix*: Non-Heteronormative Sex, and Forthcoming Translation." *Societas Magica Newsletter* 34 (2016): 1–6.

Bendersky, Gordon, and Susan C. Ferrence. "Therapy with Saffron and the Goddess at Thera." *Perspectives in Biology and Medicine* 42, no. 2 (2004): 199–226.

Bever, Edward. *The Realities of Witchcraft and Popular Magic in Early Modern Europe*. New York: Palgrave Macmillan, 2008.

Blake, William. "The Marriage of Heaven and Hell." In *The Poetical Works of William Blake*, edited by John Sampson, 247–60. London: Oxford University Press, 1913.

Boudet, Jean-Patrice. "L'amour et les rituels à images d'envoûtement dans le *Picatrix* latin." In Boudet, Caiozzo, and Weill-Parot, *Images et magie*, 149–62.

Boudet, Jean-Patrice, Anna Caiozzo, and Nicolas Weill-Parot, eds. *Images et magie: "Picatrix" entre Orient et Occident*. Paris: Honoré Champion, 2011.

———. "*Picatrix*, au carrefour des savoirs et pratiques magiques." In Boudet, Caiozzo, and Weill-Parot, *Images et magie*, 13–24.

Boudet, Jean-Patrice, and Jean-Charles Coulon. "La version arabe (*Ghāyāt al-ḥakīm*) et la version latine du *Picatrix*: Points communs et divergences." *Cahiers de recherches médiévales et humanistes / Journal of Medieval and Humanistic Studies* 33, no. 1 (2017): 67–101.

Boudet, Jean-Patrice, Martine Ostorero, and Agostino Paravicini Bagliani, eds. *De Frédéric II à Rodolphe II: Astrologie, divination et magie dans les cours (XIIIe–XVIIe siècle)*. Florence: SISMEL Edizioni del Galluzzo, 2017.

Bowman, W. C., and I. S. Sanghvi. "Pharmacological Actions of Hemlock (*Conium maculatum*) Alkaloids." *Journal of Pharmacy and Pharmacology* 15, no. 1 (1963): 1–25.

Branca, Daniela Delcorno. "Un discepulo de Poliziano: Michele Acciari." *Lettere italiane* 28 (1976): 464–81.

Brown, James Wood. *An Enquiry Into the Life and Legend of Michael Scot*. Edinburgh: David Douglas, 1897.

Burnett, Charles. "European Knowledge of Arabic Texts Referring to Music: Some New Material." *Early Music History* 12 (1993): 1–12.

———. "Hermann of Carinthia and the Kitāb al-Isṭamāṭīs: Further Evidence for the Transmission of Hermetic Magic." *Journal of the Warburg and Courtauld Institutes* 44 (1981): 167–69.

———. *Magic and Divination in the Middle Ages: Texts and Techniques in the Islamic and Christian Worlds*. Aldershot: Ashgate, 1996.

———. "Magic in the Court of Alfonso el Sabio: The Latin Translation of the *Ghāyāt al-Ḥakīm*." In Boudet, Ostorero, and Paravicini Bagliani, *De Frédéric II à Rodolphe II*, 37–52.

———. "Le *Picatrix* à l'Institut Warburg: Histoire d'une recherche et d'une publication." In Boudet, Caiozzo, and Weill-Parot, *Images et magie*, 25–38.

———. "Talismans: Magic as Science? Necromancy Among the Seven Liberal Arts." In Burnett, *Magic and Divination*, 1–15.

Callataÿ, Godefroid de, and Sébastien Moureau. "Again on Maslama Ibn Qāsim al-Qurṭubī, the Ikhwān al-Ṣafā', and Ibn Khaldūn: New Evidence from Two Manuscripts of *Rutbat al-ḥakīm*." *Al-Qanṭara* 37, no. 2 (2016): 329–72.

———. "A Milestone in the History of Andalusī Bāṭinism: Maslama b. Qāsim al-Qurṭubī's Riḥla in the East." In Fierro, Schmidtke, and Stroumsa, *Histories of Books*, 85–116.

———. "Towards the Critical Edition of the *Rutbat al-ḥakīm*: A Few Preliminary Observations." *Arabica* 62 (2015): 385–94.

Carmody, Francis J. *Astronomical Works of Thabit b. Qurra*. Berkeley: University of California Press, 1960.

Chwolsohn, Daniel Abramovich. *Die Sabier und der Sabismus*. Vol. 2. St. Petersburg: Imperial Academy, 1856.

Darby, George O. S. "An Astrological Manuscript of Alfonso X." Ph.D. diss., Harvard University, 1932.

Davidson, Gustav. *A Dictionary of Angels, Including the Fallen Angels*. New York: Macmillan, 1967.

De Quincey, Thomas. *The Confessions of an English Opium-Eater*. London: Folio Society, 1948.

Díez, Raquel. "Alfonso X the Learned: 'Picatrix' (Vatican Ms. Reginensis Latinus 1283a), Study and Edition." Ph.D. diss., New York University, 1995.

Dorotheus of Sidon. *Carmen Astrologicum*. Translated by David Pingree. Leipzig: B. G. Teubner, 1976.

Dumas, Geneviève. *Santé et société à Montpellier à la fin du Moyen Âge*. Leiden: Brill, 2015.

Farmer, Steve A. *Syncretism in the West: Pico's 900 Theses (1486); The Evolution of Traditional Religious and Philosophical Systems*. Tempe, Ariz.: Medieval and Renaissance Texts and Studies, 1998.

Ficino, Marsilio. *De vita libri tres*. Edited by Martin Plessner and Felix Klein-Franke. Hildesheim: G. Olms Verlag, 1978.

———. *Three Books on Life*. Translated by Carol V. Kaske and John R. Clarke. Binghamton, N.Y.: Centre for Medieval and Renaissance Studies, 1989.

Fierro, Maribel. "Bāṭinism in Al-Andalus: Maslama b. Qāsim al-Qurṭubī (died 353/964), Author of the 'Rutbat al-Ḥakīm' and the 'Ghāyat al-Ḥakīm' (*Picatrix*)." *Studia Islamica* 84 (1996): 87–112.

Fierro, Maribel, S. Schmidtke, and S. Stroumsa, eds. *Histories of Books in the Islamicate World*. Leiden: Brill, 2016.

Folkerts, Menso. "Zur Frühgeschichte der magischen Quadrate in Westeuropa." *Sudhoffs Archiv* 65 (1981): 313–38.

Frank, Barry S., W. B. Michelson, K. E. Panter, and D. R. Gardner. "Ingestion of Poison Hemlock (*Conium maculatum*)." *Western Journal of Medicine* 163 (1995): 573–74.

Franklin, Howard Bruce. *Prison Writing in 20th-Century America*. New York: Penguin Books, 1998.

Genequand, Charles. "Idolâtrie, astrolâtrie et sabéisme." *Studia Islamica* 89 (1999): 109–28.

Green, Tamara. *The City of the Moon God: Religious Traditions of Harrān*. Leiden: Brill, 1992.

Hamès, Constant. "La *Ghāyat al-Ḥakīm*: Son époque, sa postérité en terre d'Islam." In Boudet, Caiozzo, and Weill-Parot, *Images et magie*, 215–32.

Hanegraaff, Wouter J. "Beyond the Yates Paradigm." *Aries: Journal for the Study of Western Esotericism* 1, no. 1 (2001): 5–37.

———. *Esotericism and the Academy: Rejected Knowledge in Western Culture*. Cambridge: Cambridge University Press, 2012.

Hanegraaff, Wouter J., and Ruud M. Bouthoorn. *Lodovico Lazzarelli (1447–1500): The Hermetic Writings and Related Documents*. Tempe, Ariz.: Arizona Center for Medieval and Renaissance Studies, 2005.

Hartlieb, Johannes. *Das Buch aller verbotenen Künste, des Aberglaubens und der Zauberei*. Translated and edited by Falk Eisermann and Eckhard Graf. Ahlerstedt: Param, 1989.

Hartner, Willy. "Notes on Picatrix." *Isis* 56, no. 4 (1965): 438–51.

Hjärpe, Jan. "Analyse critique des traditions arabes sur les Sabéens Harrāniens." Ph.D. diss., University of Uppsala, 1972.

Hudry, Françoise, ed. *Liber viginti quattuor philosophorum*. Turnhout: Brepols, 1997.

James, Robert. *A Medicinal Dictionary: Including Physic, Surgery, Anatomy, Chymistry, and Botany, in All Their Branches Relative to Medicine*. Vol. 1. London: T. Osborne, 1743.

Kahane, Henry, Renée Kahane, and Angelina Pietrangeli. "*Picatrix* and the Talismans." *Romance Philology* 19 (1966): 574–93.

Karpenko, Vladimír. "Between Magic and Science: Numerical Magic Squares." *Ambix* 40 (1993): 121–28.

Kieckhefer, Richard. *Hazards of the Dark Arts: Advice for Medieval Princes on Witchcraft and Magic*. University Park: Pennsylvania State University Press, 2017.

———. *Magic in the Middle Ages*. Cambridge: Cambridge University Press, 1990.

Láng, Benedek. *Unlocked Books: Manuscripts of Learned Magic in the Medieval Libraries of Central Europe*. University Park: Pennsylvania State University Press, 2008.

Leicht, Reimund. "Le chapitre II, 12 du *Picatrix* latin et les versions hébraïques du *De duodecim imaginibus*." In Boudet, Caiozzo, and Weill-Parot, *Images et magie*, 295–330.

Lugt, Maaike van der. "'Abominable Mixtures': The *Liber vaccae* in the Medieval West, or the Dangers and Attractions of Natural Magic." *Traditio* 64 (2009): 229–77.

Marquet, Yves. "Sabéens et Iḫwān al-Ṣafā'." Pts. 1 and 2. *Studia Islamica* 24 (1966): 35–80; 25 (1967): 77–109.

Merlin, Mark D. "Archaeological Evidence for the Tradition of Psychoactive Plant Use in the Old World." *Economic Botany* 57, no. 3 (2003): 295–323.

Moussaieff, Arieh, Neta Rimmerman, Tatiana Bregman, A. Straiker, C. C. Felder, S. Shoham, et al. "Incensole Acetate, an Incense Component, Elicits Psychoactivity by Activating

TRPV3 Channels in the Brain." *Federation of American Societies for Experimental Biology (FASEB) Journal* 22 (2008): 3024–34.

Naudé, Gabriel. *Naudeana et Patiniana: Ou singularitez remarquables prises des conversations de Mess. Naudé et Patin.* Amsterdam: François vander Plaats, 1703.

Nifo, Augustino. *Ad Apotelesmata Ptolomaei eruditiones.* Naples: Petrus Maria de Richis Papiensis, 1513.

Otto, Bernd-Christian. "Historicizing Western Learned Magic." *Aries* 16 (2016): 161–240.

Page, Sophie. *Magic in the Cloister: Pious Motives, Illicit Interests, and Occult Approaches to the Medieval Universe.* University Park: Pennsylvania State University Press, 2013.

———. "Les sacrifices d'animaux dans le *Picatrix* latin et d'autres textes de magie médiévale." In Boudet, Caiozzo, and Weill-Parot, *Images et magie*, 187–211.

Panayotopoulous, D. J., and D. D. Chisholm. "Hallucinogenic Effect of Nutmeg." *British Medical Journal* 1, no. 5698 (1970): 754.

Pasi, Marco. "Theses de Magia." *Societas Magica Newsletter* 20 (2008): 1–5, 7–8.

Perrone Compagni, Vittoria. "La magia cerimoniale del 'Picatrix' nel Rinascimento." *Atti dell' Accademia di Scienze Morali e Politiche* 88 (1977): 279–330.

———. "*Picatrix*: Une philosophie pour la pratique." In Boudet, Caiozzo, and Weill-Parot, *Images et magie*, 359–72.

———. "Picatrix Latinus." *Medioevo* 1 (1975): 237–337.

Peters, Emily. "Hermes and Harran: The Roots of Arabic-Islamic Occultism." In *Magic and Divination in Early Islam*, edited by Emily Savage-Smith, 55–86. Aldershot: Ashgate, 2004.

Pingree, David. "Al-Ṭabarī on on the Prayers to the Planets." *Bulletin d'études orientales* 44 (1992): 105–17.

———. "Between the *Ghayā* and the *Picatrix* I: The Spanish Version." *Journal of the Warburg and Courtauld Institutes* 44 (1981): 27–56.

———. "Between the *Ghayā* and the *Picatrix* II: The *Flos naturarum* Ascribed to Jābir." *Journal of the Warburg and Courtauld Institutes* 72 (2009): 41–80.

———. "The Diffusion of Arabic Magical Texts in Western Europe." In *La diffusione delle scienze islamiche nel Medio Evo europeo (Convegno internazionale promosso dall'Accademia nazionale dei Lincei)*, 57–102. Rome: Accademia Nazionale dei Lincei, 1987.

———. "Indian Planetary Images and the Tradition of Astral Magic." *Journal of the Warburg and Courtauld Institutes* 52 (1989): 1–13.

———. "Plato's Hermetic Book of the Cow." In *Il neoplatonismo nel Rinascimento*, edited by Pietro Pini, 133–45. Rome: Istituto della Enciclopedia Italiana, 1993.

———. "Some of the Sources of the *Ghāyat al-Ḥakīm*." *Journal of the Warburg and Courtauld Institutes* 43 (1980): 1–15.

Plessner, Martin. "A Medieval Definition of Scientific Experiment in the Hebrew *Picatrix*." *Journal of the Warburg and Courtauld Institutes* 36 (1973): 358–59.

Porreca, David. "Apollonius of Tyana through a Medieval Latin Lens." *Magic, Witchcraft, and Magic* 9 (2014): 157–77.

———. "How Hidden Was God? Revelation and Pedagogy in the Ancient and Medieval Hermetic Writings." In *Histories of the Hidden God: Concealments and Revelation in Western Gnostic, Esoteric, and Mystical Traditions*, edited by April D. DeConick and Grant Adamson, 137–48. Durham: Acumen Publishing, 2013.

Principe, Lawrence. *The Secrets of Alchemy.* Chicago: University of Chicago Press, 2013.

Ptolemy, Claudius. *Claudii Ptolemaei Geographia.* Edited by Carolus Fridericus Augustus Nobbe. Leipzig: Sumptibus et typis Caroli Tauchnitii, 1843.

———. *Geographia Cl. Ptolemaei Alexandrini.* Venice: Apud Vincentium Valgrisium, 1562.

Saif, Liana. *The Arabic Influences on Early Modern Occult Philosophy.* Basingstoke: Palgrave, 2015.

———. "From Ġāyat al-ḥakīm to Šams al-maʿārif: Ways of Knowing and Paths of Power in Medieval Islam." *Arabica* 64 (2017): 297–345.

Saxl, Fritz. "Beiträge zu einer Geschichte der Planeten-Darstellungen im Orient und im Okzident." *Der Islam* 3, no. 1 (1912): 151–77.

Sherratt, Andrew. "Sacred and Profane Substances: The Ritual Use of Narcotics in Later Neolithic Europe." In *Sacred and Profane: Proceedings of a Conference on Archaeology, Ritual, and Religion, Oxford*, edited by Paul Garwood et al., 50–64. Oxford: Oxford University Committee for Archaeology, 1991.

Shulgin, Alexander T. "Possible Implication of Myristicin as a Psychotropic Substance." *Nature* 210, no. 5034 (1966): 380–84.

Smith, Andrew. *Porphyry—Fragmenta*. Stuttgart: B. G. Teubner, 1993.

Solalinde, Antonio. "Alfonso X astrólogo: Noticia del manuscrito vaticano, Reg. Lat., núm. 1283." *Revista de Filología Española* 13 (1926): 350–56.

Tardieu, Michel. "Sābiens coraniques et 'Sābiens' de Harrān." *Journal asiatique* 274 (1986): 1–44.

Thomann, Johannes. "The Name Picatrix: Transcription or Translation?" *Journal of the Warburg and Courtauld Institutes* 50 (1990): 289–96.

Thorndike, Lynn. *A History of Magic and Experimental Science*. Vol. 2, *During the First Thirteen Centuries of Our Era*. New York: Columbia University Press, 1923.

Tommasi, Chiara Ombretta. "Some Reflections on Antique and Late Antique Esotericism." In *Formen und Nebenformen des Platonismus in der Spätantike*, edited by Helmut Seng, Luciana Gabriela Soares Santoprete, and Chiara O. Tommasi, 9–35. Heidelberg: Universitätsverlag Winter, 2016.

Véronèse, Julien. *L'Ars notoria au Moyen Âge: Introduction et édition critique*. Florence: SISMEL Edizioni del Galluzzo, 2007.

Vickers, Brian, ed. *Occult and Scientific Mentalities in the Renaissance*. Cambridge: Cambridge University Press, 1984.

Watts, Donald C. *Dictionary of Plant Lore*. Amsterdam: Elsevier Academic Press, 2007.

Weill-Parot, Nicolas. *Les "images astrologiques" au Moyen Âge et à la Renaissance: Spéculations intellectuelles et pratiques magiques (XIIe–XVe siècle)*. Paris: Honoré Champion, 2002.

Yates, Frances A. *Giordano Bruno and the Hermetic Tradition*. Chicago: University of Chicago Press, 1964.

INDEX OF TERRESTRIAL NAMES

This index contains proper names, places, and titles of works.

INDEX OF CELESTIAL NAMES AND MAGICAL WORDS

INDEX OF SUBJECTS AND MATERIALS

For proper names, places, or titles of works see Index of Terrestrial Names.